Centers and Peripheries in Knowledge Production

This book examines the circulation of knowledge within globalization, focusing on the differences between centres and peripheries of knowledge production in the social sciences. It explores not only how knowledge is appropriated in peripheral fields but also how foreign ideas shape those fields and the trajectories of scholars, and uses actor-network theory to explain circulation of knowledge as an extension of socio-technical networks that transcend borders.

Leandro Rodriguez Medina is Associate Professor at the Department of International Relations and Political Science at Universidad de las Americas Puebla.

Routledge Advances in Sociology

For a complete list of titles in this series, please visit www.routledge.com.

83 Life Course Perspectives on Military Service
Edited by Janet M. Wilmoth and Andrew S. London

84 Innovation in Socio-Cultural Context
Edited by Frane Adam and Hans Westlund

85 Youth, Arts and Education
Reassembling Subjectivity through Affect
Anna Hickey-Moody

86 The Capitalist Personality
Face-to-Face Sociality and Economic Change in the Post-Communist World
Christopher S. Swader

87 The Culture of Enterprise in Neoliberalism
Specters of Entrepreneurship
Tomas Marttila

88 Islamophobia in the West
Measuring and Explaining Individual Attitudes
Marc Helbling

89 The Challenges of Being a Rural Gay Man
Coping with Stigma
Deborah Bray Preston and Anthony R. D'Augelli

90 Global Justice Activism and Policy Reform in Europe
Understanding When Change Happens
Edited by Peter Utting, Mario Pianta and Anne Ellersiek

91 Sociology of the Visual Sphere
Edited by Regev Nathansohn and Dennis Zuev

92 Solidarity in Individualized Societies
Recognition, Justice and Good Judgement
Søren Juul

93 Heritage in the Digital Era
Cinematic Tourism and the Activist Cause
Rodanthi Tzanelli

94 Generation, Discourse, and Social Change
Karen R. Foster

95 Sustainable Practices
Social Theory and Climate Change
Elizabeth Shove and Nicola Spurling

96 The Transformative Capacity of New Technologies
A Theory of Sociotechnical Change
Ulrich Dolata

97 **Consuming Families**
Buying, Making, Producing
Family Life in the 21st Century
Jo Lindsay and JaneMaree Maher

98 **Migrant Marginality**
A Transnational Perspective
*Edited by Philip Kretsedemas,
Jorge Capetillo-Ponce
and Glenn Jacobs*

99 **Changing Gay Male Identities**
Andrew Cooper

100 **Perspectives on Genetic Discrimination**
Thomas Lemke

101 **Social Sustainability**
A Multilevel Approach to
Social Inclusion
*Edited by Veronica Dujon, Jesse
Dillard, and Eileen M. Brennan*

102 **Capitalism**
A Companion to Marx's
Economy Critique
Johan Fornäs

103 **Understanding European Movements**
New Social Movements,
Global Justice Struggles,
Anti-Austerity Protest
*Edited by Cristina Flesher
Fominaya and Laurence Cox*

104 **Applying Ibn Khaldūn**
The Recovery of a Lost Tradition
in Sociology
Syed Farid Alatas

105 **Children in Crisis**
Ethnographic Studies in
International Contexts
*Edited by Manata Hashemi
and Martín Sánchez-Jankowski*

106 **The Digital Divide**
The Internet and Social Inequality
in International Perspective
*Edited by Massimo Ragnedda
and Glenn W. Muschert*

107 **Emotion and Social Structures**
The Affective Foundations of
Social Order
Christian von Scheve

108 **Social Capital and Its Institutional Contingency**
A Study of the United States,
China and Taiwan
*Edited by Nan Lin, Yang-chih Fu
and Chih-jou Jay Chen*

109 **The Longings and Limits of Global Citizenship Education**
The Moral Pedagogy of
Schooling in a Cosmopolitan Age
Jeffrey S. Dill

110 **Irish Insanity 1800–2000**
Damien Brennan

111 **Cities of Culture**
A Global Perspective
Deborah Stevenson

112 **Racism, Governance, and Public Policy**
Beyond Human Rights
Katy Sian, Ian Law and S. Sayyid

113 **Understanding Aging and Diversity**
Theories and Concepts
Patricia Kolb

114 **Hybrid Media Culture**
Sensing Place in a World of Flows
Edited by Simon Lindgren

115 **Centers and Peripheries in Knowledge Production**
Leandro Rodriguez Medina

Centers and Peripheries in Knowledge Production

Leandro Rodriguez Medina

LONDON AND NEW YORK

First published 2014
by Routledge
711 Third Avenue, New York, NY 10017

Simultaneously published in the UK
by Routledge
2 Park Square, Milton Park, Abingdon, Oxfordshire OX14 4RN

Routledge is an imprint of the Taylor and Francis Group,
an informa business

First issued in paperback 2015

© 2014 Taylor & Francis

The right of Leandro Rodriguez Medina to be identified as author of
this work has been asserted in accordance with sections 77 and 78 of the
Copyright, Designs and Patents Act 1988.

All rights reserved. No part of this book may be reprinted or reproduced or
utilised in any form or by any electronic, mechanical, or other means, now
known or hereafter invented, including photocopying and recording, or in
any information storage or retrieval system, without permission in writing
from the publishers.

Trademark Notice: Product or corporate names may be trademarks or
registered trademarks, and are used only for identification and explanation
without intent to infringe.

Library of Congress Cataloging-in-Publication Data
Medina, Leandro Rodriguez.
  Centers and peripheries in knowledge production / by Leandro
Rodriguez Medina. — 1st Edition.
    pages cm. — (Routledge advances in sociology ; 115)
  Includes bibliographical references and index.
  1. Knowledge, Sociology of.   2. Political science—Study and
teaching—Argentina.   I. Title.
  HM651.M43 2013
  306.4'2—dc23
  2013014862

ISBN 978-0-415-84079-8 (hbk)
ISBN 978-1-138-95739-8 (pbk)
ISBN 978-0-203-76701-6 (ebk)

Typeset in Sabon
by IBT Global.

To Gregorio and Don Manuel,
because their thrill for knowledge has transcended

To Sofía,
the most beautiful *obstacle épistémologique*

Contents

List of Figures	xi
List of Tables	xiii
List of Acronyms	xv
Foreword	xix
Acknowledgments	xxi
Introduction	1
1 Understanding the Circulation of Knowledge	10
2 A Qualitative Approach to Scientific Fields	44
3 Training Scientists in Networked Scientific Fields	69
4 Getting Started: The Beginning of Academic Careers	95
5 Towards a Plurality of Translations	129
Conclusion	170
Notes	187
Bibliography	209
Index	235

Figures

1.1	Social worlds and scholarly works as boundary objects.	11
1.2	Negotiation between symmetrical social worlds.	34
1.3	Negotiation between asymmetrical social worlds.	35
1.4	Subordinating objects, social worlds, scientific fields, and spaces of translation.	40
2.1	Research methods and techniques of data gathering.	48
2.2	A scientist's life-history as a node in a network.	51
3.1	Construction of a distinction between foreign and local ideas.	77
3.2	Sites of local student debates, and processes that obscure these debates.	85
4.1	Dynamics of a scientific career in Argentine political science.	125
5.1	Published articles in political science journals by Argentine scholars per year, 1975–2013.	142
5.2	Country of origin of co-authors' institutions.	144
5.3	Consolidated and consecrated scholars as mediators within peripheral and central fields.	167

Tables

1.1	Differences between Fields According to Structural Features	22
1.2	PhD Holders with Foreign Degrees in Argentina by Country Where Degrees Were Conferred	39
2.1	Number of Interviewees According to Gender, Position within the Field, Location in Argentina, and Holding of Local/Foreign Postgraduate Degrees	61
4.1	Title of PhD Theses Written by Argentine Political Scientists Abroad and Country Where Degrees Were Conferred	112

Acronyms

ANPCyT	Agencia Nacional de Promoción Científica y Tecnológica de la República Argentina (National Agency of Scientific and Technological Promotion)
ANT	Actor-Network Theory
APA	American Psychological Association
CBC	Ciclo Básico Común (Common Basic Cycle)
CCD	Consejo para la Consolidación de la Democracia (Council for Democracy Consolidation)
CEDES	Centro de Estudios del Estado y la Sociedad (Research Centre on the State and Society), Argentina
CEPAL	Comisión Económica para América Latina y el Caribe (Economic Comission for Latin America and the Caribbean)
CINVESTAV	Centro de Investigación y Estudios Avanzados, Instituto Politécnico Nacional (Centre for Research and Advanced Studies, National Polytechnique Institute), Mexico
CNPq	Conselho Nacional de Desenvolvimento Científico e Tecnológico (National Council of Scientific and Technological Development), Brazil
CNRS	Centre National de la Recherche Scientifique (National Centre of Scientific Research), France
CONACYT	Consejo Nacional de Ciencia y Tecnología (National Council of Science and Technology), Mexico
CONICET	Consejo Nacional de Investigaciones Científicas y Técnicas de la República Argentina (National Council of Scientific and Technical Research), Argentina
DAAD	Deutscher Akademischer Austausch Dienst (German Academic Exchange Service)

xvi *Acronyms*

EUDEBA	Editorial Universitaria de Buenos Aires (Buenos Aires University Press), Argentina
FLACSO	Facultad Latinoamericana de Ciencias Sociales (Latin-American Faculty of Social Sciences)
IADB	Inter-American Development Bank
IESALC	Instituto Internacional para la Educación Superior en América Latina y el Caribe (International Institute for Higher Education in Latin American and the Caribbean)
ILAS	Institute of Latin American Studies, University of London
IMF	International Monetary Fund
IPSA	International Political Science Association
IRD	Development Research), France
MINCyT	Ministerio de Ciencia, Tecnología e Innovación Productiva de la República Argentina (Ministry of Science, Technology and Innovation for Production)
MLA	Modern Language Association
NSSR	New School for Social Research
OECD	Organisation for Economic Co-operation and Development
SAAP	Sociedad Argentina de Análisis Político (Argentine Society for Political Analysis)
SECyT	Secretaría de Ciencia y Tecnología de la República Argentina (Secretariat for Science and Technology, it became MINCyT in 2007)
SNI	Sistema Nacional de Investigadores (National System of Researchers), Mexico
SSCI	Social Science Citation Index
STS	Science and Technology Studies
UADE	Universidad Argentina de la Empresa
UB	Universidad de Belgrano
UBA	Universidad de Buenos Aires
UCC	Universidad Católica de Córdoba
UCEMA	Universidad del Centro de Estudios Macroeconómicos de Argentina
UCSF	Universidad Católica de Santa Fe
UDeSA	Universidad de San Andrés
UNDP	United Nations Development Programme

UNESCO	United Nations Educational, Scientific and Cultural Organisation
UNGS	Universidad Nacional de General Sarmiento
UNR	Universidad Nacional de Rosario
UNSM	Universidad Nacional de San Martín
UNTREF	Universidad Nacional de Tres de Febrero
USAL	Universidad del Salvador
UTDT	Universidad Torcuato Di Tella
WB	World Bank

Foreword

Whereas traditionally the sociology of intellectuals has explored the natural sciences, there is now a growing literature on the sociology of the social sciences. This is a welcome development, which could potentially encourage reflexivity within the social sciences. Leandro Rodriguez Medina's fascinating study of political science in Argentina is a significant and incisive contribution to this emerging subfield.

As the title of this book suggests, the book isn't just about political scientists in Argentina, but about how their lives are entangled in complex arrangements which involve various imbalances of power. There is firstly the asymmetry between those who hold a Chair and exercise power, and those scholars are who dependent on their senior colleagues' goodwill and whose work conditions are precarious. There is also the asymmetry between the academic centre, still located in the United States and Europe, and the geographical 'periphery' that is in many respects dependent on the centre. Drawing on a sophisticated theoretical framework, Rodriguez Medina is able to support his bold claims about the nature of those asymmetries with rich empirical data, mainly based on a substantial number of in-depth interviews with political scientists.

Throughout the book we follow the lives of those scholars who try to balance their career choices with various domestic demands and whose choices and positioning have in the long run significant, though sometimes unforeseen, repercussions for them. Many academics will recognize this picture and see at least part of themselves in some of the moving stories. Indeed, this is not an exclusively Argentinian story, nor even specific to Latin-America. Many parts of the world—including several European countries—exhibit similar academic structures in which clientelism is the dominant form and in which locally effective strategies tend to be irreconcilable with the type of work that is internationally recognized.

This work is one of the first to come out of the programme of research on the sociology of intellectuals that is currently taking place in Cambridge. I have had the privilege to be able to follow this study at various stages in its

xx *Foreword*

creation, and I am delighted that it has now turned into a book, which will be recognised as a major contribution to this emerging field.

Patrick Baert
Reader in Social Theory
University of Cambridge

Acknowledgments

This book is a network of people and objects. I owe to the former many of the best ideas that it contains, and to the latter the possibility of materialising these ideas in order to make them public. I want to begin by thanking Patrick Baert for his support, help, and insightful comments throughout my years in Cambridge. His careful and generous reading of my work has had a longstanding impact not only on the following pages but also on the way I see, and now conduct, the supervision of postgraduate students. I thank him for pushing me always that little bit farther.

Among those who recommended me readings, suggested ideas, made me see new angles of my own research project, and criticised my arguments, I want to mention Zaheer Baber, Jose Vicente Tavares dos Santos, Tania Pérez Bustos, Elihu Gerson, Adele Clarke, Robeto Toledo, Celia Szusterman, Syed Farid Alatas, Alexis de Greiff, Guillermo O'Donnell, Gabriel Abend, Mauricio Tenorio, Arturo Fernández, David Slater, Don Ihde, Michele Lamont, Rosalba Casas, Eduardo Mendieta, Gustavo Emmerich, Lucy Suchman, Vicente Sisto, Lucas Rubinich, Julian Go, John Law, Luisa Vilar, Susan Leigh Star, Marina Frasca-Spada, Alan Scott, Suresh Canagarajah, Joan Fujimura, Mario Albornoz, Robert Rosenberger, Michel Callon, Edgardo Lander, Richard Whitley, James Griesemer, Christine Leuenberger, Ricardo Salvatore, Carlos Strasser, Adriana Aliaga, Laura Martínez, Carlos Floria, John Trent, Tove Thagaard, Carolyn Keeler, Blanca Tovías, Antoni Castells i Talens, Rosa María Blanco, Fernando Domínguez Rubio, Iris Montero Sobrevilla, and Santiago Leiras.

Some people and institutions deserve a special acknowledgement. For chapter 4 I have drawn upon one of my earlier works, the article 'Local Chairs vs. International Networks: the Beginning of the Scholarly Career in a Peripheral Academic Field', published in the International Journal of Politics, Culture and Society (online first 2013). I thank the journal for permission to use this material. Hebe Vessuri, Pablo Kreimer, Hernán Thomas, Renato Dagnino, and the researchers and postgraduate students of the doctoral school at the Instituto Venezolano de Investigaciones Científicas (IVIC) have been most provocative with their comments and suggestions. Many improvements of previous drafts are due to their criticisms. Catalina

xxii *Acknowledgments*

Smulovitz, at Universidad Torcuato Di Tella (UTDT) provided institutional support while I stayed in Argentina doing fieldwork, encouraging me to explore new research questions that I had overlooked altogether. Mercedes Kerz allowed me to participate in an inter-institutional research group that held regular meetings at Universidad de Belgrano (UB) in 2007. She has been a formidable teacher and a supportive colleague for so many years that this book is, in many ways, a form of thanking her. Patricia Torre Mejía and Alberto Aziz Nacif have opened to me the doors of the Centro de Investigaciones y Estudios Superiores en Antropología Social (CIESAS) in Mexico and given me stimulating comments on the drafts of some chapters. Additionally, CIESAS awarded me a scholarship in 2009 to apply myself to writing up the dissertation. I am very grateful for this generosity and hope to keep a long relationship with this prestigious and leading Mexican institution. In 2006 and 2009, José Antonio Hernanz Moral, on behalf of the Instituto de Filosofía at the Universidad Veracruzana (UV), provided me the opportunity to share with its members the main arguments of my research and to receive feedback that helped me to refine some of my ideas. Finally, the Universidad de las Américas Puebla (UDLAP) has provided financial aid during my time in Cambridge and, more recently, has appointed me as full-time professor at the Department of International Relations and Political Science. It has been a fantastic institution to exchange with colleagues (and apply) some of the ideas explored in this research. In particular, I want to thank Alberto López Cuenca because he gave me the opportunity to discuss with the students of the PhD in Creation and Theories of Culture some of the preliminary findings of my investigation. Last, but not least, my stay in Freiburg in 2013 as International Fellow of the research project "Universalität und Akzeptanzpotential von Gesellschaftswissen. Zur Zirkulation von Wissensbeständen zwischen Europa und dem globalen Süden" allowed me to work on the final details of this manuscript while discussing and exchanging ideas about the current state of the research on circulation of social science knowledge. I thank Wiebke Keim and her research team for their comments and suggestions.

Alejandra Racovschik, Macarena Morales, and Sebastián Erdmann in Argentina and Juan Carlos Patiño in Mexico were very helpful in transcribing the digitally recorded interviews. They worked under (my) pressure and responded proficiently. Thanks to their work, I had all the information in time to develop the qualitative analysis that sustains this research. Regarding the writing up of this book, the help of Anne Hinton, Teresa Welborne, and Emma Norman has been invaluable. Although they have transformed a poor draft into a readable, polished book, only my flawed use of the language is responsible for the mistakes that might be found in the following pages. I am also grateful to Max Novick and Jennifer Morrow of Routledge for their help and support throughout the editorial process. They have been enthusiastic about this project and I hope to make a modest contribution to this prestigious publishing house. Without Alejandra, Macarena,

Sebastián, Juan Carlos, Anne, Teresa, Emma, Max and Jennifer, this book would still be an ongoing project.

I would like to thank especially to those scholars who participated in my research as interviewees. They showed me the passion for political science, the commitment to knowledge and democracy as forms of dialogue, and the untiring dedication to a country that, more often than not, has ignored or underrated their contributions. This book is not merely a description of (some parts of) their work, but rather an attempt to draw attention to their role in the intellectual life of Argentina.

My family has been fundamental in my studies—for several thousands of reasons—since the day I decided to become a political scientist. I still doubt that they know what a political scientist does, but this has not impeded them from giving me their love and support. After many years of sacrifices, the day has arrived.

Claudia, my wife, has been the most supportive, understanding, and loyal companion throughout this journey. She has been next to me in each step, in each moment of joy, anxiety, excitement, doubt, and sadness, because developing a scholarly career is always a mixture of these feelings. Every line of this book is an acknowledgement of her encouragement and my humble request to start all over again. Do you accept?

Freiburg im Breisgau, 28 February 2013

Introduction

Study of the production and circulation of knowledge has been part of the sociology of knowledge for a long time. The main focus has been on the production of knowledge in certain places (centres) and its diffusion throughout the world (periphery), from the pioneering studies of Basalla (1967) on imperial science, to the current claims of 'global South' as a 'labile signifier whose content is determined by everyday material and political processes' (Comaroff and Comaroff 2012: 127). In this period, four standpoints can be identified and will be described to depict the general landscape.

Firstly, there is a school of thought that studies the international circulation of knowledge under the umbrella of positivism. These studies focus on the regularities found in the relationships between scientists and scientific fields (such as patterns of co-authorship). This concentrates on the diffusion of Western scientific values throughout the world, as influenced by Merton and his conception of science as a set of rules that practitioners have to respect and follow. The result is a body of literature that focuses on imperialism and the role of the metropolis in the flow of knowledge (Basalla 1967; De Gregoi 1978; Kumar 1980; McLeod 1975). More recently, but in the same epistemological tradition, some scholars have been carrying out research into the structure of international science, acknowledging that centres and peripheries are still the best way of describing how knowledge circulates (Luhmann 1992; Schott 1988, 1993a, 1998; Taschwer 1996; Wagner, C. 2006; Wagner et al. 2001). Others, showing a sensibility towards power relations in the international arena, have focused on the place that the colonies have played in the transformation of knowledge, since these areas usually provide the data and conditions for testing hypothesis and theories proposed in the metropolitan institutions (Delbourgo and Dew 2008; Ferreira Furtado 2008; Jacob 2008; Raj 2010; Roberts 2011; Schaffer et al. 2009).

A second perspective was inaugurated by studies of scientific practices in which the circulation of knowledge was somehow reduced to some central sites (e.g. universities and laboratories) that receive, classify, store, and produce new knowledge. This perspective focuses on the micro-negotiation through which scientists translate the peripheral areas of the world (i.e. a

2 Centers and Peripheries in Knowledge Production

coast in the Pacific Ocean) into devices (i.e. maps and drawings) able to transport, in a stable way, the local knowledge of faraway regions. The consequence of this approach, for the sociology of science, is a theory that proposes that knowledge is produced and circulates through networks organised around centres that concentrate information and produce theory (Latour 1987, 1988; Law 1986b; Verran 1999). This theoretical standpoint, known as Actor-Network Theory (ANT), is the current creed within science and technology studies (Golinski 2005), and has influenced, directly or indirectly, the development of studies of the circulation of knowledge. Amongst these studies, two are worth mentioning; firstly, Galison (2001)'s notion of trading zones as contact regions where different languages emerge is an attempt to shed some light on the conditions that make the circulation of knowledge possible. Galison argues that, for knowledge to travel, the emergence and consolidation of hybrid languages and creoles that allow scientists to describe phenomena using a shared vocabulary and rules to organise perception are needed. In turn, this encounter gives rise to new knowledge that can be materialised in theories, instruments, methodologies or more sophisticated creoles. Secondly, Star and Griesemer (1989) have proposed the notion of the boundary-object to understand the dissemination of knowledge between different social worlds. They have argued that there are some objects that are stable enough to travel from one context to another without losing their identity but, at the same time, are flexible enough to be interpreted by the inhabitants of such contexts. With the notion of the boundary-object, the authors offer a theory of knowledge circulation that transcends textual analysis and revolves around the importance of materiality of the process of knowledge transmission.

Another perspective, stronger in cultural studies and literature than in science and technology studies, has been post-colonialism. Post-colonial thinkers are concerned with the impact of the international colonial structure upon the economic, political, social, and epistemic conditions of the colonies. In particular, they argue that Europe has transmitted not only a set of institutions and social relations, such as liberal thought and capitalist economy, but also a complex and hierarchical organisation of knowledge in academic disciplines, according to which European science appears as a model to be imitated. By paying attention to the epistemological basis of knowledge production, post-colonialists claim that the voices of some oppressed communities and societies are usually unheard in metropolitan science, giving rise to a phenomenon described as the 'coloniality' of knowledge (Castro-Gómez 2003; Lander 2003b; Quijano 2003, 2007). As a consequence of this hierarchy, knowledge produced in the peripheral regions of the world is perceived as culture, while only that produced in the metropolitan institutions might be considered to be scientific.

The fourth and final perspective that addresses the circulation of knowledge is based on Bourdieu's field theory. Under this approach, the sciences are organised in the same way all around the world, which permits the

Introduction 3

specificities of every place to be ignored. Indeed, the conditions of knowledge production of the metropolis are implicitly accepted as a norm that should be replicated in other parts by mirroring the features of the scientific fields in the developed world. As a consequence, the international circulation of knowledge is not perceived as a relevant problem, since it responds to the same imperatives: the acquisition and reproduction of scientific capital. Bourdieu (1999a) has analysed how German philosophy was introduced into French academia by illustrating the role of some French scholars who benefited from the use of foreign theories to obtain dominant positions in their field. A similar conclusion was drawn by Lamont (1987) in her study of the introduction of Derrida's work into American literary studies. She focused not only on the originality and relevance of deconstruction but also on the network of journals and disciples that were necessary to transfer the work of the French philosopher from its original settings to the American university system. Like Bourdieu, Lamont has argued that the search for prestige and the need for reorganisation of the field of literary studies in the United States, were the driving forces behind the scholars who permitted the incorporation of Derrida's theories. In a similar vein, Nieburg and Plotkin (2004a, 2004b) relied on Bourdieu's field theory to study the construction of social knowledge in Argentina and paid attention to the influence of foreign ideas. They maintain that the acceptance and circulation of foreign ideas depends on the features of the local field, especially during the commencement of academic social reflection, when the metropolitan fields, particularly Germany, France, and the United States, were taken as models.

The landscape just described shows that the reflection concerning how ideas circulate is a current and urgent problem within science and technology studies. Be it in a historical perspective or an up to date analysis, the present sociology of knowledge is especially concerned with space and the influence of this on the conditions of production (Burke 2012; Livingstone 2003, 2005; Meyer 2010), which opens up room for debating how knowledge travels through different places, undertaking profound transformations but remaining valid, useful, and true.

1 SHORTCOMINGS OF CURRENT RESEARCH ON KNOWLEDGE PRODUCTION AND CIRCULATION

The theoretical perspectives that have dealt with the phenomenon of the circulation of knowledge present some shortcomings that are necessary to mention. They can be grouped around three main issues. Firstly, some of them ignore or underestimate the weight of the power relations that shape the relationships between nations and, as a consequence, between scientific fields. Scholars undertaking research under the positivist and Bourdieuan assumptions of an international Republic of Letters, where shared norms and values are the rule, tend to focus on collaboration or competition

4   Centers and Peripheries in Knowledge Production

between scientists and their effects at a global level. They do not ignore the existence of centres and peripheries, but they consider them as natural results of the disparity of material and symbolic resources, which transform certain areas into centres of knowledge production and relegate others to a peripheral condition. Thus, one defining feature of the periphery is that it tries to imitate the achievements of the leading countries and their scientific fields. Had they an interest in the processes of knowledge production, instead of concentrating on the papers and articles published, they would have noticed that the unevenness between regions gives rise to different practices, procedures, evaluation standards, and epistemic cultures. In short, centres and peripheries produce science differently. Recently, Camic et al. (2011) have shown to what extent practices and material objects have shaped the social sciences, but still they lack interest in other parts of the world except the United States.

Secondly, some scholars, especially those who participate in the postcolonial debate, assume that the distribution of power affects the production of knowledge and try to figure out how other alternative forms of intellectual production might emerge from the oppressed regions of the world. For postcolonial scholars, the coloniality of knowledge (i.e. the peripheral position of Latin American science) is taken for granted (Castro-Gómez 2007, 2003; Mignolo 2003, 2002; Quijano 2007). They focus on the epistemological consequences of this phenomenon by highlighting the voice and knowledge of the oppressed people whose cognitive status has been systematically underrated. However, they do not seem to explore the mechanisms through which centre/periphery relations are partially structured by peripheral academics. In so far as mainstream science rejects the knowledge produced in the periphery, the task of post-colonialist scholars seems to be reduced to a denunciation of the intellectual debates of the first world, because of the blindness of metropolitan scientists (especially social scientists) towards colonial issues. Accordingly, the post-colonial sociology of science usually criticises the ideas produced in the periphery when it follows the epistemological assumptions of the European model and only reproduces metropolitan knowledge. The role of Third World scholars in the reproduction of this international inequality is usually underrated.

Thirdly, ANT scholars, and many of the sociologists who have developed models to understand science diffusion and transmission, are insensitive towards post-colonial legacies and power relations at an international level. Whilst focusing on networks and acknowledging that some of the nodes of such networks are centres, they ignore (i) the weight of the past in the configuration of scientific and intellectual institutions and practices in the former colonies, and (ii) the constraining effect that power relations have upon the development of knowledge in peripheral regions, since the epistemic models of knowledge are foreign, and affect the form and content of locally produced ideas. As a consequence, ANT scholars usually study laboratories, universities, and research centres that are located in the

Introduction 5

metropolitan centres, providing insightful and precise descriptions of phenomena that frequently cannot be transferred to peripheral contexts in a straightforward manner. By paying yet more attention to the centres, in what Law (2006b) refers to as 'managerialism', scholars have not shed light on the peripheral areas. Peripheral nodes, such as developing countries, do not simply follow the rules imposed by developed countries. The periphery exchanges things (e.g. data) with the centres of knowledge production and such exchanges give rise to 'trading' or 'contact' zones where new knowledge may appear. The lack of research on science in the periphery seems to be a main feature of current science and technology studies and a problem that needs to be resolved (Anderson and Adams 2008).

2 THE SPECIFICITY OF OUR ARGUMENT

What do social scientists from developing countries do with foreign knowledge? How does their position, peripheral to the international division of academic labour, affect the use of ideas manufactured in the centres of knowledge production? This study explores how political scientists in Argentina utilise foreign knowledge to structure their academic careers and proposes a theoretical framework within which it is possible to observe the role of such knowledge in the scientific practices of the periphery. Understanding the relevance of foreign knowledge in the less developed countries is important with increasing globalisation and weight of knowledge in the current economy.

This study shows that the conditions of knowledge production play a crucial role in the way it circulates, is appropriated, and becomes accepted in different contexts. The place and location where knowledge is manufactured have been only recently incorporated into the debates of the sociology of science. This concern with spatiality has been based on empirical studies that, on the one hand, have analysed the importance of material environments (e.g. laboratories or libraries) and, on the other, have shed light on the constraints and potentialities that certain geographical areas (e.g. cities or regions) impose on knowledge creation and development.

Secondly, this study brings to the forefront the uneven relationship between local and foreign knowledge, which gives rise to the undergraduate students' perception that local scholars are frequently second-rate academics. Influenced by this secondary role of local knowledge, students not only build a distorted idea of local social science but also tend to overestimate the value of foreign—often metropolitan—knowledge. Therefore, it is not surprising that many talented students choose to leave their peripheral countries to pursue postgraduate studies in the centres of knowledge production, a situation that produces different opportunities for those trained abroad in contrast with those who remain in the developing country.

Thirdly, while the sociology of knowledge, or science and technology studies, focuses on knowledge production or circulation, it tends to ignore

6 Centers and Peripheries in Knowledge Production

the labour conditions of the academic profession. By disregarding this, it helps to reproduce the idea that the practice of science is more or less homogenous around the world, whilst hiding the dynamics of institutional and para-institutional strategies that are necessary where scientific endeavours are not structured according to the Western model. One of the main goals of this research is to identify these strategies and study how they affect the production of knowledge and the use of foreign ideas. Even in the social sciences, where laboratories are not involved and instruments are relatively cheap, the required set of material and symbolic resources (e.g. libraries and office space) is usually scarce in developing countries. Consequently, scholars ought to develop ways of dealing with the scarcity of resources and still be flexible enough to undertake research, teaching, and other scholarly activities. The result of this pressure creates a particular way of carrying out research, which has mostly been ignored by studies about science and technology written in the developed world.

Finally, this study responds to an issue that has been addressed many times throughout Latin American intellectual history. From the original, innovative analysis produced by CEPAL's theorist, Raúl Prebisch, concerning the structural dependence of the Latin American economy, to the recent claims made by Luiz Inácio Lula da Silva, president of Brazil, related to the necessary independence of Latin American scientific and technological systems, the region has always been concerned as to its role on the international scene. Analysing dependence is not, however, an attempt to move the burden of responsibility to the centres of knowledge production. On the contrary, this study describes the mechanisms developed in the periphery that contribute to the asymmetry between local and foreign knowledge, many of which usually work without being noticed as such by the members of the peripheral field.

A qualitative methodology based on life-history and participant observation is used in order to observe how Argentine political scientists use foreign knowledge to articulate their careers. Life histories allow us to examine scientists' trajectories, not only in terms of their personal decisions but also within an understanding of the structural constraints (such as economic crises and dictatorships) that have affected the entire discipline of political science. While this method provides a sensibility towards history, the participant observation approach contextualises the narratives of academics by relating them to the specific circumstances of local institutions. Observing scholars working, under the adverse conditions in which they usually produce and transmit knowledge, brings to the fore the process of doing science, usually obscured by the rhetorical devices that shape its outputs (e.g. research articles) in the form of objective knowledge.

This qualitative perspective is complemented by an in-depth analysis of secondary sources, classified into five broad categories. These are (i) historical studies of Argentine intellectual life, (ii) analyses of Argentine universities as institutional actors, (iii) historical analyses of Argentine political

Introduction 7

science, focusing, in particular, on the development of institutions and scientists' diasporas, (iv) studies of some of the material dimensions of cultural life in Argentina, specifically books and how they, as objects, 'tell' the history of the country, and (v) analyses of Latin American science, its conditions of production and how it has been practiced by some notable scholars or researchers.

3 OVERVIEW

This study has five parts and every one, developed in chapters 1 to 5, is focused on foreign knowledge and its critical appropriation by local scholars. Due to this angle, other features of Argentine political science have been downplayed, although this does not imply they are not important to understand its organisation or development. Thus, the use of foreign knowledge must not be seen as the only driving principle that structures the discipline; however, it is particularly relevant for this study given the nature of its central research questions.

In chapter 1 a theoretical framework for this research is presented; one that draws from field theory (Bourdieu 1988; 1999b; 2004), ANT (Callon 1986, 1992; Latour 1987, 1991, 1999, 2005; Law 2006b), social world theory (Clarke 1991; Clarke and Star 2008; Star and Griesemer 1989) and postcolonial theory (Castro-Gómez 2003, 2007; Mignolo 2000, 2002, 2007; Quijano 2003). This chapter focuses on the analytical devices employed to understand the transformation of knowledge when it travels from one place to another: social worlds, boundary objects, and translations. Equipped with this vocabulary, the chapter ends with the introduction of two additional concepts, *asymmetrical translation* and *subordinated object*, which describe what happen to those transformations when power relations, both material and symbolic, are involved.

Chapter 2 focuses on methodology, and in particular on the epistemological and ontological assumptions behind life-history. The use of research techniques, such as in-depth interviews, document analyses, and participant observation are considered in this chapter. At the same time, it deals with the ideas of credibility and reliability as the correct criteria to evaluate the pertinence of a qualitative methodology, which leads to an explanation of the representativeness of the sample and the difficulties in making generalisations from the data obtained in this research. This study uses three different, but intertwined, strategies in relation to sampling: (i) purposive sampling (Brink and Wood 1998), (ii) theoretical sampling (Honigmann 1970), and (iii) snowballing. Purposive sampling refers to the decision of the researcher to include some informants in the sample because they have some special characteristics that are highly valuable for the objectives of the investigation, while theoretical sampling indicates that the researcher has to segment the sample according to theoretical criteria that are sustained in previous studies.

8   Centers and Peripheries in Knowledge Production

These forms of sampling are useful when: (i) the population parameters are unknown, and/or (ii) there is a theoretical interest in including some informants and excluding others, and/or (iii) theory is required to stratify the sample in order to take into account relevant categories of the informants. Finally, snowballing was used to enact the networks in which interviewees were embedded and, at the same time, to contact potential interviewees with whom the researcher had no previous bonds. As a result of these sampling strategies, sixty-three Argentine political scientists were interviewed and provided a narrative of their life-histories. These interviews took place in Buenos Aires and its metropolitan area, the provinces of Mendoza, San Juan, Santa Fe, Entre Rios, and Cordoba, between December 2006 and December 2007. Informal exchange with some of the interviewees, literature review, and short visits since then have been used to update information as well as identifying changes in Argentine higher education.

In chapter 3 the focal point is the training process of Argentine political scientists at undergraduate level. This commences with a description of how students are socialised in such a way that they learn how to distinguish between local and foreign knowledge, in terms of their association with novelty, 'scientificity', theoretical level, and methodological accuracy. Then, the places where this distinction is created, the debates that shape the critical appropriation of foreign knowledge, and the difficulties of translating these debates into written documents, such as research articles, are described in detail. The chapter ends with a theoretical discussion that revolves around some epistemological consequences of the distinction between foreign and local knowledge that have influenced syllabi and curricula in the Argentine university system.

The beginning of the academic career of Argentine political scientists is the main topic of chapter 4. In this section, the argument begins by describing a particular phenomenon of Argentine academia: teaching by undergraduates. Then, an analysis of the connections of students with senior scholars in order to create networks is developed, a process described as career bonding. After this phase, young scholars face a dilemma: they must either take as many academic posts as possible (taxi-cab professors) or leave the country for full-time postgraduate education. The response to this dilemma structures the remainder of the chapter. After focusing on the scholars who have stayed in the country and developed a career based on- and around—local actors in the field, the networks of academics who leave the country for postgraduate education and search for academic capital earned in foreign fields are considered. A theoretical analysis of the process of the early academic career in Argentine political science is addressed at the end of this chapter, and the concept of *teaching technology* is explained.

In chapter 5 the consolidation of an academic career is considered and the focus is placed on scientists who have reached the point of making a living from scholarly life. The necessary conditions for ideas to circulate at an international level are explored in this section, and an explanation is provided as to why Argentine political science makes it difficult for actors to be mediators with foreign scientific fields. At the same time, an exploration is made as to how this gatekeeping role is played by foreign actors and institutions, whose research and teaching agendas tend to be favoured to the detriment of those of local academics. None the less, the landscape of Argentine political science is not homogeneous and, consequently, the last part of the chapter is devoted to showing how the dominant actors of the field have reached such positions by pointing to three conditions that scholars and their production have to meet: the intellectual, the networking, and the international conditions.

Finally, the main findings are summarised in the last chapter, and conclusions are drawn from empirical data, which indicate some of the implications and consequences of the findings. Limitations of qualitative analysis, especially those based on life-histories, are also analysed in this chapter, along with the outstanding questions for future research that have been raised from this study.

1 Understanding the Circulation of Knowledge

Science is an international activity, not only because its assertions claim to be universal, that is, valid beyond the context in which they are produced, but also because it is practised, with significant differences, in almost all countries around the world. At the same time, science is international because of the scope of its content and the location of its practitioners. This leads us to two different ways of studying the international dimension of science. Some studies focus on collaboration between scientists and assume that, although differences can be found, science is practised homogeneously around the world. In such a landscape, some countries and their scientific communities play a leading role and become centres of knowledge production (e.g. Schott 1988, 1993a, 1993b, 1998; Schott et al. 1998; Meadows 1997; Forero-Pineda 2002; Wagner, C. 2006, 2008; Ziman 2000). However, there is a growing body of literature that recognises the importance of location and concentrates on the differences between sites of knowledge production and how places alter knowledge, the way it circulates, and how it is both produced and received (e.g. Kemple and Mawani 2010; Burawoy 2008; Livingstone 2003, 2005, 2007; Latour 1987, 1988; Mignolo 2000, 2002; Delbourgo and Dew; 2008; Anderson and Adams 2008; Chakrabarty 1992; Fujimura 2000; Abraham 2000; Star and Greisemer 1989; Wallerstein 1996a; Keim 2008; Comaroff and Comaroff 2012). While scholars of the first group look at the shared, common practices that Western science has delivered across the planet, those in the second group attempt to figure out how divergent practices, academic cultures, and institutions (or networks) converge to an international scenario. From this perspective, once place is as important as reasoning, the geography of knowledge ties in with philosophical concerns of epistemology.

The main hypothesis of this research is that scholars in peripheral fields use knowledge from central fields in order to structure their academic careers. This use of foreign ideas is understood as a translation, following ANT's theoretical approach; that is, it is a process by which academics at peripheral institutions incorporate new foreign elements (books, articles, conference proceedings) and scholars into their networks to strengthen their position within the local scientific field.[1] Translation includes not only

Understanding the Circulation of Knowledge 11

the expression of ideas in a different language, but also the process through which 'the identity of actors, the possibility of interaction and the margins of manoeuvre are negotiated and delimited' (Callon 1986: 6). Objects elaborated in central fields are negotiated in the peripheral ones and these negotiations contribute to set up the identity of the actors inhabiting both fields. Therefore, translation is an instrumental process in generating centres and peripheries of knowledge production, as will be discussed in sections 1.4 and 1.5. The main concepts analysed in this research come from ANT and its more recent developments, although other theoretical perspectives are taken into account, such as Bourdieu's theory of field or postcolonial studies of science and technology. Actually, ANT serves as a theoretical framework into which other viewpoints may be incorporated.

This chapter is structured into five sections in which concepts and theories that are relevant to the research are discussed and a vocabulary is developed to understand the phenomenon of the circulation of knowledge. In section 1.1 science is presented as a culturally embedded human activity. This context illustrates that fields are in constant competition and negotiation in regard to the setting of their boundaries and, by so doing, to include some members and exclude others. A discussion of scientific fields and their main features (rules of the game, conditions of entry, capital, and objects) is presented in section 1.2. A typology is proposed in section 1.3 according to the level of institutionalisation of scientific fields, and this classification allows for a distinction between science as practised in the developed world and the developing world. In section 1.4 the circulation of scientific

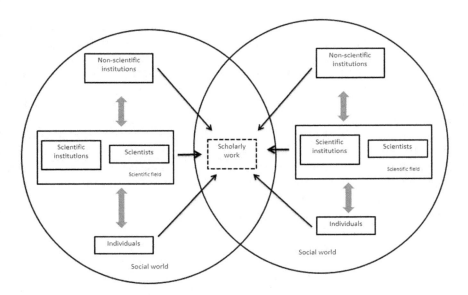

Figure 1.1 Social worlds and scholarly works as boundary objects.

12 Centers and Peripheries in Knowledge Production

knowledge and the transformation of the actors involved (producers, products, and receivers) is discussed. Then, an ecological perspective is proposed, forcing us to observe the characteristics of the objects that can aptly move from their place of production to other sites in order to be appropriated by different actors. Finally, scholarly works, one type of such objects, are presented and analysed in section 1.5. By focusing on scholarly works as objects that travel between social worlds, unevenly endowed in terms of material and symbolic resources, this section leads to a theoretical discussion that sheds some light on the specificity of the circulation of knowledge between asymmetrical social worlds and scientific fields. A schematic representation of the structure of the chapter is presented in Figure 1.1.

1.1 SOCIAL WORLDS

Science operates within a context. Scientists are connected with people beyond the scientific field, from the administrative staff of their university to senators in a commission on science and technology. Science and its context are perpetually shaped and re-shaped by each other in such a way that both are continually changing their boundaries. The way science and its context are related at a particular moment is a matter of negotiation (Gieryn 1999; Lamont and Molnár 2002).

The context in which science is embedded will be referred to as the *social world*.[2] This term refers to 'activities and processes' (Fujimura 1992: 169) whose outcome is a negotiated order in which fields are established as 'dynamic, shifting stakes and not as purely static institutions' (Keating et al. 1991: 5; quoted in Fujimura 1992: 169). According to Clarke and Star, 'the social world's framework focuses on meaning-making amongst groups of actors—collectives of various sorts—and on collective action—people doing things together and working with shared objects, which in science and technology often include highly specialized tools and technologies' (2008: 113). In the social world, 'various issues are debated, negotiated, fought out, forced, and manipulated by representatives of the participating' fields (Strauss 1978: 124). Thus, the main characteristic of a social world is its conflictual nature. Actors are constantly debating and negotiating issues related to their activities, affecting their own identities in the process. Furthermore, this is an approach that seeks 'to understand the nature of relations and actions across the arrays of people *and things* [. . .] representations [. . .], processes of work (including cooperation without consensus, career paths, and routines/anomalies), and many sorts of interwoven discourses' (Clarke and Star 2008: 113; emphasis in the original).[3]

Since the context (social world) and science are constructed in the very process of their mutual negotiations, a constructivist approach is proposed at a theoretical level. Neither the social world nor science is a monolithic entity, for this reason neither of them can be used to explain the other

Understanding the Circulation of Knowledge   13

(Latour 1988, 2005). The consequence of such a perspective is the need to focus on practices, on activities, and the processes by which some actors produce knowledge (Camic et al. 2011; Knorr-Cetina 1981; Latour and Woolgar 1986; Collins 1985). Thus, one of the tasks of the sociologist of science is 'to elucidate which [fields] come together . . . why, what their perspectives are, and what they hope to achieve through collective action' (Clarke 1991: 133).

Social worlds are not, *sensu strictu*, societies. The main difference is that social worlds emerge in relation to particular issues. They group diverse fields according to certain problems or concerns. Clarke has pointed out that a social world 'may form where all the groups that care (in the pragmatist sense) about a given issue come together' (Clarke 1997: 70). For this reason, the social world is a construction of the sociologist who must decide who participates in it, in what way they do so, for what reasons, and with what expectations.[4]

The theoretical importance of the concept social worlds is manifold. First, they allow us to treat the differences between countries or societies as differences between social worlds. This implies that, for example, scientific knowledge as a problem can be addressed in different ways not only because there are many diverse scientific fields but, also, because science is produced in different social worlds. The distinction between central and peripheral science comes not only from the conditions of knowledge production within scientific fields but also the relationships between such fields and other fields (economic, political, cultural, or religious) that constitute a social world.[5] Furthermore, it is at the level of social worlds, as well as at the level of scientific fields, that a centre/periphery structure may be observed: Argentine science is peripheral because Argentine society is peripheral (Sigal 2002; Miller 1999; Altamirano and Sarlo 1983).

Secondly, the notion of social worlds opens the possibility of incorporating an interdisciplinary dimension into the analysis of science. Saying that science happens in a location highlights the interconnectedness of science with other human endeavours, such as economy (Foray 2006; Mignolo 2000; Delbourgo and Dew 2008), the military (Rappert et al. 2008; Winner 2004; Rappert 2006), law (Jasanoff 2008, 1995; Lynch and Jasanoff 1998; Foucault 1979), politics (Hess et al 2008; Bucchi and Neresini 2008; Anderson and Adams 2008; Gray 2002), and religion (Zanca 2006; Sarlo 2001; Polkinghorne 2007; Wallace 2007). The connection between social worlds does not imply that science and other human activities are completely different or absolutely identical. Social worlds contain fields that permanently reshape themselves, changing boundaries according to the issues at stake, the resources available, or the interests involved (Clarke 1997: 70; Lamont and Molnár 2002). However, as long as boundaries are observed by actors inside and outside a field it is possible to talk about specific activities, be it scientific, economic, political, or religious.

14   *Centers and Peripheries in Knowledge Production*

Actors (e.g. politicians) and objects (e.g. newspapers) of the social world located outside the scientific field constitute the public of science, whose importance influences many different aspects of scientific development and organisation. Firstly, the public influences scientific development and government support on science through a 'set of situations and activities, more or less spontaneous, organized and structured, whereby nonexperts become involved, and provide their own input to, agenda setting, decision-making, policy reforming, and knowledge production processes regarding science' (Bucchi and Neresini 2008: 449). This public participation in science and technology is relatively new and has contributed to shaping the path of research in areas such as AIDS investigations and environmental studies (Epstein 1996; Diani 1995). Secondly, the public impacts on science by determining 'who can be considered a scientific expert, or even what counts as "scientific proof"' (Bucchi and Neresini 2008: 455; also Jasanoff 1995) in courts, where legal knowledge crosses scientific facts and procedures. Thirdly, public involvement in science has opened a debate as to the very nature of expertise, the role of experts, and what lay people do in relation to expert knowledge. As Evans and Collins have argued,

> [e]xperts may be the best people to decide certain matters of fact, but they are not necessarily the best people to make value judgments about the utilization of that knowledge. Conversely, lay citizens are not experts, but this is also their weakness and their strength. While they are not best placed to answer those questions that belong more properly within esoteric expert communities, precisely because they lack such membership, they are, paradoxically, the best placed to make the crucial judgments about what should be done with such knowledge (2008: 623).

Finally, the public matters for an epistemological reason, mentioned by post-colonialists: according to Santos 'scientific knowledge has intrinsic limits regarding the type of intervention [. . .] on the real world. These limits are the result of scientific ignorance as well as the inability to recognise alternative forms of knowledge and interrelate with them, from the beginning, in equal terms. [. . .] The search for knowledge does not imply discrediting scientific knowledge. It simply implies its counter-hegemonic use' (2009: 115).[6] From this point of view, public participation in science is the guarantee that many other divergent voices, especially those ignored by mainstream research, will be heard, respected, and utilised. The recent reversion to the use of traditional medicine, for example, illustrates the role and influence of the public in the choices made.

Fourth, since science is situated and happens in certain places, social worlds where science takes place are one of the symbolic and material constraints for scientific practice. Symbolically, scientists negotiate the boundaries of science and the specificity of scientific knowledge with other groups, ranging from politicians to journalists. Materially, scientists develop their

Understanding the Circulation of Knowledge 15

daily tasks in particular sites such as museums, libraries, laboratories, universities, and research centres. The importance of these sites forces us to pay attention to space as a category with implications for the development of science. As Livingstone points out, '[c]ertain socially produced spaces are privileged sites because from them emanate discourses that exercise immense power in society . . . It is thus critically important to attend to those venues that have generated knowledge-claims and then wielded them in different ways. No less is this the case on the reception side of the equation. *Where* ideas and theories are encountered conditions *how* they are received' (Livingstone 2007: 73; emphasis in the original). This spatial and material turn of the study of science has been a recent development and formulates interesting challenges to the traditional idea of science as a reflection that develops from nowhere (Golinski 2005).

Finally, the notion of social world permits an understanding of the structural changes of science. Processes of competition, conflict, negotiation, and exchange between fields shape the social world, modify the boundaries of each field, and make them highly fluid. These processes are the dynamic dimension of social worlds because they help to explain why scientific fields change and how science changes other fields. Moreover, for countries like Argentina, because of these processes, policies on science and technology are not always rationally planned by a national authority and scientists but are, rather, the product of diverse forms of negotiation between competitive actors at national or international levels (Albornoz 2007; Villanueva 2002).[7]

This section has shown that science as a particular field is situated in social worlds and that social worlds serve as a context for scientific activities. The different fields shape themselves, and each other, in a dynamic tension according to negotiations, conflicts, exchanges, and competition. One of the outcomes of such processes in relation to science is the establishment of two groups: scientists (and scientific institutions) and non-scientists or the public (and non-scientific institutions), the latter being a heterogeneous group that may influence science through public policies and private involvement. Another crucial result is that science is considered a situated activity, both in symbolic and material terms. Thus, scientific knowledge is not only the product of the scientists' minds but, rather, the outcome of the interrelationships of scientists with people (colleagues, the public, actors of different fields) and objects (books, libraries, technologies). By taking into account social worlds in which science is embedded, it is possible to understand the peripheral situation of some societies, beyond the strict landscape of science. At this point, it is necessary to shift our focus to the specific activities of science.

1.2 SCIENTIFIC FIELDS: PEOPLE, INSTITUTIONS, AND IDEAS

This section turns now to a discussion of Bourdieu's notions of field and capital. It is argued that both notions need to be altered in the light of

16 Centers and Peripheries in Knowledge Production

insights from interactionism and ANT. The importance of Bourdieu's theory, which has been used to arrange the arguments that follow, lies in its recognition of the structuring effects of the organisation of science.[8] Such structuring effects have been partially underestimated by interactionists and ANT theorists, yet they are crucial to understand science, at an international level, as an arena of centres and peripheries of knowledge production.[9] The argument of the section departs from Bourdieu's ideas of a scientific field, capital, and habitus, according to which scientific activity is determined by the agents, their practices (conditioned by the habitus), and their capital (conditioned by their strategies, past and present) within a space of forces in which conflict is the organising principle (Bourdieu 1988, 2003b, 2004). However, these theoretical concepts need to be modified according to two theoretical insights of Science and Technology Studies (STS). Firstly, the interactionists' notion of communication (within the field and between fields) as an organising principle of the social life, even when actors compete and struggle for recognition—and other material and symbolic resources (Clarke and Star 2008; Clarke 1991, 1997; Gerson 1983). Secondly, an ANT approach that pays attention to the networks of interconnected humans and non-humans in order to produce knowledge in specific sites and through particular practices (Callon 1992; Latour 2005; Law 2006b). The result of this dialogue is not only the introduction of our revisited idea of field but also the recognition of a distinction between institutionalised and networked scientific fields. At the same time, the dialogue depicts the advantages and shortcomings of Bourdieu's theory in the light of (i) a stronger sensitivity towards the actual interactions of members of the field (not only the interactions presupposed by the structural features of it) and (ii) a deeper understanding of the role of materiality in such interactions (not only as the manifestation of social relations in the form of objects and technologies).

The use of theories that are prima facie opposing perspectives requires us to take some parts of them and re-frame them into a different general framework. In this sense, an inductive perspective that allows us to find structural features of the field permits to combine Bourdieu's theory and the interactionists' approach, a strategy used by Lamont (2009) in her analysis of academic cultures of interdisciplinarity (see also Lalaki 2007). At the same time, this inductive strategy needs to take into account how materiality affects the actual interactions between people and by so doing it opens up the possibility of using ANT. For these perspectives to be assembled, it has been necessary to introduce changes in the meaning of some crucial theoretical concepts, such as structure and field, that allow us to avoid logical inconsistency, as well as utilising a methodology flexible enough to accommodate the prescriptions of all these theoretical perspectives (see chapter 2).[10]

The structuring effects of science, according to Bourdieu, lie in the interplay between two theoretical concepts: field and capital.[11] The former is 'a structured field of forces, and also a field of struggles to conserve or

Understanding the Circulation of Knowledge   17

transform this field of forces' (2004: 33). In such a space, 'agents . . . create, through their relationships, the very space that determines them, although it only exists through the agents placed in it, who, to use the language of physics, "distort the space in their neighbourhood", conferring a certain structure upon it' (Bourdieu 2004: 33).[12] In the fields, scientists are taught how to solve some problems, how and when to criticise scientific knowledge, how to produce new knowledge, and why and how to accept and respect certain rules of the game. Scientific practice in this research will be considered a structuring, and structured, activity and will be studied from bottom to top, that is, from the interactions between actors and objects to the construction of arrangements or assemblages.[13]

When practitioners accept the rules of the game and play it they are also creating the boundaries for the field, giving rise to some practices that they—and the members of other fields—will call scientific activities.[14] Once this happens, the scientific field can be considered autonomous, that is, a space with structural features that distinguishes it from other fields (Gieryn 1995, 1999).[15] Autonomy is consolidated through a 'ticket of entry'; the condition that individuals have to meet to become members or agents of the scientific field. Formal requirements, such as holding a PhD and mastering the technicalities of academic writing, may intertwine with informal ones, such as personal affinity or political commitments. In addition, tickets of entry tend to vary with the discipline.

> Social sciences . . . have an object too important . . . , too controversial, for it to be left to their discretion, abandoned to their law alone, too important and too controversial in terms of social life, the social order, and the symbolic order, for them to be granted the same degree of autonomy as is given to the other sciences and for them to be allowed the monopoly over the production of truth (Bourdieu 2004: 87).

The conditions of entry in the sciences vary according to the context, so they must be taken into consideration in order to explain any particular field. Even within a particular field, they are not definitively established and change as time passes. Thus, they are permanently negotiated amongst the dominant agents of the field, according to their capital and interests (intra-mural negotiations) and between scientists and non-scientists (extra-mural negotiations). In this sense, the autonomy of any field depends on the field's self-enclosure, that is, its capacity for establishing and maintaining more or less strict conditions of entry or boundaries. This situation emphasises the importance of dominant agents because, by controlling the conditions of entry, they regulate the field and its relationship with external (local or foreign) actors.

The second fundamental theoretical concept, capital, complements this spatial approach: '[T]he structure of the field, defined by the unequal distribution of capital, that is, of the specific weapons or assets, bears on all

18 *Centers and Peripheries in Knowledge Production*

the agents within it, restricting more or less the space of possibles that is open to them' (Bourdieu 2004: 34). The field appears as the product of the actions of agents and their attempt to monopolise material and symbolic resources, giving rise to the idea of dominant positions within the field. Thus, a 'dominant agent is one who occupies a place within the structure such that the structure works in his favour' (Bourdieu 2004: 34). The notion of capital rests on communication between scientists which oblige us to two clarifications, one related to the role of communication within the field and the other concerning the relevance of objects that make communication (and other scientific activities) possible.[16] These clarifications, in turn, force us to incorporate other theoretical approaches, such as ANT and interactionism.

Although for some scholars academic communication is mainly concerned with the exchange of information through formal media (Gross et al. 2002; Meadows 1997), for us, and introducing a crucial insight from interactionism, scientific communication is a constitutive process of the field and transcends the institutionalised media and the goal of communicating new knowledge. Consequently a field can be defined seen as a 'universe of regularized mutual response, communication, or discourse; it is not bound by geography or by formal membership but by the limits of effective communication (Clarke 191: 131). Communication in scientific fields is not only a way to make public new findings, theories, or methodologies but also a process through which the scientists set boundaries and acquire their identity by including some actors as interlocutors and excluding others. 'Through extended communication, participants in (fields) characteristically generate, adopt, or adapt ideologies about how their work should be done and debate about both their activities and others' actions that may affect them' (Clarke 1991: 131–32). It is from the centrality of communication within a field that the notion of capital, be it scientific, academic, or intellectual, finally emerges.

The idea of scientific capital rests partially on the objects that facilitate communication and mediate between scientists, from journals to grants to office space. By focusing on the social relations within—and beyond—the field, Bourdieu has underestimated the role of technological devices and of other objects used in scientific activities. In order to shed some light on this, it is necessary to focus on recent studies in STS, especially ANT and the social constructionist approach.

Recent developments in the sociology of scientific knowledge and STS focus on the role of non-humans in science (Hackett et al. 2008; Golinski 2005; Latour 2005; Law 2006b). STS scholars have been studying how technologies influenced by the social world evolve but, at the same time, how that social world is influenced by technologies. Each shapes each other in an endless process. The capacity of objects or technology to shape the social world, however, has divided scholars. More radical scholars have suggested that the differences between humans and non-humans have to be

Understanding the Circulation of Knowledge 19

diminished, replacing the idea of causality by that of translation and the dichotomy between nature and society by the notions of network, envelope, and collectives (Bijker 1995; Callon 1986; Latour 1987, 1988, 2005; Latour and Woolgar 1986; Law 1986b; Pickering 1995). At the opposite extreme there is a long tradition of scholars who have defended the thesis of technological neutrality, according to which objects have meanings and functions given by their producers and users (Bunge 1979, 2000; Carnap et al. 2003). In the middle ground, influenced by phenomenology and departing from ANT and positivism, a group of academics argues that only humans have the ability to produce effects because intentionality is always involved. For them, it is necessary to study materiality and technologies but with a different philosophical status to that of humans. Ihde summarised this position by stating that

> there is, indeed, a limited set of senses by which the nonhumans are actants, at least in the ways in which *in interactions with them, humans and situations are transformed and translated.* I do not want to extrapolate this agreement too far but rather argue that while there are some situations of clear symmetries, these are often limited, and there remain many situations that are asymmetrical (2003a: 100).

Given the awareness of the role of objects and technology in shaping social life and scientific activities, it is necessary to modify Bourdieu's notion of field and introduce materiality as a fundamental dimension of scientific practice. The field, as it will be referred to in subsequent chapters, is a particular arrangement of actors and objects that are connected to undertake activities that, in turn, produce new knowledge. Printers, computers, books, and desks, as well as hormones, race, and mass media are amongst the non-humans within the scientific field, which likens it to what Bijker (1995, 2001) has called socio-technical ensembles and Hodder (2012) has called entanglements. Taking into account objects and people at the same time does not imply their symmetrical treatment. Even ANT theorists have recognised some differences between elements of the network. 'It is impossible to make an absolute distinction between an actor and an intermediary [such as an object], except for the attribution mechanisms attached to the former: an actor is an intermediary attributed with putting other intermediaries into circulation. Thus, an actor can be described as a transformer' (Callon 1992: 80).[17] As far as the research presented in this book is concerned, only humans can be responsible assigning intention, as well as meaning, to transformations, which means that only humans may have the interest of looking for recognition and acting consequently.

Bourdieu had already pointed out a crucial organising element of the symbolic and material dimensions of scientific activity to which I now turn: the habitus. Although struggle for recognition is the driving force within scientific fields, scientists have to respect the 'rules of the game',

20 *Centers and Peripheries in Knowledge Production*

e.g. publishing conventions, rhetorical styles, or presentation of data even when they are struggling for recognition. In addition, they have to master the practical side of science, i.e. they have to understand current theories and be able to make the correct distinctions that such theories demand, and solve the problems presented in the field. In order to highlight the practical dimension, Bourdieu introduces the concept of habitus, which is

> a 'craft', a practical sense of the problems to be dealt with, the appropriate way of dealing with them, etc. . . . There is always an implicit, tacit dimension, a conventional wisdom engaged in evaluating scientific work. This practical mastery is a kind of 'connoisseurship' which can only be communicated through example, and not through precepts (unlike methodology) (2004: 38).

According to Bourdieu, when agents internalize their position within the social structure, they have to choose from a set of possible actions in specific situations. The choices they make depend on their predispositions: 'the real principle of scientific practices is a system of largely unconscious, transposable, generative predispositions, which tends to generalize itself' (2004: 41). This principle, which conditions how an agent sees the world, and what choices she or he can make, is determined by several factors, such as sex, social class, professional trajectories, and country (Bourdieu 2004: 42). Habitus becomes a normative concept, by permitting scientists to determine who can be a 'peer' within the field, which makes it useful for evaluating the performances of scientists. Some people endowed with the necessary institutional authority must decide how, and after what process, someone has the necessary mastery of science to become a member of the field. There are at least two differences between Bourdieu's notion of habitus and the notion presented in this book.

The first difference refers to the capacity of the members of every field to make distinctions based not only on their position in society but also in their situation within particular fields. However, unlike Bourdieu, my use of the notion of habitus involves dispositions that are connected to one's position in specific fields, such as a scientific field or an economic one. People go through two processes of socialization: a primary and a secondary process. Both processes develop the capacity to make distinctions. Second-order distinctions, taught in institutional spaces, such as schools, companies, or universities, refer to theoretical and practical knowledge belonging to those particular fields. This interpretation relies on Bourdieu's idea of scientific relevance. He argues that 'to exist scientifically is to have a "plus" in terms of the categories of perception prevailing within the field, that is to say, for one's peers ("to have contributed something"), to have distinguished oneself (positively) by a distinctive contribution' (2004: 55). That 'plus' is what we refer to as 'second-order' distinctions.[18] The actors' ability to produce second-order distinctions is the result of being socialised

Understanding the Circulation of Knowledge   21

in different fields within the social world, and not solely a product of the social world as a homogeneous entity (Bourdieu's social structure). In addition, by mastering other activities in different fields, actors may acquire other forms of capital, such as economic or social, to be exchanged in the scientific field. This is one of the main reasons for introducing the interactionists' perspective. Clarke argues that

> a social world may be composed of a number of organizations and a number of cross-cutting subworlds wherein numbers of those organizations and other participate. Further, formal organizations may also participate in a number of social worlds. Social worlds/arenas theory aims at capturing, describing, and thus rendering susceptible to analysis the multiple simultaneous organized actions of individuals, groups of various sorts, and formal organizations (1991: 131).

The other difference between Bourdieu's and our notion of habitus revolves around the indicators of educational capital. In Bourdieu's (1988) analysis of French academia, educational capital depends on: (i) secondary schooling, (ii) graduation from the *Lycée*, (iii) the location of higher education, (iv) studies overseas, and (v) prizes. Bourdieu found that most of the professors of Science (85.1 per cent), Arts (91.6 per cent), Law (89.6 per cent), and Medicine (91 per cent) did not study overseas, which means that 89.1 per cent of his sample did not leave France for graduate or postgraduate studies. Bourdieu, therefore, did not make a special study of the impact of overseas education on the members of the field, their positions, and accumulated capital. A different approach is proposed in this research. Where disparities between scientific fields are concerned, postgraduate studies in metropolitan centres open up possibilities for scholars at the periphery that differentiate them from their 'local' colleagues because 'the source of ultimate cultural validation (in the periphery) lies outside the domain of the nation, and instead in the more developed world' (Miller 1999: 29). Central and peripheral scientific fields may have the same structural components but they differ in terms of the influence of overseas education.

This section has shown science as a self-regulatory activity that produces knowledge about the—constantly changing—social and natural world. Becoming a scientist is a process that involves meeting some conditions of entry, respecting the rules of the game, communicating with other members and with people from other fields, and possessing a certain amount of capital, be it strict scientific, academic, or intellectual.

Finally, taking into account institutional features, a classification of fields is suggested. Fields can be broadly organised as *institutionalised fields*, on the one hand, or as *networked fields*, on the other (see Table 1.1).[19] There are four criteria used to classify scientific fields: (i) conditions of entry, (ii) number of actors, (iii) sources of capital, and (iv) level of autonomy (alternative criteria are suggested in Keim 2008). Institutionalised fields have strict conditions

22 Centers and Peripheries in Knowledge Production

of entry, which imply not only formal requirements (such as holding a PhD in the discipline), but also informal ones (such as personal contacts). These fields include a high number of actors and, probably more importantly, are differentiated in terms of their role within scientific and intellectual fields.[20] Thus, institutionalised fields have strong universities, government agencies, large philanthropic organisations, powerful publishing houses, professional associations, and an extended network of scholarships, professorships, and other means to intensify the circulation of students and academics. One crucial characteristic of the institutionalised field is that the source of capital is local; that is, the material and symbolic resources to legitimate a 'proper' academic career originate in the field. As a consequence, academics in these fields only look beyond their local context when they want to undertake empirical research in faraway places or when they are specialised in a particular region. Finally, the fourth feature of institutionalised fields is the high level of autonomy. Although there is always a close relationship between the social sciences and other intellectual fields (such as journalism or politics), in the developed world the social sciences are considered a valid, authoritative form of producing knowledge that guarantees, among other things, proper conditions of work. Moreover, autonomy makes it possible for social scientists to freely establish the conditions of entry to the field and the requirements to develop a successful career.

On the other hand, networked scientific fields have relaxed conditions of entry, which explains why members of these fields have very different qualifications. In Argentina, for example, holding a PhD is not a necessary condition of entry to lecture at the undergraduate level. Moreover, as will be shown in chapter 3, students usually begin their academic careers before they graduate.

Networked fields usually have a small number of participants and they are rarely specialised, because the academic job market and consumers of social scientific knowledge, such as the State, do not require this type of scientist. Science and technology are developed mainly in the university system, mostly at public institutions. The private sector and philanthropic organisations do not play a relevant role in research, which forces scientists to compete for the scarce university posts available to develop their careers. In addition, institutions such as publishing houses or journals do not have

Table 1.1 Differences between Fields According to Structural Features

Criterion	Institutional fields	Networked fields
Conditions of entry	Strict	Relaxed
Number of actors	High	Low
Sources of capital	Local fields	Local and foreign fields
Autonomy	High	Low

Understanding the Circulation of Knowledge 23

enough material and symbolic resources to become important organisations of the field, relying on—and reproducing—individual contacts in order to publish relevant literature.

The source of capital in networked fields usually comes from the developed world and from more advanced scientific fields, although some local institutions may provide some capital to their members. Obtaining a grant from philanthropic institutions of the metropolis is a distinctive sign of prestige for peripheral scholars, since it implies a difficult, competitive, and fair process of evaluation that includes applications from all over the world. The same occurs in terms of prestige: even when scientists in the periphery recognise the necessity of publishing in local journals to develop their careers, they also acknowledge—as well as many of the government agencies on science and technology—that publishing in metropolitan journals or publishing houses gives more prestige to the scientists and guarantees a wider distribution of the publication and, consequently, a more extensive circulation of the knowledge produced locally. Finally, autonomy in networked fields is low because the influence of other fields—such as economy or politics—usually affects the standards of scientific production. Universities are easily penetrated by political cleavages and the system of science and technology depends on provisional policies that change when the president leaves the office. Because of this, scientists cannot always set up conditions of entry and other formal requirements that homogenise the members of the field and provide standards to evaluate their production and careers. The lack of autonomy of the social sciences in the developing world seems to be one feature of the more general characteristic of the absence of long-term policies and strong institutional arrangements that make possible enduring decisions.

While most of what has been said so far is related to institutionalised fields, the subsequent section will deal with the specificities of the networked ones. The following chapters will address the relationships between the two types of fields.[21]

1.3 NETWORKED FIELDS

Most sociologists have paid attention to institutional fields instead of networked fields. For Merton and his disciples, science is a community in which shared principles regulate scientific practices. For them, communities are 'closed entities in which agents feel the pressure to conform to social rules or roles . . . Inside communities, communication has a self-referential component: at every moment, boundaries and identities of community are reaffirmed through language and communication, so that communication inside communities can be visualized as a centripetal force that channels the new knowledge production vertically' (Dal Fiore 2007: 870).[22] Maintaining a sharp distinction between the community and the outer world

24 Centers and Peripheries in Knowledge Production

results in the appearance of an 'external' and an 'internal' history of the community. Applied to science, the distinction produces a stark division between what happens in the scientific fields and its specific sites (museums, universities, laboratories) and what takes place beyond their boundaries. While 'the internal factors include those changes which occurred within science and rational thought generally; the external include a variety of social factors' (Shapin 1992: 340).[23]

The post-Mertonian sociology of science challenged many of Merton's assumptions, but it continued to focus on institutionalised fields. Bourdieu, for example, criticised Merton because 'the scientific analysis of science as Merton practices it justifies science by justifying scientific inequalities, by showing scientifically that the distribution of prizes and rewards is in accordance with scientific justice since the scientific world proportions scientific rewards to scientists' scientific merits' (Bourdieu 2004: 13). Unlike the Mertonian sociology of science, Bourdieu focuses on the conflictual nature of science, the power relations involved in scientific practices materialised in its awards and recognition system. By so doing, he departs from functionalist assumptions inspired by Parsons' theory of society as a system oriented toward equilibrium that had moulded pioneer studies of scientists and their activities. Thus, for Bourdieu, the 'scientific field, like other fields, is a structured field of forces, and also a field of struggles to conserve or transform this field of forces' (2004: 33).

Latour and Woolgar also use the notion of field but in an individualistic way. To them, a field 'denotes the effect on an individual of all others' moves and claims rather than a structure or an organisation' (Latour and Woolgar 1986: 232). Actors move, according to their capital accumulated, interests, and contacts, from one position to another, which they regard as the best possible one. What defines a particular moment of a discipline is the specific configuration of its members in different positions. These point 'to the intersection of individual strategy and field configuration, but neither the field nor the individual are independent variables' (Latour and Woolgar 1986: 211). Furthermore, a field is the arrangement of the positions occupied by scientists within a space—not geographically delimited but still situated. The field is always in the making, in constant transformation, rather than a fixed structure (Bourdieu 2004) or a community (Merton 1973). Its fluidity, however, does not hinder the effects that the field has over its members, because the interplay of actors brings about what Bijker (2001) has called a semiotic power structure that conditions their strategies and decisions.

However, as empirical studies in STS have focused on laboratories, museums, research centres, universities, and other research sites in developed social worlds, they have described different domains of institutionalised scientific fields. A lack of research into less institutionalised science seems to be a feature of STS (Anderson and Adams 2008). To understand networked scientific field the theoretical focus has to be moved from the boundaries of the field to the heart of it, which is the set of actors, objects, and the relationships between them that shape the field.[24]

The first feature of networked fields is the isolation of academics and research groups, that Whitley (2006) has analysed through two variables: functional and strategic dependence.[25] The first refers to the 'extent to which researchers have to use the specific results, ideas, and procedures of fellow specialists in order to construct knowledge claims which are regarded as competent and useful contributions', while the second points to 'the extent to which researchers have to persuade colleagues of the significance and importance of their problem and approach to obtain a high reputation from them' (Whitley 2006: 88). In networked fields researchers accept (i) that their work is evaluated by peers, but they do not need their immediate colleagues' work (e.g. they cite foreign colleagues but only rarely local academics), and (ii) that sometimes it is necessary to clarify how important a new idea, problem, or methodology is for the field as a whole (e.g. presenting epistemological pleas that are not necessary in those fields where scientific criteria are widely shared, respected, and institutionalised). The consequence is that networked fields are characterised by low functional dependence and high strategic dependence (Whitley 2006).

The second characteristic of this type of field is the high degree of task uncertainty, i.e. the variability in the possible results of scientific practice. If science is mainly concerned with the production of new knowledge, and if new knowledge cannot be algorithmically deduced from established knowledge, then scientific activity always implies a relatively high degree of uncertainty. The employment of the skills that scientists are taught 'will not result in definite, clearly bounded outcomes but rather in the production of particular types of knowledge which can be variously obtained and understood . . . The nature of the product is difficult to specify clearly in advance and is subject to negotiation when it has emerged' (Whitley 2006: 17).

Task uncertainty is always reduced by postgraduate education within certain theoretical frameworks or paradigms. After studying PhD students at work, Delamont and Atkinson have shown that postgraduate studies aim at mastering craft knowledge but also at dealing aptly with unstable, unpredictable phenomena, fieldwork failures, problems in replication, and personal frustration. In other words, becoming a scientist means learning to work with uncertainty. In a similar sense, Caffarella and Barnett (2000) and Campbell (2003) have extended the scope of uncertainty to include the process of peer review. While studying the training stage of scientists, they pointed out that postgraduate students do value the peer review process, but some of them find the process emotionally stressful. 'While (postgraduate) students found the direct interaction with others and the iterative process of revision to be extremely valuable, they also found the process emotionally draining and often frustrating' (Campbell 2003: 912).

The third defining element of networked fields is job instability. In peripheral scientific fields, scholars not only need to master the formal requirement

26   Centers and Peripheries in Knowledge Production

of their discipline but also the changing rules of the game, most of the time imposed by colleagues through informal mechanisms and personal connections (Sisto Campos 2005). These working conditions are worsened by poorly paid salaries that force scholars to choose between being appointed to many positions, obtaining alternative jobs outwith the academic realm or leaving the country for full-time postgraduate studies. Ad honorem work is also a strategy that many universities in peripheral contexts have developed, since the number of students has increased disproportionately to the number of posts available (Rodriguez Medina 2008a). A survey carried out by the Organisation for Economic Co-operation and Development (OECD) in 2000 shows that 'insufficient research activity and excessive time spent in non-university activities by many professors' (Schiefelbein and Schiefelbein 2007: 170) are some of the most urgent problems of Latin American higher education, which corroborates the underprivileged working conditions of scholars in the periphery. For, as García de Fanelli has shown, 'the legal framework determines the institutional conditions for the development of permanent and limited-term labour contracts, [but] social practices do not follow these formal institutional agreements' (2007: 272, and also 2009). As a consequence, 'informal universities' have grown, and the Argentine social science establishment has

> shifted away from renowned but decaying universities to a congeries of small independent centres run on co-operative lines and financed by a combination of contract work and research grant—mostly from Canada, the USA and Europe. What started as a 'coping' response to repression and expulsion from official universities, as well as the budgetary famine affecting most of them, has now established itself, and will continue to exist, and indeed flourish, whatever the future political conditions (Lehmann 1990: 183).

Another feature of networked fields is the weight of informal communication and the presence of 'house' journals. As task uncertainty is high and there are many different groups, communication between them is difficult and the evaluation and comparison of research results beyond the group is hard. Due to this, formal media of communication lose their relevance within the field and personal contacts become necessary. Non-institutionalised personal interaction is important in this context because it allows scientists the opportunity to exchange research results and theoretical perspectives without requiring journals, conferences, or other formal channels. In addition, 'the importance of personal contact and knowledge for integrating research results and projects, coupled with the need to demonstrate their general significance, encourages the formation of sub-units around different approaches to intellectual goals' (Whitley 2006: 177). Thus, personal contact reinforces—and is reinforced by—the constitution of small groups or schools within which different theoretical and empirical approaches are established.[26] In such groups there is a proliferation of 'house' journals, that is, publications that include research completed under the theoretical assumptions of a certain school. In Argentine political science these journals are tied to people (not institutions, schools, or groups) and frequently when the person in charge of the journal leaves the project, the journal rapidly disappears.

A fifth attribute of the networked field is that specialisation is not encouraged, except within the research school. Therefore, 'where appointments are tied to teaching posts which are not highly specialised, scientists have to be able to cover a wide range of material and to be proficient in general knowledge. This, in part, explains the highly theoretical nature of the field' (Whitley 2006: 178) and separates the social sciences from their natural counterparts.[27] By discouraging specialisation, these types of fields force scientists to compete for the few posts available under the assumption that a wide knowledge of the discipline is required. In turn, this situation leads scholars to the 'classics', that is, the set of highly reputed authors who represent the core of the discipline. Instead of being oriented towards theoretically and empirically relevant problems, academics in the networked social sciences must focus on ideas—generally foreign—that constitute the basis of speculative reflection.[28] Consequently, much of the knowledge produced in the field is considered irrelevant by colleagues, or by the public (Alatas 2001).[29]

Another feature of networked fields is that they tend to rely on non-standardised procedures, which link the knowledge produced in the field with everyday descriptions of phenomena and ordinary language. The lack of standardisation allows the public to participate in the field, usually as a source of legitimacy for some of the groups, and the use of ordinary language makes the boundaries of the field more porous and diminishes the degree of autonomy. The specificity of scientific knowledge is challenged not only by scientists but also by members of other fields, such as journalists or politicians, who claim a legitimate right to participate in the intellectual exchange (Chew 2005). This situation, in which the degree of formalisation and technical terms is low and there is more controversy because of the participation of non-experts, is a crucial feature of the social sciences (Whitley 1985; Bourdieu 2004).

One of the most important features of networked fields is the lack of solid institutional frameworks for science and technology.[30] Vessuri has described peripheral, Latin American science by arguing that 'it is common knowledge that most developing countries lack a scientific tradition and that few places provide a favourable context to pursue scientific research. Although the universities have been frequent *loci* of research in Latin American countries, this does not mean that they were apt for the growth of *research as an institutional activity*' (1997a: 311; emphasis added). Research as an institutional activity means research as it is conceived in developed countries, that is, in institutionalised scientific fields. Latin America does have institutions for science and technology, but they are usually weak, penetrated by a

28　Centers and Peripheries in Knowledge Production

disinterested State, surrounded by a public not much informed about them (Polino et al. 2003), and subjected to economic and political fluctuations.[31] Accordingly, members of the scientific field have to trust other forms of support, from family ties to international funding (Vessuri 1997a; Sebastián 2007b) giving rise to substitute forms of institutionalisation (O'Donnell 1996; Miller 1999). The lack of institutions does not impede scientists' work; rather, it forces them to carry out scientific endeavours in alternative ways, such as circulating articles through e-mail or face-to-face encounters instead of submitting them to refereed local journals. The shortage of efficient institutions means that scientists at the periphery have had to develop novel strategies to produce and promulgate knowledge. Historical experience has shown that family ties, political bonds, personal links, master/disciple relationships, academic contacts established during postgraduate studies, and even age usually replace the absence of institutional settings (Sebastián 2007b; Kreimer 2000; Vessuri 1997a).

The feature of contacts mentioned above is backed up by analysis of the scale-free distribution of contacts between scientists (Wagner, C. 2006, 2008; Wagner et al. 2001). In these networks, 'a few elements are extremely large or frequent or well connected, and the vast majority are very small or rare or essentially isolated' (Wagner 2008: 41).[32] Hidden behind this technical vocabulary, empirical studies find that networks are organised in terms of centre (nodes highly connected) and periphery (isolated elements) structures. Consequently, these 'networks are fairly resilient to accidental injury but can easily be paralyzed by the removal of a few major hubs' (Wagner 2008: 42).[33] These networks grow by 'preferential attachment', which means that 'entrants choose the actors with whom they want to connect when joining a network' (Wagner 2008: 42). Evidence shows that new members try to link with those who are better known and connected, reproducing the centre/periphery structure. Finally, scale-free networks usually grow faster and longer through 'weak ties', because they 'play a crucial role in bridging clusters within social networks. In science [. . .] a researcher's strong ties [. . .] tend to work in the same lab, institution or field. If he wants to reach outside his own community and communicate with scientists in another discipline, a weak tie—say , a visiting speaker [. . .]—is more likely to form a crucial link' (Wagner 2008: 43–44).

Where there is a lack of strong institutions (or completely different institutions), the sociologies of sciences, as understood in the developed world, seem to be unproductive. Miller's analysis of intellectuals in 19th century Spanish America shows the limitations of Bourdieu's theory and points at the fundamental problem, i.e. institutions.[34] Justifying her theoretical assumptions, she states that

> the difficulty in applying this kind of approach (Bourdieu's theoretical approach) to Spanish America is that what Bourdieu referred to as to the 'intellectual field' was clearly defined and highly institutionalized

Understanding the Circulation of Knowledge 29

in France, whereas in Spanish America it was not. In France, the route to cultural distinction traversed membership of the Academie Française and mention in the *Larousse*, publication in a paperback series (Gallimard's '*Idées*' or Sueil's '*Points*') [which conferred] a kind of classic status, membership of the editorial committee of intellectual reviews, and finally connections with the popular media, television and widely read weeklies (*Le Nouvel Observateur*). Apart from the periodicals, there was no real equivalent of this anywhere in Spanish America (Miller 1999: 28).

In 21st century Argentina, for example, intellectual fields are still weak and science and technology are always in danger. Albornoz claims that 'to formulate a public policy on science, technology and innovation in a country like Argentina, at present, is a task for which there is no ideological certainty because the country no longer has the general framework of a "theory of development" and *solid and predetermined institutional systems*' (2007: 22; in translation, emphasis added). However, even in such a difficult context, some scholars manage to produce scientific knowledge of considerable quality.

Understanding the networked nature of scientific fields in peripheral social worlds may advance a new idea of critique applied to the sociology of science. As Latour (2005: 250–51) suggests, sociology needs to abandon many of the concepts with which it describes the social worlds in order to gain a critical edge. Instead, it has to combine the use of the traditional categories of its repertoire and attempts to see the associations that make social worlds possible. By doing so sociology can maintain a critical perspective and de-fragment what is already assembled, in order to produce new assemblages. It is necessary to have the rich and useful vocabulary of social worlds and fields at hand as long as we are ready to leave it behind when faced by actors who do not respond as expected. In such cases, likely to be found in non-institutionalised fields, following the actors' traces, questioning them, and listening to them would be the right thing to do (cf. Latour 2005).

Thus far, the social worlds in which different fields can be found have been described. A characterisation of fields has been proposed, supplemented by the specific features of *networked fields*, a useful concept to explain contexts of poorly institutionalised social worlds, such as Latin America and other peripheral regions. Nevertheless, the main characteristic of networked fields, from an epistemological point of view, has not yet been covered. When exchanges between uneven social worlds and scientific fields are taken into account, knowledge that travels from one world to another is *not* negotiated because actors of less developed social worlds usually cannot debate in the international scenario (e.g. mainstream journals and international world conferences) the knowledge produced in the most prestigious institutions—and the theoretical, methodological, and ontological assumptions that it involves.[35] In this sense, translation of foreign knowledge by peripheral scholars is possible even if there is no negotiation at

30 *Centers and Peripheries in Knowledge Production*

the international level.[36] Negotiation, as will be shown, takes place locally, under the rules of the peripheral scientific field whose networked nature shape the translations produced. The next section will focus on translation as a necessary process to understand the internationalisation of science.

1.4 TRANSLATIONS AND TRANSLATORS

In STS translation is a concept that came to the fore with the work of some of ANT's pioneers. Callon's (1986) description of fishermen and scallops in St. Brieuc Bay, Law's (1986b) analysis of 15th and 16th century Portuguese expansion, and Latour's (1988) pasteurization of France are the basis of a research program that has reflected a Gestalt change in STS (Anderson and Adams 2008: 190). In these works, translation appears as a fundamental process through which some actors—actors of a network—are able to enrol other actors, forcing them to act in a certain way that is convenient to the enroller's interests.[37] This section will be devoted to exploring the claims on translations mentioned above, to analyse the differences introduced by Star and Greisemer (1989) and Clarke and Star (2008), and, finally, to introduce a new perspective that we shall call *asymmetrical translation*.

Callon (1986) has argued that translation involves four moments: (i) problematisation, (ii) interessement, (iii) enrolment, and (iv) mobilisation.[38] The first moment incorporates the required definition of a problem for each and all of the actors involved. The problem, in turn, is presented in such a way that its resolution is usually an acceptance of one of the actors' standpoints, which means that they become 'obligatory passage points'. Once the problem has been stated, typically in technical terms where scientists are involved, the second moment consists of assigning every actor a 'role' established previously by the programme (the enrollers' interests and decisions). Moreover, enrollers have to try to lock the other actors into their roles in order for the programme to reach its goals. If it is possible to show that acting in a certain way will bring benefits for all the actors, then the second moment has been accomplished. Dominant actors have to make the assigned roles work through different strategies, that is, the *interessement* will be successful in so far as the enrolment can be achieved. Callon designates enrolment as 'the device by which a set of interrelated roles is defined and attributed to actors who accept them . . . To describe enrolment is thus to describe the group of multilateral negotiations, trials of strength and tricks that accompany the *interessement* and enable them to succeed' (1986: 206). The last moment is mobilisation and refers to both the epistemological concern on induction and the political notion of representation. Since translations include some representatives only (usually actors work with samples, not with universes), it is necessary to know whether these representatives will be able to mobilise the other actors represented by them. However, translation does not end here.

Understanding the Circulation of Knowledge 31

In addition to the inductive problem mentioned previously, all the actors must be able to be displaced and then reassembled at another place at a particular moment for mobilisation to take place. 'The scallops are transformed into larvae, the larvae into numbers, the numbers into tables and curves which represent easily transportable, reproducible, and diffusable sheets of paper' (Callon 1986: 210). Translation thus involves the transformation of something into something else that retains some features but changes others, making the new object more transportable, durable, or combinable. These new objects, that Latour (1987, 2005) calls *immutable mobiles*, can be classified, stored, and archived, and the sites where these objects are kept, from libraries to national archives, become centres of calculation (Latour 1987, 1988). The importance of centres of calculation lies not only in their capacity to gather and maintain information but also on the possibility of long-distance control, which, for Law (1986b), is one indicator of successful translations.

In his original analysis Callon presented a four-step procedure to understand translation, but in a later work (1992) he simplified this and described it as a two-step process in which, firstly, some actors attribute some properties, capacities, or actions to an element. By so doing, the actor predicates on the enrolled nodes of the network, granting these nodes identity. Secondly, actors enrol the material intermediaries that make translation—and its analysis—possible. Thus translations are always materialised; they, are inscriptions that link two elements by indicating what relationship(s) they have.

The operation of translation is performed by an entity A on another entity B. Both A and B can be actors or intermediaries, humans or nonhumans. The statement 'A translates B' can have two different meanings. First of all, it means that A provides a definition of B. In so doing, A may input B with certain interests, projects, desires, strategies, reflexes, and afterthoughts. A chooses amongst all these possibilities, but this does not mean that A has total freedom. What A does or proposes is consequent to a whole series of intertwining translation operations, some of which determine ensuing translations to the point of pre-programming them. The general rule is that one actor translates several others, between whom it establishes relations. [...] These [translations], and this is the second dimension of translation, are always inscribed in intermediaries. [...] These intermediaries can equally well be round-table discussions, public declarations, texts, technical objects, incorporated skills, or money. It does not make any sense to speak of translation in general: one has to start by defining the medium, the material into which it is inscribed. [...] Clearly translation involves three terms: A → I (intermediary) → B (Callon 1992: 81–82)

Latour (1987) has analysed in detail the idea and functioning of networking and enrolling. He accepts most of Callon (1986)'s arguments

32 Centers and Peripheries in Knowledge Production

concerning the dynamics of translation and incorporates a clarification on the possibilities of enrollers to organise their allies. Latour mentions that enrollers can do away with the 'explicit interests' of those enrolled by resigning some original goals and accepting new ones, more or less close to the original. In order to do away with actors' interests, the enroller can interpret them in different ways, invent new (shared) objectives, invent new groups of actors, and render this 'detour' from the original goals invisible. In other words, Latour assumes that enrollers may advance their own agenda with a certain degree of independence from the interests of those actors already enrolled. That is why the enroller must have the ability to see what strategy suits him or her best and has to take the right steps or moments and why humans tend to have pre-eminence after all. The result is, as in Law's work, that it is possible to act at a distance, that is, to become an obligatory passage point around which a network or environment is organised.[39]

Useful as it was, the original theory of translation as advanced by Callon (1986, 1992) and Latour (1987) has been improved by later development in ANT. One shortcoming of the preliminary accounts has been pointed out by Star and Greisemer (1989: 389–390) and refers to the centrality of some actors in the process of translation. For example, in Latour (1988) Pasteur plays a central role—historically and theoretically speaking—that contradicts the idea that ANT treats objects and people symmetrically: at the end of the day Pasteur translates, Pasteur organises, and Pasteur wins. In an opposite direction, in an analysis of the Museum of Vertebrate Zoology at the University of California, Berkeley, at the beginning of the 20th century, Star and Greisemer state that actors 'from more than one social world are trying to conduct such translations simultaneously. It is not just a case of *interessement* from non-scientist to scientist. Unless they use coercion; each translator must maintain the integrity of the interests of the other audiences in order to retain them as allies' (Star and Griesemer 1989: 389). This ecological perspective does not award primacy to one position over the others. Instead, it appears as a 'many-to-many mapping, where several obligatory points of passage are negotiated with several kinds of allies' (Star and Greisemer 1989: 390). Only if we are allowed to observe not just the central nodes of the networks (the Pasteurs) but also the less important actors (the periphery) will it be possible to understand phenomena such as the international circulation of knowledge.

The second development within ANT refers to the study in depth of the nature of what is being translated. Here again, some scholars in STS, influenced by social world theory, have paid attention to the intermediary role of some objects that are appropriated differently in various social worlds, as well as their features and attributes. As a consequence, they introduced the concept of the *boundary object*.[40] Originally developed by Star and Greisemer (1989), the concept describes 'things that exist at

Understanding the Circulation of Knowledge 33

junctures where varied social worlds meet in an arena of mutual concern' (Clarke and Star 2008: 121). Boundary objects range from political treaties (Clarke and Star 2008), software programs (Sapsed and Salter 2004), and museum specimens (Star and Greisemer 1989) to visual representations (Henderson 1999), antiseptic technologies (Fox 2011), and information infrastructure (Bowker 2005). The usefulness of boundary objects is that they can be 'very important to many or most of the social worlds involved and hence, can be sites of intense controversy and competition for the power to define them. The distinctive translations used *within* different worlds for their own purposes also enable boundary objects to facilitate cooperation without consensus' (Clarke and Star 2008: 121; emphasis in the original).[41]

The ecological perspective mentioned above questions another assumption of translation in ANT: what is the translation for, or, who is going to use the translation and for what purpose? It seems that ANT theorists do not distinguish between those who participate in the translation, and those who validate the translation. For these theorists, both groups are composed of the same members: the actors of the network. In fact, the criterion advanced by Law to identify a successful translation (long distance control) denies the possibility of differentiating the groups because it forces us to believe that all the members of the network *really know* that they have been enrolled. Is there an alternative? Could it be possible that actors of one social world enrol others from other social worlds who do not know that someone else is speaking in their names? What if boundary objects do in fact belong, at the same time, to different worlds but can be negotiated within each world, only between local actors?

When actors from two social worlds, equally endowed in terms of material and symbolic resources, negotiate the meaning or identity of a boundary object, they get involved in a sort of dialogue, in a communicative situation in which rational outcomes can be expected. From its origins, the Museum of Vertebrate Zoology at the University of California at Berkeley showed the results of this negotiation (Star and Greisemer 1989). While amateur naturalist and philanthropist Annie Alexander considered the collection of specimens as a contribution to the preservation of California's natural diversity, Joseph Grinnell was mainly concerned with advancing his own evolutionist theory. Both, however, were able to negotiate and benefit from each other. The exchange between Alexander and Grinnell was possible because each had something that the other needed in order to put forward his or her own project. Alexander lacked Grinell's scientific knowledge and Grinell lacked Alexander's economic resources. Although both possessed a different kind of capital, they needed each other. This translation required symmetrical actors who recognised each other as an alter-ego and that the space of negotiation was actually the intersection of both worlds, as Clarke and Star (2008) have shown and Figure 1.2 schematises.[42]

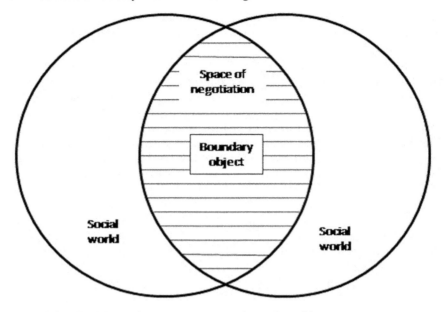

Figure 1.2 Negotiation between symmetrical social worlds.

The case is different when actors from different social worlds, unevenly furnished in terms of material and symbolic resources, have to deal with boundary objects. In his theoretical approach to translation, Demir has argued that

> [h]istorically constructed and subsequently reproduced hierarchies and asymmetries are 'real' in the sense that they dictate the pecking order of thought systems, including a hierarchy of styles of reasoning, what a 'correct' classification is, what counts as a 'rational' mode of inquiry, what counts as an 'acceptable' research question, as well as in which language to carry out the exchange. These hierarchies inevitably structure and shape epistemic values and the method and type of interaction, and consequently have a bearing on what can or cannot be exchanged (2011: 19).

In such a situation, neither the handicapped nor the powerful considers the other as equal.[43] Negotiation between them is impaired by the unequal contexts in which they are situated. It is not only a matter of language or cultural heritage, but also of access to information, material resources, highly qualified people, institutions, prestige, and technologies.[44] They live in different social worlds and work in dissimilar fields. Nevertheless, this does not imply that the boundary object is accepted in a straightforward manner. Negotiation happens, but within the receptive

Understanding the Circulation of Knowledge 35

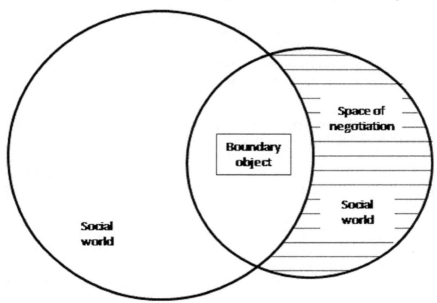

Figure 1.3 Negotiation between asymmetrical social worlds.

social world or field (see Figure 1.3). Negotiation is an internal affair that puts in motion the structure of the field, forcing actors to create alliances, and leaving traces inasmuch as it produces some new associations and breaks some older ones.[45]

What we will call asymmetrical translation is the translation of a boundary object whose validation is determined, after internal negotiations, in only one of the fields.[46] The identity or meaning of the object, then, is not the result of an inter-social agreement, but is a sort of debated appropriation. Asymmetrical translations give rise to a boundary object being inserted into a network, whose main feature is that the actors enlisted, or assembled, do not necessarily know that they have been enrolled. Thus, they may be used, manipulated, given new identities, and transformed as long as the negotiation continues to be an internal process.[47] However, when social worlds and their fields develop and become institutionalised, negotiation can be displaced from the isolated social world or field to a new site: the 'international' or 'inter-social' domain.[48]

The theoretical framework is now almost complete. We departed from social worlds, as understood in an interactionist perspective, went through institutionalised fields and networked fields, and arrived at translations. By introducing the unequal distribution of symbolic and material resources into the picture, we made a distinction between symmetrical and asymmetrical translations. The former are located at the intersection between equivalent social worlds, fields and actors;[49] the latter are the result of an

36 Centers and Peripheries in Knowledge Production

encounter between disparate social worlds, fields, and actors that locates the processes and acts of translation on the less powerful side. While the outcome of symmetrical translations has the appearance of a boundary object, the result of asymmetrical translations is what we will call subordinating objects. The remainder of this chapter addresses this concept.

1.5 FROM BOUNDARY OBJECTS TO SUBORDINATING OBJECTS: SCHOLARLY WORKS

The concept of the boundary object was introduced, and discussed extensively, by Star and Greisemer (1989) to deal with the problems faced by actors from different social worlds who need to coordinate their work. [50]

> When the worlds of these actors intersect difficulty appears. The creation of new scientific knowledge depends on communication as well as on creating new findings. But because these new objects and methods mean different things in different worlds, actors are faced with the task of reconciling these meanings if they wish to cooperate . . . (Thus) [s]cientists and other actors contributing to science translate, negotiate, debate, triangulate and simplify in order to work together (Star and Griesemer 1989: 388–389).

As mentioned earlier, one appealing feature of this theory is the fact that differences between social worlds—and between the fields they contain— can be taken into account. These differences explain not only why negotiation and debate are necessary, but also allow power relations to emerge, presenting a more complex landscape in which translations take place. Consequently, scientists compete and cooperate at the same time. They compete for assigning meanings or defining the identities of the objects or methods at the intersection of their social worlds. They cooperate because they translate and negotiate in a shared space (see Figure 1.2), enabling 'boundary objects to facilitate cooperation without consensus' (Clarke and Star 2008: 121).

According to Star and Griesemer (1989) boundary objects have to meet two criteria. First, they need to be flexible enough to move from one social world to another but, at the same time, they have to be robust enough not to lose their identity between sites. Second, 'they are weakly structured in common use, and become strongly structured in individual-site use' (1989: 393). As a result, a boundary object can change its meaning or identity when transported to a different world but it must remain the 'same' object. If this does not happen, then communication between social worlds is not possible. [51]

The idea introduced by this research is that *scholarly works*, from scientific articles to textbooks, *have to be considered as boundary objects.* For the purposes of this research, a scholarly work is any embodied or

Understanding the Circulation of Knowledge   37

materialised idea produced in any scientific or intellectual field in accordance with the required formal and informal conventions. Scholarly works, along with the academics who produce, circulate, and use them, are also nodes in networks which allow the analyst to follow their traces, describe their connections, and report the arrangements of the people and objects enacted. In this sense, scholarly works are what Star and Griesemer have called 'standardised forms'; a type of boundary object that has specific features in order to make it possible to carry an idea or knowledge from one site (of production) to many sites (of consumption or appropriation) without significant changes. For, as Busch has put it, 'looking at the world of people and things, of material objects and thoughts, of ideals and realities, of social structures and human agencies, through the lens of standards provide us with one perspective, one vantage point, one means of understanding' (2011: 5).

There are at least three reasons to support the idea of scholarly works as boundary objects. First, scholarly works usually travel from one field to another, from one social world to another and by so doing they are negotiated, and not just directly internalised. Secondly, scholarly works must respect some of the fields' standardised procedures and constraints. Amongst the procedures, the peer reviewing process is worth noting, because it has strong effects not only on the content of the publications but, also, in the long term, on the scholars' careers (Meadows 1997; Abel and Newlin 2002; Deneef and Goodwin 2007). Amongst the constraints, the field forces the scholars to be acquainted with the rules of the game (Bourdieu 2004) and also to know that 'they have to publish in the right journals, and they manage to do so only if they write in an appropriate fashion, backing up their own claims with equally contentious references, further referring to other articles, and so on *ad infinitum*' (Baert 2005: 148). Formal and informal restrictions make scholarly works a sort of standardised form. Thirdly, as long as scholarly works are negotiated between members of diverse social worlds, they are a medium of communication without the mandatory requirement of consensus. Academics may variously evaluate the relevance, contribution, and importance of a scholarly work, but it still remains an object that can be recognised as such by the different worlds across which it may have travelled. It is robust enough to know that it is embodied knowledge from a specific context, but it is flexible enough to be adapted, in different ways, to new environments. This adaptation is what some scholars call 'interpretation' and others 'translation'.

A problem arises concerning the idea of the boundary object when dealing with asymmetrical translations. Negotiation or debate as to the meaning or identity of the object, in this case a scholarly work, does not take place. Although sporadic encounters at international conferences or some publications in a prestigious U.S. or European university press by scholars from peripheral contexts do actually occur, academics do not seem to share an international scientific domain. Moreover, such a domain may not

38 Centers and Peripheries in Knowledge Production

exist—but this does not necessarily impede internationalisation of science from taking place.

Even though international collaboration in science may have increased in recent decades, the motivation for scientists to participate in co-authored works remains local. Scientists look for colleagues in other social worlds with whom to collaborate because of the local constraints and demands of their field. Thus, using network analysis, Wagner and Leydesdorff have shown that:

> The networks examined here have self-organizing features, suggesting that the *spectacular growth in international collaborations may be due more to the dynamics created by the self-interests of individual scientists rather than to other structural, institutional or policy-related factors* that have been suggested by others. The many individual choices of scientists to collaborate may be motivated by reward structures within science where coauthorships, citations and other forms of professional recognition lead to additional work and reputation in a virtuous circle. Highly visible and productive researchers, able to choose, work with those who are more likely to enhance their productivity and credibility (2005: 1616; emphasis added)

If the scientist is not motivated by personal or institutional demands there will be no reason to collaborate in international projects or publications, especially in the social sciences where collaborative work is a more or less recent phenomenon. Then, since weak institutions in developing social worlds rarely require international publications for their scholars, the prevailing reason to participate in international projects is personal. Empirical data presented in chapters 3 to 5 of this book will show that this is usually the case, at least for Argentine political scientists.

Furthermore, to argue that there is something like 'international science' or 'international exchange' is a rhetorical confusion, usually seen in the analysis produced on this topic in developing social worlds. The notion of 'international science' demands a set of specific features that emerge as result of the exchange between the different scientific fields (and their respective perspectives on scientific activity), and cannot be reduced to the extrapolation of some countries' ideal of science to the rest of the world. One example may serve to illustrate that 'foreign countries' are readily reduced to 'metropolitan countries'. In her study of scientists' training in Latin America, Vessuri states that 'postgraduate students have been encouraged to do their PhDs in *foreign countries*. Sometimes the State has given them support for long stays in *foreign universities* during training periods; sometimes international cooperation has been decisive' (2007: 18; emphasis added) In the paragraph, 'foreign' seems to be a more or less homogeneous area outside Argentina but what, exactly, do 'foreign countries' and 'foreign universities' mean? In a study on the South American political scientists' diaspora,

Understanding the Circulation of Knowledge 39

Malamud and Freidenberg have found that 'the preferred destination for PhD is the United States: half of the Argentine and Uruguayan scholars and two thirds of Brazilians (of the sample) chose it. Second, at a distance, the United Kingdom (for Argentinians), then Mexico, and finally Spain and Brazil, being this last option chosen by Argentine and Uruguayan academics' (2012: 8; in translation). Luchilo (2010) has analysed the mobility of Argentine scholars and found a preeminence of United States as the favored destination for PhD studies, as Table 1.2 shows. Thus both studies present evidence that 'international', when referring to postgraduate education in Argentina, means the metropolitan centres.

Finally, there is a theoretical reason to maintain the argument that 'international science' may not exist. From an interactionist perspective, social relations must be traced from people's interactions in local, specific settings. If such traces are correctly reported, then it is not necessary to turn to predetermined 'collectives', such as class, structure, or field, unless the 'collective' is still functioning as a shared, rhetorical device that refers to solid, stable interactions. Due to this theoretical position and, as Wagner (2008) has pointed out, the changing nature of present international science, this label does not depict a set of stable interactions and consequently cannot be used to explain the strategies of the actors involved in science around the world. Furthermore, international science has yet to be described in detail, by following the traces left by the material and human actors when they are enrolled in networks that transcend their local origins.[52]

Given the reasons for believing that the international arena of science *sensu strictu* may not exist and taking into account the power relations

Table 1.2 PhD Holders with Foreign Degrees in Argentina by Country Where Degrees Were Conferred

Country	#	%
United States	130	31.0
Spain	97	23.2
France	44	10.5
Germany	33	7.9
Brazil	27	6.4
United Kingdom	24	5.7
Italy	15	3.6
Canada	9	2.1
Mexico	8	1.9
Others	32	7.6
Total	419	100.0

Source: Luchilo (2010)

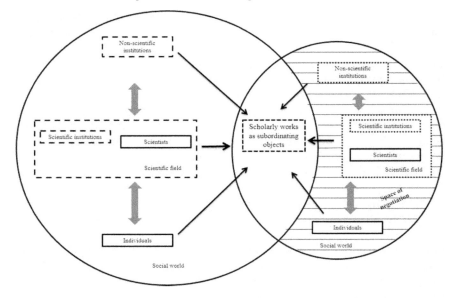

Figure 1.4 Subordinating objects, social worlds, scientific fields, and spaces of translation.[53]

between social worlds (Wallerstein 1996a) and scientific fields (Alatas 2003; Baber 2003), the theoretical concept of boundary objects needs to be replaced by *subordinating objects* (see Figure 1.4).

Subordinating objects share the defining characteristics of boundary objects but they are not negotiated or debated between equal actors. In the intersection of unevenly endowed social worlds, where scientific and other fields meet, there is no boundary object. Instead, subordinating objects, from journals and conferences to visiting scholars, inhabit that territory and become nexuses between the worlds.[54] These nexuses, however, may be subjected to passionate and rational scrutiny as soon as they enter the weak field. For that reason, assuming that power relations always underlie academic exchange does not inevitably imply academic dependency or the imperialism of categories (Rudolph 2005; Alatas 2003). Empirical data from both this research and other studies show that scientists in peripheral settings are rarely passive subjects who incorporate foreign ideas. Rather, they are responsible for abridging local and foreign knowledge in innovative ways (Anderson and Adams 2008; Shinn et al. 1995; Vessuri 1997b; Saldaña 2006). Scholarly communication within and across unequal scientific fields is possible and surely necessary. It carries with it, nonetheless, the disparities of power between the social worlds and the fields involved, forcing actors to develop skills and abilities to deal with such asymmetries.

Subordinating objects, such as scholarly works produced in the metropolitan centres, can be analysed by paying attention to the impact of texts

Understanding the Circulation of Knowledge   41

and their conditions of production and circulation. For example, Lesgart (2003: 103–48) studied the influence of a series of books (O'Donnell et al. 1986) on the notion of transition to democracy that materialised from a research project developed at the Wilson Centre in the beginnings of the 1980s. She mentions that the books

> inaugurated a new area of reflection in Political Theory and a change in the level of analysis (. . .) [it meant] a new way of thinking concerning political change in the Southern Cone of Latin America, incorporating some intellectuals and some areas of the social sciences (. . .) into the systematic activity of comparing several political regimes (Lesgart: 2003: 103–4, in translation).

The effect of the book can be easily perceived: it structured some areas of the social sciences, especially in the southern region of Latin America, and gave intellectuals a metaphor (the very idea of transition to democracy) that they used in order to understand the phenomena observed in the early 1980s. According to Lesgart, the subordinating effects of this work seem to depend on its intellectual contribution: a theory that summarises the asymmetrical dichotomy 'authoritarianism vs. democracy'. However, in the same chapter, she recognises the relevance of the social, political, and economic conditions that surrounded the production of this theory. She points out the appeal of the Wilson Centre in the United States for those intellectuals whose space of reflection was reduced because of the dictatorships in Argentina, Chile, and Brazil. She also argues that, along with their training at universities of the metropolitan centres, the work at the Wilson Centre allowed social scientists to accept the requirements (and benefits) of an academic career as understood in the developed world (Lesgart 2003). By focusing on this sociological dimension, Lesgart acknowledges the relevance of the conditions of knowledge production, although she does not consider them as influential in the acceptance of the ideas in the social sciences of the Southern Cone. To some extent, she seems to accept a separation between the intellectual content of an idea and its conditions of production and circulation. Such a separation, however, prevents her from appreciating the subordinating effects of the work.

> This trajectory [of Latin American intellectuals] was made possible because of labour conditions that were available outside the limited area of Latin America and depended on the reorganisation of the institutions devoted to Latin American Studies [in the developed world] . . . The academic experiences abroad, the structure of postgraduate studies, the features of the research centres and research groups, (and) the requirements of funding agencies, all contributed to the transformation of the state of institutional, thematic, and methodological organisation (of the social sciences) (Lesgart 2003: 111; in translation).

42   *Centers and Peripheries in Knowledge Production*

As the previous passages show, a scholarly work is a subordinating object when it is structured as a network of material objects (e.g. grants and research centres) and people (e.g. intellectuals thrown out by dictatorships) that produces meaningful contributions (e.g. the value as a theory that transcends traditional theoretical dichotomies) with the capacity of setting the research and teaching agendas of the fields in which it is incorporated (see also Rodriguez Medina 2013).

1.6 PRELIMINARY CONCLUSIONS

This chapter has adopted an ANT perspective in which some of Bourdieu's concepts are incorporated in order to sketch a theoretical framework to understand the circulation of knowledge between uneven scientific fields. At first, the notion of social world was introduced and explained in order to present the broadest picture and to contextualise scientific fields. Then, an analysis of scientific fields was developed and the conflictual nature of science was shown as well as the crucial importance of communication and practices (habitus). To conciliate Bourdieu's theory with recent studies in STS, I focused on the relevance of materiality which forced me to incorporate objects as constitutive elements of the field. This decision, however, does not commit me to symmetry between humans and non-humans, since only the former can express their interests (which usually are behind the decision to enrol some actors and exclude others) and struggle for recognition.

To show how science is organised in developing countries (periphery) I introduced the notion of networked field, one in which informal mechanisms are used to guarantee the dynamics of the field. Networked fields are linked to strong, institutionalised, developed scientific fields not in a symmetrical way. Instead, scholars in the weak fields usually use knowledge produced in the metropolitan centres and by so doing they shape those centres (as sites of knowledge production), the peripheral field (as sites of knowledge consumption), and their own careers (as dependant of a specific type of device, the foreign scholarly work).

The notion of asymmetrical translation was proposed to describe the particular phenomenon of peripheral scholars transforming metropolitan knowledge into different forms of intellectual and academic products with the purpose of advancing their careers and searching for recognition. Since knowledge only travels in form of people and objects (e.g. research article) I have referred to them as metropolitan or central scholars and subordinating object respectively. In both cases, the main feature is that they are part of strong networks, symbolically and materially endowed, which are able to have a world-wide scope and to set the research and teaching agendas or peripheral scholars, programmes, and institutions. The final result of this picture is an international division of academic labour in the social sciences

Understanding the Circulation of Knowledge 43

that is organised in centres and peripheries. This structure is responsible for—but also shaped by—the decisions and actions of scholars at both sides as well as guaranteed by the material network that supports it and the symbolic disparity that frequently justifies it. In the next chapters I will show how Argentine political scientists develop their careers, illustrating this complex picture and providing empirical, qualitative data to back it up.

2 A Qualitative Approach to Scientific Fields

The social world is made up of fields whose boundaries and shapes are constantly negotiated, as was shown in the previous chapter. The negotiation involves scientific and non-scientific institutions and people, and usually also includes foreign participants. Negotiation involves not only the exchange between actors but also the diverse changes in the nature of the actors themselves. Their identity is transformed by negotiation and the result is new participants, that is, an assemblage or network with new members (people and objects), who have new properties and features.

The different connections between members of a field, locally and internationally, can be studied from different perspectives, with diverse methodologies, and focusing on a variety of material and non-material entities. First, bibliometric analysis (Schott 1988, 1991; Wagner, C. 2006; Wagner and Leydesdorff 2005), for example, concentrates on the production of co-authored works, assuming that the necessary translations required to produce such works are commonalities of the life of scientists. Second, analysis of correspondence (Bourdieu 1988) is based on the social features of the members of a field (such as place of birth, matrimonial status, degrees obtained, and honorary distinctions) and how these characteristics are associated positively or negatively in statistical terms. Third, qualitative, ethnographic approaches have been used prolifically to study science and technology, especially since the appearance of Latour and Woolgar's (1986) study of the Salk Institute. Ethnographic studies permit observation of the dynamics of science by focusing on scientists' daily activities. Most such works are based on observation at specific scientific sites—usually laboratories and museums—and address the interplay between the material and symbolic elements of the scientific environment. Scientists' work is seen as a continuous process of translations, from dead animals to statistical charts, and from papers to conferences. In these analyses, the task of the researcher is, as the stranger who arrives at a place, to follow the actors and observe how they change throughout the processes occurring in that specific scientific site.

There are at least three problems with use of the traditional ethnographic approach in science studies. First, it deals with scientists over only a short period of time. Although one or two years might be considered a long period for an individual researcher undertaking her fieldwork at a laboratory, that time may turn out to be too short to appreciate some tendencies and structural features of the field in which the laboratory is located (Kreimer 2005). The interrelationships between the site and its contextual network are as important as the specific features and dynamics of the place of production of knowledge. By criticising laboratories studies, Bourdieu (2004) has argued that one main characteristics of scientific sites is that many of their properties derive from their situation in a field, which forces sociologists of science to locate a laboratory in relation to other sites and, by so doing, enacting a particular configuration of actors that constitute a field. Second, ethnographic studies do not necessarily pay attention to the biographies of the people studied. Ethnographers have to observe, describe, and understand what is going on during the daily activities of the group under study, but they rarely focus on the history of these people, and the personal and professional opportunities and constraints that they have had to face. Consequently, some ethnographic reports fail to account for the intersection between the individual agency and the broader context throughout a lifetime (Yarrow 2008). Third, the ethnographic perspective is partially based on the cultural distance between the researcher and the group studied. It is assumed that prior cognition of the technical matters taking place in the laboratory—or any other scientific site—is not a prerequisite to understand the activities of the actors (Latour and Woolgar 1986). The sociologist or anthropologist appears as a newcomer whose main task is to be acquainted with the practices observed and to describe how these practices give rise to transformations of objects and people. In other words, the problem with the ethnographic method is that it is not possible to observe structural or collective limitations, so it is difficult to appreciate the historical background of the members of the group and maintain the cultural distance needed as a methodological requisite for objectivity.

A combination of life-history and ethnographic analysis is utilised in this research. This approach, elsewhere called 'biographical ethnography' (Payne Katt 1997; Reed-Danahay 1997; Yarrow 2008), grasps the dynamic of the scientific field in a particular context by inquiring about the decisions that certain members of the field have made during their careers. In this sense, scientists' trajectories not only result from individual choices but also help to reconstruct the social exchanges that, at the same time, narrow the scope of options for scientists and enhance their chances of developing a successful career. Life-history also permits researchers to deal with known, familiar environments since it introduces the scientists' narration of their life as a distance understood in two different ways. On the one hand, interviewees' recapitulation of their lives appears as an extraordinary situation in which the researcher intentionally takes them out of their ordinary activities. This creates an unusual context that helps to induce a gap useful for reflection. On the other hand, the differences between the trajectories of

46 Centers and Peripheries in Knowledge Production

the interviewees and that of the researcher become evident and it is easier to appreciate the divergent paths followed by both actors. In terms of ANT, the interview allows the researcher to observe in what network the interviewee is situated and what distance really exists between such a network and the one in which the interviewer himself is located. In this sense, a previous knowledge of the field and the people becomes a necessary condition to guide the interviewees through their own lives.

While life-history gives ethnography a sensibility towards history, a method to reconstruct the characteristics of the field, and an alternative to the notion of 'anthropological strangeness' (Latour and Woolgar 1986: 29), the ethnographic approach provides a mechanism to help understand the process according to which knowledge is produced. By so doing this approach may overcome the difficulties of grasping the technicalities of the scientific activity through its final products (i.e. articles). These objects usually hide the processes of production by using a set of rhetorical devices that let the facts 'speak for themselves' (Latour 1987; Shapin and Schaffer 1985; Adelstein and Kuguel 2004; Cubo de Severino 2007). In fact, a crucial step towards mastering science is the writing of research reports that consciously pass over failures and other adversities found during the empirical analysis (Delamont and Atkinson 2001), which produces a standardised and stylised account of the scientific activity. Thus, the better the report, the more difficult it is to trace its conditions of production (Canagarajah 2002; Latour 1987).[1]

The focus on how science works leads to the use of methods that show the complexities of the activities of scientists. First, it demands that we stay and see what scientists do, how they relate to each other, and how they interact with their material and symbolic surroundings. This first-hand involvement can easily be achieved by participant observation. Through this method, the researcher is able to immerse himself into the social reality chosen for study and to become acquainted with the rules of the game as it is really played by the actors of the field. Secondly, the focus on scientific practice forces the investigator, on occasion, to follow scientists beyond the usual boundaries of their academic activities (Knorr-Cetina 1981). To study the natural sciences, sociologists stay in scientific laboratories (or other scientific sites), following scientists for long periods. This gives rise to *laboratory studies* (Doing 2008; Latour and Woolgar 1986; Pinch 1986; Lynch 1985; Knorr-Cetina 1981). In the social sciences, following scientists means shadowing them through their many activities and the sites in which these activities take place. A lecture room or a university café are possible sites of scientific practice. Obviously, other more traditional places, such as a classroom or an office in a university department, must also be included.

In addition to participant observation in different settings, in-depth, open interviews are also necessary to gather data on scientists' lives. These interviews are useful to grasp scientists' perceptions about the field and about themselves in relation to the field. In a way, they are a dialogue between the researcher and the interviewee in which the latter reflects on her/his life and the field as a whole. In-depth interviews can be structured or open and the researcher has to choose one type according to the nature of data required. For example, the present study calls for detailed data concerning the academic careers, professional and personal decisions and influences, perceptions of the field and the place the interviewee occupies within it , and reflections about personal and institutional links with colleagues within and beyond the field. Another reason for open interviews is that many interviewees have a long trajectory that may shape the interview, if they are allowed to lead the dialogue. Moreover, interviews may end up being dialogues about issues impossible to anticipate by the interviewer, such as family tragedies or acts of corruption, despite the fact that a list of questions could have been constructed to serve as a guideline for the interviews, as Holstein and Gubrium (2002) suggest.

Argentine political science is a field with a relatively short history (Bulcourf and D'Alessandro 2003; Leiras et al. 2005), so interviews may also be used to reconstruct this field from its commencement. Almost all professors who launched the degree in political science at the Universidad del Salvador (USAL) and Universidad de Buenos Aires (UBA) are still alive—and many of them are still working. Life histories, as a research methodology, capitalises on the privilege of having at hand people who were actively involved in the emergence of an academically organised reflection on politics in Argentina.

Finally, this research is also based on the analysis of written documents. Amongst such documents there are official statistics on higher education, science, and technology; laws and other regulations; biographical and autobiographical accounts of local social and political scientists; qualitative and quantitative reports made by universities and other institutions; studies in the history of Argentine social and political science; studies of local labour conditions in academia sponsored by the State and labour unions; institutional brochures; scientists' CVs; and reports of Argentine scientific production by national agencies (National Council of Scientific and Technical Research [CONICET], Ministry of Science, Technology and Innovation for Production [MINCyT], and National Agency of Scientific and Technological Promotion [ANPCyT]) and international organisations (Inter-American Development Bank [IADB], World Bank [WB], and United Nations Development Programme [UNDP]).

Secondary literature concerning social sciences in Argentina and Latin America were also identified and incorporated into this research. These texts can be classified into five broad categories. First, there are texts that analyse Argentine intellectual life historically, in which the debate about political science as a discipline is subordinate to the study of political thinking (Blanco 2004; Sarlo 2001; Sigal 2002; Lehmann 1990; Terán 2004; Devés Valdés 2000, 2003; Beigel et al. 2006; Zanca 2006; Quiroga 2003; González 2000; Dieterich 2000; Sánchez Ramos and Sosa Elizaga

2004). A second group of texts is composed of analyses of Argentine universities as institutional actors in the social world, the intellectual field, or the higher education system (Barsky et. al 2004; Del Bello et al. 2007; Suasnabar 2004; Riquelme 2006; Consejo de Decanos de Facultades de Ciencias Sociales y Humanas de Universidades Nacionales 2005; Coraggio and Vispo 2001; Araujo 2003; Naishtat et al 2001; Krotsch 2002; Plotkin 2006; Pérez Lindo 2003; Buchbinder 2004). Other scholars developed a wider, comparative look at the university system, with a focus on Latin America as a region (Fernández Lamarra 2007; López Segrera 2006; Rinesi et al. 2005; Kent 2002; Krotsch 2001; Vessuri 2006a; Mollis 2003; Gentili and Levy 2005; Gandarilla Salgado 2007). A third set of texts includes historical analyses of Argentine political science, focusing, in particular, on the development of institutions—from universities to research centres and professional associations—as well as the role of some scholars as gatekeepers and diasporas of scientists (Bulcourf and D'Alessandro 2002, 2003; Fernández 2002; Lesgart 2002, 2003; Kandel 2002; Lesgart and Ramos 2002; Leiras et al. 2005; Malamud and Freidenberg 2012; Murmis 2005; Serrafero 2002). Fourthly, there is a small group of texts devoted to the study of some of the material dimensions of cultural life in Argentina, specifically books and how they 'tell' the history of the country (Invernizzi 2005; Invernizzi and Gociol 2003; de Diego 2006; Blanco 2007). Finally, there is a group that contains texts that consider Latin American science, its conditions of production, and how it has been practiced by some notable scholars or researchers (Saldaña 2006;

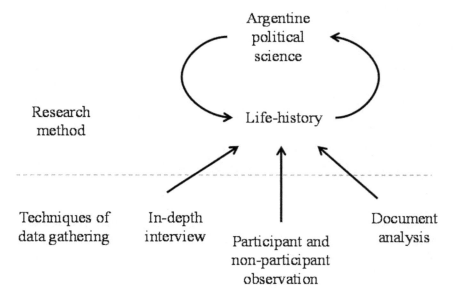

Figure 2.1 Research methods and techniques of data gathering.

A *Qualitative Approach to Scientific Fields* 49

Vessuri 2006b; Cueto 2006; Cabral 2006; Sebastián 2007a; Albornoz 2007; Luchilo 2007; Licha 2007; Beigel 2010).

The main techniques of data gathering used in this research are in-depth interviews, participant and non-participant observation, and analysis of written documents. These allow the researcher to elaborate or reconstruct scientists' life-histories. It is worth noting that the life-history of scientists is the result of this triangulation process (see Figure 2.1). The voices of scientists are complemented by information provided by written documents and participant observation. Section 2.1 deals with life-histories in more detail and explains the reasons for the use of this approach to study Argentine political science, as well as the theoretical and philosophical assumptions. In section 2.2, identification of settings and informants is discussed, along with the employment of theoretical sampling, how contacts with scholars were established, how, and with what instruments, data were analysed, and specifications in relation to interviews. This section revolves around the idea of credibility, that is, the necessary confidence that any reader of qualitative research must feel in order to trust the data and analysis. Finally, section 2.3 deals with Argentine political science, and discusses the reasons as to how and why this case was chosen for study.

2.1 LIFE-HISTORIES AS A RESEARCH METHOD

In this research, life-history is understood as the account of the process of reconstruction of past events by people who (i) make sense of their past, (ii) from the perspective of their present, and (iii) in the light of an anticipated specific future. Construction of a life-history requires gathering information about events from different sources, such as in-depth interviews, diaries, letters, 'and other "personal" and "human" documents' (Robertson 2002: 34). The construction is not an individual endeavour undertaken by the researcher alone but, rather, the assemblage of a network of related elements that enact certain past and current events. The stronger the network is, the greater the veracity of the past events. There is no point of view from which an impartial, neutral reconstruction of 'truth', 'past', or 'reality' can be made. All points of view, and the knowledge produced, are situated, as well as the researcher him/herself.[2] However, even though the biographical approach is focused on individual histories, it does not preclude an understanding of structural features, such as culture, society, or a specific field.[3]

Some scholars have pointed out that life-histories are a tool for dealing with culture. Marshall and Rossman propose a definition of the life history as 'a deliberate attempt to define the growth of a person in a cultural milieu and to make theoretical sense of it. One understands a culture through the history of one person's development or life within it' (1995: 88). Robertson (2002) also points to the same direction by stating that a sociological approach to life-history calls for recognizing individuality within a social

50 *Centers and Peripheries in Knowledge Production*

context, while Ferraroti claims that any biographical account is a 'horizontal or vertical section of a social system' (2003: 29). From this perspective, the individual is embedded in a social context which itself is the subject matter of the sociologist. The individual becomes the means of access to society, but it is the society itself that has to be explained or studied. However, these definitions do not shed light on how the life of a person intertwines with those of other people in order to shape society.

This last question has been answered by symbolic interactionists. Their interest in society as the result of human interactions, leads to the postulation that social realisation

> has to be viewed as the product of a continual interaction of individual consciousness and objective reality. In this connection the human personality is both a continually producing factor and a continually produced result of social evolution, and his double relation expresses itself in every elementary social fact (Thomas and Znaniecki 1958: 1831 cited in Kohli 1981: 63)

If society is reduced to human interactions, then the study of such interactions explains society by describing the behaviour, interests, and motivations of a group of people. When structures arise they are the result of solid connections between people and the methodology used has to address this by paying attention to the micro-sociological aspects of human life. Attention thus changes from society 'to the subjective reality or the social interaction of daily life' (Robertson 2002: 35) and a new interest in 'meanings' and 'motivations' emerges. The focus on interactions, however, does not prioritise the subjective side of human action over the objective one. Bertaux and Thompson point out that 'in choosing particular courses of actions, structural constraints such as economic needs interact with value orientations, moral obligations, self-determined goals, and the individual's own perception of the situation and choices ahead. The actor's subjectivity, and the subjectivity of others in a close relationship, are part of the objective situation' (1997: 17).

Nevertheless, the ontological commitment of symbolic interactionists is biased. If the interactions that constitute reality only refer to human interaction, then the material side of the process of construction of society and nature seems to be missing. Consequently, we have assumed a commitment to materiality of scientific practices that oblige us to focus on both humans and non-humans although granting them a different philosophical status (Collins and Yearly 1992a, 1992b; Hacking 1999; Ihde 2003a). Paraphrasing Hitchin and Maksymiw, it could be said that we have used 'a materially sensitised and biographical lens [focused on] infrastructure, objects, situations and lives' (2012: 75). This position presents a complex picture of society and nature and that seems to be the main reason for moving beyond the traditional methodologies of the social sciences (Law 2006a).

A Qualitative Approach to Scientific Fields 51

If society is the result of interactions, and if interactions have to include both humans and non-humans, the life-history is, at best, a way in to the network of science.[4] A life-history, as narrated by a scientist, cannot have pre-eminence over other elements of his or her career. Bertaux has pointed out that 'each life story, but also each statistic, each piece of evidence, should be made to contribute to the understanding of a given network of social relations. When this network is clearly understood, the analysis is completed' (1981: 40). A sociologist may begin the study of a discipline, a university department, or a research group by talking to the members and reconstructing their careers. Then, she may have to move to the teaching classroom, to private libraries, to the Ministry of Education, to cafés, and to any other relevant place because this helps reconstruct the actors and the network at the same time.[5] If anything, a structure will consist of the relationships among scientists, and between them and their material environment. Therefore, what is social and what is material in any relationship is enacted in the very act of tracing connections and observing relationships taking place. That is why life-histories are about identity or, as Bertaux and

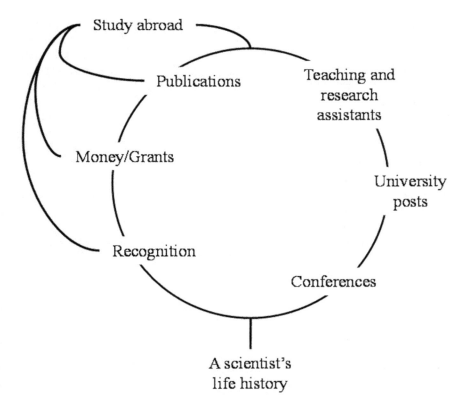

Figure 2.2 A scientist's life-history as a node in a network.

52   Centers and Peripheries in Knowledge Production

Delcroix put it, '"anthroponomic production", that is, the production of human beings themselves' (2000: 75).

When scientists narrate their life, they are making sense of the past events but they can only do so as far as their symbolic and material environments support their narration. It is possible to say that I graduated from Harvard until the moment at which this is nullified by the university records. It is not a matter of true or false statements; it is about the resistance of a fact, an idea, a story, or, as Latour (1988) put it, it is a matter of 'trial of strength': 'real' is what resists the pounding of other assemblages, of alternative 'realities'.[6] The task of the sociologist, when constructing the network of a life history, is to show how strong a scientist's story is.[7] Does it resist the opinion of other scientists in the field, information from archives, and accounts provided by historians of the discipline? These are some of the questions according to which a methodology has to be chosen.[8] They also point to a crucial feature of life-history: it explores processes, rather than merely static structures or people (Rustin 2000). The interview is a situation in which both participants are producing an account of a life; one by asking, and the other by self-reflecting and answering.

It is not only the career of scientists that is relevant, but also their views and perceptions of themselves, the field, and the social world. Subjective as they may appear, they are as powerful or objective as the network of humans and non-humans that supports them. When they resist enough, a solid and stable history arises and the identity of the scientist is revealed. Therefore, 'life histories are . . . not a collection of all the events of the individual's life course, but rather "*structured* self-images"' (Kohli 1981: 65; emphasis added) that produce, at the same time, the life of the scientist and its context. In turn, these images respond not only to the reconstruction of the life made by the scientist but also to the requirements of the interview, that is, the dialogue situation in which the life is being enacted (Hammersley and Atkinson 1989). Moreover, when several life-histories are put together the details provided contribute to the reconstruction of a network, a collective, (Latour 2005) and its history. While an individual life-history can show particular adaptations made by extraordinary people, life-histories (of the members of a group) 'put (. . .) bonds at the very centre of the picture and look at the development of such bonds over (. . .) the long term as they unfold and change through historical time' (Bertaux and Delcroix 2000: 73).

This interaction between interviewee and interviewer makes explicit that in life-history narratives, 'the interviewee takes over the control of the interview situation and talks freely' (Bertaux 1981: 39).[9] Interview-guides are sometimes required to help the interviewees talk about relevant issues. These guides may be based on prior information given by other interviewees rather than on preconceived ideas about the subject. The accumulation of data thus produces a saturation process by which each new testimony assesses previously gathered data (Bertaux 1981: 37). However, the guidelines have to be flexible enough to permit the unexpected to come to light. The life of the interviewee is the organising element around which

A *Qualitative Approach to Scientific Fields*   53

the dialogue must turn. Therefore, 'the precise form of question cannot (. . .) be fundamental to the method of analysis; so that to develop new questions, or to sharpen and shift their focus as the inquiry proceeds does not threaten the integrity of the enterprise' (Thompson 1981: 294).

The interaction produced in the interview also determines the scope of the life-history. Although this research is based on data about the careers of Argentine political scientists, different notions of careers were brought about. For some their academic life includes their family, their parents' influences and desires, political commitments, religious principles, and economic constraints. For others their career involves scholarly activities and decisions, exclusively. While the former presents a more integrated description of their lives, the latter tends to present disparate spheres of their life, not always making explicit the bridges between them. The diversity of appreciations about careers shows that 'the evidence in each life story can only be fully understood as part of the whole life' (Thompson 1981: 292; Porter 2006). One of the main problems of qualitative social research, i.e. dealing with the complexity of human life, is also one of its main attractions. Porter, referring to the British mathematician Karl Pearson and his multifarious interests, observed that

> he viewed his disparate pursuits as episodes in the formation of a tense and conflicted but coherent self, stages in the *Bildungsroman* of his life. I was enchanted by the themes that resonate through, even if they could not quite harmonize these disparate intellectual activities and what they showed about the relations of his personal to his scientific life (2006: 318).

In more general terms, Nye adds that 'while historians of science often use biography as a vehicle to analyze scientific processes and scientific culture, the most compelling scientific biographies are ones that portray the ambitions, passions, disappointments, and moral choices that characterize a scientist's life' (2006: 322). A career, as situated within a life, not only appears as rich and multifaceted, it also arises as a consequence of the moral judgements usually shadowed by scientific activity.

The next section addresses technical aspects of this research. Detailed information concerning the interviews, the sample and its 'representativity', and the case under study, is presented. Finally, the approach used for the analysis of empirical data is explained.

2.2 FROM RELIABILITY TO CREDIBILITY

How reliable is a life-history? This question has several, complex answers. Some scholars have claimed that reliability is attainable 'where the study of a topic remains close to an actual context' (Plummer 1983: 101). This historical closeness seems to permit the researcher to triangulate the

54   *Centers and Peripheries in Knowledge Production*

information, taking into account documents, witnesses, and other means to confirm the life-history. Denzin (1970), on different grounds, has sustained that 'validity requires that the case used for generalization is representative of the population and that restriction of time and place are taken into account' (Robertson 2002: 39). Validity is thus a consequence of correct sampling and the researcher must consider the 'historical conditions' that represent the environment in which the life-history is situated. Blumenfeld-Jones has claimed that, from an aesthetical point of view, 'fidelity' could be a better criterion to use to measure the accuracy of a life-history. He claims that truth is '"what happened in a situation" (the truth of the matter)' and fidelity is '"what it means to the teller of the tale" (fidelity to what happened for that person). Truth treats a situation as an object while fidelity is subjective' (Blumenfeld-Jones 1995: 26). The main problem with this definition is not only that it contradicts our ontological assumptions but, rather, that it assumes the existence of a sharp distinction between objective and subjective views. However, for the purpose of the present research, the story told by an interviewee is considered to be true if (i) it is densely connected to other material elements (i.e. written documents, historical accounts, and official statistics) that support the story, and consequently (ii) it can resist the test of different stories told by other members of the field. Subjectivity and objectivity are, in the long term, a matter of resistance.

It seems, as Miles and Huberman (1994) have pointed out, that 'there are no agreed-upon canons or heuristics for evaluating a qualitative study. Each reader must necessarily judge the credibility of a qualitative study for him—or herself' (Taylor and Bogdan 1998: 170). From this perspective, the only possible strategy for qualitative researchers is to make every step of their research as transparent and explicit as possible. Readers require all the basic information, and need to be able to evaluate whether data are correctly gathered, that the sample is representative, and that the analysis can be logically inferred from the data, in order to trust life-histories or any qualitative study.

2.2.1 Time and Length of Study

Fieldwork was done in Argentina between December 2006 and January 2008. Interviews were conducted in the city of Buenos Aires, its metropolitan area, and the provinces of Mendoza, San Juan, Santa Fe, Entre Rios, and Cordoba. Empirical data collection for this study was done in Argentina, United Kingdom, Mexico, and Germany from 2006 to 2013.

Participant observation was conducted at many sites during fieldwork in 2007. However, most data were gathered at the Universidad de Belgrano (UB) and the Universidad Torcuato Di Tella (UTDT). Appointments as Lecturer in political theory at the former, and as Visiting Researcher at the latter, were fundamental to be present at meetings, participate in conferences, discuss some of the findings on an informal basis, and attend events regularly. While the appointment as Visiting Researcher was for one year, the post at the UB is still held.

Finally, observation *in situ* was made at the VIII Annual Conference of Argentine Society for Political Analysis (SAAP), held at USAL between 6th and 9th November 2007.

2.2.2 The Nature and Number of Informants and Settings

Fieldwork involved very different settings. Interviews were conducted in cafés (thirty-one), university offices (nineteen), boardrooms (six), homes (four), and professional offices (three). Participant observation was conducted in university settings, such as meeting rooms, conference rooms, and classrooms.

The informants were university scholars working in departments of political science in higher education institutions in the city of Buenos Aires and the provinces of Santa Fe, Entre Rios, Buenos Aires, Cordoba, San Juan, and Mendoza. I knew some of the participants beforehand, so they became key informants in the sense that they allowed me to contact other scholars and get institutional affiliations at UB and UTDT. They were told to talk about their lives and a list of open questions was used as a guideline to guarantee a common ground for all interviews. However, as explained in section 2.1, the informants led the interviews and provided insights that enriched this research, but may also complicate comparisons.

There were sixty-three informants who were interviewed in-depth to relate their life-histories. In addition, occasional encounters with other scholars, students, researchers, authorities, and experts in local science and technology provided valuable information that helped triangulate interviewees' life-histories. The anonymity of the interviewees was guaranteed in order to permit them to express themselves in an open manner. However, all of them signed a written consent form, permitting use of any part of their testimony in this book.

2.2.3 Recording Data

Data recording was a technology-assisted process. A digital recorder was used to record interviews with explicit authorisation from the interviewees. Although there were some 'off the record' comments, interviewees rarely asked to turn the recorder off. Occasionally, they made clear that some pieces of information could be used by the researcher but not quoted or written down. Immediately after some interviews, and privately, some personal observations were recorded (e.g. about the mood of the interview, the conditions of the office, and possible new questions).

Digitally-recorded interviews were then transcribed by research assistants. A group of four people, all of them advanced students in the social

56 Centers and Peripheries in Knowledge Production

sciences, transcribed the interviews and received a payment of around £9 for each transcription.[10] These documents, in turn, were uploaded to Atlas. Ti, software for qualitative analysis that permits researchers to select quotes from the texts, categorise quotations, establish links between categories and between quotations, and, finally, analyse the material selected as relevant.

A digital recorder and notebooks were used for participant observation. Where possible, meetings or conferences were recorded digitally and only some selected moments were transcribed. On other occasions, notes were taken concerning specific situations, conversations, lectures, attitudes and gestures of informants, and the material surroundings. Sometimes notes included personal comments to be taken into account during the analysis at a later date. Notebooks were labelled in numerical order, pages were numbered, and every observation was assigned a number. Thus, a three-number code identified every note taken during fieldwork.

Both field notes and interviews were conducted in Spanish. A preliminary evaluation of this research suggests that it was a crucial advantage for the researcher to speak the same language as the members of the field. Among other reasons, the importance of language as an element to link scientific fields was highlighted by many interviewees, as well as the different means by which English has become a *lingua franca*, that threatens the use of other languages. Speaking the same language gave rise to familiarity, which, in turn, led to better predisposition toward the researcher and the study.

2.2.4 Sampling and Representativity

The usefulness of examination of life histories depends on how representative the sample is of the population being studied. However, the relationship between sample and population is not based on statistical 'representativity'. Bertaux notes that we have to go through

> a process of saturation of knowledge. This process confers a completely different meaning on the idea of 'representativity'. In short, we may say that our sample is representative, not at the morphological level (at the level of superficial description), but at the sociological level, at the level of socio-structural relations (*rapports sociaux*) (1981: 37, emphasis in the original).

According to this sociological notion of 'representativity', the problem is not how many people one need interview, but, rather, who the interviewees are, and how they make sense of their own life histories and of their relationships within the wider social and material context.

While quantitative studies require the selection of cases on the basis of statistical probability, qualitative studies rely on alternative ideas of sampling, such as judgment sampling, opportunistic sampling (Honigmann 1970), purposeful sampling (Patton 2001), purposive sampling, snowball sampling (Brink and Wood 1998), and theoretical sampling. What lies behind all of these forms of sampling are the following assumptions: (i) the population parameters are unknown, (ii) there is a theoretically informed interest in taking some informants into account, and (iii) the population has to be theoretically stratified in order to consider all relevant categories of informants. For the purpose of this research, a mixture of theoretical, judgment, purposive, and snowball sampling were used.

Theoretical sampling 'refers to a procedure whereby researchers consciously select additional cases to be studied according to the potential for developing new insights or expanding and refining those already gained' (Taylor and Bogdan 1998: 27). The researcher should present as many diverse cases as possible in order to broaden the scope of the research and guarantee the usefulness of the theoretical analysis. In this view, theoretical sampling is 'to determine beforehand what is wanted from the study and who or what can best provide that information' (Brink and Wood 1998: 321).

According to Brink and Wood, a purposive sample is used 'when specific members of the population are desired as study participants. The criteria for sample selection are listed, and study participants are sought to meet those criteria from whatever source is available' (1998: 319). Given the multiplicity of methods being used to include participants, screening is rigorous and it is necessary to take into account all the relevant criteria that have been chosen. Insofar as those criteria are determined by the theoretical framework and the purpose of the research, this type of sampling responds to the needs and interests of the researcher, focusing on an 'emphasis on in-depth understanding [that] leads to selecting *information-rich cases* for study in depth' (Patton 2001: 46; emphasis in the original).

Theory is not the only important factor for choosing the participants; their personal and social characteristics are also elements to be taken into account because the researcher values some experience, qualities, or knowledge that some informants possess (Honigmann 1970). However, the researcher is able to characterise their informants only when s/he is doing fieldwork, so the process of sampling is perpetually readjusted. The better the researcher knows the group under study, the more accurate the categories for classification of its members, making the sampling more precise.

Snowball sampling was necessary to establish contacts with key informants. Although the researcher knew the local field, after each interview, scholars were asked to suggest some other political scientists to be interviewed according to some predetermined criteria. By asking for possible interviewees, the researcher was able to visualise the different networks in which each participant was located.

The combination of different types of sampling for qualitative research obliges us to stratify the universe and to introduce theoretical categories in which it is possible to classify the members of the field. Furthermore five features of Argentine political science have to be taken into account in order to proceed to sampling: (i) the orientation of the university system towards

58 Centers and Peripheries in Knowledge Production

teaching, whilst acknowledging research as one of the professors' responsibilities; (ii) the influence of foreign postgraduate education on establishing international connections; (iii) the differences between public and private universities; (iv) the organisation of the university system in Chairs according to areas of knowledge; and (v) the disparities between Buenos Aires and other regions of Argentina that may affect research capabilities.

First, Argentine political science is produced mainly in local universities, with a strong bias towards public institutions (Albornoz 2007; Del Bello et al. 2007; SECyT 2007). Further, the Argentine and Latin American university system is oriented toward teaching, not research, and 'the idea of a university as a research centre that generalised in the developed countries in the 19th century arrived much later in Latin America' (Ribeiro Durham 2002: 12, in translation). Moreover, the Argentine higher education system juxtaposes science and technology in such a way that it is impossible, in practice, to refer to the former without implicating the latter (Villanueva 2002). Consequently, university professors are, by definition, researchers, although they do not always have the resources to develop a career on both fronts. This historical and theoretical framework forces us to sample the universe according to university departments or careers and to attempt to interview scholars from every institution at which political science is taught in Argentina.

Secondly, in a study concerning the international connections between scientific fields seen from the perspective of peripheral social sciences, an important issue is postgraduate education abroad. Some scholars have shown that collegial ties represent strong bonds between academics. Schott, for example, has argued that the 'particular influence upon one community from another is facilitated by their collegial and educational ties' (1988: 231). Crane has referred to these ties as an *invisible college* that links academics from different settings, and forms networks of scholars. When academics share experiences, such as postgraduate studies, they tend to establish stronger bonds, which, in turn, are reinforced by the common vocabulary they have been taught (1972: 105).

The methodological conclusion to be drawn from these theoretical ideas is that the sample had to take into account whether scholars had obtained degrees at local or foreign institutions. Consequently, twenty-seven scholars who hold a degree from a foreign institution were interviewed, as well as thirty-five whose degrees were awarded by local institutions. The scholars who undertook postgraduate studies abroad went to the United States (nine), Spain (five), the United Kingdom (four), Italy (three), Mexico (three), Chile (two), Brazil (one), and Belgium (one). One of these scholars holds a master's degree from a UK institution and a PhD from an Italian university, so he has been counted twice.

Thirdly, the distinction between public and private universities has been a long-debated issue in Argentine higher education and has to be considered when sampling (Del Bello et al. 2007; Sarlo 2001; Plotkin 2006). Unlike other social sciences in Argentina, political science has been particularly

A *Qualitative Approach to Scientific Fields* 59

strong in the private institutions (Leiras et. al. 2005). In fact, the idea of political science introduced by Carlos Floria at USAL in the 1960s had an impact on several public and private institutions in subsequent decades (Murmis 2005; Bulcourf and D'Alessandro 2003). This situation, nevertheless, does not hide the fact that social science research in Argentina is conducted mostly in public institutions and funded by the State (Araujo 2003; Barsky et al. 2004; Gentili and Levy 2005).

In accordance with the public/private distinction in the Argentine university system, the present investigation includes interviews with scholars at public institutions (thirty-five), private universities (twenty-seven), and international universities (one) which attempted to reflect the balance of institutions providing degrees in political science (fourteen public universities, eighteen private universities, and one international university). The bias towards scholars working at public institutions can be partially explained by the size and relevance of some departments of political science, such as those at UBA or Universidad Nacional de Rosario (UNR). Nevertheless, it is worth noting that many scholars work at the same time in many universities, making it impossible to classify them exclusively in one category or another.[11]

Fourthly, Argentine universities are organised around Chairs, a stratified group of scholars who lecture on a particular area of knowledge (i.e. Chair in political theory).[12] Further, the head of Chair is the highest recognition for a scholar within the university system. In this organisation, seniority implies both age and the position within a Chair. For our sample, data were available only for the faculty at UBA. According to this institution, 59.8 per cent of the academic staff are forty-five years old or younger, while 40.2 per cent are older. In quantitative terms, these figures separated the sample into two approximately equivalent groups, thirty-seven juniors and twenty-six seniors. In terms of positions within a Chair, the sample included twenty-nine scholars who hold Chairs at public and/or private universities and thirty-four who occupy other positions within that structure. The combination of both criteria shows that, although some junior scholars may become head of Chair, it is common that as time goes by scholars reach the highest positions within a Chair, which means that age and position are positively associated. However, empirical data collected during fieldwork made the distinction between senior scholars and junior scholars even harder.

While complete details of every group will be provided in subsequent chapters, data showed that there are three groups of scholars according to the place they occupy in the field, the time spent in the academic realm, and the type of scholarly job (part- or full-time). There are what we shall call 'newcomers', those who have been incorporated recently into the university system and/or have held a university post for no more than ten years. They usually have ad honorem or poorly paid academic positions and depend on family support and/or on non-academic jobs, which means that they are part-time scholars. What we shall call 'consolidated scholars' are those who

60 Centers and Peripheries in Knowledge Production

have been able to make a living exclusively from academic jobs and reach higher positions within one or more Chairs—at one or more institutions—and may have held administrative positions (such as head of department or dean). Within this group, a subset of scholars is made up of what we will call 'consecrated scholars', the most relevant, prestigious, and recognised academics who occupy the dominant positions of the field. They have frequently led research teams, have held administrative positions, and/or developed their career mostly in one institution, though keeping in contact with a variety of local and foreign colleagues. Within this threefold classification, the sample for this research is made up of nineteen newcomers, forty-four consolidated scholars, and three consecrated scholars.

Finally, diversity between geographic areas had to mirror differences in the sample because the international structure of centres and peripheries is also reproduced within any particular society. Shils argued that 'no periphery is homogeneous [. . .] For some parts of the periphery, like some parts of the centre, are more central than are others; other parts of the periphery look more at other parts of the centre' (1988: 256). The proliferation of centres and peripheries is the result of continuous changes 'in opportunities to acquire or control acknowledged resources, such as wealth, or in belief which led the centre or the periphery to decide that the existing distance is unsatisfactory' (Shils 1988: 258). At a national level in peripheral societies, the 'inequalities or concentrations in the distribution of authority, power, wealth, knowledge, creative achievements, religious qualification, [and] moral distinction' (Shils 1988: 260) produce cities or regions which appear as new centres. The history of Argentina illustrates this pattern and the emergence of Buenos Aires, Cordoba, and Rosario (the largest Argentine cities located in the heart of the most prosperous part of the country) as local centres obliges us to take into account the local relationships between unevenly developed areas. This situation led to interviewing academics in many of the most important universities in the hinterland. While forty interviews were conducted in Buenos Aires and its metropolitan area, twenty-three were carried out in the provinces of Buenos Aires, San Juan, Mendoza, Cordoba, Entre Rios, and Santa Fe. The importance of having interviewed scholars in some of these provinces cannot be underestimated. One of the interviewees explicitly stated that he feels that Buenos Aires' political scientists sometimes forget that many universities in the hinterland have developed relevant research traditions. Moreover, the fact that the first degrees and faculties of political science in Argentina were established in Rosario and Mendoza is usually overlooked.[13]

Table 2.1 summarises the sample used in this research. It can be seen that only four of the twenty-eight scholars (14 per cent) who obtained a postgraduate degree at a foreign institution are newcomers. This proportion suggests that the impact of a foreign postgraduate education can be evaluated predominantly by consolidated scholars. For many newcomers, having a foreign postgraduate education is more a project than a past

A Qualitative Approach to Scientific Fields 61

Table 2.1 Number of Interviewees According to Gender, Position within the Field, Location in Argentina, and Holding of Local/Foreign Postgraduate Degrees

		Newcomers		Consolidated Scholars	
		Men (N=7)	Women (N=12)	Men (N=35)	Women (N=9)
Provinces (N=23)	Foreign degrees (N=7)	0	2	3	2
	Local degrees (N=16)	2	5	5	4
Metroploitan Area of Buenos Aires (N=40)	Foreign degrees (N=21)	2	0	18	1
	Local degrees (N=19)	3	5	9	2

experience. It is also worth noting that women may be underrepresented within the group of consolidated scholars (six out of thirty-two). The difference between men and women may be assigned to the late participation of the latter in the market in general, and in the science and technology system in particular (Zubieta 2007: 88). However, there were no data to determine the real universe of this research. The only institution that groups political scientists, SAAP, did not have complete records of its members by the time fieldwork was done and this made it impossible to determine how many women and men should be interviewed.[14] Finally, the predominance of Buenos Aires' scholars in the sample corresponds to the fact that most of the institutions at which political science is taught turned out to be in Buenos Aires and its metropolitan surroundings (eighteen out of thirty-one). Consequently, this bias does not correspond to an *a priori* assumption about the quality or quantity of political knowledge produced in Buenos Aires and the provinces, but reflects the actual location of political science programmes.

The decision as to how many people (sixty-three) needed to be interviewed obeyed the principle of saturation. This means that a point was reached at which the researcher considered that much of the theoretical variation of the study has been accounted for (Marshall and Rossman 1995; Marradi et al. 2007). When informants from every theoretically informed category had been interviewed and the researcher observes that additional informants do not provide new data (variations) that suggest new categories, it can be said that theoretical saturation has occurred. An indication of this moment is that every additional participant only contributes biographical specificities but these do not provide new insights concerning the structural features of the group. Thus, in terms of ANT, saturation is the moment at which the researcher gives the network its temporary closure.

2.2.5 Choosing Universities and Scholars

The Argentine government created a website on which all information related to education has been uploaded.[15] This official website contains a list of Argentine public and private universities, and information as to what degrees are offered in each. From this list, a sub-list was obtained of all the universities at which a degree in political science at undergraduate or graduate level is offered.[16] Then, authorities and scholars at each institution were identified through the Internet or personal/professional contacts. An e-mail explaining the research was sent to them as well as requests for interviews. On occasion a phone call was used to reach some of the scholars whose e-mails could not be obtained. The response rate was around 90 per cent and just one scholar openly refused to be interviewed without further explanations. Other practical reasons, such as travel or available time, made it impossible for some academics to participate, although they showed interest in the research.

According to the information gathered, thirty-one institutions of higher education offered degrees in political science in Argentina in 2007. Only five of these could not be incorporated into the sample because of lack of funds to travel to further provinces or lack of contact with the academics there. Thus, two public universities (one in the province of La Rioja and the other in the province of Rio Negro) and three private institutions (one in the province of Santiago del Estero, another in the province of Tucuman, and one in the city of Buenos Aires) were ultimately excluded from the sample.

The reason for choosing scholars according to their place of work is related to the fact that Argentine political science is mainly produced at universities (Albornoz 2007; Villanueva 2002; SECyT 2007). At a theoretical level, Whitley has already pointed out that 'it has become seen as "natural" and "normal" for science to be located in universities and the common model of professionalized science assumes the dominance of university employees' (2006: 57). The location of science in universities cannot obscure the fact that CONICET is also in charge of promoting and funding science and research in Argentina. However, CONICET requires scientists to have an institutional affiliation with a research centre or university, public or private.[17] Consequently, researchers at CONICET are usually members of departments or research centres at the universities and, as such, have been included in the sample.

2.2.6 Data Analysis

The analysis of empirical data was an ongoing process. Field notes and sections of interviews were analysed immediately after they were conducted. This permitted the interviewer to remember details about the interview situation, the mood of the interviewee, the material features of the place where interviews were conducted, and ideas that emerged during the dialogue but were not related in a straightforward manner to the life-history recorded.

A Qualitative Approach to Scientific Fields   63

Then, after transcriptions of all interviews were finished, they were uploaded to Atlas.Ti for qualitative analysis. Following the principles of grounded theory, analysis implied: (i) a selection of relevant passages, (ii) the codification of such passages, (iii) a comparison between quotations and between codes, and (iv) re-codification and conceptualisation.[18] The emerging patterns (i.e. the construction of a distinction between local and foreign ideas) were analysed through the theoretical vocabulary derived from symbolic interactionism, field theory, actor-network theory, and boundary-object theory (see chapter 1). When data could not be interpreted through the concepts of these theoretical frameworks, minor conceptual innovations were suggested and discussed. Nevertheless, the main objective of the empirical analysis was to make sense of testimonies, to link them in a coherent and meaningful way, and to observe whether the features of the field and the processes of translations came to the fore.

The empirical analysis shed light on the organisation of Argentine political science as a field. Indeed, data indicated that the senior/junior divide was not adequate to systematize the information and this forced us to develop the arguments contained in this book in three steps, one developed in each chapter. First (chapter 3), the focal point is the training of new political scientists and how the production of foreign fields is incorporated through textbooks or the bibliography for course work. Then (chapter 4), foreign production is seen in the process of incorporation into the academic market through which young scholars have to pass. This process is followed by consolidation (chapter 5) within the field, which allows observation of the atomisation of connections with foreign colleagues and knowledge. This phenomenon, in turn, is associated with whether or not scholars went abroad for postgraduate education, and their experience in other fields. For a small group of scholars, the final moment of a career is consecration in which international and local connections are articulated in order to gain scientific and academic capital and to create strong networks that eventually give rise to new institutions (e.g. university programmes).

2.2.7 Autobiographical Notes

A claim for situated knowledge implies acknowledgement that the researcher is part of what is being enacted. An autobiographical note will serve as clarification of the personal situation of the present researcher.

I was born in Argentina in 1977 and studied political science at UB between 1995 and 2000. I began to teach, as a student-auxiliary, on political theory at UB in 1998, and in 2000 I was appointed as *Jefe de Trabajos Prácticos* (Chief of Teaching Auxiliaries). Some months after graduation, I was hired as Assistant to the President of the same university, which meant a full-time position and opened up the possibility of focusing exclusively on academic activities. During my time as Assistant to the President, I took a master of arts in epistemology and history of science at Universidad Nacional de Tres

64 *Centers and Peripheries in Knowledge Production*

de Febrero (UNTREF), in the city of Buenos Aires. My interest in the philosophy of the social sciences was awakened when I wrote my *Licenciatura* thesis on hermeneutics and the hypothetic-deductive method, analysing Robert Dahl's notion of economic democracy. For my master's thesis I dealt with a Kuhnian reconstruction of Gaetano Mosca's theory of elites and became familiar with some debates in the philosophy of technology (e.g. Hacking 1999; Haraway 1989). Influenced by the material turn in the philosophy of science, I went to New York to take another master's degree at the State University of New York at Stony Brook, under the supervision of Dr Don Ihde. In 2006 I began a PhD in sociology at the University of Cambridge, where I carried out most of the present research on Argentine political science under supervision of Dr Patrick Baert. It is worth noting that I received no scholarship, although Universidad de las Américas Puebla, where I am still working, partially supported my doctoral studies. My independence to choose a research topic might have been connected with this lack of financial support from international agencies (such as British Council) or from the University of Cambridge and/or its colleges. I have returned several times to Argentina since 2003, but I have never moved back permanently. Since 2004 I have been working at Universidad de las Americas Puebla in Mexico, being appointed as Assistant Professor in 2009 and promoted to Associate Professor in 2010 in the Department of International Relations and Political Science. Finally, in 2013, I have been an International Fellow at the Institute für Soziologie at Albert-Ludwigs Universität Freiburg, where I have done research on circulation of social scientific knowledge between centres and peripheries.

My view of Argentine political science has been shaped by my own experience, by the personal perceptions of my professors at the UB, by the texts I read as a student and teacher, and my interest in the history and sociology of the discipline. Further, in 2007, I was visiting researcher at UTDT, one of the most prestigious Argentine universities. The appointment gave me access to the library and all the academic events organised by the institution. Neither office nor stipend was provided, but Catalina Smulovitz, head of the Department of Political Science and International Studies, was really supportive of my research and encouraged me to attend conferences and meet the scholars who worked at, or visited, UTDT. Although nobody openly stated as much, this appointment might have affected some of the participants' answers because of the perception that they might have had about the institution. While some people in the field argue that UTDT is one of the few places at which political knowledge is produced in Argentina, others tend to have a more critical view, based on ideological differences, principles related to the distinction between public and private education, or the tendency towards the US idea of political science that this university actually supports (e.g. this is one of the few institutions where faculty is organised in academic departments, following the US university model). Whatever their opinions, all recognise the quality of the scholars in the Department of Political Science and their advantageous labour conditions.

A Qualitative Approach to Scientific Fields   65

At the same time, my status as a PhD student at the University of Cambridge might have counterbalanced such a bias as well as the fact that I have been living abroad for several years.

2.3 THE CASE STUDY: ARGENTINE POLITICAL SCIENCE

What is the context of Argentine political science and why is it relevant? The criteria used to select Argentine political science as a case to study and the reasons behind such criteria are the topic of this section.

The case study employed in this research was not selected to prove any theory. Sociologists sometimes take a theoretical framework and examine how well it describes a specific portion of reality. In such cases, the theory is reduced to one or several hypotheses, the hypotheses are reduced to indicators, and the case study is the source of data for those indicators. This top-bottom process, associated with deductive reasoning, requires the case to have some particularity or be representative of a universe of cases. George and Bennett, for example, argue that researchers 'may . . . come upon cases that have many features of a most- or least-likely case, a crucial case, or a deviant case' (2005: 83). In more general terms, they state, 'cases should . . . be selected to provide the kind of control and variation required by the research problem' (George and Bennet 2005: 83). Whatever the case, it has to be theoretically relevant.

In an inductive, bottom-top process, the researcher typically goes in the opposite direction, that is, theories are selected that make sense of data. In this situation, the researcher 'is guided by initial concepts and guiding hypotheses, but shifts or discards them as the data are collected and analyzed' (Marshall and Rossman 1995: 112). Thus, the case is the centre of attention and theories are chosen or discarded according to empirical evidence. Theory is introduced to make sense of data or, as Latour (2005) has put it, to make the account or network stronger and more stable. This research was conceived as an attempt to understand Argentine political science as a mode of knowledge production in specific conditions. The search for such conditions led us to explore theory (see chapter 1) and motivated us to make some minor conceptual innovations.

The peripheral position of Argentina and its scientific production has been demonstrated widely (Vessuri 1994, 1997b; Kreimer 2000, 2006; Schott 1988; Wagner and Leydesdorf 2005; Mignolo 2000; Lander 2003a; Saldaña 2006). A similar situation occurred in Argentine social sciences, embedded in the context of the peripheral Latin American social sciences (Cerutti Guldberg 2000; Maerk 2000; Mignolo 2007; Garcés 2007; Lander 2003b; Castro-Gómez 2003). There is no literature concerning the relationship of Argentine political science with the centres of knowledge production, except that of Lesgart (2003), who has analysed in detail the process through which some scholars gave birth to the notion of 'transition to democracy'.

66 Centers and Peripheries in Knowledge Production

She recognises that theoretical innovations in the problem of transition to democracy came from foreign scientific fields, such as those in Chile, Brazil, the United States, and France, in which most of the Latin American social scientists developed their careers during the last Argentine dictatorship. She also points out that such innovations were made possible by the labour conditions that these scholars found in some countries. She states that

> [scholars were close] because of their vocation and the scientific profession; they lived for science and tried to make a living from it. To do so, they had to follow the established patterns of scholarly careers, specialise, obtain research grants, and hold visiting professorships (Lesgart 2003: 111; in translation).

In a recent autobiographical account focusing on the history of the social sciences in Argentina, Murmis has pointed out the influence of foreign fields through acknowledging the transcendence of debates concerning the use of funds from American philanthropic institutions (2005: 262–63). However, his is an institutional history of the discipline that understands the internationalisation as a two-way process without focusing on the power relationships underlying such a process. Leiras et al. (2005) and Bulcourf and D'Alessandro (2003) follow a similar pattern.

'Peripheral' and 'periphery' need some clarification. It is now accepted that categories such as 'periphery', 'the South', and 'Third World' have been under scrutiny (McFarlane 2006). It is quite obvious that Zimbabwe, Albania, and Uruguay all belong to the 'periphery', but it is not so clear what distinctive feature all of them have in common; in all probability, they have nothing in common (Shils 1988: 256). McFarlane (2006) recognises that the heterogeneity of peripheral countries does not have to obscure the disparities and asymmetries between these countries and 'the North', the 'First World', or the 'centre'. She prefers the economic labels 'rich', and 'poor', countries which seems adequate but insufficient, as economic resources are not the only source of disparity between both groups. Her labels, however, show that whatever definition is used, centres and peripheries are relational concepts, and they refer to specific connections between some sites (usually in the North) and others (usually in the South).

This research utilises the idea of 'periphery', 'Third World', 'emerging', and 'developing' to refer, in descriptive terms, to the science produced under the influence of 'a largely Anglo-Saxon and, to some extent, a continental (French and German) . . . dominant tradition' (Alatas 2001: 19; Wallerstein 1996c). In practice, both 'West' and 'non-West' sciences are heterogeneous entities that include a variety of practices, philosophical assumptions, methodologies, technologies, and even modes of arguing (Abend 2006). According to Keim, 'from a global perspective, sociologies in Western Europe and the United States appear to constitute the centre of our discipline, whereas those from the global South, despite claims for the internationalisation and globalisation of the discipline, occupy today a rather peripheral position' (2008: 22). 'Peripheral' is not an intrinsic feature of certain fields, networks, or scholars, but rather a position within an international scenario of social scientific knowledge production. This study makes a contribution to the understanding of the practices in one of the peripheral scientific fields, Argentine political science.

Notwithstanding the differences between peripheral scientific fields, some of the findings of this research could be transferred to other cases. The transference, however, 'rests more with the investigator who would make that transfer than with the original investigator' (Marshall and Rossman 1995: 143). The richness of the description of practices, assumptions, perceptions, and attitudes in qualitative research always counters the ready transference of its results. The application of the findings of this research to other geographical or historical contexts involves judgements concerning the adequacy of the concepts and relationships advanced in this investigation that cannot be made a priori. However, as Alatas (2003), Baber (2003), Saldaña (2006), Altbach (2007b), and Schiefelbein and Schiefelbein (2007) have demonstrated, similarities within the group of countries or scientific fields that are usually called 'peripheral', 'developing', or 'Third World' can be found, making it possible to transfer, with caution, some of the findings of this research to other peripheral contexts.

Therefore, the question as to how Argentine political science represents larger theoretical or empirical units (e.g. 'peripheral social science') is not important in this research.[19] Instead, the challenging question is whether the available theories explain the peripheral situation of Argentine political science by an understanding of its structural features and observing how its relationships with foreign fields are established. This book is a contribution to this last question.

2.4 PRELIMINARY CONCLUSIONS

This chapter complements the previous one by the addition of a methodological strategy to enact the networks that constitute a scientific field. It introduces a bottom-top approach, according to which personal decisions and actions are shaped by—and mould—the structural features of the field. This inductive view allows us to focus on the life of political scientists as a way in to the field and obliges us to obtain and analyse additional information (i.e. historical accounts and university reports) with which triangulation can be produced. When triangulation is completed, a network of people and objects is enacted, one that also includes the researcher himself.

The complexity of Argentine political science has been studied by sampling the field according to local characteristics of the members of the field, such as age, geographical location, institutional affiliation, and place of postgraduate education. Sampling meets the requirements of qualitative

68 Centers and Peripheries in Knowledge Production

research according to which theoretical categories and research interests have to be taken into account. In addition, the personal and professional experiences of the researcher, along with snowball sampling, have allowed the investigation to capitalise scholarly contacts and by so doing it was possible to interview dominant and non-dominant actors of the field.[20] This situation gives rise to a broader picture and richer understanding of Argentine political science and permits us to observe the struggle between scholars and networks to control the field.

The methodology proposed is useful to understand the micro-exchanges that concretise the mechanisms of production of a peripheral condition, as it employs an inductive strategy in dealing with the complex landscape of Argentine political science. Although a geopolitics of knowledge at an international level actually exists (Alatas 2001, Baber 2003, Connell 2007), each field deals with such a situation differently, due, in part, to the specificities of their conditions of knowledge production. The strategies and mechanisms used by Argentine political scientists to face the peripheral conditions (constructed in the very process of becoming a political scientist) depend on local institutional constraints that shape the scientific and scholarly practices. A description of how those conditions are produced and reproduced, from undergraduate studies to consecration, is the subject matter of the subsequent chapters of this book.

3 Training Scientists in Networked Scientific Fields

It is generally assumed that a career in science begins in the university, a site in which students receive not only theoretical instruction but also practical education in order to master the skills that a discipline requires. In addition, university professors and researchers show students a set of accepted behaviours and rules that they must follow during their careers as well as a series of images of what it means to be a good scientist. Students draw explicit knowledge about specific topics or problems in their discipline from theoretical instruction. They learn by means of practical exercises how to deal with theoretical knowledge in order to appropriate it and use it.

The outcome of theoretical, practical, and moral knowledge is a twofold image. On the one hand, the image is of an ideal scientist concerned with social and political problems and ready to produce and disseminate relevant knowledge. On the other hand, students also acquire a realistic image of scientists by observing the obstacles and benefits that their professors face in practice. The first image is associated with the texts that students read, but the second image is connected to the scientists who stand before them in the classroom. This second image has been analysed by Kuhn under the label of 'normal science', which 'can be determined in part by the direct inspection of paradigms, a process that is often aided by but does not depend upon the formulation of rules and assumption' (Kuhn 1962: 44). Polanyi (1958), however, had already studied this form of transmission of knowledge and called it 'tacit knowledge', because it is acquired through practice and cannot be explicitly articulated.

The training process through which students become political scientists in Argentina is examined in this chapter. The analysis focuses on the role played by foreign ideas in the enculturation of students at Argentine universities at the undergraduate level.[1] Foreign ideas are materialised in many ways, from books and articles to pamphlets and encyclopedias, and they constitute what we called *subordinating objects* in chapter 1. The decision as to what texts should be taught will be analysed in later chapters, since that choice is attached to the trajectories of professors and researchers.

The present research focuses on the theoretical courses of undergraduate programmes, in order to study the training process of Argentine

70 Centers and Peripheries in Knowledge Production

political scientists, for three reasons.[2] First, as most interviewees have pointed out, theoretical courses are the core of these programmes; they give specificity to political science as a discipline and a profession.[3] Second, theories not only introduce concepts and relationships between them, but, rather, they also 'formulate a broad vision of the social' (Connell 2007: 28) and the political and, by so doing, they provide specific worldviews that condition human perception and understanding. In this way, they are more than an epistemological device; they provide a particular ontology (Law and Urry 2004). Third, theories are usually presented as ungrounded knowledge, i.e. a body of ideas whose value lies in its capacity to make sense of phenomena from *any* part of world. Were this epistemological assumption true, theoretical courses should reflect a geographical diversity of authors—or even a bias towards local ones—that, nevertheless, has not been found. Instead, the ideas of central scientific fields are always the heart of the syllabi of these courses, banishing local theories from students' minds.

The points made in this chapter are set out in three sections. Firstly, the construction of a distinction between local and foreign ideas is analysed, focusing on how students, in ANT's terms, translate those ideas into convenient strategies. However, the ideas are not incorporated into the local field in a straightforward manner but, rather, through debate and negotiation. This second section also shows that translations resulting from such negotiations involve actors from other fields, such as political parties and non-academic journals. The last section discusses the theoretical relevance of these findings and argues for a critical understanding of the appropriation of ideas by students in peripheral scientific fields.

3.1 CONSTRUCTING THE DISTINCTION

When political scientists in Argentina finish their training process at undergraduate level, they tend to differentiate between local and foreign ideas. For all of them, the differentiation implies values and some moral judgements as to the adequacy, relevance, complexity, and quality of both types of ideas. This section focuses on the processes through which this difference is produced at the undergraduate level. The effects of this process on scholars are studied in more detail in the subsequent chapters, since judgements concerning local and foreign ideas help scholars to organise and structure their careers.[4]

For some scholars who were interviewed, the distinction is clear in relation to the place that local and foreign ideas occupy within the curriculum. While the work of US and Western European scholars is studied in courses such as political theory, comparative politics, or the history of political thought, the writings of local and Latin American scholars are part of courses such as Latin American political thought, Argentine social and

Training Scientists in Networked Scientific Fields 71

political thought, Latin American problems, and the history of Argentina and Latin America. In extreme cases, theoretical courses introduce only foreign texts and students think that there is no local theoretical production in the discipline, which for some senior scholars seems to be the case (Strasser 2012). The lack of local production within the syllabi of political theory or other core courses suggests, more implicitly than explicitly, a seeming inability of local thinkers to carry out scholarly activity.

> [In some courses, professors] have this belief, this myth that 'Latin Americans' are not 'suited to' scholarly life, whereas Europeans are. So, let's be trained as Europeans to be closer to them, to European academics, and not to Latin American [scholars] (57: 55; in translation).

A mature scholar at a public university stated in the clearest manner the idea that there is no local production in political science. He acknowledges the predominance of Western scholars and points out an international division of labour between the periphery and centres of knowledge production. Moreover, he defends a classic distinction between basic and applied knowledge and argues that the former is produced in central institutions—generally in developed countries—and scholars in the periphery can just apply that knowledge in local situations. Teaching, for him, is precisely the application of such knowledge to specific local or regional problems. Thus, the pedagogical decision of choosing texts for a syllabus becomes an ontological commitment, together with certain ideas of what it is to be a (peripheral) scholar.

> In my syllabus on Contemporary Theory, I do not use one Argentine scholar. Not one. And if anything, I use Acuña's text to show the 'chicken game' [as exemplified by the] constitutional games in the 1994 National Constitutional Convention, as a practical piece of work. What else can I use? Is there any important Argentine political theorist? Will I use Portantiero's and Nun's texts? I teach Taylor [and] Hall (6: 163; in translation).

For students, on the other hand, applying foreign political knowledge to local situations identifies such knowledge as universal, and the goal of the researcher is to be able to use it adequately in different contexts, which is a poor original endeavour. Even though these ideas may be completely useless at first, a successful political scientist in peripheral contexts is the one who makes the hermeneutic effort to adapt the ideas to the case studied. This process of adaptation is usually preferred over the detection, tracking, and use of local theories and knowledge, a procedure that consumes more of the researcher's time and resources. Consequently, asymmetrical translation, i.e. the enrolment of foreign texts into a new, local network to produce an explanation of local problems, is a necessity for research which takes

72 Centers and Peripheries in Knowledge Production

place in contexts where there is a lack (or ignorance) of local theoretical production and important time and resource constraints.

> It was great because I realised that the concepts I had learnt were not useful to understand Africa. They couldn't be applied to [the situation in] those countries. But [I also realised that] with everything I had read [. . .] I could adapt [these concepts]. It is like a structure that one has in one's head . . . tools . . . so everything I had read, everything I had been taught were tools to deal with [this situation] . . . And I was lucky enough to get a post [in the Ministry of Foreign Affairs] and to be able to analyse [African problems] (51: 20; in translation).

What is a social fact of the international dynamic of knowledge for some scholars becomes disappointment for others who regret the paucity of local production and the dependency on foreign publications. Disappointment reflects, at the same time, the perception of the US influence on local political science and the distortion introduced by the use of English as the lingua franca for political scientists.

> There are only a few [Argentine] texts, as recommended or mandatory readings, in our syllabi [in theoretical courses]. If one reads any of our syllabi, 70–80 per cent of the texts, not old but new, are from foreign publications, especially US publications, and it seems that it is the fashion for students to have to read in English (48: 71; in translation).

A subtle process, through which some theories become canonical for understanding the local situation, is repetition. Some texts are used and re-used in many courses and this reiteration brings about the idea that those texts are part of a fundamental core that defines political science.

> In the undergraduate programmes in political science in Buenos Aires students discuss the same topics and read the same texts from their first year to their fourth or fifth year. Therefore, there is a repetition in the programme, and a repetition of authors, of articles (45: 109; in translation)

Repetition, by itself, may not be relevant for an analysis of the introduction of foreign ideas into peripheral fields. However, when seen in relation to the paucity of local production in the syllabi of theoretical courses, repetition means reiteration of theories produced abroad, generally in centres of knowledge production. The consequence is a twofold process of instituting a canon and positioning foreign theories in the very heart of such a canon.

Probably the most recurrent process in producing the distinction between local and foreign production is the explicit differentiation of both levels within a course or an undergraduate programme. By splitting the syllabi

Training Scientists in Networked Scientific Fields 73

into two stages, for example, professors tend to make students believe that such stages represent epistemological differences.

> The four first units [of the syllabus] are strongly theoretical . . . [they include] Luhmann, complexity theory, Wallerstein, for [students] to have a macro perspective, with different views, and to see how they renovated the theory of systems . . . [Students] look at me [surprised] . . . Inputs, outputs. The fifth and sixth units [of the syllabus] are more theme-oriented and we focus on Latin America, yet we try to root every unit in theory in order to avoid having a free-floating theory up there, in the air (3: 59; in translation).

Professors tend to separate local and foreign production in terms of science and non-science, resting on epistemological differences. While science is linked to foreign approaches, such as those proposed by behavioural theoreticians, local production is presented as more rustic, primitive, and simple. Consequently, the programme is grouped according to this difference and the last years of training are perceived as a refinement of the analytical abilities of the student. Going from classics to foreign contemporary theoreticians is to follow a trace from proto-science to highly formalised reasoning.

> Aristotle, Machiavelli, history . . . that fascinated me at first. [Then] I began to read Rex, Parsons, Merton; I was put in front of 'science'. I read Galtung [. . .] Those authors opened my mind . . . political science appeared in the fourth and fifth years . . . *there was a political scientific refinement* . . . Huntington, Easton, Apter, Almond, and obviously Sartori, and Bobbio (34: 15; in translation; emphasis added)

It could be argued that the sharp distinction between science and non-science was a feature of Argentine political science in the 1960s and the 1970s, when debates as to the level of 'scientificity' of political science abounded (Murmis 2005; Bulcourf and D'Alessandro 2002, 2003). Nevertheless, young scholars mention that it is still the case that some texts are associated with the core of the discipline, these being texts mainly produced in central fields, while other local texts are taught as applications.

> The first and second years [of university] are when [professors] teach the *scientific and methodological bases*, which are the core of the discipline, and you can then talk about what political science is [. . .] In the third and fourth [years], it is possible to deal with [specific topics] and [that's when] we read most Latin American authors (51: 24; in translation; emphasis added).

In practice, another means of differentiating local and foreign production is by choosing some of the texts as obligatory reading and others as

74 *Centers and Peripheries in Knowledge Production*

complementary. In this case, professors do not ignore local production, but they consider it as second-rate scientific outputs or mere applications of foreign theoretical ideas. This difference contributes to the asymmetry by forcing the students to become familiar with the former, but not necessarily with the latter.

> [To approve a course] it was mandatory to write a paper to pass Cavarozzi's seminar. For the paper Cavarozzi gave you a long list of Latin American and Argentine bibliography. He included *El Orden Conservador*, some documents produced at CEDES [Research Centre on the State and Society] and there were some texts of Latin American literature. So [we read] . . . Cardoso and Faleto . . . some works by Delich. So, yes, *these texts were not mandatory bibliography for this seminar* (15: 158; in translation; emphasis added).

When local and foreign ideas are situated at different levels, science is perceived as an attribute of texts written by foreign authors and students are puzzled by the fact that a Latin American or Argentine scholar is also able to produce theory.[5] This situation indicates that, consciously or unconsciously, students link texts, authors, and places of production of knowledge, and think of science as a result of such a configuration. Students perceive science as the outcome of the interconnection between some people (metropolitan scholars) working under certain conditions (the centres' scholarly institutions) and producing a particular kind of text (the scholarly work, mainly scientific articles and monographs). This perception not only reinforces the centrality of certain places, people, and institutions but also underestimates their own field and scholarly activities, because the production of those working at other places appears as peripheral in terms of importance, relevance, and universal application. Thus, by perceiving things this way and acting accordingly (e.g. choosing metropolitan institutions to undertake PhDs), students contribute to enact a network through which political knowledge concentrates on centres (production) and flows to peripheries (use).

> The biggest problem that Political Science, as it is taught at UBA, has is that it is too broad; it focuses on nothing. Above all, we read many European and US authors and very few Latin American ones. So one ends up being . . . I ended up being a supporter of Guillermo O'Donnell. Not because I like what he writes, but because he is one of the few Latin American authors that we read as undergraduate students. [. . .] Besides *O'Donnell creates concepts, develops theories . . . reading his works is so great that you finally end up appreciating him although you don't really like him.* We see many European authors, much Italian, British, and Spanish political science and very few [authors or theories] from here (57: 54; in translation; emphasis added).

Training Scientists in Networked Scientific Fields 75

Another means of producing a distinction between local and foreign ideas is to present the latter as a novelty. This occurred at the commencement of Argentine political science, but not exclusively at that time. Novelty was crucial in the context in which local production on political issues was permeated by law, history, and philosophy. The empirical turn introduced by some scholars (e.g. Germani in sociology and Floria in political science) was fundamental to giving local political science a scientific status and taking it away from the domain of other social sciences. However, the introduction of foreign ideas as novel approaches to politics was also characteristic of the period in which several social and political scientists returned to Argentina, after the re-establishment of a democratic regime in 1983. In the 1990s novelty was associated with public choice and rational choice theoreticians and nowadays seems to be linked to social network analysis and the research agenda set up by terrorism and international security. The point is clear: at any given time, some theories or methodologies are presented as novel and; by so doing their supporters enhance their own positions in the local field.

The importance of novel ideas for local career strategies was mentioned by interviewees. For some, novel foreign ideas were relevant for keeping in touch with colleagues abroad because they channelled the academic exchange. Commenting on, or translating, a colleague's article, for example, made it easy to stay in contact with other political scientists abroad and let them know not only the predisposition to collaborate but also the possession of the required abilities to undertake such a critical analysis. In peripheral fields, novel ideas allow some scholars to establish new links with local publishing houses, which, sometimes, are not involved in translating texts in political science due to the costs or the lack of interest of metropolitan academics to publish in such fields.

Novelty is empowered by its connection with scientific methods.[6] The link between novelty and scientificity can be strong because Argentine political science has attempted to be an autonomous discipline by emphasising its methodological rigour and its epistemological status. Furthermore, foreign authors, who focus on issues of empirical methodology and conceptual accuracy—frequently unexplored by local production—attract many students and become icons of the scientific study of politics.[7] The behavioural revolution in the 1960s, for example, impacted on the Argentine social science field by introducing a sharp distinction between political science and law and philosophy.[8] The professors who introduced the work of behaviouralist researchers, such as Easton and Powell, relied on the importance of empirical evidence and methods, and presented their texts as scientific and methodologically grounded.

In 1968, and before that [. . .], *there was already a more empirical perspective on social sciences, more scientific, more methodological, and separated from philosophy and law . . . And this situation coincided with the time when professor Floria arrived at this university.*

76 Centers and Peripheries in Knowledge Production

> He was returning from his postgraduate studies in political science in the United States and called other people who also had done postgraduate studies abroad: Natalio Botana, Mariano Grondona . . . and others. [. . .] They formed a team here and began the cycle of 'political science', not in the plural (political sciences) but in the singular; that is, it was not a compendium of courses from other disciplines that focused on the political reality, but, rather, a science with its specific focal point, independent of neighbouring disciplines. I was here at that moment (23: 9; in translation; emphasis added).

When novelty is accepted as a criterion for use in evaluating teaching and research, students tend to identify good teaching with an up to date bibliography.[9] In the context of a paucity of local production and easy access to foreign journals and books—through online databases—the criterion forces professors to rely on publications from abroad in order to keep their syllabi up to date.[10] As a consequence, the pressure for new ideas becomes a pressure for foreign texts.

> As you advance in your studies, you read, compare, and realise [that there are] some professors who use bibliographies from the 1980s and [others] who give you the most up to date texts. You see? The bibliography that a professor uses is [a] determinant [factor of the quality of his or her teaching] (9: 34; in translation).

Novelty is not only related to ideas, but also to people. In some contexts, such as the first years of the programme of political science at the Universidad de Buenos Aires, professors who are coming back from long periods abroad introduce new ideas, new debates, and new methodologies. By so doing debate is enriched at the local level—which highlights the relevance of the repatriation of scientists who have gone abroad for postgraduate education—and scholars use novel ideas to progress within the local field. The consequence of such a process is a multi-paradigmatic political science with strong influences from many fields, from the US rational choice to the French structuralism.

Even when foreign ideas are not new, students may be enticed towards them because they are taught by prestigious, widely recognised, professors whose cutting-edge knowledge shows the complexity of the discipline as well as its future. The prestige of professors attracts students even though such an attraction is sometimes not thoroughly conscious but, rather, the product of a long, subtle process through which some students become disciples of recognised scholars. In other cases, students clearly realise that some professors have an academic capital that distinguishes them from the other scholars because they have a broader scholarship or a distinguished career. In both cases, prestigious scholars usually create a 'circle' of students with whom they establish solid and long standing bonds, helping them to develop their academic careers. For their disciples, the career of these scholars is the exact definition of professional success, making these academics appear to be as a model to be imitated, and the ideas they transmit as knowledge to be propagated to other generations. Thus, prestige travels from people to texts and this intertwining of ideas, professors, and students gives rise to a network that tends to enact a specific idea of political science, its theoretical foundations, and its methodological assumptions.[11]

Prestige, however, is not the static property of some scholars. It is a dynamic phenomenon, the outcome of the interplay between actors of the field—usually peers—which endows some of them with recognition by reading and citing their works. For students, productive professors are perceived as a particular kind of scholar, and are highly valued because they have their names in print and because students have read their texts. In this sense, prestige is the result of scholars being translated by their pupils through the texts they have produced. The influence of such scholars may begin in the first meeting, but it often continues for many years, as several interviewees report. The impact involves not only the acquisition of some state-of-the-art knowledge in the discipline but also the encouragement of an academic career.

> In 1986 I attended a seminar course that changed my life. It was Comparative Political Systems, with Marcelo Cavarozzi. [. . .] We have been friends for fifteen years, a great guy . . . a great motivator and team-builder. [Some years later] when I was doubtful about applying for a PhD, Cavarozzi went as Visiting Professor [to the University of North Carolina, Chapel Hill] and, when he returned, he said to me: 'It is extraordinary; beautiful . . . the department [of political science] is very good . . . they don't have much money but it doesn't matter. Just apply there' (52:25; 52:45; in translation).

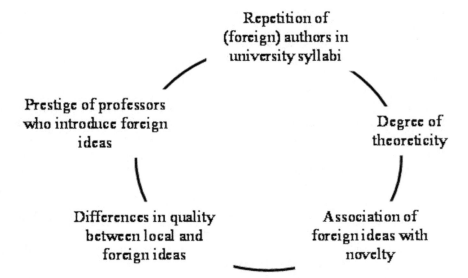

Figure 3.1 Construction of a distinction between foreign and local ideas.

78 Centers and Peripheries in Knowledge Production

Figure 3.1 summarises the findings concerning a difference between local and foreign ideas and theoretical production. Interviewees drew out five mechanisms through which professors and scholars create such distinction: (i) differentiation of quality, (ii) differentiation of degree of 'theoreticity', (iii) prestige of academics who introduce foreign ideas, (iv) repetition of (generally foreign) texts, and (v) association between foreign ideas and novelty. Regardless of its individual weight, which deserves separate study, each process tends to differentiate between local and foreign authors, their ideas (texts), and, implicitly, the conditions of production of such ideas. However, these are not one-way processes but, rather, conflictive negotiations. Students discuss these ideas, debate them with their peers, and confront scholars as to their relevance or adequacy. These discursive confrontations happen in relatively isolated spaces, such as a classroom or a national conference, so the output from them is not necessarily known in the developed world. The following section is devoted to the debates and how these can be considered to be translations of the knowledge produced in central institutions.

3.2 CRITICAL APPROPRIATION: NEGOTIATIONS AND TRANSLATIONS

Debate and discussion of ideas seems to be crucial in political science, even during the training process. Debates take place in dissimilar locations, but empirical findings allow us to present three: (i) the classroom; (ii) the political group, consisting of the student centre, labour unions, and political party; and (iii) non-institutional settings. The classroom is the quintessential place of transmission of knowledge and an obvious site for discussion of ideas. However, political circumstances in the history of Argentina make it impossible, sometimes, to exchange ideas freely and rationally in the classroom. Many historians of Argentine social sciences have shown that the university was a victim of the dictatorships and the classroom was one of the many battlefields (Lehmann 1990; Suasnábar 2004). The political groups, especially the student centres, were, and still are, strong organisations within the Argentine university system. Inspired by the university reform of 1918, student centres have consolidated on their powerful position in the governance structure of public universities, influencing every aspect of their institutional life. Finally, non-institutional settings mainly involve the café, which is a fundamental part of the academic landscape, and homes.

These places appear as spaces of negotiation. When the distinction between foreign and local ideas is produced, both need to go through a process of critical appropriation that involves discussion, debate, analysis, and only occasionally written reports. While local production is usually oriented towards local problems, foreign texts need to be contextualised, that is, linked to other historic, political, social, and economic accounts

Training Scientists in Networked Scientific Fields   79

of the problem that allow students to understand their local environment. Moreover, students not only make sense of national reality through foreign ideas but are also able to criticise local production in political science.

Texts from abroad are also used to classify and order local intellectuals by grouping them around topics (e.g. dependency theory in the 1970s and transition to democracy in the 1980s), foreign scholars, (e.g. John Rawls), and classic texts (e.g. Hobbes' or Locke's). With their indexical function, foreign ideas organise not only the theoretical debates but also their own notion of disciplinary progress and force peripheral political scientists to see themselves through the lens of those debates.

> [His] lecture course clicked with me to the point that it finally became a part of my PhD thesis. He had proposed that we read the [works of the] theoreticians of the transition to democracy in Argentina and Latin America as classic texts . . . and we had to read classic texts, such as Hobbes', Locke's, Rousseau's, and Monstequieu's, as if they were contemporary texts. That intersection really made sense because a part of the literature that we read, including texts by Juan Carlos Portantiero, Emilio de Ípola, Jose Nun, or Lechner [. . .] was related to re-readings that were being done, or had been done, not in the countries where they had been born but where they were [living] because of political reasons, exiles, or migrations. [They were] re-evaluating some readings that would have been unthinkable some years back. They proposed a new reading of Hobbes, of Locke, of contractualists and neo-contractualists, of Rawls, of Gramsci . . . but Gramsci read in relation to other questions, to other political urgencies. So it made sense to read classic authors as if they were contemporary authors because many of them provided answers to the questions [posed by] our Argentine or Latin American political scientists [and] sociologists. That course clicked with me in the sense that it encouraged me to read topics that I was already reading and discussing (14: 17; in translation).

The debate, and its subsequent translation, may take place outside the classroom, but it is still a critical appropriation. Student politics in Argentina have, to some extent, been influenced by ideas from abroad. It can hardly surprise anyone that theories such as Foucault's disciplinary society or Habermas' deliberative democracy have been used by students in the very process of debating the governance of public universities or their role within the democratic society.

> [While I was in the Student Centre] there were two authors who were frequently cited in speeches. One was Foucault and the other was Habermas . . . I think that we tried to intellectualise the political militancy and also to politicise the intellectual discussion. So it was something really interesting. In the assemblies, during the discussion, there

80 Centers and Peripheries in Knowledge Production

> were theoretical quotes and the opposite too, when we studied for an exam. Reading was strongly marked by the turn of events (22: 28; in translation).

In some hostile contexts, especially during the years of dictatorship, the debate needed to be displaced to other sites. Workshops, informal meetings, and even football matches were mentioned as places where politics was discussed heatedly. The ultimate aim was always the same: to analyse the local events through the categories or concepts of the available theories.

The informality of the meeting affects as much the nature of the exchange— making it more flexible and less hierarchical—as the emotional impact on students. The result is not only education but also inspiration.

> We doorstepped Dotti, took him to have lunch, every time to the same restaurant, and we talked for two, or three hours. For us, that was highly instructive . . . for us it was *inspirational* and an opening (22: 50; emphasis added; in translation).

The dialogue in a public space, such as a coffee house or a restaurant, has at least three important consequences. First, it contributes to the idea of a public sphere, 'a realm of social interaction vital to the emergence of critical sociability, rational dialogue, and the exchange of information' (Livingstone 2003: 84). Coffee houses allow for an open dialogue where non-academics are usually members of the public, providing a non-hierarchical context that favours a flexible exchange between participants (cfr. Chew 2005). Second, meetings at coffee houses frequently become a sort of proto-institution in which some relations are established and maintained over time. In fact, given the lack of office space for scholars at many universities, the coffee houses have become a proto-office for many scholars, as indicated by the number of interviews conducted in such spaces. Third, the relaxed nature of the encounter in theses spaces helps to produce a different bond between academics and the public, who are often students. Professors may link their scholarly work with family or personal situations, giving rise to a more realistic image of the scholar. That is why these meetings are frequently inspirational.

Be it limited by institutional arrangements or by public gaze, the debate, more often than not, is oral, and written documents are rarely the outcome of the discussion. However, the oral discussions have a prerequisite: students must read and become familiar with the text, otherwise discussion is perceived as non-theoretically funded and sterile.

> You know that, when taking the exam, you have to repeat the text, because that is what the teacher expects from you. [S/he wants to] see if you have read it. But s/he will never ask you what you think about it. This is the question, and only some teachers may ask you for some

Training Scientists in Networked Scientific Fields   81

personal innovation but they all want you to know [the text] for you then see what you can do with the text, how you can re-think it from other places, how you criticise it—or not. There is a moment of incorporation and a moment of production and that is pretty clear (25: 52; in translation).

The moment of incorporation, as we have tried to show, is the translation into oral reports, the process through which a text, an idea, or an author is critically appropriated by the students. The second moment, production, refers to the materialisation of such debate in written works. Regrettably, the second moment, if it exists, seems to be one of the weaknesses in the training of Argentine political scientists at undergraduate level. While heated debates can be found in almost every classroom, at every institution, the next step is not as common as thought. Students hardly ever seem to be able to channelize systematically the efforts of discussion into new written ideas. Empirical evidence shows that they rarely attend national and international conferences. Students are evaluated through exams that do not encourage them to produce new ideas, and they have no journals or other means to make their production available for public scrutiny.[12] In addition, they lack knowledge as to the structure of articles as written in developed scientific fields, which is an impediment for the scope of their production to transcend local contexts.

The senior and mature scholars interviewed hardly ever attended national conferences when they were students because that was not common practice. They did attend some public lectures by foreign scholars, such as Alan Rouquié, Fernando H. Cardoso (19: 53), Guillermo O'Donnell, Ernesto Laclau (32: 28), Giorgio Alberti (34: 30), Robert Dahl, Hans Morgenthau, Sergio Cotta (13: 56), Noberto Bobbio, and Giovanni Sartori (37: 57). These multitudinous public lectures took place at universities, such as the Universidad de Buenos Aires and the Universidad del Salvador, but also in public theatres, such as the Teatro General San Martin, in Buenos Aires. The structure of the academic conference was consolidated in Argentine political science by the biannual meeting of the SAAP. These conferences have been the meeting point of Argentine political scientists since 1993. Their growing relevance can be measured by the numbers of attendees. While in the first meeting, held in the Universidad Católica de Córdoba in 1993, there were 400 participants, in the ninth conference held in Universidad Nacional del Litoral and Universidad Católica de Santa Fe in 2009 there were 1,239 participants.[13]

Nevertheless, for mature and senior scholars, the SAAP biennial meeting has lost part of its original meaning. Although nobody questions that it is the most important event in the local field, the relevance of the debates and discussions that take place there has been disputed, especially by established and consecrated scholars. While the first meeting brought together some of the most prestigious researchers and introduced many long-lasting

82 Centers and Peripheries in Knowledge Production

debates, recent meetings have seen a growing participation of students and the absence of many 'big names' in the discipline.[14] The first consequence is increasing concern about the usefulness of the conference as a locus of debate and discussion which, indirectly, discourages students from participation. Students choose to attend the conference because of the opportunity for exchanging ideas amongst themselves but also, and fundamentally, with mature and senior scholars. If an academic meeting is not able to draw together young and senior researchers, it becomes meaningless for both (Fortes and Lomnitz 2005). The second consequence is that the original and novel ideas debated by students do not inform the research agendas of their professors. This contributes to the illusion that local and foreign ideas are inculcated directly by scholars and obliterates the process of critical appropriation by political science students.

Most interviewees agree that promotion of writing by professors is far from a common feature of the training process. Examination in a university usually involves one or more mid-term exams (*parcial*) and a final exam. Both are usually written, but the final exam is sometimes oral.[15] Written exams generally aim to identify the main argument of the texts discussed in class and rarely criticise the premises of such an argument, or its theoretical and methodological assumptions. Consequently, students hardly develop the necessary skill to criticise analytically the arguments of the texts of their professors and fellow students. This handicap hinders the academic exchange with people in other fields in which the academic writing style is taught from the very beginning of the training process.

> The *handicap* that we, Argentineans, have when facing the Anglo-Saxon academic culture is, in particular, that we don't know how to write. I experienced that and I am a victim of it now: I'm still a little illiterate (34: 34; in translation; the emphasized word was expressed in English by the interviewee).

Some interviewees have claimed that the promotion of writing is a recent tendency in Argentine higher education. However, young scholars have argued that the situation has not changed and students are frequently asked to repeat the main arguments of a text.

> [Nobody] encourages us to do research, to write. In the fourth year Prof. A compels us to write [. . .] But that is the criticism of this programme. It is about swallowing [texts] and repeating [them] in the exam (9: 19; in translation).

When compelled to write a piece, usually in the final years of the programme, students attempt to produce a sound analysis of some topics discussed in the classroom, but their work usually lacks the quality needed for publication. There are various reasons for this, from the number of students in the classroom to insufficient office hours to meet professors or researchers. The production of knowledge by students is generally a non-guided activity.[16] Further, the work does not follow the somehow canonical structure that would favour diffusion of the article. This situation is due to (i) a tradition of essay-style writing in Argentine academia (González 2000), (ii) the paucity of up to date libraries where students can access online databases and other electronic and print resources, (iii) the almost non-existence of office hours in most higher education institutions, (iv) the lack of awareness of writing guides for production of uniform academic work, and (v) the lack of empirical analysis, usually replaced by hermeneutical exegesis, of canonical texts.

> The difference I see, now compared with when I was a student, between [Argentine political science] and, let's say, the British tradition, is that in Britain [professors] rapidly put the structure of the paper in our heads. You have to write a piece for a seminar and that piece has to have the format of a journal article. You have to have an introduction, *literature review, methods & results, discussions*, all that. And they put in your head the writing guides, *Harvard system* or whatever. By contrast, here there was an essay-style thing. There was no instruction as to how to present [a paper] even though [the papers may have had] empirical contents or empirical analysis; each [student] had to make out as s/he could. And this is still the case in most places. Students don't include the state-of-the-art, strictly speaking, in their works. They don't have the idea of 'state-of-the-art', of exploring databases for recent articles directly related to the topic on which they are working (32: 20; 32: 22; in translation; the emphasized words were expressed in English by the interviewee).

In cases in which students are able to produce good work, they face the obstacle of a lack of local publications. All interviewees agree that *Desarrollo Económico*, a journal devoted to social sciences in general, is the most prestigious publication in Argentina, but they also point out that the journal is inclined towards discussion of the economy and economic policy. Interviewees also mention *POSTData*, the *Revista Argentina de Ciencia Política*, the *SAAP Journal*, and some others published in the hinterland: *Studia Politicae* in Córdoba and *Temas y Debates* in Rosario. The small number of journals makes it very difficult for students to publish their work because they have to compete with professors and consolidated researchers for the small publication space. In turn, this contributes to the impression that students do not participate in the academic debate of local and foreign ideas.[17] A unique attempt to create a journal for junior researchers was made in the mid-1990s, but the goal of the journal changed rapidly, for economic reasons.[18] The beginning of *POSTData* illustrates the nature of problems that a journal has to face when there are a few members actively participating in academic activities and there is a shortage of material resources. It

84   *Centers and Peripheries in Knowledge Production*

shows that advanced undergraduate students and young scholars are not attractive in commercial terms because the market is too small. Segmentation of the market, as postgraduate student-run journals in the developed world exemplify, requires a market large enough to present the specific needs of each group.[19]

> *POSTData*'s beginnings were different. We wanted to create a journal to publish [the work of] junior researchers, but then this changed. Obviously, it was an unfortunate commercial strategy: who was going to buy a journal in which [the senior researchers] did not publish? . . . There was, once in a while, a good article, but . . . so, how did we do that? We did it by trying to publish works written by members of the Chairs. Then, those texts would be part of the bibliography of those Chairs and a market would emerge. But peer-reviewing was a problem, because we couldn't say 'Send me an article . . . but I will peer-review it' . . . and it happened. Negative evaluations appeared and, what could one do? (20: 167; in translation)

There is another reason that obscures the translation process of new, foreign ideas by Argentine political science students. Senior scholars, and many mature scholars, do not always teach at undergraduate level, though appointed to do so, and for many students they are only names, not people with whom they can discuss their ideas.

> I began my studies and took courses with some professors, Atilio Borón (. . .) Arturo Fernández. Time went by, many auxiliaries appeared and professors didn't show up. There are some professors that I haven't met, I haven't seen their faces—widely known professors and associate professors with whom I would have liked to take a lecture series, but I don't even know their faces (1: 60; in translation).

This absence of professors impedes students from establishing academic and intellectual bonds with senior scholars.[20] Without such bonds, discussion of local and foreign ideas by students cannot reach the top of the field and it seems that student debates are not relevant to the discipline. Something similar occurs in relation to the international projection of local student debates. Interviewees point out that there were no foreign visiting professors during their undergraduate studies. In some provinces, scholars mention that visiting professors from Buenos Aires are part of the academic staff because some universities have not been able to recruit scholars from the local surroundings. This situation affects many of the recently created programmes (e.g. Universidad Nacional de Río Cuarto and Universidad Nacional de Villa María), but in the past affected other institutions that now have consolidated programmes (e.g. Universidad Nacional de Rosario). The paucity of foreign visiting professors complicates the international

Figure 3.2 Sites of local student debates, and processes that obscure these debates.

diffusion of local student debates and forces students to use the institutionalised mechanisms of formal publications that, as mentioned earlier, are almost closed for them.

The findings of the first two sections of this chapter are summarised in Figure 3.2. Debate of foreign ideas takes place in different environments in Argentine political science. The classroom is the quintessential site of discussion, but non-institutional settings (e.g. cafés or homes), workshops, and student centre meetings are also loci for theoretically-informed dialogues. However, many such debates never turn into written documents and this situation seems to obscure the effervescence of local discussions concerning foreign ideas. The lack of undergraduate publications, the absence of professors in the classroom (usually replaced by auxiliaries or other assistant teachers), the discouragement of writing, the paucity of foreign visiting professors, and the style of academic writing more usually developed by students (the unstructured essay) tend to make it difficult for student ideas to materialise in texts or to reach the research agendas of mature and senior scholars.[21] The next section contextualises these findings in the theoretical landscape of scientific training and higher education.

3.3 DISCUSSION

The process of training of Argentine political scientists is comprised of two stages, from the point of view of foreign ideas. The first involves the production of a distinction: students are taught that foreign ideas have pre-eminence over local production. In the second, students are seen by their professors and by themselves as able to question foreign knowledge. Questioning foreign knowledge is the result of the effort of adapting foreign ideas to local contexts. This hermeneutical task seems to be at the core of the training process, in that students are usually forced to explain local realities with the concepts introduced by their professors. Thus, this training process is an example of what we called *asymmetrical translation* in chapter 1.

ANT's notion of translation involves not only incorporating something from outside, such as a shift from one vocabulary to another, but also the

86 Centers and Peripheries in Knowledge Production

'displacement, drift, invention, mediation, the creation of a link that did not exist before and that to some degree modifies the original two' (Latour 1999: 311). In this sense, by introducing foreign ideas and presenting them as universal, professors are making a bond, a link that did not exist before and that will contribute to position him/her within the local field.[22] That bond is a result of translations, 'the process or [. . .] work of making two things that are not the same [i.e. local and foreign texts], equivalent [i.e. bibliography of university courses]' (Law 1999: 8). By making these bonds, professors contribute to the process of generalising Western political knowledge. However, a book just released in any Western academic market is transformed as it travels to a non-Western university as a textbook for a course. The difference between one and the other lies in the network—or bonds—that link the book with the entire academic and intellectual fields. In this way, networks territorialise the international arena of political science: here versus there, local versus global, knowledge versus culture. The explicit process through which translations are successfully produced, and these links are strengthened, is repetition or, in different terms, the construction of a canon. As Brown and Capdevilla have shown,

> that which happens only once (the solitary accident) is properly nothing or 'no-thing'. Yet when the accident occurs *again* repeatedly, and these repetitions are grasped as a series, then an ordering or organization seems possible. A single accident is simple fate, a series of accidents starts to look like a programme. [. . .] What is repeated becomes a basic element, a rhythm which is discernible as such and not as noise. Rhythm marks out time through a simple ordering achieved by a spacing between elements. In so doing it becomes located in a rudimentary space. Something like a 'territory' is formed (1999: 35–36; emphasis in the original).

From this point of view, the notion of translation is useful to understand the construction of a distinction between, and critical appropriation of, foreign and local ideas. First, it puts in the background the content of ideas, highlighting the fact that the difference between ideas is not (only) about their substance but also about their packaging (article, book, or thesis). 'Foreignness' is associated with the journey of a materialised idea more than with the idea itself. Be it a Marxist analysis of exploitation or a Neo-liberal study of the relationship between the State and the civil society, the salient feature is that ideas are travelling embedded in networks strong enough to reach far-away places.

Second, translation allows us to grasp the ontological transformation of an idea when it leaves its context of production. Such transformation, however, does not impede observation of a certain resemblance with the original. For example, PhD education at a metropolitan university becomes a new syllabus at a peripheral institution. To what extent are these two

Training Scientists in Networked Scientific Fields 87

elements equivalent? They are the same insofar as professors organise their courses using the texts read during their postgraduate education abroad. Moreover, academics may produce another translation by presenting foreign texts as mandatory bibliography, reinforcing their importance and putting aside local production as optional reading.

Third, translation implies the possibility of enrolling actors in a network and the enroller appears as the active node of such a network. When professors choose the texts for their courses, they are enacting a network, enrolling other academics, giving rise to particular phenomena (democracy, civil society, or the State), and solidifying their position within the local field. However, while metropolitan academics enact networks by enrolling local texts and colleagues (a North-North dialogue), peripheral networks commonly contain some actors of the developed world (which are obligatory passage points in a South-North asymmetrical translation) without letting them know about their participation, that is, without dialogue. Thus, using Sartori's *La Política* in a classroom in Argentina involves enrolling Giovanni Sartori in the network, but only to the extent that his work is considered a valid translation of the scholar.

Finally, the notion of translation, along with ANT's concerns with spatiality (Law and Hetherington 2002), permits us to recognise the relevance of the sites where knowledge is produced, debated, and circulated. It has been shown in this chapter that in specific places certain translations are allowed (e.g. using European theorists to think the role of universities in the democratisation of civil society) while others are forbidden (e.g. discussion in the classroom of Marxist bibliography during the last dictatorship). At the same time, the analysis of space opens up the possibility of perceiving displacement as a necessary precondition for translations to be produced. The encounter of students with professors at cafés or restaurants exemplifies the need for non-institutional settings in order to debate some political ideas.

Nevertheless, ANT's concept of translation has an important weakness. By incorporating foreign bibliography in local syllabi, professors make local and foreign ideas appear to be knowledge about a single social world in which differences between them—and their constitutive fields— are overcome by the general nature of scientific knowledge and the power of the scientific method. However, this knowledge is, most of the time, Western knowledge, which leads to the 'asymmetricality' of such a translation. Insofar as foreign texts are presented as superior, that is, as general knowledge applicable anywhere, and local production is always rooted in specific realities—that of the peripheral societies—the translation does not produce equivalence (cfr. Law 1999) but difference (Alatas 2001). This difference is, at the same time, the product of the international division of academic labour and an important cause of its reproduction worldwide. Therefore, while the ANT's notion of translation allows us to expect ontological transformations of the ideas travelling from one field to another, it tends to overlook power relations as something already established and

88 *Centers and Peripheries in Knowledge Production*

working, insofar as ideas are connected and re-connected with different actors and objects. Even though 'power [. . .] is the final product of a process and not a reservoir, a stock, or a capital that will automatically provide an explanation' (Latour 2005: 64), once power relations have toughened, they have to be taken into consideration as a sort of weak structure that affects the relationships taking place within that context. In other words, against Latour, some structures exist, are the natural outcome of power relations, and contribute to explain certain phenomena, as the establishment of centres and peripheries in science.

Distinction and repetition make students organise their own perception of the social world, especially with regard to the discipline they practice. As Swartz argues, a 'distinction determines our mode of apprehending the social world; it predisposes us to organize the social world according to the same logic of polarity and thus to produce social as well as cognitive distinctions' (1997: 87). From this perspective, it is almost impossible for students to avoid the hierarchy that the distinction may insinuate. Some scholars refer to this by calling into question the ability of local academics to produce relevant knowledge. Moreover, this distinction is crucial to understanding the reasons and potential destinations of those who leave Argentina for postgraduate studies, which will be analysed in the next chapter.

In distinguishing between local and foreign scholarly works, students are conditioned into a particular way of understanding their scientific practice, because theory and practice are both required to be able to master knowledge. As Bourdieu recognises, 'the difficulty of initiation into any scientific practice (. . .) lies in the fact that a double effort is required in order to master the knowledge theoretically but in such a way that this knowledge really passes into practice' (Bourdieu 2004: 40). When these second-order distinctions, which have been structured within the scientific field, and transmitted through theoretical and practical training, are appropriated by the students, a particular, locally-reproduced habitus is perpetuated. One main feature of this habitus, for Argentine political scientists, is the ability to differentiate between local and foreign knowledge, giving rise to an explicit hierarchy between those forms of knowledge and, implicitly, between the fields and social worlds, in which every type of knowledge is produced.[23] In turn, this implies the capacity to decide whether or not foreign knowledge can be applied at all to the local reality.

The empirical evidence also shows that the training process of political scientists includes relationships with members of other fields within the social world. The active participation of students in political debates in student centres or political parties, particularly strong during the 1960s, 1970s, and 1980s, leads to the strengthening of the network by incorporating actors such as politicians and activists. At the same time, these actors are able to influence the discipline and, indirectly, teaching and selected bibliography. In the 1980s, for example, the attempt of President Alfonsín to reform Argentine presidentialism gave rise to the Council for Democracy

Consolidation (CCD) and encouraged local political scientists to discuss alternative forms of institutional design. Foreign scholars, such as Juan Linz and Guido Calabressi, who were then professors at Yale, and Giovanni Sartori, participated in some events organised by CCD (Bulcourf and D'Alessandro 2003: 159). This debate influenced the discipline by putting some new texts in the bibliography of seminars and courses. What is now known as the 'Presidentialism vs. Parliamentarism' debate introduced, in almost all the undergraduate programmes in Argentina, texts such Linz's *Democracia presidencialista o parlamentaria: ¿Hay alguna diferencia?* and Lijphart's *Democratización y modelos políticos alternativos*, both published in 1988 by Eudeba, UBA's own publishing house. This example illustrates that the process of training scientists is always 'embedded within larger socio-political discussion' (Mody and Kaiser 2008: 380; Erickson 2005: 134) and that the reproduction of scientists is one part of the larger process of social reproduction. That is why training 'is the central arena within which various communities craft and then reinforce their "moral economies"—often tacit conventions that regulate how members of their discipline should interact and behave, allocating resources, research programs, and credit' (Mody and Kaiser 2008: 381). By determining training styles and contents, professors not only transmit explicit and tacit knowledge but also set the boundaries of political science and separate it from other non-scientific fields (Gieryn 1999; Lamont and Molnár 2002).

Insofar as discussion of local and foreign ideas happens in a context, the material environment has to be taken into account because discipline is sometimes exercised through architecture (Foucault 1979; Goodsell 1988) and materiality (Hodder 2012). While the classroom is the most prominent site of student debates, non-institutional settings play an important role as they tend to eliminate hierarchies and open public debates between scholars and students. Moreover, participant observation in many discussions suggests that interdisciplinary dialogue is more likely to take place in this context than in departmental meetings. In addition, discussion outside the university is problem- or topic-oriented, while classroom debates are usually text-oriented. This difference accentuates the critical appropriation of texts, which are read through the lens of local, specific circumstances.

Another aspect of discussing foreign and local ideas is that by doing so, accompanied by professors, students tend to assimilate the main intellectual, emotional, and social elements of scientific life (Fortes and Lomnitz 2005: 114). Empirical evidence shows that reading and discussing foreign texts are processes of identity-building in the sense that students internalise a specific idea of both the local and foreign fields in political science. They feel confident enough to speak of British political science or US political science and this allows them to place Argentine political science in relation to other fields, usually as a subordinated field. However, identity-building is not only an individual process through which students construct their position within a discipline, locally and internationally. It also enacts a local discipline crossed

90   Centers and Peripheries in Knowledge Production

by the national/international distinction at its core. This happens because 'personal and collective identities are mutual and interrelated. There cannot be personal identities without collective identities and vice versa. [. . .] Individuals are defined in their social relations and [the field] reproduces itself and changes through individual actions' (Larrain 2000: 30).

At the same time, the process of identity-building is partially shaped by the scholar who introduces the foreign theory. Prestigious scholars, those who have published and/or hold PhDs from central universities, usually attract students and strongly affect their education. That is why, for the purpose of this research, prestige, research grants, or education at centres of knowledge production cannot be separated. In practice, they are part of what Latour and Woolgar (1986: 187–234) call a circle of credit, to which the training responsibilities and pedagogical strategies have to be added, especially for contexts in which most higher education institutions are oriented towards teaching rather than research, as García de Fanelli (2007) and Ribeiro Durham (2002) have pointed out.

The empirical evidence in this chapter counters some widely accepted ideas as to the imperialism of categories (Rudolph 2005) or the impossibility for the subaltern to speak (Spivak 1988). Burawoy, for example, has pointed out that 'Northern "standards" become the benchmark for evaluating Southern sociologists, drawing them away from local issues' and that 'contesting domination at all levels depends on the valorisation of local, national and regional sociologies, allowing voices from the periphery to enter into debates with the centre' (Burawoy 2008: 443). According to this passage, the periphery seems to have no voice because it does not debate with the centre. That is partially true. Foreign ideas are imposed in local debates as subordinating objects through the force of the network that supports them, from institutions, philanthropic organisations, national systems of science and technology, and prestigious journals. However, because they are objects appropriated by thinking subjects, debates do take place, but not in the international arena of world conferences, usually populated with First World scholars. Instead, the debate, as shown in this chapter, takes place locally and, most of the time, orally and outside the institutional settings. In this sense, the second stage of the training process, the obscuration of the debate, impedes local student ideas, as well as their professors' ideas, from reaching the research agenda and journals of developed scientific fields. They exist, even though they cannot be read, and occasionally allow academics in developing countries to play a relatively important role in metropolitan debates (e.g., dependency theory in the 1960s), which suggests that the centre/periphery distinction is not always as clear-cut as Burawoy implies.

The data presented in this chapter seem to support the notion of *border thinking* proposed by Mignolo (2000). In his analysis of travelling theories, Mignolo argues that theories do not have to be the centre of attention when studying the (possibility of) circulation of some ideas. Instead, the question has to be addressed in terms of the locus of enunciation, that is, the

Training Scientists in Networked Scientific Fields 91

possibility of thinking from a border (or peripheral) perspective (Mignolo 2000: 174). Unlike theories, usually presented as universal due to the 'mechanisms to lay aside prejudices and presuppositions and to guarantee objectivity by leaving the local behind' (Livingstone 2003: 1), thinking is a situated process constrained by the local conditions of intellectual production, by the general context of the social world, and by the exchange with other fields of symbolic production. The problem does not seem to be whether theories travel, but rather if the way that some people think—and communicate their ideas—is considered as legitimate in international dialogues. This process of thinking, embodied in discussions and debates, in classrooms and outside them, has been observed in Argentine political science, at least at the level of undergraduate studies. However, what Mignolo calls the colonial difference, that is, the self-awareness of the 'border thinking' and the necessity of using alternative methodologies and concepts, because of the postcolonial reality, seems to be absent in Argentine political science. Influenced by foreign texts, usually produced in the United States and Western Europe, students set geopolitical boundaries to their debates. Moreover, the lack of promotion of empirically-grounded writing at undergraduate level induces a discouraging context for theoretical and methodological innovations. While the adequacy of foreign ideas is debated, the empirical test of applying them (e.g. doing empirical research and publishing results) in order to understand local realities is usually neither produced by students nor motivated by professors.[24] Debates remain oral and many students hardly develop the necessary writing skills to participate in academic exchanges.

When students overcome these obstacles, however, a structural feature of the field may still hinder the publication of written works. Due to the differences between research groups, departments, or university Chairs, 'groups publish in their own separate "house" journals' (Whitley 2006: 178) which tends to reduce the possible space for publications. This characteristic of networked fields becomes worse if resources are scarce and there is no space at all to publish the work of a group or school.

Notwithstanding the geographical origin of texts discussed at undergraduate level, data suggest that the classroom has to be seen as a valid space of production, and not merely a location for the transmission of knowledge. As Mody and Kaiser (2008) have claimed, 'the student is also creating a kind of knowledge by pointing out alternative interpretations. Thus, in the classroom, like the laboratory, knowledge is simultaneously taught and created' (2008: 377). Evidence confirms similar findings from an analysis of scientists training in Mexico. Fortes and Lomnitz (2005) have shown that discussion in the classroom is a means of reading critically, evaluating novel ideas, and opening up alternative readings of facts and texts.

> Through discussion, [professors] transmit messages such as: the student is able to think by him/herself and criticise everything and everyone; the student has as much potential as his/her professors; things

92　Centers and Peripheries in Knowledge Production

> have to be looked at from many different points of view; [students] have to have many ideas and can be creative; it is possible to disagree with other people; it is important to question every spoken or written word; there are no absolute truths; everything is fallible and improvable; there is not only one interpretation of facts; [and] the researcher experiences daily a test of his/her capacities (Fortes and Lomnitz 2005: 124; in translation).

The critical translation of foreign ideas produces a dynamic of classroom discussions that leads students to test and evaluate their professors' ideas.

> I never skive off a class . . . I would have to be dead to skive off a class because I like what I do. I say to my students that I hate it when they don't work, and don't participate in class, because I, particularly, work with them. I use them as a sounding box. [. . .] When they point to a failure in my thinking, it is useful for me, because sometimes one cannot make a distance from oneself, even if one tries hard. [That's why], for me, there can be neither research without teaching nor teaching without research (41: 83; in translation).

Given the short tradition of postgraduate studies in Argentina (Fernández Lamarra 2007; Barsky et al. 2004; Plotkin 2006) and the possibility of unfolding an academic career without a PhD, the training of Argentine political scientists takes place during the undergraduate years. This situation challenges the investigations that focus on PhD training as the time in which scientists acquire their identity and are socialised within the scientific field (Wagner, C. 2006; Campbell 2003; Delamont and Atkinson 2001) and confirms many of the findings of research concentrated at the undergraduate level (Fortes and Lomnitz 2005). However, many of the features of the PhD training process can usually be found in undergraduate education, such as recruiting students, teaching and training, and influencing career decisions (Campbell 2003). Moreover, in those institutions in which undergraduate research, leading to a thesis of *Licenciatura*, is required, professors also become supervisors or tutors and they influence the students' selection of research topics (Campbell 2003).

Many studies of the training of scientists overlook the central role of foreign ideas within the curriculum, which empirical evidence in this research illustrates. The distinction between foreign and local ideas—and local and foreign scientific fields—reinforces an international division of labour in the social sciences. Firstly, the distinction and the training process situate peripheral production as geographically rooted, and US and Western European works as general or theoretical, as pointed out by Baber (2003) in his analysis of the titles of articles in prestigious international journals. Reading Argentine or Latin American authors in a course on Latin American social thought, but not in one devoted to political theory, enhances

Training Scientists in Networked Scientific Fields 93

the idea that foreign ideas can travel while local ideas remain local (Alatas 2003: 607).

Secondly, the tension between the stage of constructing the distinction of, and that of debating, foreign ideas illustrates the subordinated place of Argentine political science in the international division of intellectual labour. Encouraging indigenous debates, though affected by foreign ideas, is one of the strategies used by some peripheral social sciences fields in countries such as Germany and Japan. Alatas claims that

> generally, the Japanese social science establishment, while very much influenced by western models, does not gauge success according to publications in western periodicals and western languages. There is, in a sense, an opting out of that game. The same is true of the German social sciences. In both cases, great prestige is to be derived from publishing in the national language in nationally recognised periodicals (2003: 606).

Recognising the necessity of skilled scholars and abundant funds, the argument proposed by Alatas (2001, 2003), points to the existence of a tension between academic dependency—which makes the boundary scholarly object a subordinating object—and the local schemes that can be used to deal with it and counters the international uneven distribution of symbolic and material resources in academe. Thus, acknowledging a peripheral position and encouraging local written (journals) and oral (conferences) debates creates a productive tension that may contribute to the growth and reinforcement of local scientific fields.

Finally, empirical evidence shows that many Argentine political scientists acknowledge the irrelevance of foreign ideas, and also some locally produced theories, in the explanation of local issues. Following Alatas' (2001) conceptualisation of irrelevance, data suggest that many theories produced in the developed world are perceived by Argentine political scientists as inapplicable, alienated from local social needs, and mystified through the use of jargon. As an interviewee stated, 'very bad arguments—with a couple of numbers—are sometimes published. I think that a good share of my work is related to this [situation]' (20: 169; in translation).

3.4 PRELIMINARY CONCLUSIONS

The research presented in this chapter has shown that subordinating objects—foreign ideas embodied in people or texts—are the core of the training process of Argentine political scientists. These texts usually displace local production to peripheral seminars or courses within university undergraduate curricula, such as Latin American history or Latin American political thought. Peripheral needs to be understood in the same sense

94 Centers and Peripheries in Knowledge Production

that political science programmes suggest, that is, there is a core of courses in the programme composed of political theory courses around which other topics or perspectives (the economy, sociology, philosophy, and history) converge. The scholars interviewed agree that they were more impressed by foreign literature than by local work. In some cases, they recognise that foreign ideas 'changed their lives', 'opened their minds up', and 'left a long-lasting impression on them'. By connecting local authors with a geographically defined area—Argentina or Latin America—and foreign authors with the theoretical core of the discipline, students produce, and reproduce, a distinction that defines a particular type of habitus.

However, the distinction does not imply a straightforward acceptance of foreign ideas. Data show that discussion flourishes, not only in the class-room or local conferences, but also in non-institutional settings, such as cafés, and in politically engaged groups, such as political parties or student centres. Thus, the defining feature of Argentine political scientists is not their reception of foreign ideas as a revealed truth but, rather, a tension between ideas produced in other scientific fields—usually in the United States and Western Europe—and the local situation to which they must adapt these theories and methodologies. Mastering this tension, and making it tacit but fruitful, is the benchmark of Argentine political science students. The impact of this tension on graduate students and scholars will be explored in the following chapters.

4 Getting Started
The Beginning of Academic Careers

The beginning of academic careers has been the focus of many studies, most of them in the developed world (Deneef and Goodwin 2007; Welch 2007a; Ziman 1994; Becher and Trowler 2001). Introduction into the academic labour market is a standardised process, from the search for available positions to interviews at national conferences (Wilbur 2007; Shetty 2007). The search for posts is, itself, a standardised process in countries such as the United States and the United Kingdom, in which the *Chronicle of Higher Education*, *Jobs.ac.uk*, and the *Times Higher Education* (formerly *Times Higher Education Supplement*) are, in practice, almost obligatory passage point (Wilbur 2007: 123). An academic career is the logical continuation of the completion of the PhD. The beginning is not easy, but a pattern can be distinguished:

> The first year or two of a position is intellectually, psychologically, and physically exhausting. Life may be lonely, too. The graduate student's social life may be very different from the life of a single assistant professor in a department where everyone else is over thirty and has two kids and a house. But everything gets easier. In the second or third year you will have a good chance of moving up. Your doctoral research should be published or in press; you should have a new direction to your research independent of that of your old adviser; and, most important perhaps, you should have a realistic view of academic life and your own evaluation of the relative importance of teaching and research (Wilbur 2007: 134).

The main aim of new academics is to produce novel ideas, publish them, and expect them to have an impact on the discipline. They obtain support from the university (e.g. offices, libraries, software, travel grants) and from other institutions within the science and technology system (e.g. National Science Foundation) in order to become established in the field. Material conditions are given, so academics can develop their ideas in a context in which freedom of speech and job stability is provided as well (Finkin 2007; Ziman 1994), although some studies have shown the increasing

96   Centers and Peripheries in Knowledge Production

importance of fixed term contracts in the higher education sector of many developed countries (Bryson and Barnes 2000; Tight 2000). Furthermore, evaluation of academic performance attempts to determine whether scholars make progress and deserve promotion or other types of material and symbolic rewards. If they work as expected, the path to a tenure-track position is secure, although some new obstacles related to the recent fiscal crisis have been put forward (Altbach 2007a). The whole process not only shows a pattern in academic beginnings but also highlights the importance of institutions, such as journals, research grants, conferences, professional organisations, and universities, for the job-search process. In other words, the standardisation of academic careers implies the consolidation of institutions and, in turn, institutions contribute to strengthen the conditions of entry into the scientific field.

Notwithstanding some superficial similarities, the process of beginning an academic career in Argentine political science differs widely from the pattern described above. Firstly, academic posts are rarely announced openly through newspapers and other specialised media, which makes the search for opportunities entirely a personal effort and allows networks to work subtly in order to guarantee their control of the local academic positions.[1] Secondly, the small number of posts available and the division between schools that have their own particular academic views tends to monopolise the posts into the hands of a few mature and senior scholars who occupy dominant positions in the field. Thirdly, newcomers must usually pass through a stage of *ad honorem* (Rodriguez Medina 2008a; Hobert 2007), or poorly paid work, that forces young scholars to either get a job outside academia or to accumulate as many courses as possible to teach, trying to stay exclusively in the academic milieu, usually in many universities at the same time (Schiefelbein and Schiefelbein 2007; García de Fanelli 2005). In this way, while senior and mature scholars face the demands of increasing accountability for research and teaching, many of the required activities are developed by unpaid young scholars, producing and reproducing what Clark (2006) has called the pre-capitalist model of social relations within the university system.

The fourth difference between the beginning of an academic career in developed countries and Argentine political science is that newcomers in the latter have to deal with foreign ideas and scientific fields in order to locate themselves within the local scientific field. This is due not only to the distinction between local and foreign production, analysed in chapter 3, but also to the imposition of research agendas, theoretical models, and methodologies that, as subordinating objects, penetrate the local fields. Like their students, scholars understand that it is almost impossible to remain unresponsive to foreign ideas but also consider that they are able to contest or expand that knowledge. The tension between the international division of academic labour and the opportunity for producing new ideas in order to understand a local reality is usually ignored by theories produced in metropolitan academia (Alatas 2001, 2003). This tension articulates, and is partially shaped by, the relationships between newcomers of peripheral fields and knowledge produced abroad.

This relationship is developed in four steps in this chapter. It begins with the participation of undergraduate students in teaching and research activities, which implies a commitment with, and an interest in, academic life. Then, the career-bonding process is analysed in order to describe the establishment of networks. Two types of network are at work at this stage: there are locally-oriented networks, strongly devoted to teaching and only tangentially to research, and there are internationally-oriented networks, in which research is more highly valued and research agendas, theories, and methodologies are entangled with those produced abroad.

This chapter finishes with two sections that challenge common understanding regarding the two types of networks. While some studies have focused on the individual characteristics of scholars in local and international networks (Welch 1997, 2007c), evidence presented here shows that both networks are the result of a process through which newcomers understand that, in order to be able to make a living from academia, they have to organise their work to be as productive as possible in a context of symbolic and material scarcity. If they manage this they are likely to become what are referred to in this book as 'consolidated scholars'. However, centrifugal forces, such as poor salaries, lack of social and political recognition, institutional pyramidal hierarchies and bottle-necks for promotions, and family pressures, are at work during this particular stage of academic life and tend to push many newcomers out of academia, not necessarily because of lack of interest, vocation, or intelligence. A conceptual suggestion is presented in the concluding section that addresses the management of such centrifugal forces by scholars, and, by so doing, enables them to advance from being newcomers to mature academics.

4.1 RESEARCH AND TEACHING BY UNDERGRADUATES

Students have to deal with searching for a job within or outside academia before they finish their undergraduate studies. The decision to begin an academic career is usually made well in advance, because there are some non-formal procedures that students identify and have to follow. Almost all the scholars interviewed in the course of this research were engaged, as undergraduate students, in teaching or research.

Teaching by undergraduates is common practice, both at public and private Argentine universities, although some differences have been found. At public universities this may require the student to be in charge of the class—preparing lectures, designing practical work, and grading exams. In highly populated Chairs, the professor who holds the Chair sometimes prefers not to be in the classroom and there is loose supervision. At some

98   *Centers and Peripheries in Knowledge Production*

private universities teaching by undergraduates is permitted, but professors must be in the classroom when the student is lecturing. In fact, although the lecture is the responsibility of the student the professor is the person who is paid for the class. In this way, teaching by undergraduates is perceived only as a training process through which professors contribute to the education of new generations of academics. However, this perception runs counter to the lack of supervision at public universities and the absence of a salary at many private institutions at which this practice is encouraged, which limits its pedagogical effects.

It is often professors who actively recruit students because they have appointments in several institutions or Chairs and need colleagues to do the teaching. The academics interviewed, who were rapidly recruited by a professor during their undergraduate studies, recognise their involvement as auxiliaries as being problematic when they ended up in charge of a class. In 1983, soon after the return to democracy, there was an increase in the enrolment of students at both public and private universities in Argentina. At this time, many professors were forced to recruit young political scientists who ended up teaching before they graduated. However, the situation has not changed in recent years. At UBA, for example, around 14 per cent are full-time and half-time remunerated faculty, while 72 per cent are part-time teachers, for whom research represents a minor part of their work (García de Fanelli 2007: 273; 2009).

Teaching by undergraduates depends heavily on a professor's decision as to the bibliography. Advanced students involved in teaching just lecture or supervise practical work, but rarely, if ever, participate in the process of deciding what texts are taught. One important consequence of this situation is that the newcomers' contact with theories and methodologies remains attached to the professors' interests. Thus, foreign ideas are subordinating objects in two different, but intertwined, senses. They are imposed on peripheral scientific fields by the international division of academic labour, according to which theory is produced only in Western academia (Baber 2003; Alatas 2001, 2003), and are imposed on auxiliaries by the local division of academic labour that prioritises a professors' research and teaching agenda.[2]

> I was an auxiliary in Romero's Chair from 1985. Q: How did your involvement occur? A: I took his course, Argentine History I, and at the end of that year the [Common Basic Cycle] CBC and the demand for auxiliaries increased enormously and he asked me to become a student-auxiliary.[3] I was in my third year and was already an auxiliary . . . a massive responsibility, because, to tell the truth, I had read the same texts just one year before, and some additional stuff, but in practice I had no formal training at all. And that gave me teaching practice, so to speak . . . I now have twenty years' experience as a university teacher and am forty-four years old . . . it's crazy! (52: 24, in translation).

Getting Started   99

Teaching by undergraduates has a meaning and a function within the logic of Argentine academia. It is the beginning of the career and the possibility of judging if the activity is as rewarding as it seems for those interested in the possibility of pursuing a scholarly life. Further, it is perceived as a necessary step toward the required recognition to become member of a Chair.

A mature scholar at a public university in Buenos Aires considers that the period as an ad honorem auxiliary was a chance to improve his abilities as a scholar, and acknowledges the importance of this first approach to academic life. Ad honorem teaching is perceived as a training process by which undergraduate students learn how to teach.

> At the end of my undergraduate studies, Prof. P. invited me to become his auxiliary [. . .] Q: Was there any formal appointment? A: Yes, there was an appointment, but it was completely *ad honorem*. I think I was two years as an *ad honorem* [auxiliary], but this is something that still occurs frequently and that you take basically as a *challenge*. Those who teach have first to learn in order to be able to teach. It was a way of re-reading and preparing your classes. Further, [I had to] *pay my dues [as] a means of obtaining a Chair* (37: 32; emphasis added; in translation).

This first step in the academic career in Argentine political science shows the centrifugal forces that enhance the chances of talented young political scientists in becoming established scholars. These forces operate throughout the career of academics, but it can be argued that their strength lessens when scholars obtain permanent positions and a decent salary. However, it is at the beginning of their careers that it is more difficult for young scholars to stay in the academic domain, since they have almost no academic capital and they need to have alternative jobs or family support. As Bourdieu has pointed out, 'posts in higher education tend to depend at least as much on the scope, diversity and quality of academically profitable social relations (and thereby on place of residence and on social origins) as on academic capital' (1988: 143). The centrifugal forces that push many people out of academia are accepted as natural. Persistence, which in itself can be seen as a positive attribution of any scholar, as Hermanewicz (2007) has shown, is confused with economic and social relations that make it possible for someone to pass through a period of ad honorem work that may extend for several years. A newcomer at a private institution in Buenos Aires recognised this when she states that

> it is complicated when you are still an undergraduate student . . . [Student-auxiliary] was a controversial post . . . I was a student-auxiliary but as time goes by you have to win your place, that is, it is because of persistence that you stay [in academia]. *There are people who may be offered [a post] but can't stay because they need to look for a job or because they say 'This is not for me'; [some] don't like it. [It is all*

100 Centers and Peripheries in Knowledge Production

> *about] persistence and earnestness and the respect you earn from students*, as well as working on a topic, so when I graduated I was already an auxiliary in two Chairs (51: 27; emphasis added; in translation).

Student-auxiliaries see themselves in a transition, from undergraduate level to their first job(s) in academia. When many interviewees relate their academic life-histories, they are able to give this moment a specific, well-defined, meaning: it is the required ticket of entry to scholarly work. Contrary to analyses of the beginning of academic life in developed countries (Bourdieu 2004; Delamont and Atkinson 2001; Hermanewicz 2009; Whitley 2006), the empirical evidence presented in the present research shows that the ticket of entry to academia is neither a PhD nor a Licenciatura diploma but, rather, the connection between undergraduate students and one or more professors who recruit them as members of the Chairs. In networked fields, such as Argentine political science, formalities such as a diploma are subordinated to personal connections and these connections function as pedagogical institutions in the sense that they 'can either encourage or interrupt the flow of certain types of students [. . .] into the professional pipeline' (Mody and Kaiser 2008: 380). Without these connections, and in the context of the paucity of institutions, advanced students have no chance of obtaining a post at public or private universities in Argentina.

What seems to be a self-evident problem has to be framed in order to grasp its deepest consequences. The paucity of institutions is not only a feature of Argentine political or social sciences but, rather, a structural characteristic of Argentina and other developing societies (O'Donnell 1992, 1996, 1998; Miller 1999). Professors usually rely on their own criteria to judge the quality of the next generation of scholars and take very seriously the selection of new members of a Chair. Since every Chair is materially and symbolically linked to the name—and prestige—of the professor who holds it, the members of a Chair form a team and are usually evaluated as such by students and authorities. This team can be roughly divided into two groups: one made up of auxiliaries and the Chief of auxiliaries who are all in charge of practical work, setting exams, and grading, and another one made up of professors, who usually decide the texts to be taught and the theoretical inclination of the Chair as a group.[4] Thus, the lack of solid institutions does not imply a lack of criteria to assess the quality of scholars, although it does mean that professors who hold a Chair have more power to decide who will be recruited according to their own idiosyncratic and personal criteria, what Hobert (2012) has called 'academic clientelism'.

Informal mechanisms linking advanced students with professors force students to develop their productive capacities as soon as possible during their undergraduate studies. Amongst students leaning towards academic life, it is possible to see an interest in getting an up-to-date bibliography, in attending lectures and conferences, and in extending the network on which they will rely in order to be appointed. As a mature scholar recognises, when comparing his undergraduate studies with those of his students today,

> Now, those who are inclined towards an academic career are already publishing when they are twenty-two or twenty-three, because they have some schemes [. . .] such as Chairs' research teams and I don't know what else, that didn't exist in my time [as student] (32: 68; in translation).

Nevertheless, the quality of local production is strongly affected by this fact, because undergraduate programmes, as was shown in chapter 3, are not focused on research and do not provide any means for students to improve their writing abilities. The final issue is the difficulty of writing scholarly works—at least as they are understood in Western scientific fields—and of publishing research in local or international journals.

When students oriented toward the academic world graduate they have usually taught and done research for some months or years. They have incorporated not only the explicit, theoretical, knowledge, but also the tacit and implicit knowledge that teaching and research experience brings about (Mody and Kaiser 2008; Kuhn 1962). Advanced students have no influence on the selection of texts or foreign ideas to lecture as these are chosen by the professor who holds the Chair. During this period the energy of students is focused on acquiring teaching and research experience, extending their social and academic networks, and graduating. The transition into the academic market for those who want an academic career, facilitated by connections made during undergraduate studies, takes place immediately after graduation; this is explored in section 4.2.

4.2 CAREER BONDING AND NETWORK-BUILDING

Isabela Wagner argues that in the world of elite scientists and musicians a process can be observed 'which concerns the parallel professional routes of two or more actors who cooperate [. . .] during the time necessary for them to change their rank in their respective professional worlds' (2006: 78). She calls this process 'career coupling' and in her analysis '"coupling" means that the actors, who are involved in this process, build their careers jointly. Without this close collaboration they do not evolve in their professional worlds' (Wagner, I. 2006: 79). In Argentine political science, career coupling becomes career bonding, since newcomers have to link their professional trajectories to several consolidated or senior scholars. Influenced by their professors, especially those with whom students have had a close relationship for academic, ideological, or personal reasons, newcomers know that immediately after graduation, if not before, they will have to become members of as many Chairs as possible if they want to become full-time academics. In this context, the expression 'full-time academic' does

102   *Centers and Peripheries in Knowledge Production*

not imply a single full-time position at a private or public university but, rather, multiple positions in one or many institutions that allow newcomers to make a living from academia. This type of full-time academic has been described as a 'taxi-cab professor' (Altbach 2007a: 154) and this label is common amongst scholars in Argentina.

Career bonding involves three phases, (i) matching, (ii) active collaboration, and (iii) passive collaboration, following I. Wagner (2006)'s description of career coupling. Matching, in Argentine political science, usually takes place during the final years of undergraduate study when professors actively recruit new members of their Chairs or when students approach professors in search of job opportunities. Empirical data in the present research points to three main reasons to participate in teaching or research at undergraduate level: (i) academic interest, (ii) ideological similarities, and (iii) lack of external job opportunities. It is widely accepted that the process of ad honorem work described above is a necessary requirement to enter the academic labour market, both at public and private institutions (Rodriguez Medina 2008a; Hobert 2007, 2012).

Active collaboration is the second phase and, because of the lack of posts available, includes a process of bonding with many professors at one or several institutions. However, newcomers face informal incompatibilities when occupying several posts; that is, personal differences that condition academic development by forming closed groups (Whitley 2006; Villanueva 2002). A mature scholar at a private university in Buenos Aires illustrates this when he states that

> I joined Prof. C's Chair. And that caused me big trouble with Prof. R. (a professor who held a Chair to which the interviewee was previously appointed) because there was that thing: 'If you are with me, I [will] hassle the other [professor]' and this really made me fed up because both courses were offered in different semesters and there was no problem (52:27; in translation).

The main feature of the second phase of bonding, active collaboration, is the increase in the number of posts, all under precarious conditions, to which newcomers are appointed. Newcomers move through the network of their contacts, generally gathered during undergraduate studies, and the main goal of this phase is to be able to concentrate personal effort on academic activities. In order to reach this goal, the distinction between public and private education is put aside. The lack of material resources at any institution and the multiplication of jobs prevent scholars from having enough time to do research. The evidence uncovered during this research corroborates other empirical studies (Altbach 2007a; García de Fanelli 2007; Schiefelbein and Schiefelbein 2007), and makes clear the orientation towards teaching in developing countries and the inherent tension between teaching and research when there is no structure of full-time

Getting Started 103

posts. However, the lack of alternatives weakens the tension, since it is widely accepted that this a normal situation due to the crisis imposed by the 'transition [. . .] from elite to mass higher education, and [the] backdrop of a substantial decline in funding support' (Welch 2007b: 1).

Every new post implies previous academic or personal contacts, which makes clear the networked nature of Argentine political science. A full-time commitment with academia, at least in Argentine political science, is the result of the stability of a network, not the pre-existing institutional post to which a scholar may apply—as happens in other more developed scientific fields (Shetty 2007; Wilbur 2007).[5] The more stable and solid the network is, the more this strengthens the position of the scholar within the field. Like tenured positions in the United States and other developed countries (Finkin 2007), full-time multiple appointments rest on the idea of freedom of teaching, research and extramural activities, and economic security that can be summarized in the phrase: don't put all your eggs in one basket.[6]

A mature scholar at a private university remembers the beginning of his career and supports the idea that surviving in Argentine political science requires the ability to follow (older) scientists:

> I went to the Universidad T. with my work about The Federalist and Alberdi, knocked Prof. M.'s door [. . .] and said to her 'Look, I wrote this and I'm here to work.' Q: Was it just that? A: Yes. I had seen her at the SAAP Annual Meeting that had taken place in Mendoza. I attended the conference when I got the scholarship, but I had gone before to the meeting in 1993 and I had seen her there. I was not an absolute stranger whose name she didn't know . . . I went to give her the work [on] Alberdi and the Federalist [. . .] and she ended up appointing me under her Chair in the Introduction to Political Science at Universidad T. [. . .]. And then I met Prof. S. and became an auxiliary there. I think I left one of the courses at Univ. B. I always kept something at Universidad B. . . . *I was teaching Political Development with Prof. F., and at one particular moment I was lecturing three courses, two at Universidad B. and one at Universidad T. And I also taught a course of Introduction to Economics for [the programmes] of Economics and Political Science. So I was teaching [three courses], and doing research; that is, I was a like a full-time* (54: 33–34; emphasis added; in translation).

Active collaboration usually implies participation in meetings with members of the Chairs, and teaching at undergraduate level. Occasional publication of some works may take place, but this depends on funds for publication being especially assigned by the university or other governmental agencies, such as CONICET, MINCyT, ANPCyT, and even personal savings. Such publications may include textbooks, or *cuadernillos* (folded sheets), that complement the mandatory bibliography of the courses. The recent expansion of the publishing industry in Argentina, after the economic crisis of 2001, allows

104 *Centers and Peripheries in Knowledge Production*

some Chairs to publish a book sporadically. However, empirical data confirm the idea that publication is more an individual predisposition—sometimes transmitted explicitly by professors—which some newcomers follow from the beginning of their careers, as Wagner and Leydesdorff (2005) have demonstrated in an analysis of international collaboration using the ISI's Web of Science and Science Citation Index version 2000.

In terms of the Argentine university system as a whole, dispersion of activities may push young scholars out of academia in search of job opportunities. Job diversification is the natural result of insufficient posts in the field of political science in Argentina and increases the likelihood that talented newcomers will leave the country for postgraduate studies due to the paucity of institutional support. The universities are usually unable to keep the next generation of scholars within the institution and force them to look for a job outside, as a senior scholar acknowledges

> *When concursos[7] are eventually organised, they are so late that the people who obtain an appointment as an auxiliary do not take the job because they are doing something else.* For example, the *concurso* [auxiliary appointment in the course] for *Fundamentos de Ciencia Politica* was won by Prof. A. [However,] nowadays she is a big name in a non-governmental organization, so how is she going to be an auxiliary? (63: 76; emphasis added in translation).

Even when university appointments are achievable, they may not include a salary, or provide only a poor income that is not enough to meet basic personal or family needs. Then newcomers have to make a decision; either they stay in Argentina, accumulating as many posts as possible and perhaps relying on jobs outside academia in order to devote time to scholarly work, or they leave the country for postgraduate studies abroad. It is in the context of this decision that foreign fields appear in the discourse of the scholars who were interviewed. Those who remain in the country attempt to strengthen their local networks and translate their connections into job opportunities and publications. Those who go abroad establish an international network that allows them to translate their connections into letters of reference, scholarships, and postgraduate degrees.

4.2.1 Local Networks

Some groups, organised by and around some senior scholars, have more access to information and opportunities for postgraduate studies in centres of knowledge production than others. However, newcomers in local networks generally argue that remaining in Argentina is a carefully evaluated, conscious decision that takes into consideration personal situation, family, job opportunities, and pressure from the academic environment, i.e. the network in which they are involved.

The relationship between costs and benefits is crucial here because it is widely accepted that going abroad for postgraduate studies implies leaving behind non-tenured posts at local universities, which in turn impacts on the careers of scholars when they try to return to Argentina. The high costs of leaving the country make some scholars refuse the advice of Argentine consolidated academics and develop an alternative local network that is based on multiple positions held at the same time by a scholar and his/her closest colleagues. Further, leaving frequently includes discarding previous personal and professional projects, within and without academia, and may not be compensated by the degree obtained abroad because the local field is not structured according to meritocratic criteria that favour those trained at prestigious foreign institutions, but is shaped through personal contacts and networks.

> [In the 1980s], there was the first wave of 'those who don't study abroad are stupid,' at least in some circles. 'You have to go abroad, you have to go abroad.' But . . . I have many friends, partners, acquaintances from those years that went abroad, and it was 'going abroad' that cost your life. Those who were not abandoned by their scared wives got divorced abroad [. . .]. It destroyed your life, especially the United States, where a PhD takes three, or four years of courses. It is not like Europe where you have [to take] a few courses and then you can go back and forth. So [the PhD] destroyed their lives . . . We were all at the same level at that moment, but there was that external pressure ('You have to go abroad'), along with being at research centre EA, with a guy such as Prof. B. who says to you 'You have to go abroad' . . . Internally, personally, I didn't see it . . . The cost/benefit relationship was not clear (19: 90; in translation).

> To be a full-time postgraduate student, to some extent, isn't convenient. So unless you have kept an active social capital that allows you to return to some contacts, to some places where you [had] worked, [where] you are identified, it is very difficult (10: 70; in translation).

In Argentine political science at present, postgraduate studies are now beginning to be considered as a basic requirement for an academic career, and the decision to stay in Argentina does not necessarily postpone the requirement for further education after graduation. However, empirical evidence shows that scholars who undertake postgraduate studies in Argentina, even if they have been awarded a scholarship, retain their several academic posts, making it extremely rare to find postgraduate students in political science who are full-time students. Empirical data also suggest that postgraduate studies are seen as complementary to the academic and professional career of scholars and almost never as a step that requires full-time involvement.

106 *Centers and Peripheries in Knowledge Production*

> There is one part of the experience (of doing a PhD) that depends on you, I mean, I took advantage of it, I feel I'm not the same as before (doing it). For me, it was a possibility, a growth. I also know, because of the experience of a friend who went to Notre Dame for his PhD, about the differences. In his emails he did not mention any other things apart from his doctorate, because it was his life. His life was devoted, from Monday to Sunday, to the PhD. So, obviously, [. . .] besides what I have just told you about having no [time for my] personal life, I could tell him about my child, my jobs, in plural, so for me the difference was palpable. One thing is when you are full-time dedicated [to your PhD] and how you can grow [. . .]. It is absolutely clear that if I could have done a PhD on which I could have been totally focused, I would have grown ten times, so to speak, academically (39: 96; in translation).

The lack of strict conditions of entry into Argentine academia discourages students from becoming involved in a long, demanding and poorly-rewarding doctorate that does not guarantee a post at either public or private institutions. Moreover, for those who have recently benefited from CONICET's scholarship for doing PhD in Argentina, the problem will be the insufficient available posts neither in public nor in private universities that will push them out of the academic field as soon as they finish their postgraduate studies. In other words, postgraduate education in the local scientific field is frequently seen as an opportunity to enlarge the CV and not as a phase of original production of novel ideas and improvement of methodological skills.[8]

> During 2005 I was wondering what to do with my life; whether I'd go abroad . . . Andres said to me 'Just go,' Maria Laura said to me 'Just go' . . . At that moment, a friend of mine phoned and told me 'Juan [a professor from the university where I had studied] is offering us a scholarship at Universidad U.' *When I asked Andres he told me 'U. is good, very good in management. I recommend that you do the master's; it will be good for your CV.' So, that was it. I did it because of this . . . I didn't look for it actively, I didn't even know that Universidad U. existed* (1: 112; in translation).

Some newcomers see postgraduate studies as a phase, after graduation, in which they can still be connected with academic life without a formal appointment in any institution. In this regard, they seem to play the same role as postdoctoral positions in developed scientific fields. The lack of opportunities, along with scholarships or personal savings, pushes newcomers to do a master's or PhD in which they continue their training and move forward while they seek a permanent position in the academic job market. A newcomer at a public institution exemplifies this situation.

Getting Started 107

[I thought] 'Well, I have this money. The money will have no value tomorrow, [I don't have] any real chance of getting a job . . . *everything was just there.*' So I took advantage of my [free] time and did a master's (46: 37; emphasis added; in translation).

Geographical differences in Argentina give rise to a reproduction of the centre/periphery structure within the national territory, in which Buenos Aires is a pole of attraction for local scholars. In the hinterland, the lack of academic opportunities is reinforced by the paucity of master's and PhD programmes in the social and political sciences. In Argentina, for newcomers working in the provinces a postgraduate degree is generally the result of an institutional decision to bring some pre-packaged programme from Buenos Aires (and sometimes from other countries).[9]

> During the process [of institutionalisation of higher education in Argentina] it was obvious that one needed a postgraduate degree to keep on studying. What the [Universidad R.] did was to make an arrangement with the research centre F. to bring [here] its master's in Social Sciences with an orientation towards Sociology or Political Science. *That gave me an opportunity, because my kids were too young, of studying here because [it was impossible to go to] Buenos Aires [due to the] costs and time* (47: 41; emphasis added; in translation).

Local and foreign ideas are filtered by the professors in the Chair of which newcomers are members and teaching only reinforces, to some extent, the subordination by forcing scholars to teach ideas introduced by the older members of the Chair. This filter, along with the international division of academic labour that produces a local canon makes newcomers reproduce the distinction between central and peripheral knowledge that characterised their own undergraduate education (see chapter 3). In addition, if we take into account the difficulties of publishing in local and international journals and of attending national or international conferences due to the shortage of resources, it could be argued that the voices of newcomers are subject to the control of a tightly networked environment, i.e. the members of the Chairs and some colleagues, and a paucity of widespread debates in written (journals) and oral (conferences) means of communication.

The Chair is, sometimes, a space where debates may take place, even if the voice of newcomers is seldom heard. Since the Chair-system resembles the departmental structure of the Anglo-Saxon university system, in that members of the Chair participate, occasionally, in internal debates on readings, practical work, and even on the syllabus itself. Discussion, however, is permeated by the power relations within the Chair, as a mature scholar at a public university remembers,

108   *Centers and Peripheries in Knowledge Production*

> Basically, it is the professor who gives you a list of authors, a list of topics. At first you are not in front of the class, but with him. At a particular moment you begin [to teach] a practical work that you may have proposed to the professor. You talk with him about the practical work and when he gives you the OK or makes the required corrections and suggestions, then you, in a more practical than theoretical perspective, begin your teaching experience, in some cases with the presence of the professor [in class], in others, alone (7: 70; in translation).

The description of the functioning of a Chair by a newcomer at a public university illustrates the articulation of roles that the system requires, sustains and reinforces. He says that

> In the Chair here (. . .) I generally have meetings, perhaps monthly. We [the members of the Chair] work together on a research project and the specific [teaching] activity is practical work. Sometimes I teach a theoretical topic, once a year, and the professor is next to me [in the classroom]. The roles are clearly defined. I and another guy are in charge of practical work; the professor and the assistant professor are in charge of theoretical topics. This year [the research project] was finally presented. It's individual work, that is, everyone has to do his/her own work. It is a big project that allows us to introduce our [particular] interests that are very dissimilar under the umbrella [of] the project (29: 46; in translation).

When professors are not able, usually for reasons of multiple appointments, to meet with other members of the Chair periodically, the control loosens and the participation of newcomers becomes more active and decisive. Newcomers may influence the syllabus and contribute to the selection of texts for undergraduate courses. Further, when this happens, they rarely need to coordinate their choices with the professors' decisions about texts because auxiliaries are left to evaluate which authors should be taught and the pedagogical strategy that should be employed. This higher responsibility, as the following passage exemplifies, is not always welcomed by newcomers, since it implies previous knowledge about topics and pedagogy that they usually ignore or with which they are only vaguely acquainted.

> Q: Do the members of the Chair discuss readings, authors, and the syllabus? A: There is no discussion . . . I decide everything! [. . .] When I began [. . .] I met Cristian [a member of the Chair] who had an idea about the topics [for the course] and he said to me: 'Let's compare this with other courses; *Fundamentos de Ciencia Política, Introducción [a la Ciencia Política]* at other universities.' And then we prepared a basic syllabus, with the authors I knew and liked. As time went by, I read other texts and thought 'I'll change that' . . . but nobody else touched

the syllabus. It is not arrogance, I swear, it is a burden for me (1: 104; in translation).

A halfway point between absolute control of the bibliography and topics, on the one hand, and the delegation of all responsibilities, on the other, seems to be possible and is used by some Chairs. In such cases, members of the Chair meet regularly and discuss some topics but the texts are still selected by the professor. A senior scholar at an international university claims that his role as professor in a Chair on political science included coordinating meetings and exchanging novel approaches.

> With associated [professors], assistant [professors], and auxiliaries I had a long list, of around fifteen people that, I now remember, used to meet in a Chair's seminar during the first two years [since I was appointed]. [W]e met in the home of one or other member of the Chair . . . We always found a place. Q: Did you discuss the bibliography of the course? A: No. Each of us presented what he or she was doing. We discussed topics, we established a topic, in general, and every one explained what he or she was working on, but we exchanged [. . .] novelties (16: 136, in translation).

Previous passages have shown that members, who are in local networks of Chairs and oriented towards teaching at undergraduate level, translate foreign knowledge according to the choice of the professors, whose interests newcomers tend to reproduce and strengthen.[10] In this sense, a first translation is produced by professors (by selecting certain authors to be taught) and is followed by a second translation by newcomers (by teaching selected texts) who incorporate the foreign texts as subordinating objects but also leave room for oral debate and discussion in class. In both translations foreign ideas are introduced by some consolidated scholars, but they remain the nexus between the local field and the foreign scientific fields. In this way these scholars in peripheral fields enrol their colleagues in foreign fields by using (e.g. teaching and citing) their production. At the same time the wide gap between fields, due to unevenly distributed economic and symbolic resources, transforms these scholars into mediators, actors within the field who increase their capital by monopolising, at this stage, the relationships with the centres of knowledge production, through controlling the bibliographies of courses taught.[11]

It is worth noting here that translation can take place even though scholars in the developed world may be absolutely ignorant of the trajectory of their texts and of how they become subordinating objects as a result of their appropriation by mature and senior scholars in the developing fields. This situation is possible because the materialisation of ideas permits them to travel and to influence other people and fields beyond their context of production. Paradoxically, the worldwide spread of electronic technology

110 *Centers and Peripheries in Knowledge Production*

accentuates the opportunity for knowledge to travel and reach remote fields in which individuals may appropriate them without the resources to discuss them internationally but with the possibility of debating them at the local level. Put differently, the new technology seems to enhance the tension between the international division of academic labour, which helps some ideas to travel further, and the local production of knowledge through critical understanding, mainly orally and outside mainstream journals and conferences (Gläser 2003; Duque et al. 2005; Thompson 2006).

While the first strategy of Argentine political scientists seems to be to remain in the academic domain, by obtaining as many posts as possible, a second option involves getting a job outside academia that sustains, on the one hand, personal and family expenditures and, on the other hand, one important part of the professorial labour, especially at many public institutions. As an academic secretary at a public university recognises, 'teaching activities couldn't possibly be carried out if there weren't a number of ad honorem auxiliaries' (37: 71; in translation). The testimony of a mature scholar referring, to the time when he could finally leave his non-academic job in order to pursue an academic career at a research centre in Buenos Aires, illustrates the second strategy.

> I was keeping a distance [from politics] and devoted time to finishing my undergraduate studies, and that is why my first job at the research centre C. was my first period of calm. It was something that made sense to me. I liked it very much, I had an income. *Until then I had worked in a bank, [so] leaving the bank, and earning more money in order to read books, write papers . . . that was wonderful!* (5: 51; in translation)

The symbiotic relationship between newcomers who are trying to survive in the academic arena and mature scholars who seek to reinforce their position in the local field may be observed with greater clarity when newcomers attempt to go abroad for postgraduate studies. The analysis of this relationship is the focus of section 4.2.2.

4.2.2 International Networks

In institutionalised fields, such as scientific fields in developed countries, the search for postgraduate studies is highly standardised. Firstly, a proliferation of rankings of universities and departments makes it easier for graduates to choose a programme that meets both their interests and accumulated economic and symbolic resources. Secondly, the existence of university guides and specialised magazines facilitates a comparison between programmes and helps identification of the specificities of any PhD or master's programme. Thirdly, standardised exams, such as GRE and GMAT, establish basic criteria according to which the range of institutions to which an individual applicant can apply will be determined, reinforcing the idea

Getting Started 111

of habitus as based on a 'logic of circular causality which arises between positions and dispositions' (Boudieu 1988: 99). Fourthly, the number of academic staff in many developed countries, especially the United States where there are 500,000 full-time scholars and scientists (Altbach 2007a: 148), encourages specialisation. Responding to this demand, universities tend to segment the marketplace of postgraduate studies by focusing on particular topics, theoretical frameworks, or methodologies. The segmentation of postgraduate studies produces a subsidiary segmentation of the professoriate according to their research topics. It is sufficient to read the *Chronicle of Higher Education* or *Times Higher Education* to realise how specific the search for new scholars is and to deduce the consequences for a scientific field in which, as Whitley (2006) recognised, novelty and originality are required. Fifthly, as a consequence of segmentation, the faculty of any university is oriented towards some particular problems and uses some specific methodologies, which justifies the rankings by areas, such as American politics, comparative politics, political theory, or international relations. If these five features of institutionalised fields are so obvious that everyone takes them for granted, it may sound weird that none of these are observed in networked, poorly institutionalised fields, such as Argentine political science.

Although this is slowly changing, Argentina does not have a structure for postgraduate studies that is attractive to many newcomers, even though they may end up registering in some programme in any social science because of the desire to stay in the academic world until they can obtain a post at a university.[12] Local postgraduate programmes rarely have funding support for their students and while a few studentships may be available they are subject to the rules of the network that offers them. CONICET has emerged as the main provider of financial support for postgraduate students in Argentina in recent years, but mainly at the national level (Albornoz 2007). In 2011, CONICET awarded 7,087 scholarships for local students to undertake postgraduate studies in Argentina and no one single scholarship for an Argentinean to study abroad at doctoral level.[13] The cutback in support for Argentineans to undertake postgraduate education in other countries is a tendency that began in 2001,[14] and forces newcomers to rely on foreign agencies (e.g. the Fulbright Commission, or the British Council) or the universities of the centres of knowledge production, especially US universities that have more funds for postgraduate students as well as a structure of teaching and research assistantships. Along with foreign support, of course, there are a series of topics that are prioritised by foreign agencies and universities (Parmar 2012; Pereyra 2004; Welch 2007c; López Segrera 2006) and that may have nothing to do with local problems or needs (Alatas 2001).

Some newcomers choose a different strategy to reach their goal from within academia: they apply for postgraduate studies at universities in the metropolitan centres. Indifferent to the specificities of the labour market in

112 *Centers and Peripheries in Knowledge Production*

the centre, peripheral newcomers make their decision influenced by the lack of opportunities in the local field and use their contacts and networks to obtain any form of material (scholarship or loan) and symbolic (letters of reference) resources. The main argument of this section is that, for those who returned, the reason to go abroad for postgraduate education is the same as that which forces other scholars to hoard academic posts, i.e. to remain in the academic environment—usually to study Argentine socio-political phenomena—under the most advantageous conditions available.[15] They go to the North, but think about the South, as Table 4.1 makes clear.[16]

Table 4.1 Title of PhD Theses Written by Argentine Political Scientists Abroad and Country Where Degrees Were Conferred

Title (in alphabetical order)	Country
Between Knowledge and Politics: State Water Management Reform in Brazil	United States
Bureaucracy and Environment: On the Productivity of Public Administration in Uraguay	United States
Cuatro paises de América del Sur, cuatro gabinetes presidencials: Argentina, Uruguay, Chile, Brasil, (Four Southern Cone Countries, four presidential cabinets: Argentina, Uruguay, Chile, Brazil)	Italy
Distritos y escaños: malaporcionamiento y representacion partidaria en perspectiva comparada (Districts and seats: malapportionment and partisan representation in a comparative perspective)	Mexico
El final del bipartidismo argentino y la formación del partido Frente Grande (The end of Argentina bipartisanism and the formation of Frente Grande Party)	Mexico
El presidencialismo en el sistema politico argentino (Presidentialism in Argentine political system)	Spain
Entre las experiencias y las expectaivas: producción intelectual de la idea de transición a la democracia (Between experiences and expectations: intellectual production of the idea of transition to democracy)	Mexico
La nascita del concetto di corrlazione nella teoria statistica inglese (The birth of the concept of correlation in British statistical theory)	Italy
Models of Economic Liberalization: Compensating the "losers" in Argentina, Spain and Chile.	United States
Nuevos liderazgos politicos en America Latina. Estilo populista, estrategia decionista. Los caso de Carlos Menem en Argentina (1998–1999) Fernando Collor der Mello (1990–1992) en Brasil (New political leaderships in Latin America. Populists style, decisionist strategy. The cases of Carlos Menem in Argentina (1998–1999) and Fernando Collor de Mello in Brazil (1990–1992)	Spain

(continued)

Getting Started 113

Table 4.1 Continued

Title (in alphabetical order)	Country
Opposition and government in Argentina: The Frondizi and Illia Years	United States
Parties, provinces and electoral coordination: A study of the determinants of party and party system aggregation in Argentina, 1983–2005	United States
Partis Politques et Confits de Classes. Le cas argentin (Political parties and class conflicts. The case of Argentina)	Belgium
Policy Making by a Military Corporation: Argentina, 1976–1983	United States
Politica y econimia: reformas estructurales e inversion extranjera directa en Argentina (1998–2001) (Politics and Economy: structural reforms and direct foreign investment in Argentina (1989–2001)	Spain
Politica y Tragedia: Hamlet entre Hobbes y Maquiavelo (Politics and Tragedy: Hamlet between Hobbes)	Brazil
Relaciones entre empresarios y politica en Argentina (Relationships between entrepreneurs and politics in Argentina)	Italy
The Politics of Military Intervention in Argentina (1880–1999) Comparing Cycles of Coups and Subordination	United Kingdom
The Politics of Taxation in Argentina and Mexico	United States
The two princes. A comparative study of the political emergence of Vargas in Brazil and Peron in Argentina	United Kingdom
Three to Tango. Prenegotiation and Mediation in the Reestablishment of Anglo-Argentine Diplomatic Relations (1983–1990)	United States

The nature of the links between centres and peripheries changes when the decision to go abroad is made. Suddenly, the authors of the texts students and young scholars have been reading are materialised in terms of letters, e-mails, phone calls, and face-to-face meetings. Specific sites of knowledge production come to the fore, e.g. a research team at Columbia University, the JFK School of Government at Harvard, and the National Centre of Scientific Research (CNRS) in Paris. Sites and people allow the prospective students to situate knowledge geographically and socially. Materialised foreign ideas are approached from a completely different perspective, one in which newcomers not only have to be able to establish and stabilise a contact—usually through the network that they have set up in the local field—but also, most importantly, they have to be able to engage in a meaningful exchange. The application process requires applicants to submit their accreditation in the form of a complete CV (Latour and Woolgar 1986: 35–43; 1986: 208) and to write a research proposal and provide a piece of published or original work. The relationship with authors and ideas of the centres of knowledge production is transformed. Newcomers are expected to read an up-to-date bibliography, to propose new ideas, to

114   Centers and Peripheries in Knowledge Production

show mastery of the methodologies used in the discipline, and to criticise (metropolitan) colleagues' arguments to fortify their own ideas. Further, the decision to study abroad implies the recognition of the predominance of a written culture over an oral academic tradition, as Canagarajah (2002) has demonstrated. Newcomers realise that their entire network has to be mobilised for them to meet the requirements of the institutions abroad.

To observe how the network acts, it is necessary to examine the specific translations that take place and allow the newcomer to leave Argentina, as well as the failed translations, the enrolments that ultimately do not happen and force newcomers to attempt detours, extending the network and including new actors. Failed and successful translations show the contingency of network building.

Newcomers seem to be aware of the importance of the symbolic capital that they need for their goals to be accomplished. They are able to map the field, to recognise dominant actors, to foresee prospective dominant actors, and to delineate strategies to participate in the networks in which such actors unfold. They are also able to evaluate if networks are strong and large enough to reach particular objectives. In this sense, evidence shows that the ability to understand how the dynamics of the discipline functions (e.g. mentorships) does not mean that scholars can shape the networks at their will (e.g. obtaining a letter of recommendation). Sometimes, the interests of actors cannot be translated by other actors from the assemblage, making the accomplishment of individual aspirations impossible and showing that some networks may be useful in relation to a specific circumstance (e.g. an undergraduate course), but ineffectual for other types of translations. The story of a newcomer illustrates the construction of networks and describes the difficulties to enact them:

> I attended, just to listen, along with Dario and Marcelo, who were in Prof. G.'s and Prof. M.'s Chair [. . .], a course taught by Prof. G. [at UBA's Faculty of Philosophy and Letters]. Why [were they there]? Because they studied philosophy with [these people], who have been their professors. Prof. G. signed [letters of] recommendation to them. But [he would] never [have signed one] for me. I noted that. It is still the same today. Let's say I was an outsider [from Buenos Aires' academic field], an absolute outsider from all those places. I hadn't been [Prof. M.'s or Prof. G.'s] student as an undergraduate. I was coming [to the course] as a graduate student. The [professors] felt that they had not educated me. Furthermore, I didn't have access to the symbolic resources that these guys already had [because] they had been Prof. G.'s students when they were seventeen or eighteen years old. So, that made an impression on me. It was good that I was learning, but I have never been able to get into that circle (6: 85 in translation).

When networks are not solid enough to give rise to the necessary translations to study abroad, newcomers have to attempt alternative moves. By

Getting Started 115

exploring other institutions' faculty, attending conferences, approaching foreign visitors, transforming personal support into letters of recommendation, and setting formal or informal circumstances in which their interests can be expressed, newcomers shape new networks, capitalising, at the same time, on their previous experiences. During an informal conversation with one of his professors at Latin-American Faculty of Social Sciences (FLACSO) Buenos Aires, a newcomer said:

> [I said] Hey, what a great [author] Prof. L. is! The guy is Argentinean—Prof. S. said—he was my classmate and is at University E. [in the UK]. Why don't you go [there]? In 1995, I met Prof. L. He came to the Universidad de Buenos Aires to teach a course and I asked him for an interview. I told him that I had been recommended by Prof. S. and Prof. L. told me what I later heard from him thousand times: 'Well, apply and send me a project.' I sent a project to him [. . .] Q: [. . .] do you remember who signed a letter of recommendation on your behalf? A: Prof. T. signed a letter of recommendation and [. . .] well, Prof. S.! (6: 75–78; in translation)

Successful networking also requires mastering academic writing according to metropolitan standards, enrolment of objects (e.g. books), transformation of personal contacts into letters of recommendation, and overcoming linguistic incompetence. Some interviewees have recognised the importance of the lack of training in academic writing by highlighting the relevance of their experience as research assistants during undergraduate studies or after graduation. Actually, it seems possible to claim that one reason to accept ad honorem posts is the awareness of the possibility of learning implicit skills that can only be acquired through practice (Rodriguez Medina 2008a). However, if we take into account the textual and para-textual conventions that regulate academic writing in Western academia (Meadows 1997; Cubo de Severino 2007; Weidemann 2010) and are unknown to many scholars in the periphery (Canagarajah 2002), then the picture can be even darker, because only by being connected with people who studied abroad can newcomers learn the specific conventions of the centres. In turn, this reinforces the power of local scholars who obtained degrees at metropolitan institutions.

Networks are not only a matter of human beings enrolling other human beings but also about enrolled objects, such as specific books or highly cited articles. The connection between the applicant and the metropolitan field is not only mediated by people—such as local professors or translators—but also by texts, which play an intermediary role. Texts permit the applicant to place foreign scholars and institutions within their field, something necessary for a prospective student to be accepted at any metropolitan university. Texts also structure letters of application by quoting the necessary authors to fortify one's scholarly position (Latour 1987: 33) and to demonstrate a

116   *Centers and Peripheries in Knowledge Production*

mastery of academic technicalities. Further, by using specific texts, the new-comer has to mobilise even those actors who are not personally involved in the network in order to enrol those members actually outside the network: the professors who evaluate their applications. Finally, acquiring and reading some texts has been thought of as outcomes of previous networks at work, e.g. the undergraduate courses, or personal academic contacts. Thus, the trajectory of a book influences—and is affected by—the trajectories of the people who use it, or quote from it.

Translation may have a linguistic component that cannot be ignored, as many studies have shown (Ortiz 2004; Mignolo 2000; Montgomery 2000; Weidemann 2010). The corrections made by the professor of English are a fundamental part of the process of application since the use of the language expert may prevent the application from being rejected due to its informal language. Canagarajah has pointed out that 'for center [scholars] [. . .] the appearance of our texts typically indicates sloppy writing, linguistic incompetence, or a shabby lack of professionalism' (2002: 165) and these may damage the chances of admission into graduate schools in the institutions of the centre. Success is, as the next passage shows, one possible outcome of a network:

> In order for the New School of Social Research to offer you a scholarship, [you had to] present a fifteen-page paper . . . and I hadn't written a paper in my whole life! In 1993- 1994, the New School accepted [my application] and I still remember that I received a [the acceptance] letter from Richard Bernstein . . . I had read [Habermas'] *Perfiles Filosófico Políticos* . . . so [. . .] I knew who Bernstein was! [. . .] And the guy accepted me, but without a scholarship. However, I wrote a letter about the three versions of Ethics, a paper influenced by McIntyre, whose [works] I had been studying at [UBA]. No . . . They didn't give me the scholarship, but I remember going to the home of a professor of English who taught at UBA's Language Laboratory for him to correct my paper. The guy charged me a lot of money to correct my work. That is, I invested, I lost much time, much life, and much money from the little money I had and earned, in that application process (6: 101; in translation).

4.2.2.1 Why is it Necessary to Leave? What is to be Found in the Centres of Knowledge Production?

The election to undertake postgraduate studies abroad responds more to local needs and opportunities than to an abstract cost/benefits analysis of the international options. The need for proper working conditions to do research, for local personal contacts (with international projection), and for financial aid, has encouraged scholars to leave Argentina for postgraduate studies abroad. At the same time, the current development of higher education and science and technology systems of certain semi-peripheral countries, such as Brazil and Mexico, permits us to observe a centre/periphery structure within the periphery:

> And when I returned to Argentina, [. . .] Prof. A. introduced Prof. C. to me. Prof. C. came from University G. [in the United States] and he had opened [. . .] the PhD programme at the research centre F. at Mexico City. And the professors who were lecturing there interested me. There were others . . . Fabian, Antonio from La Plata, and Juan Manuel, who had been a militant like me, who had applied . . . Juan was younger. The other two were taking courses [at that research centre] and recommended the programme to me. I applied, and was accepted on to the course, but I said 'That's fine. Until I get funds [to attend other better options] I won't reject it.' And I was awarded a scholarship from the Ministry of Education of Argentina and another one from the Ministry of Education (sic) of Mexico for going to study at research centre F. . . . And I pondered a lot! Q: Why? A: Because I was waiting for opportunities at other universities. Q: Do you remember which universities? A: Yes. I had [the option] of [University of California] San Diego. [I wanted to] see if I could apply those scholarships to San Diego. I received an acceptance from the University of London, the [Institute of Latin American Studies] ILAS again . . . but that didn't interest me very much . . . and [University of California] Berkeley, for public policy. But I wasn't sure (20: 77; in translation).

The stories narrated by the scholars interviewed, and observation of the application process for postgraduate studies of newcomers, allows us to infer that (i) there is not much consideration of the specificities of each institutions in terms of research traditions or academic strengths, and (ii) the main reason behind the decision is to reduce the dispersion of efforts that teaching in many Argentine institutions demands, impeding scholars from doing research under proper conditions. Furthermore, the preeminence of practical reasons over theoretical or methodological motives indicates that some scholars in the periphery, especially at the beginning of their careers, seek to overcome local working constraints—epitomised by multiple teaching positions and low salaries—by foreign favourable environments that enable them to investigate original topics, to publish in the mainstream journals of the discipline, and consequently to obtain international recognition.

> Q: Why not Latin America? I mean, why not Buenos Aires or a Latin American university? A: I think that the main reason was . . . Undertaking a PhD here [would have implied] having to do it in the middle of the maelstrom of the seventy-eight courses I was in charge of. [Leaving] implied being undisturbed, with your head and energy [. . .] put on that. I think that it was the right decision, because I finished everything

118 Centers and Peripheries in Knowledge Production

> there. Besides, with the lifestyle you have there you can study and do all that an academic life includes; that is, travel, go out, [having a] social life that you can't have here (55: 42; in translation).

While searching for proper working conditions was the reason behind the decision to leave the country for postgraduate education, those who earned a PhD at the metropolitan institutions mention such conditions as the most valuable aspect of their time abroad. Full-time involvement in academic work, understanding the relevance of networking, and the weight of funding in scholarly life (perceived through the need for scholarships) transforms the idea of academic jobs for peripheral scholars.

> The great difference is that the one who stays in Argentina studies and works; the one who goes to study abroad gets a scholarship. And that scholarship means that 'You can go, but you have to be a full-time student, and you have a deadline, you cannot take five years. It has to be in one or two.' And that helps a lot. It allows you both to be a full-time student and to have deadlines and create specific commitments with whoever is sponsoring you. It is for this reason that I think it is advantageous for an Argentine student, recently graduated, to go abroad, because s/he passes through that process. From looking on the Internet for the opportunities for getting a scholarship to [letters of] recommendation, these are things that mould and develop people's ability to develop in the academic world (5: 96; in translation).

In addition, the idea of an academic life—instead of merely an academic job—libraries that allow comparative studies due to their impressive amount of data, the habit of having and respecting deadlines, and specialisation (through discovering unknown disciplinary areas) have been mentioned by interviewees as elements that shape working conditions in metropolitan fields:

> The main difference [between Argentine and US academia] was the idea of immersion. This was not only immersion into study activities in which I was involved. This was a university that is [located] in a university town. It is a big university town, but it still is a university town, so apart from one's own interests, one is forced to study. [. . .] The second thing was the library. The discovery that libraries existed and were useful, and that one could find things . . . I think it was equivalent to discovering Google today. [. . .] Also, the fact that one could enter the library, walk around its bookshelves and find surprising things. I found weird things about Argentine history [. . .] [The third thing] was the deadlines for research and writing, and being able to have a product. I don't understand how [. . .] I was able to write those things and produce something averagely reasonably, I'm not saying publishable, but I mean . . . This thing of having three or four courses and having three or four papers per term [. . .] And well, in terms of professors, curiously I think that

Getting Started 119

those who impacted me weren't the professors in my [research] areas because I think that [my] undergraduate education [. . .] was superior to, and more specialised than, the one in the United States. *So, actually, what surprised me most was not Latin America, knowledge about Latin American issues*, but, for example, the sociology of organizations, and American politics; topics that surprised me because they were not known to me (15: 161; in translation; emphasis added).

For other scholars, working conditions abroad permit exchanges with people from many different regions, and this underpins a more multicultural approach to topics discussed in the classroom. Interestingly, and contrary to the findings of many studies, Altbach (2007a), Welch (2007b), Schott (1998), and Crane (1972), that consider the 'centre' as the place where great scholars concentrate, peripheral scholars are not particularly impressed by their professors abroad. Scholars recognise, however, that they opened the scope of topics and sub-fields of the discipline, something that can only be achieved in highly institutionalised and specialised academic labour markets. Therefore, the network in which the people are embedded, from libraries to classmates to scholarships, looks like the organizing structure that not only enables the flow of knowledge, but also—and most importantly from the point of view of developing countries—gives rise to the fertile ground on which peripheral scholars can produce knowledge:

[At the University of California, Berkeley] I had no master classes. I remember attending master classes by Prof. F. or Prof. T. here [in Argentina]. It wasn't the case that Prof. C. or Prof. E. was in front of me [lecturing] and I said 'Ohhh.' I said something, but [the difference was most related to] the material resources. For me, what was crucial was sharing [the classroom] with a Korean, with someone from Eastern Europe. You go to the library and have [books] . . . *It's the way that people work in the First World* [especially those] who want to engage in [academic work]. It changed me in terms of infrastructure and comparative politics (54: 46; in translation; emphasis added).

4.2.2.2 What is the Importance of Working Conditions?

Evidence from the present research shows that robustness is not only the outcome of logical connections between arguments but also the result of certain working habits (e.g. focusing on your research, having an up-to-date bibliography at hand, and discussing ideas with colleagues and classmates) that the scholar had to acquire. Consequently, interpretation of ideas— what we have called translations—is embedded not only in theory but also in the conditions of production.[17] In fact, it could be said that working conditions determine the range of possible interpretations or translations that can be effectively produced. What many scholars in STS seem to ignore is that the real number of possible translations, connections, re-articulation,

120 *Centers and Peripheries in Knowledge Production*

and new networks is determined by the symbolic and material resources to be rearranged and reassembled and that these resources are unevenly distributed around the world.

The robustness of the ideas emanating from centres of knowledge production appears as the structural consequence of solid, stable, and extended networks to which scholars from the periphery attach, as Kreimer (2000, 2006) has shown. This attachment, in turn, is the condition for translation to take place, because every act of translation, for example, a paper, is the result of the network at work. A mature scholar at a public university describes the association between robustness of ideas and working conditions:

> [The PhD was] a sharp change in my way of working in academia. It was a short but intensive PhD. I started [every day] at 9 am and finished at 1 pm. You ate something and then, at 3 and 5 pm you had another course to which you had to return. [Then you had to] go home quickly because you had to read the couple of books that [professors] had given for the next day. Read, read . . . I loved it! It was a powerful experience in terms of robustness. I went there to look for robustness. Everything I talked about—[political] parties in general—I read there [in the PhD programme] (33: 74; in translation).

The magnitude of the difference in working conditions between developed and peripheral scientific fields is perceived by scholars who return to Argentina with their PhD.[18] Their reinsertion is not only a matter of networks and contacts (chapter 5) but also of accepting the precariousness of their work in academia and how it transforms their practices, intellectual production, and expectations. A consolidated scholar at public and private universities coined the term 'argentinisation' during the interview to describe the effect of returning to Argentina. 'Argentinisation' refers here to the necessity for multiple positions to make a living from academia, the shortage of resources to pursue scholars' research interests, and the adverse institutional environment in which theoretically-informed debates and high quality publications cannot flourish. The persistence of this situation throughout the academic career is always a centrifugal force that pushes people out from the local academic domain into other jobs or scientific fields abroad.

> Today I'm disappointed with the academic career [. . .] even though I'm a member of CONICET. I'm disappointed with the academic career because [. . .] it is very difficult . . . I came from England to [here], so, of course, I came from a place in which I was [. . .] living full-time for five or six years. I spent five years seeing people who were devoted to this full-time, in which they discussed research every day and here, you know, you can't put together two guys to discuss anything in a month. So, it is like, I have 'argentinised', but nevertheless I still have that [gesture of frustration] (6: 102; in translation).

The perception of the lack of opportunities in Argentine academia can explain statistical data that measure the number of graduates who attempt to stay in the United States after obtaining their PhDs. Luchilo (2007) has shown that Argentineans are amongst the most ready to make plans to stay in the United States after completing their postgraduate studies. While Chinese (96.6 per cent) and Indians (90.1 per cent) are at the top of the list, Argentineans (64.9 per cent) are well ahead of other Latin American nationalities, such as Colombians (50.9 per cent), Mexicans (38.2 per cent), and Chileans (36.4 per cent) (Luchilo 2007: 74). The reason for these answers may be found, as Altbach (2007a) suggests, in the attractive US academic market, but also in the lack of perceived opportunities in the country of origin (Mollis 2003; Buchbinder 2004; García Fanelli 2007). That is why the recent appearance of a programme to repatriate Argentine scholars who have gone abroad for postgraduate studies can be thought of as an attempt to reverse this situation.[19] The programme offers a one-year postdoctoral scholarship after which the scholar has to be accepted into a scientific career at CONICET. If the candidate is not accepted by CONICET, s/he loses his or her monthly stipend. However, the programme ignores the fact that since CONICET requires academics to be associated with a research centre or university, an effective repatriation requires other institutions to share CONICET's goals and to hire the repatriated academics. Although some institutions give postdoctoral scholars a non-permanent position, this does not guarantee the repatriated academic a tenure-track position at the university or research centre. Furthermore, no matter how institutionalised the repatriation process may be, in the long term it still depends on the networks and personal connections that scholars need to have strengthened in order to obtain a post at an Argentine higher education institution. This kind of uncertainty differs from the often studied notion of science as an activity oriented towards uncertainty as well as novelty (Whitley 2006; Delamont and Atkinson 2001; Campbell 2003) and points to the basic, minimal, labour conditions under which scientists have to work in Argentina and other peripheral fields (Buchbinder 2004; Vessuri 2006a; López Segrera 2006; Canagarajah 2002).

From the General Coordination [at research centre F. in Mexico] I began to link strongly with research centre F.'s regional offices. I began to participate in the meetings of the Board of Directors, the Superior Council, and the Assembly and I began to become a friend of the director of research centre F. in Argentina. We talked and I mentioned to her about my wish to return [to Argentina]. [. . .] Here the [academic] activity is linked more with teaching than with isolated studying in your office. And this is true. I'm teaching all day long. [. . .] I accessed the [CONICET] website, filled out the forms and [. . .] one month and a half later I was told my application was successful. [. . .] Q: Did you have to develop your research at a higher education institution?

122 Centers and Peripheries in Knowledge Production

A: Yes. I'm doing my postdoctoral studies at research centre F. in Argentina. The meeting [I had had] with people from this centre was important [. . .] I'm teaching, I'm lecturing at postgraduate level and those courses are fairly well paid according to local standards. So we are fine. We have not the robustness, the confidence that this [situation] will last, but we are fine (20: 182; in translation; emphasis added).

4.3 PRELIMINARY CONCLUSIONS: TEACHING TECHNOLOGY TO MINIMISE DISPERSION

Seen from the centres of knowledge production, the relationships between scientific fields are usually represented as networks whose central node is situated in the top Western research universities or networks where the centres monopolise control of 'specimens, maps, diagrams, logs, questionnaires and paper forms of all sorts [to be] used by scientists and engineers to escalate the proof race' (Latour 1987: 232). These relationships are perceived as 'invisible colleges' (Crane 1972) that tie scholars from different locations who legitimise the predominance of certain fields because their 'achievements [. . .] become exemplars for research in the periphery' (Schott 1993a: 204). A top-down view prioritises the cognitive factors, takes for granted the materiality that makes them possible, and presents the hierarchy of scientific fields as a natural phenomenon based on the control and monopolisation of symbolic and material resources.

The view from below, however, is more complicated. Firstly, it shows that the connection between scientists, at least during the first years of their career, as exemplified by Argentine political scientists, is the outcome of fortuitous and sometimes accidental decisions. The lack of information about postgraduate programmes and the asymmetrical job market structure makes it difficult for scholars in the periphery to think in terms of the motivations and paths that govern the academic career in many developed countries. Due to this situation, the decision about where to apply for a master's or PhD in the metropolitan fields becomes more complicated, idiosyncratic, and hard to describe.

Secondly, the reason to apply for postgraduate education abroad is not different from that which leads scholars to accumulate as many posts as possible: to survive in the academic field under adverse conditions. Study abroad does not seem to be a matter of acknowledgment of metropolitan institutions as sources of original, innovative ideas (Schott 1993a). Instead, the process observed in Argentina suggests that newcomers simply perceive metropolitan fields as sites where research is possible and encouraged. It is less about imitation and recognition, as Altamirano and Sarlo (1983) and Sigal (2002) have suggested, and more about the conditions of work described as 'a combination of rigid, often endogamous and/or nepotistic, hierarchical structure, with either too stable or too precarious and almost always poorly paid academic jobs, which stifle[s] the research potential of many academics' (Rodriguez-Pose 2006: 609).

Thirdly, the view from below defies the idea argued by some Actor-Network theorists that the periphery is just an element in a network controlled at a distance to fulfil the expectations of the centres. Although it seems to be true that the only important movement in science is 'a cycle of accumulation that allows a point to become a centre by acting at a distance on many other points' (Latour 1987: 222), empirical evidence from peripheral locations forces us to depart from traditional ANT perspectives and suggest a more complex process of accumulation than this. Data presented in this chapter indicate that centres of knowledge production are used by peripheral scholars to remain in the academic domain through unfavourable circumstances in the local field, appropriating symbolic and material resources from central ones. These resources are usually devoted to establishing connections with colleagues in the developing world in order to channel grants or financial aid and to open up research and publication opportunities. This depicts a more active and significant role of these scholars, since they can usually be the bridge between uneven scientific fields, favouring the circulation of knowledge and resources and influencing the research agenda of their metropolitan colleagues. Thus they can become knowledge brokers (Sverisson 2001; Bielak et al. 2008; Meyer 2010). As Rossi has argued, these scholars have a commitment

> to mediating between different scholarly and cultural 'traditions': first, in terms of individual and mutual recognition and legitimisation within the context of different academic spheres, and of their differing institutions, rules, and conventions; second, in terms of ways of thinking, of articulating thoughts and of presenting research findings, and spelling out political and theoretical arguments within academia and the public realm (2008: 402).

At the same time, the analytical focus of many STS accounts on the gathering and processing of information by the centres, i.e. 'bias towards centering, ordering [and] managerialism' as Law (2006b) has put it, may obscure the power that peripheral scholars can exert over the international circulation of science and some possible consequences, such as contact zones (Galison 2001; Canagarajah 2002: 69, 70; Pratt 1991), border thinking (Mignolo 2000), post-rationalist learning (McFarlane 2006), or subaltern studies (Beverly 1999).[20] Science developed in the centres is often the result of an encounter between scientists from different countries, many of them from the developing world.

Instead of centres controlling peripheries through gathering data from all over the world, empirical studies (Wagner et al. 2001; Welch 2007a; Altbach 2007a, 2007b) have demonstrated the absence of interest in foreign ideas by metropolitan academics. Welch has argued that 'the very low value

124   *Centers and Peripheries in Knowledge Production*

placed on international contacts in the USA [. . .] may be both a product of the weight of that university system, together with associated research opportunities and publications outlets' (2007c: 84). Altbach supports these findings and adds 'American faculty seem to feel that US higher education is at the centre of an international academic system. The world comes to the United States and therefore international initiatives are superfluous' (2007a: 148). In their analysis of collaboration amongst scientists through co-authorship of papers, Wagner et al. state that 'in general, [. . .] scientists in advanced countries are most likely to collaborate with those in other advanced nations' (2001: xii), which indicates that the focus on peripheral regions is secondary. Furthermore, the interest in the far sides of the world that many Actor-Network theorists show should be taken cautiously because it obscures the fact that power is, at the same time, the outcome of a network (the 'traditional' ANT view) and a (structural) condition for the actors of such a network—(the postcolonial gaze). In other words, if science is the outcome of a network whose central nodes or obligatory points of passage (Law 2006b) 'act-at-a-distance', then its actors are subjected to the rules and conditions imposed by such nodes, (re)producing an international structure of centres and peripheries. Latour (1987, 2005) is right to highlight power as a social and technical construction, but he does not seems to recognise that power, once established through a stable network, is a structural feature of the field within which any practice is actually developed. This is why Anderson and Adams have argued that '[the circulation of ideas] is far more than the multiplication of contexts or the creation of networks or arenas, more than standardization or enrolment, more than dominance or submission. Postcolonial investigations of proliferating modernities, or "development", might offer some guidance for scholars in science and technology studies, yet they are largely ignored' (2008: 183). However, as Bijker has argued, it is possible 'to distinguish two aspects of power—a *micropolitics of power*, in which technology may be used as instruments to build up networks of influence, and a *semiotic power structure*, which results from these micropolitics and constrains actors [from doing certain things, but enables them to develop in other directions]' (2001: 28). Accordingly, recent studies have shown that this power structure that enacts centres and peripheries in science can nevertheless coexist with contact zones and exchange processes (Delbourgo 2011; Schaffer et al. 2009).

The focus on relationships between scientific fields through life-histories has given rise to a plausible new form of understanding of a scientific career in Argentine political science. Figure 4.1 illustrates this by combining courses, institutions, and time.

The development of a scientific career implies the control of dispersion, that is, the possibility of reducing the span of institutions at which political scientists work, and at which courses are taught throughout time in order to (i) undertake teaching responsibilities, (ii) do research and develop a research tradition, (iii) read and write, and (iv) take part in other academic

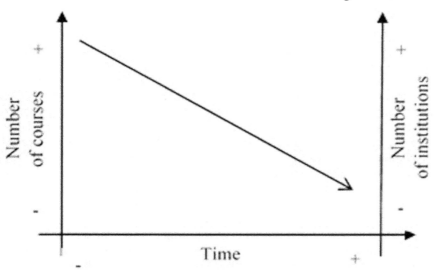

Figure 4.1 Dynamics of a scientific career in Argentine political science.

tasks, such as management, service, and local and international conferences. Although time 'is a background variable to scientific activity that does not usually catch our focused attention' (Weidemann 2010: 367), it is a crucial aspect of the organisation of scholarly life in peripheral regions, where instable working conditions force scholars to deal with multiple positions and/or specialise in only one element of academic practice (teaching, research, management, service), which Macfarlane (2010) has called the 'para-academic'.[21] The combination of these activities with the material resources required to undertake them and the personal and institutional relationships that somehow frame them has to be thought of as a particular type of technology.[22]

According to Bijker (2001, 1995), technology cannot be reduced to objects and has to be studied in relation to the social environment in which it emerges. At the same time, society has to be understood, at least partially, as produced by technological systems. This co-deterministic view gives rise to what he calls socio-technical ensembles, which capture the philosophical assumptions of our notion of technology.

> Instead of technical artifacts, the unit of analysis is, from now on, the socio-technical ensemble. Each time 'machine' is written as a shorthand for 'socio-technical ensemble', we should, in principle, be able to sketch the (socially) constructed character of that machine. Each time 'social institution' is written as a shorthand for 'socio-technical ensemble', we should be able to spell out the technical relations which go into making that institution a stable set-up. Society is not determined by technology,

126　*Centers and Peripheries in Knowledge Production*

nor is technology determined by society. Both emerge as two sides of the socio-technical coin, during the construction process of artifacts, facts, and relevant social groups (Bijker 1995: 274).

Bijker (2001) argues that every technology is negotiated by different groups whose interests are an important element of the network enacted. What a particular artefact means depends on the struggle between those groups in their attempt to fix its particular and more or less definitive meaning. Once a meaning has been stabilised by closing the dispute, technology 'cannot be changed easily, and it forms part of an enduring network of practices, theories and social institutions' (Bijker 2001: 28). For the actors involved in the network that set up the meaning of the technology, 'there is no life without the artifact, but there is a lot of life within it' (Bijker 2001: 29). They need the technology and organise their (social) relationships according to it and the 'obduracy of technological ensembles presents itself as the technology, being all-pervasive, beyond questioning, and dominating thoughts and interactions' (Bijker 2001: 29). On the contrary, those low-included actors have only a 'take-it' or 'leave-it' strategy to deal with the new technology. 'Leave-it' implies to be excluded of the networks that produce and use a given technology. Since every technology links several relevant social groups, the 'take-it' decision 'results in being included into [. . .] a semiotic power structure [. . . and . . .] being subjected to power relations that one would otherwise [. . .] be immune to' (Bijker 2001: 29).

We shall call the complex ensemble of humans (scholars, administrative staff, students, editors of journals), non-humans (office space, computers, software packages, classrooms, libraries), and relationships (mentorship, taxi-cab professorship) that allows political scientists to remain in the academic field in a peripheral context 'teaching technology'.[23] This idea rests on the notion of technology as knowledge-producing tools (Shapin and Schaffer 1985: 25), which permits the combination of rhetorical devices with hardware and objects. The consequence of the proficient use of this technology is not only fact-making (i.e. papers, courses' syllabi, exams, and lectures) but also the stabilisation of the academic career in terms of the possibility for newcomers to structure time in order to minimise dispersion of efforts and resources.[24]

Time is not an abstract or universal entelechy within which actions take place but rather the outcome of specific configurations of socio-technical ensembles. 'Such ensembles are characterized by their own proper time, which, when viewed as performative [. . .] also affect—at least potentially—the proper times of other ensembles' (Michael 2006: 145). In the context of a poorly institutionalised field, under the pressure of multiple and diverse academic jobs, and pushed by the need to meet deadlines and criteria to remain in the academic realm, newcomers face the need to optimise time. To do it they rely heavily on foreign ideas, because they are more widely spread out around the world, easier to obtain, packaged in

Getting Started 127

standardised forms (e.g. research articles), endowed with prestige, and the result of an 'international' research agenda set in the metropolitan centres. In other words, foreign knowledge is fundamental to produce local (academic) time.

Foreign knowledge forces local newcomers to make a 'take-it' or 'leave-it' decision.[25] By leaving-it, they are remaining 'outside' the international landscape of the discipline, ignoring the novel methodologies and theories, and producing parochial knowledge that can hardly transcend local settings. Most scholars who choose this strategy usually speak of the necessity to concentrate on home problems and propose possible solutions, which leads them to publish locally and sometimes to point to a broader public (e.g. as columnists in newspapers). By 'taking-it', scholars are making a twofold decision.

On the one hand, they are setting their own research and teaching agendas in relation to debates nurtured by the institutions of the centre. Further, they become familiar with cutting-edge methods, and acquainted with new theoretical approaches which inform their papers, articles, and syllabi. In addition, they acquire a worldwide view of political science, one that shows an international arena of discussion even when disparities in symbolic and material resources are acknowledged (Schott 1998; Schott et al. 1998; Wagner 2008). On the other hand, they are placing themselves in a marginal position within the semiotic power structure that Bijker (2001) describes, because, in such international networks they play a subordinated, peripheral role. However, the decision to use foreign knowledge is usually justified by its prestige and recognition, which are highlighted strongly during the training years. In this sense, the choice of being attached to the international semiotic power structure seems to be counterbalanced by the possibility of legitimising their own careers in terms of the international networks in which they are embedded.

The relationship between members of peripheral scientific fields with their colleagues in the metropolitan world during the first few years of an academic career is subjected to the requirements of the former fields for mastering teaching technology and, subsequently, to strengthening the position and obtaining one (or several) posts at academic institutions. Leaving Argentina for a postgraduate degree is one of the strategies, as the stories of members of international networks illustrate, the other being the accumulation of posts and responsibilities in the local field. Those who go abroad for postgraduate education find, when they return, that the adverse conditions of academic work in Argentina force them to accept the logic of the field. Networking becomes fundamental, as some examples in the previous pages have shown, because the field, as Whitley (2006) has theoretically depicted, is divided into schools or groups that tend to control monopolistically some symbolic or material resources. The returning scholar has to accept the real rules of the game and try to find available posts and combine them in advantageous ways. Teaching at postgraduate level is preferred by those who obtain a PhD abroad because many members of local networks

128   *Centers and Peripheries in Knowledge Production*

cannot find the time and space to do their postgraduate studies, remaining excluded from the networks that control the postgraduate programme market.[26] Social capital may be important, along with the academic one provided by a degree at a metropolitan university, since family or personal connections may be the last resort to obtain a post at a local institution. In the case of public universities, the broader political context is also a determinant of the real possibilities of members from both the local and international networks to enter the academic job market.

The first phase of the academic career in Argentine political science is complete when scholars are able to sustain their personal and family needs with the income provided exclusively by academic work. For this to happen, scholars are involved in teaching activities and tangentially in research, especially in those few institutions at which research and publishing are encouraged, as Vessuri (2006a), Barsky et al. (2004), Del Bello et al. (2007), and Buchbinder (2004) have concluded. In the second stage, the bonds with their senior and mature colleagues weaken due to the degree of relative independence that the newcomer has reached. A phase of 'passive collaboration' is then characterised by the fact that 'collaborators do not work together intensively, but the development of the ex-collaborator's career continues to influence the reputation of the partner' (Wagner, I. 2006: 70). The process through which a newcomer gains a certain degree of independence has been summarised by a senior scholar at a public university in Buenos Aires:

> In my Chair [. . .] there were two brilliant guys who led the Radical [Party] and the Peronist [Party]; Prof. M. and Prof. A. [They] came with me. Both began as Auxiliaries, then they were Chief of Auxiliaries, then Associate Professors, and then they left, logically. They wouldn't spend their whole lives there (63: 100; in translation).

The data obtained in the course of the present research challenges the idea that passive collaboration 'would correspond to the introduction of a young professional into the labour market' (Wagner 2006: 89) since newcomers depend on career bonding from the beginning of their career to enter the academic job market. Passive collaboration, however, is when the relatively independent scholar may show a personal record of research and teaching that at the same time links him or her with some senior or mature scholars and separates him or her from their academic patrons. Nevertheless, it is worth noting that the identity of newcomers is usually associated with the groups to which they belong (Fernandez' Chair at UBA or Yannuzzi' Chair at UNR), whereas the definitive identity of the scholars is only achieved in the second phase of the academic career; consolidation, which is the focus of chapter 5.

5 Towards a Plurality of Translations

In the same way that light is required to observe cells through the microscope, the circulation of foreign ideas allows us to examine a curious phenomenon: in networked fields, such as Argentine political science, although there are dominant actors, only a few actors can obtain the material and symbolic resources to establish a permanent, steady connection between some local networks and their foreign counterparts. Further, the acquisition of academic posts, such as Head of Department or Dean, is particularly important, because only from these institutional positions can international connections be maintained through time. This is one important reason why local scholars usually take administrative posts even when they know that by so doing they probably will not have enough time to develop their research and teaching careers (cfr. Bourdieu 2004).

In networked fields, the weakness of institutions and the personification of relationships illustrated in the groups gravitating around some consolidated scholars are obstacles to monopolisation of the circulation of ideas by any one individual or group. Such a monopolisation would require formal rules (institutions), the acceptance of peer-review as the process to ensure the quality of research, and a culture of the written diffusion of research findings (Canagarajah 2002).[1] More importantly, the control of the circulation of ideas would require the factual capacity for some actors to exert power over the other members of the fields, forcing them to accept certain rules of the game. Without this process of becoming an obligatory passage point (Latour 1987; Callon 1986), only a few actors may become mediators between different scientific fields.

The scarcity of scientists who control the international circulation of people and knowledge does not imply democratisation. Rather, the field seems to have a disarticulated structure, with many simultaneous international connections that respond to the personal abilities and interests to keep them in place. Democracy suggests that a few highly reputed representatives would decide the allocation of material (grants) and symbolic (awards) resources based on merit. Disarticulation implies the weakness of such a leading group, or a system of recognition based on meritocratic criteria, and the absence of institutional mechanisms to channel relationships with other local and foreign fields.

130 *Centers and Peripheries in Knowledge Production*

Even with few mediators in the field, the members have different levels of resources and capital with which to participate in local and international debate. It was shown in chapter 3 that undergraduate students are virtually excluded from this debate, while being trained in the appreciation of local and foreign ideas as essentially, and primarily, distinct cultural products. Chapter 4, in addition, presents empirical evidence that illustrates how newcomers, especially those in local networks, are subjected to the will of consolidated scholars; a control reinforced by the Chair-system (Scott 2008) and the lack of opportunities to publish and debate original ideas. Nevertheless, the situation changes radically once scholars achieve a relative degree of autonomy from their academic patrons, which usually takes many years. The autonomy consists in mastering teaching technology, i.e. the articulation of as many posts as possible in order to make a living from academic activities. If this is not possible, scholars usually resort to extramural activities, such as consultancy, non-university education, translation, and advisory work, but always retaining the goal of minimising dispersion. When the autonomy that multiple appointments brings about is achieved, scholars are in the second phase of their academic career: consolidation.

During the consolidation phase, scholars begin to publish in a more systematic way, focus on academic activities, participate in research teams as leaders or coordinators, occupy some administrative positions alongside full-time engagement in one institution, and develop a network of personal and institutional contacts. Once scholars attain autonomy they tend to establish contacts with foreign colleagues, especially if they have studied abroad. The contact with foreign scientists and ideas is thus filtered by the local needs of scholars, as well as by the personal and institutional resources available. This does not avoid what Caroline Wagner (2006) has called preferential attachment (which leads to centres and peripheries) but forces us to see these relationships, at least in part, as responding to some of the needs and interests of peripheral scholars.

To argue that there are few mediators amongst consolidated scholars in Argentine political science is to acknowledge that the relationships between local political scientists and foreign knowledge are not subjected to specific, highly hierarchical structures. In this context any local scholar is a valid translator who may be able to appropriate foreign ideas with the objective of solidifying his or her position in the network. Furthermore, the acts of translation are frequently fortuitous, accidental, and opportunistic, rather than rationally and carefully judged and decided (cfr. Bourdieu 1999a). Many networks are at work simultaneously and people pursue their own agendas, forcing scholars to simply identify the opportunities and take advantage of them. The scarcity of material resources, along with the relatively low degree of functional dependence (Whitley 2006: 88) allows academics to be more or less isolated and to strive for their own particular research and teaching agendas. These opportunities, the mechanisms used

Towards a Plurality of Translations 131

to take advantage of them, and the management of their personal connections (in order to be integrated or isolated) are constitutive parts of teaching technology, as discussed in chapter 4.

The argument contained in this chapter is organised into three sections. Section 5.1 focuses on ideas materialised in texts (mainly books and scientific articles) and shows the situation of the publishing industry in Argentina and how it affects the academic labour force. Section 5.2 concentrates on people as embodied ideas drawing attention to the presence of foreign political scientists in Argentina, as well as local scientists going abroad (e.g. visiting professorships and conferences). The importance of personal contacts between political scientists and the administrative constraints of exchanging knowledge internationally is illustrated in this section. Section 5.3 analyses the careers of some political scientists in Argentina who have been able to obtain recognition abroad, becoming dominant actors of the local field. Finally, the utilisation of teaching technology in this phase of the academic career, and depiction of the landscape of consolidated scholars in Argentine political science, and how they connect their needs and expectations with foreign ideas, are presented in section 5.4.

5.1 MATERIALISATION OF FOREIGN IDEAS: SCHOLARLY TEXTS

Materialised foreign ideas are introduced into a field as texts. The main format of scientific texts is the scientific article (Gross et al. 2002; Cubo de Severino 2007). However, in the social sciences, a book is also a major means for exchanging research output (Meadows 1998) because the article is a relatively late innovation that follows the rhetoric strategy that the natural sciences have been using since the 17th century.[2] As Bazerman has pointed out,

> those communities concerned with issues of human mind, society, and culture have been moved to adopt (and adapt) what they perceive to be the methods of the physical and biological sciences. Just as natural philosophy gradually was reorganized as the natural sciences over the seventeenth and eighteenth centuries, many other parts of philosophy since the late nineteenth century have been in the process of being reorganized into what are called variously the *social sciences* (2000: 257; emphasis in the original).

In this sense, a study of the international relationships between academics is, in part, an analysis of the access of local scholars to foreign knowledge through books and articles. In this chapter, the bidirectional flow of ideas, focusing on the external control of the Argentine publishing industry and the difficulties of obtaining foreign contributions to local journals, is illustrated. Section 5.1.1 relies mainly on secondary and statistical information,

132 *Centers and Peripheries in Knowledge Production*

but section 5.1.2 is based on interviews with founders, editors, and editorial board members of some of the Argentine journals in political science.

5.1.1 Books, Publishing Industry and Circulation of Ideas

Empirical evidence concerning political scientists in Argentina supports the contention that most consolidated scholars buy academic texts in local bookstores (Centro de Estudios para la Producción 2005; Clemens et al. 1995).[3] Other forms of acquisition, such as online shopping, represent minor distribution channels.[4] The importance of bookstores was explicitly highlighted by scholars in the hinterland who recognise the need to take advantage of colleagues' trips to Buenos Aires for acquiring new books.[5] By so doing, they recognised the 'key gate keeping [. . .] performed by bookstore buyers who are attentive to commercial as well as scholarly concerns' (Clemens et al. 1995: 448) and also the reproduction of a centre/periphery structure within a peripheral country such as Argentina.

The access to new ideas is mediated by those scholars who, for personal or professional reasons, travel to Buenos Aires and visit bookstores. This mediation is, in practice, a first translation to which the scholars in the hinterland are subjected. The interest of the academic who travels and acquires new bibliography is prioritised over other scholars who can only participate at a secondary level. More importantly, in some cases the person who travels to larger cities in Argentina or abroad is a student or a newcomer, so the access to up-to-date bibliography by some scholars is again subordinated, at least partially, to that of the traveller. Furthermore, the scarcity of resources to keep a university library up-to-date brings about the multiplication of actors who are involved in this type of translation of ideas (Rodriguez Medina 2008b).

> Today, as with those who were my professors, [someone] goes to Buenos Aires and buys three or four books and returns. 'One is for you [. . .]. This is for me. This is for so and so.' And our books end up being used by the students, because the book is not in the [university] library (62: 13, in translation).

The situation is even more complicated if the texts available in local bookstores are taken into account as subordinating objects, that is, as the product of asymmetrical contacts between publishing industries and cultural fields. Firstly, the control of the Argentine publishing houses by foreign companies, such as Random House Mondadori and the Planeta Group, introduces authors and ideas into the local field who respond to the logic of their origin, which is mainly Spain.[6] Thus, 'the acquisition of [Argentine] publishing houses by foreign companies, that cannot be considered cultural agents in the traditional sense, [. . .] promotes policies of production and circulation of the book as an object that modify considerably its behaviour

Towards a Plurality of Translations   133

in terms of its cultural impact' (Botto 2006: 209, in translation). The cultural impact of the imported book is more related to the fields of production (Spain and, by means of translation, the English speaking field) than to the field of consumption, where alternative local publishing efforts are difficult to establish (De Sagastizábal 2005). As a consequence, two interrelated phenomena are seen. The network of publishing houses allows us to observe many overlapping centres and peripheries, as Carelli Lynch (2013) has described recently. While the English speaking world is, in quantitative terms, responsible for most of the academic publications and the centre of knowledge production and distribution, Spain plays a double role on the periphery. Spain is a secondary publishing industry in comparison with that of the United States, or the United Kingdom, but, through its publishing houses, it is also a centre for Latin American intellectuals and scientists due to the cultural and linguistic similarities, as well as private and public economic interests. This explains why 78 per cent of all books sold in Argentina are imported (Ceriotto 2012).

The overlapping centre/periphery structures contribute to the phenomenon of segmentation of production leading the publishing houses 'to focus on the internal market of the country in which they operate, which means that they can impose the products imported from headquarters—especially Spain—but there is not the same permeability into Argentina of the production of other Latin American countries' (Botto 2006: 217, in translation). This situation accentuates monopolisation of the sector and makes Argentina dependent not only on the cultural production of metropolitan centres but also on the consequences of economic and marketing decisions in those centres. At the same time, the flow from the centre of production to the periphery of consumption threatens multidirectional flows that can connect peripheral areas even when these areas share cultural and linguistic characteristics, as do the Latin American countries. Consequently the dialogue South-South that some scholars think as a necessary strategic step towards a more independent intellectual field (Mignolo 2000; Santos 2009) is almost impossible or, at best, is mediated by metropolitan academics and institutions, with their own interests and goals.

Local editors are faced with the problem of promoting local production in a context that favours foreign authors and texts. A former president of the Cámara Argentina del Libro, Hugo Levin, recognised that Spanish publishing houses are obstructing proposals from many Argentine houses to create the Instituto Nacional del Libro Argentino, following the example of the Instituto Nacional del Libro Español (Lago Carballo and Gómez Villegas 2006). Since a book is not only a commodity but also a cultural product, this obstruction has two sides; one economic (Perelman 2003; Centro de Estudios para la Producción 2005) and one cultural. The cultural side implies, amongst other things, that access to foreign ideas by Argentine political scientists is frequently beyond their control. Further, the monopolisation of the publishing industry and the imposition of economic

134   *Centers and Peripheries in Knowledge Production*

criteria (De Diego 2006), the weight of Spain in the dominance of the Spanish-speaking book market, the lack of university library resources (De Sagastizábal 2005; Kent 2002), the low usage of the internet for online book shopping (Uribe et al. 2005), and the cost of foreign books in relation to academic salaries (García de Fanelli 2007; Hobert 2007) all help to fracture the academic field by increasing the number of actors who participate in the circulation of ideas.

> [F]or the book world [in Argentina], the Spanish editors are the [. . .] most significant ones. So, it is imperialism that is the central country in the world of the Spanish speaking book. Against whom are we going to fight? The Mexicans? The Chileans? No. We have to fight [the Spanish editors]. They are the only ones who can put a foot on us with authority and power [. . .]. So the vision is one of a peripheral country with regard to a central one. And even the independent [editors], the small [editors] . . . are part of the central power (Levin quoted in Lago Carballo and Gómez Villegas 2006: 123, in translation).

Translation of foreign ideas into Spanish is also mediated by Spanish publishing houses which have greater economic resources to meet the costs of translation and copyright. More than 24 per cent of the books published in Spain are translations, mainly from English, French, and German (Nadal and García 2005). Therefore, 32 per cent of the money paid for copyright in Spain goes abroad, which means that €1 out of every €3 obtained by the Spanish publishing industry is due to foreign authors (Nadal and García 2005: 108).

A shift of focus from commercial publishing houses to the university press scene does not change the general picture. Empirical studies of the Argentine and Latin American publishing industries have shown that the academic production of universities is minimal in terms of global production and consumption. Moreover, the consumption of academic literature is nurtured by foreign universities and the commercial press.

> Latin America and the Caribbean have a large number of university students who may be consumers for texts. Many of those texts may be written by university professors from the region, but the reality shows that, in general, most of what is purchased (especially in relation to books) comes from foreign universities and commercial publishing houses, both from the region and from abroad (De Sagastizábal 2005: 44, in translation).

The growth of the university system, along with the consolidation of mass higher education, has opened up a potential market of readers and consumers, but many obstacles have appeared. De Sagastizábal (2005) points to (i) inadequate distribution, (ii) lack of commercial and economic autonomy, (iii) scarce human resources, (iv) financial and budgetary restrictions, (v) high costs of raw materials and operations, (vi) general problems of infrastructure, and (vii) lack of experience of directors and managers. A vicious circle emerges: the weaknesses of the university press affect the quality and quantity of their production, discouraging local consumption which, in turn, has a negative effect on the publishing houses. The result is twofold. Firstly, it indirectly promotes the consumption of foreign bibliography and thus contributes to the consecration of foreign scholars. Secondly, it reinforces a 'colonial mentality that reproduces an auto-discriminatory culture, characterised by despising *a priori* knowledge produced by national authors, and underestimating and undervaluing their contributions in favour of those of foreign authors' (De Sagastizábal 2005: 126, in translation).

The predominance of foreign texts over local ones (chapter 3) in university syllabi, and the failure of university publishing houses to attract foreign authors, generates a gap between the production and consumption of texts. De Sagastizábal has found that 'the university [in Latin America] does not edit the mandatory readings that teachers ask their students to read' (2005: 53, in translation). As a consequence, 'the few students who acquire books buy imported commercial editions and, to a lesser extent, local commercial editions' (De Sagastizábal 2005: 54, in translation).

In theoretical terms, the complex landscape of the publishing industry in Argentina contains a multiplicity of networks and translations. Dominant actors in the Spanish cultural field are dependent on other foreign economic actors, such as the publishers Mondadori (from Italy) and Bertelsmann (from Germany). Marketing strategies mean that only a small portion of the books published in Spanish are imported into Argentina and such books are frequently those that have not been sold in the local market. This tendency towards monopolisation has eliminated the need for local editors who may serve as bridges between different cultural fields (e.g. Spain and Argentina) because this role has been taken by trans-national corporations. Botto pointed out that 'trans-national groups plan the marketing of books [. . .] without regard to the specificity of the product that they produce' (2006: 215, in translation). Horacio Zabaljauregui, editor at Fondo de Cultura Economica Argentina, argues that the new publishing groups have 'a quasi-military logic of filling the spaces, without too much consideration as to with what [books]' (Botto 2006: 215, in translation). When the academic or cultural criteria to import and translate books are replaced by the economic imperative of selling as many as possible without any consideration of the cultural value of the product offered, the result is the predominance of marketing and the lack of participation of local scholars in the publishing industry on which they depend for advancing their professional careers.

5.1.2 Chasing (Foreign) Academics to Publish in (Local) Journals

In institutionalised scientific fields, the role of mediator is best represented by journal editors. They play such a role 'by funnelling manuscripts in one

136 Centers and Peripheries in Knowledge Production

direction or another or rejecting material entirely. In this way, the journal editor has an impact on the professional life of every scholar' (McGinty 1999: 1) because he or she influences the research agenda of a discipline by setting boundaries between what is published (and accepted and valid) and what is not. The importance of the editor is related to the central role of periodical publications in a field, something that the Open Access paradigm in the publishing industry does not seem to weaken (Morgan et al. 2012). According to McGinty 'the scholarly journal plays the most important role in a discipline's existence, direction, and shape. This, in turn, shapes the careers of individuals within that discipline. The centre of this universe is occupied by the journal editor' (1999: 8).

The editor may shape the journal contents and, by so doing, the direction of part of a discipline, but at the same time the journal may influence the editor. Firstly, editors usually report that 'they experience time pressures, particularly during certain periods' (McGinty 1999: 31). The tasks and responsibility of editors take time from other academic activities, mainly research and teaching. Moreover, learning about editing academic journals also demands time and most editors know almost nothing about the business when they are appointed (Garciadiego Dantan 1998). Secondly, an appointment as editor offers the opportunity of extending personal networks. The relationship of editors with reviewers and editorial boards gives them higher visibility and academic capital, strengthening their position in the field. Thirdly, a subtle influence of journals over editors is the reproduction of a certain viewpoint about the discipline. McGinty has found that 'one of the ways in which the desired comfort [with the appointee] finds expression is in the appointment of colleagues with like-minded sensibilities. If a journal has a job opening, the editorial board members cast about for people they know' (1999: 21). In this sense, journals tend to stay, as objects, linked to certain groups, schools, or scholars for lengthy periods, helping to create a sense of community 'that sets standards and provides incentive for scholars, regardless of their geographic location' (McGinty 1999: 2).

In networked fields and those with low levels of institutionalisation the landscape is different. The scarcity of material and symbolic resources, together with the low numbers of people working in the field, are obstacles to the existence of academic journals. Not only is the peer-reviewing process almost impossible, because only a small portion of the field has the time and knowledge to review new articles, but also the appearance of the journal on a regular basis, and its national or international distribution, is systematically hampered by circumstances.[7] A consolidated scholar and editor, referring to the weakness of the most important local university press, points to the inability of the press to distribute the journal—one of the most prestigious in the local field—and how this forces the editor to actively engage in the distribution process. Involvement of the editor in diffusion of the journal is accomplished by face-to-face contacts with other academics at national or international conferences. The networked

Towards a Plurality of Translations   137

nature of the field appears to be a necessary consequence of the weakness of institutions. Personal contacts between scholars fill the spaces that weak publishing houses leave empty. Consequently, there is a lack of confidence in the peer-review process, which is presented as an informal procedure by which some referees 'take a look at' the articles submitted.

> We were evaluated by CONICET. We obtained 4 out of 5 and 2 out of 5 on diffusion, in regard to the [journal's] relevance, because university press U. does not disseminate anything. These are the pathetic things that force one to spend so much time at home with the phone and pay the bills. We pay university press U. for the journal, but we get the journal ready for university press U. to distribute. The press has to distribute it, to have it in the stand at the Book Fair or in conferences or bookstore. [However,] as bookstores never pay for the issues they receive [. . .] they receive the journal [but] the publishing houses only give one book as a sample which they replenish on demand. But university press U. doesn't have the staff to do this. In conclusion: it doesn't distribute and we retain 100 issues because we pay for them. Anyway, what we pay is cheap in relation to the printing cost. This is very, very luxurious. University press U. decided to do it that way; it isn't important for us. [The editing] is more luxurious than that of American or British journals. It makes no sense. But for libraries, for collections, it is important. I noticed that the guys of journal P. distribute the journal via a distributor.[8] Because I can't, with funds from University U., pay 50 lots of postage, I give [the issues] to the more important academics, straight into their hands at conferences. And the other 50 issues are sent to the key sites: [bookstores] near FLACSO, in the Faculty [of Social Sciences at UBA], which means that [we do] what university press U. doesn't. In this way [the journal] keeps on circulating. The price of the journal is risible; 15 Argentine pesos, and it is a book, not a journal. Recently, [we] have published two numbers in one issue. So many contributions are submitted while we try to get funds that we always end up making thick, annual, issues. But we stay in circulation. People [from the editorial board] keep on appearing as referees. Sometimes they read something or take a look at something: 'biased reading', as Portantiero called it ironically. Elsewhere this is a paid activity, as it is to be an examiner (63: 42; in translation).

Therefore, the legitimacy of peer-reviewing is strongly questioned because it appears as a process based on personal contacts and favours. Scholars tend to criticise the opinion of their reviewers, which discourages the appearance of a culture of mutual evaluation.

> We are in a gradual process [of becoming a peer-reviewed publication] because it takes too much time [for scholars] to understand the value

138   *Centers and Peripheries in Knowledge Production*

of the peer-reviewing process. We have had people who were upset with us and never talked to us again after the results of a peer review. A culture [of] peer evaluation has to be established, and that's not easy (53: 32; in translation).

Along with the problems mentioned above, the lack of personnel to undertake editing of an Argentine political science journal means that this is a task managed by scholars, for whom the journal is just one amongst many other academic activities. Moreover, due to the absence of full-time staff working on the journals, editors recognise that the quality of each edition is not as good as it should be.

Nobody is devoted full-time to [the journal]. It is impossible to do something good when you have to do twenty different things [at the same time] (53: 47; in translation).

[The members of this journal] don't have widely separate activities. First [we need] to look for articles because the journal is small [. . .]. *It's necessary to go out to promote the request to people to send us articles to publish* (53: 47; in translation; emphasis added).

The inadequately institutionalised peer-reviewing process, the difficulty of publishing on a regular basis, the scarcity of material resources to guarantee a wide distribution, and the inadequate time and staffing levels make Argentine journals in political science unattractive for Western authors. However, there are foreign articles, translated into Spanish or coming from other Spanish speaking countries, in almost every number of every journal. How does this happen? The answer is in the ability of editors to take advantage of the few opportunities to request contributions from foreigners when they meet at conferences or other academic gatherings. Empirical evidence shows that the appointment of foreign scholars as director or co-director of local postgraduate programmes means that they visit the university regularly and become a target for the editors who want to publish the work of foreign authors. Occasional visits of foreign academics to conferences in Argentina are also used by editors, but they are rather infrequent in the field. In other words, one important feature of local journals is to actively look for prospective contributions and take advantage of institutional and personal contacts to obtain them. This informal procedure reinforces the lack of institutionalisation, as well as undermining the peer-reviewing process, since articles that are requested rarely undergo thorough review. At the same time, the procedure strengthens existing networks and makes it difficult for newcomers to publish in the few local academic publications. For many locally prestigious scholars, the situation is the same since their publications have generally been on request.

If there only a few local journals in the field of Argentine political science and editors invite scholars to submit work, are they not mediators? Theoretically, they are mediators if they use the space in the journal to pursue their own agendas, their own academic interests, and to solidify the networks in which they are involved (McGinty 1999). However, the lack of material and symbolic resources makes it necessary to take advantage of *any* scholar, and *any* article, not only those who would fortify their own position in the field.[9] An editor only becomes a mediator if s/he is able to determine what is included in, and excluded from, the journal and such decisions have to be coherent throughout time, as the history of the US political science journals illustrates (Renwick Monroe 2005). Further, only if the editor has a large number of submissions can s/he make a selection that at the same time guarantees the quality of the publication and strengthens his or her position in the field. When just any contribution is necessary, when selection is reduced because of the lack of articles or resources to publish them, the editor becomes a manager; a powerful actor, but not a mediator.[10]

The way that editors of Argentine journals in political science deal with the scarcity of resources and the paucity of institutions is reflected in the procedures used to minimise dispersion, referred to as teaching technology in this book. While scholars tend to take advantage of multiple positions in order to teach and, if possible, to do research, editors tend to capitalise on their chances of obtaining articles, especially from foreign fields, by requesting contributions at conferences, academic meetings, and informal reunions. Sometimes editors call for previously published pieces that can be translated into Spanish by some students or colleagues in order to include articles from abroad in the issue.[11] In any case, it seems that local journals necessarily have to contain foreign contributions to be attractive to local readers, probably because local readers, as described in chapter 3, are more familiar with foreign knowledge and authors than with local scholars and their production.

Mediated access to foreign ideas through local publications is filtered by the opportunistic strategies of local editors, but direct access to foreign journals is very difficult as libraries are not up to date. According to Coraggio and Vispo (2001), 85 per cent of the university budget is devoted to the salary of academic and administrative staff, while Saviola (2008) raises that to 90 per cent. Whatever the exact figure may be, higher education has not been a political priority for any government since 1983 (Chiroleu 2005). The State is mainly responsible for investment in this sector (Barsky et al. 2004) and public investment in academic and administrative salaries leaves no room for the necessary improvements in infrastructure, such as buildings and libraries (Delfino 2004).

Given the poorly-equipped libraries, scholars usually resort to alternative strategies in order to access novel foreign and local ideas. The first alternative is photocopies of books brought to Argentina by colleagues from abroad,[12] whose experience is valued as mediation to foreign knowledge for the members of the networks in which they are embedded. The access to data while being abroad is a condition of developing some comparative studies that, otherwise, would be impossible because they require enormous financial support.

140 *Centers and Peripheries in Knowledge Production*

> I was visiting professor at Stanford from January to May and there . . .
> I bought a suitcase full of books and material about other countries,
> not Argentina, to be able to publish about them. In the article that I'm
> writing now, I want to add [data] about countries other than those I
> studied in my thesis; Brazil for example, and I brought [those data]
> with me from Stanford (54: 70; in translation).

Other scholars utilise the free sample offers that many publishing houses in
the First World employ to promote their journals. This situation has many
implications. First, the access to bibliography is mediated by the marketing
strategies of the powerful publishing houses based in the developed world,
and such bibliography is usually translated as course syllabi bibliography
rather than the basis of a literature review for new articles or research.
Thus, instead of research technology, the interplay between the internet,
computer, publishing houses, academic journals, and peripheral scholars
gives rise to teaching technology.[13] The priority of scholars is to acquire up
to date knowledge to disseminate it in order to let students know original
theories, methodologies and empirical analyses. In that context, scholars
tend (or are forced) to ignore copyright and other restrictions of use of
foreign publications: they use whatever is available which meets certain
quality standards (Rodriguez Medina 2009). Scholars recognise implicitly
the diversified academic fields in some developed countries, the place their
specialised journals occupy, and the need for understanding such diversification in order to identify their target journals with greater accuracy. Only
those who have mapped the field of political science in metropolitan fields
(usually those who studied abroad or who have strong links with foreign
colleagues and/or with those who have done this) are able to submit their
work to the specific journal in which the piece fits best. As Canagarajah
pointed out, 'many periphery scholars are denied the ability to screen journals in order to choose those that are appropriate for their submission.
[Thus] the proliferation of journals in the West is often confusing to local
scholars, especially when most of them cannot be seen/read there' (2002:
160–61). In ANT's words, by ignoring the existence of some journals,
peripheral scholars are reducing the likelihood of enacting the necessary
network that allows them to enrol the most adequate metropolitan publication, its editors and editorial board, its peer-reviewers, and the entire
structure of scholarly journals in order to publish their work.

> The biggest problem is with journals. [. . .] But with Internet you have
> more opportunities. I have arranged an impressive library in my hard
> disk that I use a lot, especially in postgraduate [courses]. [It is] in Eng-
> lish, Spanish, French, in any language. For example, I'm now teaching
> a postgraduate course, that is an update on Social Sciences, and I pre-
> pared a CD with the mandatory articles and also the complementary
> ones, just in case [the students] need them one day. Some things are

Towards a Plurality of Translations 141

free access, but others aren't, or have been closed down [. . .] I'm pretty opportunistic. Every journal offers you, in general, especially those written in English, a free sample. That I obviously take. And then, another of the [methods] I found [to get foreign bibliography] is that some journals offer a free subscription for 30, 60, or up to 90 days. So on one day I download everything. I download everything that looks familiar and file it. Afterwards I see if it is useful, if I'll use it at any moment, because otherwise you have no time. These are the things that permit access to interesting journals, even to those that one didn't know existed. One tends to subscribe to widely known journals, but suddenly [you realise] that there are a lot that you had never heard of. And subscription is really expensive, especially since 2001 (47: 74; in translation).

The data in sections 5.1.1 and 5.1.2 show that the introduction of foreign ideas into peripheral fields is not as straightforward as is usually assumed. Although the weight of Spanish publishing houses, and the preference of local editors of journals for foreign texts, has been highlighted, it is also worth noting that the translations by which foreign knowledge is incorporated involve negotiations (e.g. between local and foreign publishers) and a subordination (e.g. the request for articles from foreign scholars or translations of previously published work). This subordination, in turn, is based not only on the interests of local journal editors but, rather, on the sporadic opportunities that they have to meet foreign scholars and obtain their contributions. The other side of this situation is the challenge for Argentine political scientists to reach an audience beyond the local field; the topic of the next section.

5.1.3 Argentine Ideas in Foreign Publications

If the introduction of foreign ideas is a complicated process in peripheral scientific fields, the exportation of local knowledge to foreign fields is even harder. Notwithstanding the problems raised by language and the textual and para-textual conventions of metropolitan publications (Canagarajah 2002), the ISI Web of Knowledge data show low representation of Argentine political scientists in international debates. According to the Social Science Citation Index (SSCI), between 1975 and 2013, 416 articles were published by scholars working in Argentina, as Figure 5.1 shows.[14]

The analysis of political science journals, according to the SSCI, shows that the impact of Argentine authors is rather minimal: 60.8 per cent were not cited, 11.5 per cent were cited only once, 9.4 per cent were cited twice, 1.9 per cent were cited three times, and 16.3 per cent were cited four or more times in thirty-eight years. Not surprisingly, the few multi-cited articles are those that have appeared in the *American Journal of Political Science*, *Comparative Political Studies*, *Political Communication*, *Studies in*

142 *Centers and Peripheries in Knowledge Production*

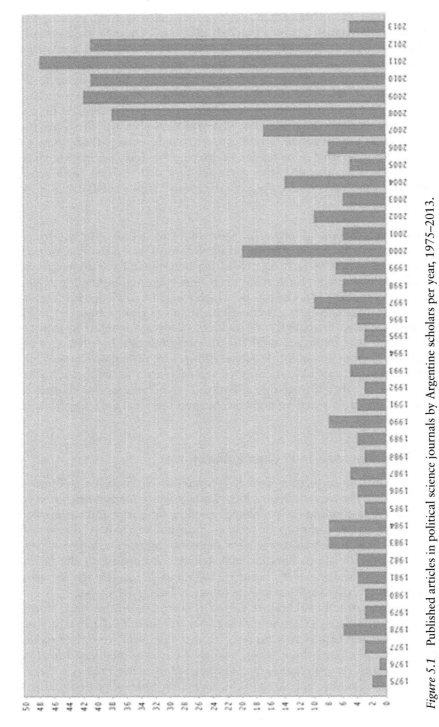

Figure 5.1 Published articles in political science journals by Argentine scholars per year, 1975–2013.
Source: ISI Web of Science, accessed March 2013

Comparative International Development, and *Human Rights Quarterly*; major journals in the field. Even less surprising is that the most cited articles have been co-authored with colleagues working in metropolitan fields.[15] The most cited co-authored articles were written by Argentine scholars in collaboration with political scientists from the University of California, Los Angeles; University of California, Berkeley; Northwestern University; Michigan State University; New York University; University of Michigan, Ann Arbor; University of Miami; and University of Houston.

A glance at the most cited article in political science written by an Argentine scholar and foreign co-authors illustrates some of the particularities of asymmetrical translations.[16] The article was written by scholars at Universidad de San Andres (Argentina), the University of California, Los Angeles, and the University of California, Berkeley. Thus, the most cited article from this short list supports the idea that belonging to highly respected metropolitan research institutions increases the chances of being published in top journals (Canagarajah 2002; Becher and Trowler 2001).[17] At the same time, it also supports the idea that the prestige of the current academic location of the authors affects the recognition that the article may receive, as Oromaner (1983) and Lightfield (1971) have suggested. Further, the article exemplifies one of Wagner (2008)'s findings about collaboration: scholars in peripheral fields tend to co-author articles more frequently with colleagues in the First World than with other scholars of developing countries; what she has referred to as 'preferential attachment' (2008: 42–43). Figure 5.2 shows this attachment in relation to all articles published in political science journals by Argentine scholars between 1975 and 2013. Instead of empowering some less developed regions of the world, co-authorship seems to accentuate the importance of centres of knowledge production, as well as diminishing the opportunity for collaboration between scholars of peripheral regions.

The title of the article, 'Judicial Independence in Unstable Environments, Argentina 1935–1998', illustrates the kind of geographical awareness that metropolitan academia requires from peripheral scholars, while reserving universalistic claims for metropolitan texts. As Baber has pointed out, 'an article or book produced by a scholar situated in a non-metropolitan society and reporting on research conducted on a non-metropolitan site will almost invariably disclose the identity of the location in its title' (2003: 617). Even though the first part of the title seems to refer to a general topic—the judicial in unstable environments—the last part clearly points to a specific environment, namely Argentina between 1935 and 1998. The reference to a particular region or country appears in every title of the articles that cite this work, reinforcing Barber's claims: Russia, Mexico, Brazil, Malawi, Zambia, Turkey, Bolivia, Latin America, Argentina, and Italy. Nevertheless, two scholars from the United States cite this article in their work 'Modeling motivations: A method for inferring judicial goals from behavior', a title with no particular geographical delimitation. What is worth noting is that

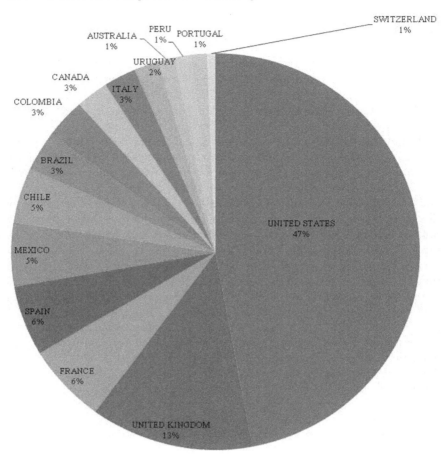

Figure 5.2 Country of origin of co-authors' institutions.
Source: ISI Web of Science, accessed March 2013

the authors rely on the data gathered in the original article concerning the Argentine judicial system to infer the behaviour of the judges of 'the rest of the world', as the abstract claims. While scholars working in the periphery refer, in their articles, to specific contexts, metropolitan scholars make generalisations based on the same data, which promote their work to the level of universal applicability.[18]

> The consensus among most scholars of American politics is that judges are policy seekers. *Yet we know very little about what motivates judges in other parts of the world.* To begin to address this gap, we develop a systematic method for inferring goals from behavior. Using a simple game-theoretic framework, we generate a series of testable propositions linking behavioral outcomes to goals for four ideal types of judges:

Towards a Plurality of Translations 145

loyalists, policy seekers, institutionalists, and careerists. We illustrate the power of our method with *original data on individual and collective judicial decision making in the Argentine Supreme Court* (1976–2000) (Helmke and Sanders 2006: 867).

It may also been seen, from the most-cited article co-authored by an Argentine political scientist, that publication in top Western journals requires respecting the methodological inclinations of the journal (Canagarajah 2002; Renwick Monroe 2005). The *American Journal of Political Science* has a clear preference for formalised models (Kasza 2005; Hill and Leighley 2005), which favours those university departments, theoretical schools, and research agendas that are strong in formalised political science. In order to meet this requirement, the authors of the article clearly state that they develop a simple model, but also claim that legal procedures in Argentina make it 'almost impossible' to obtain enough information.

> We develop a simple but useful model which we empirically implement later in the article. The simplicity of the model is driven by the unavailability of roll calls in the Argentinean Congress which makes it almost impossible to attempt to develop independent measures of legislators' preferences, and hence of justices' ideology (Iaryczower et al. 2002: 700).

Empirical evidence from the present research suggests that the conditions of knowledge production in metropolitan centres are as important in relation to publishing abroad as the prestige of the foreign journals or their potential worldwide impact. A full-time faculty position, along with involvement in peer-reviewing, is crucial for scholars in continuing the process of quality control for new publications.

> I submitted an article to the US journal *Comparative Politics* and I received four pages from a referee that killed us. But, well, s/he was absolutely right about everything, in everything s/he has pointed out. We modified it, re-submitted it, and it came out. And it was beneficial. Also, for me [the referee] was profoundly respectful because s/he had taken time to read the article fussily, to point out each and every thing that s/he thought wrong. For me, if an article is reviewed and I only received compliments it is disrespectful; it's not good, because it means that [the reviewer] didn't read it, or [the referee] didn't read the article critically. Science progresses by questioning what already exists. If not, there wouldn't have been a Galileo, a Copernicus. It's like that. [In] political science [. . .] it is the same (37: 77; in translation).

For those who studied abroad, the logic of publish or perish was internalised during their time as postgraduate students, but this logic is not

146   *Centers and Peripheries in Knowledge Production*

extended to the field of Argentine political science, except at a few universities. At one of these, a consolidated scholar recognised the requirements of many top journals in the metropolitan academia, which is shaping his current work: generalisation (Canagarajah 2002; Baber 2003). Although focused on Argentina, he presents his article as the current state of labour in the age of globalisation, a subject that invites universalistic claims. More importantly, the scholar mentions that the co-authorship is based on the necessity to keep in touch with foreign colleagues even though data gathering and writing may rest with the local political scientist. The differences in theoretical perspectives encourage some scholars to keep looking at foreign colleagues, journals, and institutions in order to continue publishing their research. Simultaneously, the possibility of ignoring the contributions made by local colleagues—due to the networked nature of the field—along with detours that scholars may take in order to avoid going through a particular local school, journal, or scholar, tends to impede the appearance of more mediators in Argentine political science. Facing a local context in which some theoretical frameworks are ignored or downplayed, interviewees have stated that they have no problem with bypassing the local members of the field and contacting foreign colleagues to publish their work.

> This article is about Argentina, but I'm submitting it to *Politics & Society*, because it is a case study with a more general view. If it hadn't been, we couldn't publish it there. We compare the relationships between government and labour unions under Kirchner, in post-liberalism, with the salary negotiation models of Europe and with what has been traditional in Latin America, and in Mexico; the more traditional state corporatism. Even though it is a work that I have put together with information from Argentina, I co-authored it with a professor from there [the United States], but just to keep in touch and because I talk with her about comparative politics. I'm still thinking like I did in the United States, in terms of debates. The introduction [to the article] is what is about labour in the age of globalisation; I'm not talking about Argentina. [. . .] I'm in limbo because I'm not there any longer and they have stopped replying to my e-mails and I have no relation with the research environment here. [Local researchers] think in local terms and are less related to US literature. Those who actually think in terms of foreign literature are influenced by the French model, [. . .] more by Bourdieu [. . .] and by political sociology (54: 65; in translation).

The current labour conditions and the features of the local field affect the actual possibilities for publishing research carried out in the periphery in journals from metropolitan centres. Scholars who refer to the tension between being in Argentina and publishing in the United States recognise that university evaluation, according to publications in foreign journals, may be unfair, taking into account the bias of many top journals. Most scholars

Towards a Plurality of Translations 147

in Argentine political science are not obliged to publish in foreign journals. Moreover, since equipment, space, and research grants are scarce and evaluation of academic performance is not thoroughly institutionalised, other than for the members of CONICET and professors at a few universities who are regularly evaluated by peers, local political scientists are discouraged from developing a strong record of publication. Thus, without institutional incentives to stimulate productivity, the decision to carry out research and publish is based more on personal interest than on institutional requirements, promoting teaching-oriented strategies in career development. In addition, teaching plays the major role within the academic system and forces scholars to combine multiple jobs in order to obtain benefits from every single activity, something we refer to as teaching technology.

> It's necessary to pay attention to both an age issue and the construction of a local community. [It's necessary to acknowledge] that we are here and it's not the same to publish in [US] journals from here, they don't give you the same attention, we know that it's not neutral. [Publications in the US] are meritocratic compared with journals with no evaluation but [. . .] the discipline is so segmented [that] some professors don't publish in the *American Political Science Review* because it's a journal biased towards American politics. So if you do European comparative politics you will have little chance of being published. We have to pay more attention to this, and to the fact that our work [has to] be known here (54: 68; in translation).

For those few who have been appointed full-time professors and enjoy advantageous labour conditions, the peripheral situation of working in Argentina is highlighted when reflecting on the actual chances of contributing to foreign journals. Local political scientists find that the publishing process does not have sufficient benefit for their careers, due to the hard work needed to publish in the most prestigious international publishing houses, the few posts in the local academic field that offer acceptable working conditions (e.g. office space, library, and full-time involvement in academic activities), and the lack of recognition for publications by university administrators. Although they do not turn down opportunities to publish abroad, they rarely take the initiative. A prolific consolidated scholar who has written book chapters for Palgrave, Cambridge University Press, Oxford University Press, the Johns Hopkins University Press, University of Michigan Press, University of Notre Dame Press, and Westview Press, recognises that

> there are two things that I know I made the effort to publish; all the other things, be it books or journal articles, I've been told to publish. One is [an article] in the *Journal of Democracy* that Prof. P. and I submitted, and the other is the book that we submitted to Pittsburgh [University Press]. I'd say that all the other opportunities just turned up

148 *Centers and Peripheries in Knowledge Production*

or I was asked to write something about that topic for a book (15: 96; in translation).

> [T]here is a tension because I think that this university must make a difference and when you come back at least you can 'score' sometimes. Here you won't be an international star, but once in a while you can do something from here. And this is possible because the university gives you an office, you have a library, they bring books in, and they pay well (54: 66; in translation).

If publication in foreign journals is difficult, it is even harder to publish a book abroad. Empirical evidence gathered in the present research suggests that most books published by Argentine political scientists abroad are based on PhD theses or other work carried out in the metropolitan centres because publishing high calibre scientific texts requires time and the opportunity to work exclusively on the topic as well as access to an up-to-date bibliography and the physical space to write. Publishing in developed countries highlights the differences between the local and foreign book industries, and the role of mediators in institutionalised scientific fields.

> [A book] is not exactly a thesis, but it is similar. So, on the initiative of my thesis director I presented [the manuscript] to a very important publishing house that has a series on that topic. [The book] is the thesis, but changed. It has other things; has a wider scope, is less technical, and is shorter. I submitted the manuscript to the committee, they approved it and sent me a letter saying that the book had been accepted. Then they sent the book to some referees and then the book came out. It was very different from what I had published in Argentina until that moment, because there was a contract, copyright, and, well, a professional publishing house. [. . .] In Argentina we publish our books, without sponsors, in home-made publishing houses, with low visibility; catalogues are not well spread . . . Recently I published a book with Emecé, part of the Planeta Group, and in that case it was similar to this [the book in Italy]. Professional proof readers, control of the proofs, designers for the cover, and mechanisms for distribution that put the book in every bookstore. [. . .] This is why I say that it's not a problem to [publish] in Europe or Argentina. [. . .] The problem is that we can't reach the big publishing houses (32: 102; in translation).[19]

It has been shown in previous sections from the circulation of printed scholarly works (i.e. journals and books), that Argentine political science, as a networked field, has only a few, isolated mediators and forces scholars to develop individual strategies that multiply their contacts with foreign colleagues and knowledge. The next two sections focus on embodied

Towards a Plurality of Translations   149

ideas, that is, people who travel and who, by so doing, carry with them knowledge from the sites of production to new environments for consumption. Embodied ideas will be studied through the circulation of academics between metropolitan centres and peripheral fields.

5.2 EMBODIMENT OF FOREIGN IDEAS

If ideas do not travel materialised in written texts, they still can move from one place to another carried by people. The history of knowledge has recognised the importance of travellers in the diffusion of ideas (Burke 2002) as well as the growing internationalisation of academic staff that has occurred since the middle of the 20th century (Welch 2007c). The reasons for the circulation of scholars are various, but 'seeking new knowledge, and students, [and] finding refuge from more hostile environments, academic and political' are amongst the most important (Welch 1997).

The circulation of scholars is the main concern of this section. In section 5.2.1 the focus is on the temporary visits of Argentine political scientists to foreign institutions, especially as visiting professors and to international conferences. In section 5.2.2 the absence of foreign scholars in the local field is explored and, from this, the local conditions of knowledge production may be understood.

5.2.1 Going Abroad: Local Scholars (and Ideas) in Foreign Contexts

Most scholars in the Argentine university system have not spent long periods abroad once they have obtained permanent jobs in the local field, due to budgetary restrictions. This situation supports Boyer et al.'s (1994) findings, according to which 86.6 per cent of Latin American scholars had not served as a faculty member abroad. The figure contrasts with the situation in many other countries, such as Israel (where 35 per cent of scholars served as faculty member abroad), the Netherlands (66 per cent), and Germany (75 per cent). In the same study, 53 per cent of Latin American scholars replied that they have not travelled abroad to study or research in the last three years, while scholars from many other places reported lower rates, such as Sweden (25 per cent), the Netherlands (30 per cent) and Germany (35 per cent) (Boyer et al. 1994).

In addition to economic reasons, there are legal factors to take into account. In Argentina, only those scholars who obtained their posts as a result of open competition and are full-time professors may apply for sabbatical leave. In most private universities, there is no opportunity for sabbaticals because the posts are related to teaching positions and academics who do not attend classes usually receive no salary even though they are part of a Chair. Thus, leaving the country is not an option for most academics in the Argentine university system.

150 Centers and Peripheries in Knowledge Production

Those who can travel abroad for longer or shorter periods usually take advantage of institutional agreements that have been signed by Deans or Chancellors (Pérez Lindo 2003). This is not only a sign of the extent to which the international connection is not necessarily under the control of the academics, but also of the tendency towards an internationalisation of higher education (Welch 2007c; Altbach and Balán 2007; López Segrera 2006). In this situation, there is no careful planning of, and control over, the flow of people but, rather, institutional bonds between universities open up the possibility for scholars to travel. Nevertheless, such links between institutions are actually between people. When scholars talk of institutional bonds, they tacitly imply that the continuity of the agreements depend on the academics who negotiated and signed them. However, once the agreement is established, the negotiator does not seem to function as a traditional mediator. The scarcity of qualified scholars who meet the necessary requirements to teach in foreign fields in developed countries forces these negotiators to keep open the channel for all the academics at the university where s/he works. When powerful actors in the field do not have enough resources to sustain a system of exclusion, and when exclusion is not possible because of the paucity of skilled people, these mediators have obstacles to maintaining their dominant position.[20] Instead, people flow through the network, taking advantage of the connections already established and bypassing the weak control of leading scholars.

> Now I'm teaching in the PhD programme at the Universidad S. [in Spain]. Q: How did this contact with Universidad S. occur? A: It was Prof. C.'s contact. Indeed, the PhD programme at this university has agreements with that of Universidad S. (4: 99; in translation).

Amongst those who can travel abroad, the personal contacts gathered during their time abroad as PhD students are crucial for obtaining invitations from foreign institutions later in their careers (e.g. visiting professorships and short academic stays). This is a conscious and demanding task that the scholar, especially one from the periphery, must undertake. Along with attending conferences and teaching some courses abroad, keeping in touch demands the effort of co-authoring articles, even though most of the work is done by the researcher in the peripheral field (Vessuri 2010). Thus, a division of academic work is perpetuated (Alatas 2001, 2003) and highlights the personal conditions that permit development of an academic career in the terms of metropolitan academia. Questioned about strategies to keep in touch with colleagues abroad, a consolidated scholar responds:

> I don't know if 'strategies' would be the word. What we have [is] the connection of having been there. I lived [in California] for five and a half years, I have a frequent exchange, by e-mail, with a professor from there. Co-authoring [articles] is one way, [attending] conferences is also

Towards a Plurality of Translations   151

a way, and going to teach abroad is another way. But it's difficult too. I can go [as visiting professor] because I'm divorced. Publishing in English with a professor from there . . . if [the article] is about Argentina, one ends up doing most of the work. I think there are ways, but they aren't free (54: 82; in translation).

When the scholar explains how he obtained the temporary position at an Ivy League university, both the personal links and the absence of mediators in the local field become evident. Since Argentina has no official programme to encourage visiting stays abroad (except for short postdoc stays for members of the CONICET), the possibility of doing so depends on previous presence in the metropolitan field, keeping contacts, and also being at a local university that values positively the experience of teaching in the developed world.[21] However, only a few scholars who hold permanent positions may undertake these short visits abroad.

A professor [who used to work at University S. and] whose research involves Europe went to University C. and they [University S.] had the expert on Latin America on leave. [. . .] So they needed someone to teach about Europe and she had read my thesis and said 'Come here.' There was no advertisement of the position. 'Can you come?' 'Yes,' I said. And I became visiting professor at University S. (54: 70; in translation).

The stay abroad, however, does not seem to be important for the circulation of ideas but, rather, for the working conditions that metropolitan universities offer. This scholar highlights the material environment (e.g. the library), the working conditions (e.g. seminars), and the students who eagerly participated in his courses, contrasting these with the local situation. The visiting professorship resembles the experience of doing a PhD abroad (chapter 4) but puts the teaching experience at the centre of the scenario. While teaching seems to be associated with the same material environment in any academic field (e.g. offices, libraries, computers), the network or socio-technical ensemble that emerges is not necessarily the same. Under full-time contracts, be they tenured or untenured, scholars relate differently with their socio-technical environment than under the uncertain conditions of peripheral academic fields. The result is not only a higher level of productivity but also a different involvement in scholarly life that allows time for other parts of the institutionalised academic field: peer-reviewing, research, writing, informal and formal contacts with colleagues, reading, and quotidian exchange with students. As the scholar recognises, by referring to the State responsibility in the institutionalisation of universities in Argentina, the system works as a whole or it does not work at all.

[At University D. in the United States] I could study, because you can't do it here, it's very difficult. I went to the library, I studied, I had the

152 *Centers and Peripheries in Knowledge Production*

peacefulness of following the topics and read things that I had never read before. I enjoyed my family. It was a paradise. There were fantastic seminars. Every day I had to choose which not to attend, because there were [seminars] about everything. [. . .] To see the eagerness of the guys is incredible. [. . .] I enjoyed a class of 10–12 students, with a diversity of ideas, ethnic backgrounds, and ideology. They read everything, and participated in class. And then I taught a postgraduate course that was spectacular. It was my most successful teaching experience. There were 22 students [. . .] I was excited! A wonderful experience. Every day I went to teach happily (52: 78–80; in translation).

We continue without a well-funded university system that helps [scholars] lead [a scholarly life] and with a division of labour to have [. . .] the guy who generates theory [. . .] and the guy who influences public policies. [. . .] But here you have neither one nor the other and nobody is thinking about this in the short term. So in a country without strong institutions there cannot be good universities and here there are no strong institutions (52: 76; in translation).

Important as they are as formal channels of communication (Meadows 1997; Becher and Trowler 2001), international conferences play a marginal role for peripheral scholars. The lack of economic resources makes it impossible for most scholars to attend international conferences, except in those cases in which the conference has been held in, or near their own country. For Bulcourf and D'Alessandro, for example, the realisation of the International Political Science Association world conference in Buenos Aires in 1991 was 'one of the most important events in the development of political science in Argentina' (2003: 164).

[Personal] production fluctuates between these things: the necessity to write something and to be present in the discipline every two years at the SAAP Annual Conference. Before 2000 I used to attend some international conferences because I was funded. Now, [I do not attend] international conferences because there aren't funds. Universities support nothing. No private university [at which I work] supports [travel to conferences] and the public universities provide less support on each successive occasion (48: 60; in translation).

Scholars need to invest their own money in order to attend international conferences without the support of universities or other bodies funding travel to conferences. The negative side of this is the frequent absence of Argentine political scientists from international forums which, in turn, reduces the opportunities to exchange ideas with foreign colleagues and to make public research done in Argentina. A more positive side is, again, the existence of only a few mediators. Scholars may freely decide which conference to attend

Towards a Plurality of Translations   153

and on which topic they submit a paper. In fact, the selection of the conference and the topic may depend more on personal issues (e.g. availability of money or contacts with people in the cities where conferences are held) than institutional or disciplinary requirements. Thus, the lack of a structure of mediators in a context of scarce symbolic and material resources reinforces the fragmentation of the field, because there is no strategic and regular participation in international fora. At the same time, the degree of mutual dependence, at the local level, decreases, since Argentine political scientists do not have to meet local criteria or standards (even in theoretical or methodological terms) to be supported to attend conferences.

Where scholars are able to acquire funds to travel abroad, the asymmetrical relationships between fields appear in their purest dimension. Their theatrical nature means that conferences are not only an opportunity to exchange information but also a place of consecration where academics recognise the work of their colleagues (e.g. referring to them as 'stars' or 'big names') through a set of rituals, the most important being plenary sessions (Wacquant 2013; Becher and Trowler 2001; Clark 2006). Furthermore, in international conferences the disparity of symbolic resources plays a crucial part. The traditional structure of conferences (i.e. keynote speakers, chairs, discussants, and paper-givers) depicts a landscape of differently-endowed academics who nevertheless share some discipline-related common features. For scholars who are usually excluded from international fora, the opportunity of exchanging ideas with leading academics in the field makes them feel the pressure of a different kind of enrolment. While texts play a more passive role in the networks, used in both citations and bibliography in syllabi, conferences, where face-to-face exchanges allow responses (e.g. rejections and disregarding), make the addition of new actors in the network more complicated. This is because the disparity of symbolic and material resources impede academics in the periphery from offering interesting opportunities to their colleagues, such as visiting professorships, space for publications, or temporary posts in a research team.[22]

> A colleague and I submitted a paper for the 1994 ISPA World Conference in Berlin. It was accepted and I was shaking for a week because the panel would be chaired by Lijphart. For me, he was someone who existed only in books. We requested a grant from the university, otherwise we couldn't have travelled there. [. . .] Because we hadn't met Lijphart, the co-author of my paper went to a stand of Oxford University Press, picked up a book by Lijphart and found a picture of him. So then we could introduce ourselves [to him]. For me, the conference was like a dream, like seeing The Beatles playing next to me, because Lipset, Linz, Lijphart, Morlino, and Bartolino were there (37: 45; in translation).

At the same time, by not attending international conferences peripheral scholars cannot use them to structure at least part of their work, such as meeting

154 *Centers and Peripheries in Knowledge Production*

deadlines, exchanging opinions with colleagues about promising new topics, or exploring new research questions (Gross and Fleming 2011).

5.2.2 Hosting Foreign Scholars

There are two main obstacles for the circulation of scholars from metropolitan fields to the periphery. The first one is related to the seeming lack of interest of the academics in central fields in leaving their countries for research or teaching. For example, Altbach has claimed that

> American academics have an ambivalent relationship with the rest of the world. They welcome scholars from abroad as visitors or as permanent colleagues and eagerly accept students from abroad in their classes and seminars. But they pay little attention to the knowledge that the rest of the world produces and are unlikely to travel abroad much for study or research (2007a: 150).

Boyer et al. reported that 91 per cent of Americans, 93 per cent of Japanese, 84 per cent of Britons, and 75 per cent of Germans responded that they have not served as a faculty member at an institution in another country recently (1994: 105). The reason for the low mobility of scholars from the First World may rest on the importance that they assign for keeping in touch with foreign colleagues. Questioned as to whether international connections are important to their professional work, 55 per cent of US scholars and 63 per cent of British scholars responded affirmatively, while 95 per cent of Chilean and 91 per cent of Korean scholars considered that their international bonds were important (Boyer et al. 1994: 106). Accordingly, Melkers and Kiopa, using a national survey of academic scientists and engineers in the United States, have found that 'it is striking (but not very surprising) that respondents who are non-US citizens and hold a foreign doctoral degree are more likely to have a close international collaborator. Conversely, US citizens who hold a foreign PhD have a negative relationship with having a close international collaborator' (2010: 409). These studies partially corroborate the thesis that 'the USA, and to a lesser extent the UK, appear to value foreign contacts far less than any other system' (Welch 2007c: 83).

The consequence of underestimation is not only a matter of staying in their home institutions and ignoring the production of the rest of the world, but also of setting the research agenda on peripheral regions taking into account only the requirements and imperatives of the metropolitan academia. As Kalman Silvert, an American political scientist and advisor to the Social Science Research Council and the Ford Foundation in the 1960s, stated, 'the reasons [for having reservations on collaborating with Latin American colleagues] had not alone to do with my habitual distrust of faddism, but also with my feelings that North American scholars should not be constrained by Latin American definitions of what is right and proper

Towards a Plurality of Translations 155

to investigate in Latin America' (Delpar 2007: 162). The counterpart to this statement has been presented by Diégues and Wood by saying that 'the [Latin American] problems studied by American social scientists "are not those which have the most direct bearing on the needs and aspirations of our peoples; nor are they problems or subjects of importance for the regional development process"'(Diégues and Wood [1967: 7–8], quoted in Delpar 2007: 161). These disagreements seem to be a crucial characteristic of the relationship between centres and peripheries.

The second obstacle resides in the peripheral field, where there are no formal or material structures to adequately organise visits, conferences, visiting professorships, and other temporary or permanent academic appointments to attract foreign scholars. Almost all the scholars interviewed in the course of the research presented in this book do not remember a visiting scholar during their undergraduate studies, although a few do mention some occasional lectures or talks. These talks take place generally because of personal contacts and the travel of metropolitan scholars funded by their institutions or government agencies. This situation has at least two consequences. It shows that the local university has no control over the people who are coming, which means that their scholars cannot be considered mediators, as they do not control the circulation of colleagues from abroad. The political agenda of international organizations, foundations or philanthropic agencies becomes more important than the academic one of the university or its faculty, introducing legal and political issues into the landscape of academic mobility because '[e]mbassy or government officials associated with ([German Academic Exchange Service] DAAD or Fulbright) programs have, on occasion, attempted to intimidate, or to threaten the employment situation of scholars who were seen as transgressing program norms' (Welch 2007c: 87–88). Indeed, political agendas tend to be far more important than scholarly interests and local needs (Parmar 2012) because they 'define how, what, who, where, and when to research and which are the satisfactory expected outcomes' (Várnagy 2010: 170).

The lack of office space for local professors impedes visiting professors from daily academic and personal exchanges that may enrich and strengthen the international connection. Further, the university uses the foreign visitor to teach some courses even though the basic income is dispensed by the foreign organisation (e.g. Fulbright or foreign universities) in which the scholar studies or works. What at first glance is cooperation (a network extending and bringing benefits for its older and newer members), ends up being a complex system of relationships that nurtures local mismanagement and reinforces the subordination of the local field to foreign organisations.

> We could convene people through the Embassy of the United States. The embassy had a centre whose name I can't remember, dependent on the cultural attaché, but they shut it down. [. . .] We usually requested them to support the travel of some Fulbright scholar or of any academic who

156 *Centers and Peripheries in Knowledge Production*

was coming from the United States. But that ended for us because this university is not a big one. It has 50 or 60 undergraduate programmes and if it were to bring in two scholars per programme, it would fall into the red. So we could do it well as long as this centre worked, but when the centre was closed, the situation changed for us, because you can't bring Sartori to lecture and ask him to pay for everything. Lately, [. . .] thanks to Fulbright, [. . .] we have received people who came on their sabbatical leave. We gave them a space for six months; they gave some seminars. But when we have to pay, when we have to support [the scholar], our hands are tied (23: 55; in translation).

The dynamics of the circulation of the scholar also illustrate how time itself is constructed and negotiated through teaching technology (Michael 2006). Management of time involves the capacity to enrol actors and overlap networks, in such a way that the 'times' of both synchronise, making it possible for scholars to establish bonds with colleagues and keep and nurture them through the use of technologies such as videoconferencing or e-mails.

There was no a systematic policy regarding foreign professors, but rather a combination of opportunity and convenience. If a professor from this university visited Boston University and he was to see Scott Mainwaring, he had an obligation to somehow get a videoconference, if [the foreign scholar] wasn't going to come to Argentina. [. . .] We did this with Mainwaring, with Touraine, with Mark Jones. Some foreign professors came here. [. . .] But we had to work on opportunity and convenience (38: 78; in translation).

Academics recognise that the only choice is sometimes to take advantage of opportunities opened up by other scholars in order to achieve international contacts that may end up being academic connections. While some ensembles work properly and the articulation of humans and objects functions smoothly, other networks may not been able to translate correctly the interests of the actors involved and the output is a failure.

[The programme of] Sociology was to invite, for its 50th anniversary, probably the greatest expert in Latin American public policy, who is also the greatest expert on Weber in Latin America. For both reasons, [this scholar] was ideal for an event like this. He was told that the university would pay the air tickets, and the hotel and would give him US$500 for daily expenses, thinking in the three or four days that he had to have lunch and dinner. Ten days ago, [I know this because] I'm a friend of his, the university sent him a note saying that instead of US$500 he'd receive Arg$500 [approximately US$160], that he would have to pay for half of his meals but that all this would be compensated by the fact that he would participate in a videoconference with an attendance of 4,000 people who would make his name known. He has recently been advisor to the United Nations! He doesn't need publicity! Conclusion: he closed the door and is not coming (63: 41; in translation).

Although scholars who spent time abroad are more likely to have and multiply their international connections (because they are better translators of their foreign colleagues' interests), this does not imply that local actors may not maintain international links, since elements like personal attitude and motivation have also been pointed out by some scholars interviewed in this research. Those elements illustrate the weaknesses of universities in establishing and keeping international liaisons. It also indicates that the local field has a high number of members who serve as filters for ideas coming from abroad. In turn, the proliferation of members who can influence the circulation of ideas makes the analysis of the flow of such ideas between scientific fields difficult because non-dominant actors appear as endowed translators, who may be indifferent to the production of their colleagues in the local fields, but not to (some) foreign production because of its symbolic power (Altamirano and Sarlo 1983; Miller 1999).[23] By introducing foreign knowledge according to their personal or group agendas, scholars contribute to the fragmentation of the field, bringing about reproduction of relatively closed groups (Villanueva 2002). Insofar as these groups are organised around specific journals and departments, the debate concerning foreign knowledge is reduced to an endogenous discussion that usually remains confined to one, or a few, sites.

> [International contacts] are related to scholars' personal bonds. I think that this is fundamental and the motivation of people also has to do with this. Obviously, having had an experience abroad facilitates things greatly. [However,] I'm still being surprised by people who, without any experience abroad, establish important and solid relationships, form networks, spaces, and obtain funds. [. . .] On the other hand, I have many examples of people who spent years abroad and seem to know nobody! Well, I think it's important, at first, to make personal links, in addition to facilitating the contribution of the university structures, such as departments of international relations. That helps a lot, but the key factor is the bonds with the professors (45: 100; in translation).

5.3 HOW TO BECOME A DOMINANT ARGENTINE POLITICAL SCIENTIST

If the previous picture of Argentine political science seems to be homogeneous, it is because only a few scholars are able to produce, extend, and strengthen their networks over time and, by so doing, become dominant actors in the field. However, the lack of awards, the youth of the discipline

158   Centers and Peripheries in Knowledge Production

(although degrees in political science have been awarded since the 1940s), the proliferation of schools, the scarce contacts between scholars (SECyT 1998), and the debility of local publications and the publishing industry make it very difficult for consecrated local members to acquire the type of recognition that is found in institutionalised fields, such as is being mentioned in encyclopedias, national awards, and translations, and as well as belonging to prestigious editorial committees (Bourdieu 1988).[24] Consecration exists, but it is more difficult for the sociologist to grasp because it depends on more informal means (e.g. word-of-mouth or through named programmes, such as Strasser's Masters).

In this section the conditions of consecration in the local field are presented. It is possible to identify three conditions from empirical evidence: (i) the intellectual condition, (ii) the networking condition, and (iii) the international condition. While the first one refers to the capacity of some academics to identify niches within the discipline and fill them in with innovative ideas, the networking conditions point to their ability to produce socio-technical ensembles in the local field that connect Argentine political scientists, institutions, and resources. However, these conditions would be insufficient if the scholars were not able to establish the preferential attachment (Wagner 2008) that allows them to be in touch with highly respected colleagues from metropolitan scientific fields. The international condition is necessary to keep up-to-date research and teaching agendas that translate into research grants, visiting professorships, conferences, scholarly curricula, and publications.

5.3.1 The Intellectual Condition

The intellectual condition refers to the capacity of scholars to open new debates and propose timely responses to the requirements of local political and disciplinary problems. Their opportune claims reflect not only their ability to understand the actual Argentine situation but also their ability to filter such observations through the lens of theoretically informed minds. The main contributions of consecrated scholars employ traditional approaches to disciplinary problems as well as international intellectual influences. In this sense, their academic capital, partially earned through degrees and scholarships in the United States or other metropolitan fields, allows them to participate in local discussion by introducing and criticising foreign ideas.

The work of Strasser illustrates this condition. His contribution was theoretical and focused on the foundation of social and political thought, as well as on the philosophical dimension of democracy. In this sense, Strasser seemed to respond to two different demands. First, he tried to ground the theoretical and empirical debates in Argentine political science by reflecting on their epistemological foundations. Strasser wrote *La Razón Científica en Política y Sociología* in which he adopts a Kuhnian approach under the

Towards a Plurality of Translations 159

influence of his mentor at the University of California, Berkeley, Sheldon Wolin. This book seems to have been a disciplinary necessity, because the positivist-oriented project of Germani's sociology in the 1950s and 1960s was replaced by Marxist-oriented production in the 1970s and this opened a profound debate as to the scientificity of the social sciences (Terán 2004) and their praxis (Bulcourf and D'Alessandro 2003; Sarlo 2002).

After initially working on taxation, Oszlak's main research was in public administration and public policy. Oszlak is another dominant local scholar. In this area, Oszlak opened and filled a disciplinary niche by being the first to explore the problem of state formation and public administration, both systematically and theoretically.[25] Oszlak was influenced by those who had been studying the State in the context of modernisation (e.g. O'Donnell) and realised that it was impossible to understand Argentine bureaucracy without the wider historic, social, economic, and political context (Oszlak 1982). He proposed an 'integral analysis [focusing on] structural factors [and] oriented towards the popular sector' (Bulcourf and D'Alessandro 2003: 155) and this contributed to the break-up of the Instituto Di Tella and the creation of CEDES in the 1970s, where Oszlak still works.[26] According to Acuña,

the explanation of the political dynamic is articulated [by Oszlak] . . . with structural logic and consequently with regional comparative perspectives. Politics, the State and its relationships with Society, its classes, Peronism, democracy, [and] military authoritarianism are situated in the [. . .] peripheral capitalism of Latin America, which is analysed comparatively for the first time (2000: 235).

The interest of Oszlak in public administration, at both theoretical and empirical levels, forced him to study Argentine bureaucracy from its beginnings. The result of this analysis, funded by a research grant from the Tinker Foundation, was published in a now classic book: *La Formación del Estado Argentino* (1982), in which Oszlak deals with the process through which the group of provinces were organised into a central, federal State during the second half of the 19th century.[27] The book was not only necessary in a field that was changing with the introduction of new frameworks to understand old problems, such as the formation of the State, but also in a context in which the State, as a political entity, was under scrutiny (Devés Valdés 2003; Lesgart 2002). The return to democracy opened up the possibility of debating what institutional design was preferable and what was required in order to proceed to a democratic modernisation. As Munck has pointed out, 'after long years of censorship, political bans, and institutional disarticulation, Alfonsin helped recreate a public space' (1992: 206). Oszlak's sensibility towards history, his deep understanding of the bureaucratic dimension of the State (especially its extractive fiscal capacity), his commitment to a structural view of the relationships between the

160 Centers and Peripheries in Knowledge Production

State and society, and his involvement in many technical studies of national bureaucratic apparatuses, as a consultant to governments and international organisations, helped to produce a vast, complex, empirically-grounded theory of bureaucracy, whose culmination is probably his recent contribution to the Handbook of Political Sociology: *State Bureaucracy: Politics and Policies* (Oszlak 2005).

5.3.2 The Networking Condition

The careers of consecrated scholars illustrate their ability to build networks that occasionally become institutions. 'Occasionally', in this context, means that the level of institutionalisation rests with the involvement of these scholars and their networks of personal friends and colleagues. The umbrella of institutions has to be understood as a physical and symbolic environment that makes it possible to undertake academic work over a certain time period. Although the programmes that these scholars have created are still offered by their institutions, the history of the discipline has shown that their quality and transcendence are closely linked to that of their directors or consecrated scholars (Bulcourf and D'Alessandro 2003).

The trajectory of Strasser, especially in his last twenty-five years, was linked to one institution; FLACSO Buenos Aires. His arrival at FLACSO also illustrates the network that he had been able to build from his time as a member of the UCR political party.

> The offer [to come to FLACSO] was made by Arturo O'Connell, then general secretary at FLACSO [while] I was in Bariloche. [. . .] Arturo was an economist, and a member of the Board of the Banco Central de la Republica Argentina. We had met during the presidential campaign of Arturo Frondizi, in 1957, 1958. [. . .] There were few political scientists in the country (16: 69; in translation).

At the time that Strasser accepted the appointment at FLACSO the Argentine university system was under the control of the dictatorial government. This situation pushed many academics away from the main public universities towards the private research centres where some scholarly work was still permitted (Lehmann 1990). FLACSO ran an MA in political science between 1974 and 1976; a programme that brought together prestigious professors such as Arturo O'Connell, Juan Carlos Portantiero, and Emilio de Ipola (Bulcourf and D'Alessandro 2003: 155). However, the coup d'état in 1976 forced FLACSO to close the programme. In 1979, when Strasser opened the Master of Arts in Social Sciences with mention of Sociology, Political Science, Education, and International Relations, the problem was still how to populate the programme with scholars, given the lack of material resources. Friends and close colleagues played a crucial role here, since the work has been usually ad honorem or poorly paid. Only when

Towards a Plurality of Translations   161

programmes become solid and successful enough to obtain funds in the form of fees, are personal bonds (partially) replaced by institutional rules (e.g. salaries and access to office space). Strasser states that

> when FLACSO was leaving Argentina because there were neither activities nor money to stay, I invented the MA in Social Sciences, with the help of people from different centres. It was the epoch of research centres, because the university was in undesirable hands. [I organised the programme] with the help of people from different centres, from Di Tella to CEDES. [. . .] This programme was taught ad honorem at first, and then it began to be funded by fees. So FLACSO stayed in Buenos Aires and was transformed [by this programme] (16: 71; in translation).[28]

The network of Strasser, from the time he organised the MA in social sciences, was already extended and solid. It included, amongst others, Francisco Delich, Carlos Floria, Floreal Forni, Manuel Mora Araujo, Arturo O'Connell, Oscar Oszlak, Juan Sourrouille, Jorge Sábato, Gregorio Weinberg, Catalina Wainerman, and Torcuato Di Tella. Through these personal contacts, Strasser also managed to group the most prominent institutions of that time: CEDES, CLACSO, CEIL, CISEA, Instituto Di Tella, and UBA. However, in a clear indication of the networked field, Strasser acknowledges that the origin of the programme required him to forget institutions and to think of people.

> There was a time, while I was in the Fundación Bariloche, when I invited three or four institutions to launch a master's programme. Mistrust and institutional difficulties were so strong that nothing could be organised. So I said to myself: 'Well, now there's nothing to be done between institutions but only between people'. And I invited people who represented the institutions (16: 76, in translation).[29]

In a recent interview published in one of the Argentine political science journals, Strasser insists that in current Argentine political science the situation remains similar: 'there's dialogue (between institutions) and it flows, but it is more personal than institutional. [But it's not a problem because] institutions generally obstacle the flow of communication, because they make it rigid, they formalise it. [. . .] The truth is that I'm not very concerned about the lack of institutionalization' (2012: 238; in translation). The networks of these consolidated scholars, that allowed them to occupy dominant positions in the field, were strengthened by the success of the programmes they created. The dissemination and recognition of the work of consecrated academics is due, in part, to the acknowledgement of their disciples, especially those who have remained in the academic world. Recalling alumni of the MA in social sciences at FLACSO, Strasser states that

162 *Centers and Peripheries in Knowledge Production*

> We had an excellent first cohort of students who are, today, academics here and there. Roberto Russell is at UTDT, García Delgado is here, Bialakowsky is at UBA, Notcheff is here (16: 80; in translation).

Many senior scholars who occupy important academic positions in Argentine political science graduated from the MSc in public administration that Oszlak still directs. Amongst the most prominent are Miguel De Luca (former Academic Secretary of the undergraduate programme in political science at UBA and current president of SAAP), Sergio Agoff (Head of the undergraduate programme in public administration at the [Universidad Nacional de General Sarmiento] UNGS), and Eduardo Kinen (General Secretary of the [Universidad Católica de Santa Fe] UCSF). The orientation of these graduates towards public administration and public policy, along with their academic positions in the field, guarantees the permanent theoretical and practical influence of the work of Oszlak in the local field. Oszlak's participation in hundreds of talks, conferences, and seminars seems to be the logical consequence of the network that he has been able to create and nurture and not only the outcome of his intellectual inheritance.

5.3.3 The International Condition

While the circulation of scholars between prestigious intellectual and scientific fields seems to be a professional experience, undertaking postgraduate education in First World institutions is an experience that changes the lives of many scholars from developing countries. In Oszlak's case, his time at Harvard University affected not only access to novel ideas but also his use of English as a second language, which, in turn, positively conditioned his continuous access to cutting-edge bibliography and his multiple exchanges with metropolitan academia. Further, his time in the United States awakened his desire to stay in the academic world, something that he had not considered before his departure from Argentina.

> That was a very important academic immersion. First, I could improve my English. Second, I had access to literature with which I hadn't had any contact. I got a postgraduate education, and that raised my expectations of continuing my studies (49: 19; in translation).

Like Oszlak, Strasser mentions not only the working conditions, which enabled him to study political science in a professional manner, but also the political climate of the late 1960s that inspired him.

> It was the most beautiful moment in my life, absolutely! [I was] studying what I really wanted, full-time, in the middle of that university, of that landscape, of that epoch, that atmosphere . . . it was fantastic! (16: 34; in translation).

Towards a Plurality of Translations 163

The disparity of material and symbolic resources between Argentine higher education and metropolitan institutions has been pointed out by interviewed dominant scholars. Strasser was the most eloquent of them in referring to the disparities between fields.

> Each time I go [to the United States] I'm impressed by the wealth of the country. It's a country that exudes wealth. In my time as a student [at University of California, Berkeley] there were *many* libraries; the libraries of the campus were amazing! The Main Library at UC-Berkeley had an entire floor devoted to Latin America, in which I could find things about Argentina [. . .] that couldn't be obtained here. [You had] all you needed. Anything new, or recently published, automatically, appeared in the libraries. That's something unique and enviable (16: 43; in translation).

The symbolic resources of metropolitan fields are closely linked to the professors and researchers whom they successfully attract and retain (Altbach and Balán 2007; López Segrera 2006; Sebastián 2007b). For this reason, consecrated scholars in peripheral fields who obtained a postgraduate degree in central fields usually tend to introduce themselves as disciples of highly respected professors. Oszlak, for example, emphasises his links with Warren Ilchman, his tutor at the University of California, Berkeley, Todd LaPorte, and David Apter. Recognition of Ilchman's influence is partially accepted by criticising Ilchman's understanding of public administration in one of Oszlak (1979)'s most noted works, *Notas Criticas para una Teoría de la Burocracia Estatal* (see also Oszlak 1984).

Floria created a different kind of bond with his colleagues abroad. He had already obtained a PhD in Law at UBA when he went to the United States as an Eisenhower scholar and formed personal bonds with his contemporaries abroad, whom he refers to as friends. Amongst the friends are Robert Dahl, Hans Morgenthau, Karl Deutsch, Giovanni Sartori, Robert Potash, and David Easton. The relationships with some of these scholars were strengthened in 1969, when Floria invited them to the *Primer Encuentro Internacional de Ciencia Política*, which was held at USAL. At that meeting, Floria and other professors at USAL publicly introduced the work of their foreign colleagues into Argentine political science by applying their theoretical frameworks to local current or historical problems.

Debate with metropolitan colleagues may take place in exceptional cases, although this is rarely a dialogue between peers but, rather, an asymmetrical translation. These occasions tend to remain as milestones in the history of the local field and be reproduced in many written accounts (Bulcourf and D'Alessandro 2002, 2003; Fernández 2002a). International conferences are some of these events. The first international conference on political science was held at USAL in 1969. Floria invited some of the scholars he had met during his time in the United States to this. In addition to the

164   Centers and Peripheries in Knowledge Production

importance of face-to-face contacts, the conference gave rise to an exercise in political analysis, because Argentine scholars organised a seminar in which Floria analysed local problems using foreign theoretical frameworks. Rafael Braun used Morgenthau's realist theory of international relations, Botana focused on Potash's analysis of civic-military relationships, and Floria utilised Dahl's modern political analysis to deal with the 1810 Revolution. Floria's experience abroad was thus translated into an international conference that ultimately made public a previous translation of foreign ideas into the undergraduate curriculum of political science at USAL. The conference, which took place in Buenos Aires, is an asymmetrical translation because (i) it translates the mainstream foreign ideas of that moment, making possible a local modernisation of the field (Fernández 2007); (ii) it gives rise to debates and exchange within the local field;[30] and (iii) those debates are absolutely marginal to the ones taking place in the centres of knowledge production.[31]

If the work, and suggestions of colleagues, were decisive in creating the first modern curriculum in political science, the funds provided by US foundations have also been crucial in the career of consecrated scholars.[32] The case of Oszlak is illustrative. Firstly, the Ford Foundation gave him a scholarship to undertake PhD studies at the University of California, Berkeley, and the interruption of funds from that foundation to the Instituto Di Tella in 1969 forced Oszlak to accelerate his return to Argentina in order to obtain one of the five positions at the Instituto Di Tella. Some years later, in 1975, a grant from the Ford Foundation made it possible for Oszlak, Marcelo Cavarozzi, Guillermo O'Donnell, and Horacio Boneo to found CEDES, where they subsequently developed a substantial part of their careers. The Ford Foundation has contributed grants to support research teams throughout the history of CEDES, together with providing funds for infrastructure, such as buying CEDES' building in Buenos Aires and updating its library (CEDES 2007).

Secondly, research grants provided by foreign institutions led to the production of important publications in the history of Argentine political science. A US$50,000 research grant from the Tinker Foundation was translated by Oszlak and a small group of collaborators into his *La Formación del Estado Argentino*, a widely circulated and read book that is a classic in the field (Bulcourf and D'Alessandro 2003; Fernández and Barbosa 1996). Another research grant, from PISPAL, allowed Oszlak to study the relationships between public administration and public policy on poverty, focused on the right to public space in an authoritarian context. The result of this investigation was *Merecer la Ciudad: Los Pobres y el Derecho al Espacio Urbano* (Deserving the City: The Poor and the Right to Urban Space), which Oszlak believes to be his best book. Finally, funds provided by UNDP were the material support for Oszlak's study of the Uruguayan public administration known as *El Diagnóstico*. This thorough study combined his academic understanding of the social and political dimensions of public administration with fieldwork that took ten months to complete. The study became not only a classic in the regional literature on public administration but also a substantial part of Oszlak's PhD thesis at the University of California, Berkeley. This summary of grants producing substantial written work is a testimony of the evaluation that Oszlak makes of his trajectory: 'my entire career was determined by funding' (49: 62; in translation). Important as they have been to consolidate Oszlak's career, funds translated into research have transcended local political science and influenced other peripheral fields. In metropolitan academia, however, Argentine political analysis has not had an impact. This reinforces the idea that there are asymmetrical translations involved in most cases.

Thirdly, the connections with foreign philanthropic foundations were made possible by the circulation of scholars in contexts which the State was not able to support (Lesgart 2002, 2003; Lehmann 1990). Strasser, for example, obtained a Visiting Professorship at the Wilson Centre in Washington, DC, thanks to the presence of Jorge Balán on its advisory board, as Chair from 1987 to 1990 (16: 127). Balán is an Argentine scholar who was appointed Programme Officer at the Ford Foundation in 1998, after twenty years at CEDES (1977–1997) and four at the Instituto Torcuato Di Tella (1973–1977). His career in Argentina resembles that of Oszlak and his moves between research centres, universities, and foundations support the findings of Turner and Turner (1990) concerning the demand for academics from particular foundations, which ends up being a self-reinforcing mechanism to sustain small networks of scholars. Thus, grants ensure publications, which, in turn, guarantee prestige and recognition in a cycle of ongoing translations (Latour and Woolgar 1986; Latour 1987).

5.4 PRELIMINARY CONCLUSIONS: ATOMISED TRANSLATIONS IN A (DISARTICULATED) NETWORKED FIELD

The role of mediators, the people who are a connecting point between local and foreign fields, has been widely studied by sociologists of science through the notion of the 'gatekeeper'.[33] According to Becher and Trowler a gatekeeper is 'the person that determines who is allowed into a particular community and who remains excluded—[and it] is a significant [role] in terms of the development of knowledge fields' (2001: 85). McGinty recognises the importance of the printed culture of academia for gatekeeping and adds that 'for hundreds of years, distribution systems (paper, printing, publishing, subscriptions, etc.) were too expensive for an individual scholar to publicize a message without going before a board to get its approval. [. . .] Nothing could be disseminated unless it was approved by the board, which controlled the "means of production"' (1999: 3). Accordingly, Cole (1983) argues that the mediators are the stars of a discipline; the big names that have the legitimacy to be in charge of the circulation of recognition.

166 *Centers and Peripheries in Knowledge Production*

> Generally, the stars of a particular discipline occupy the main gatekeeping roles. By their acts as mediators and evaluators, they determine what work is considered good and what work unimportant. For the mediators to establish consensus, they must have legitimated authority, that is, the people whose work is being evaluated must accept them as legitimate. Legitimacy is granted by virtue of one's being a star (Cole 1983: 138).

Many social sciences, and Argentine political science is an example of this, seem to have a similar structure to that observed at the research frontier of natural sciences (Cole 1983). In a field where there is a high degree of uncertainty about results, interpretations and importance, disagreement and difficulty in determining the significance of contributions are common features. At the same time, the minimal integration of research results, and the need to demonstrate to colleagues the importance of such results, is achieved by personal contacts between scientists. In this context, only a few, consecrated scholars can legitimately claim to be mediators, but there is no highly institutionalised structure of mediators since the prestige and relevance of any scientist can be challenged and diminished by the members of other groups or universities.

The current landscape of Argentine political science has been depicted in this chapter by focusing on the international circulation of texts and scholars. This landscape shows only a few mediators and contains a multiplicity of seemingly authorised translators and translations, as illustrated in Figure 5.1. The circulation of texts are mediated by the logic of overlapping networks (e.g. the Spanish publishing industry), which control the production and circulation of books in Spain and Latin America. The trend towards monopolisation of the publishing industry only accentuates the domination based partially on common language and cultural similarities. The opportunities for local scholars to participate in foreign fields have also been explored. In this case, the local conditions of knowledge production are an obstacle for the time-demanding process of publishing abroad and the need for foreign contacts becomes evident. In addition, the lack of recognition of incentives for such efforts by local universities discourages Argentine political scientists from publicising their work in the developed world.

Local political scientists depend on the ability of local editors to chase foreign scholars and obtain their contributions, as well as the possibility of accessing foreign literature through the few opportunities that the largest publishing houses occasionally offer (e.g. free samples and free online access for limited periods). While the introduction of ideas by local editors is based on fortuitous, and sometimes accidental, encounters with foreign colleagues, the reading of foreign articles is mediated by foreign publishing houses. In both cases, there is no control over the flow of knowledge. Local editors obtain whatever they can, which prevents them from selecting and choosing authors and texts according to their personal, professional, and/or disciplinary interests.

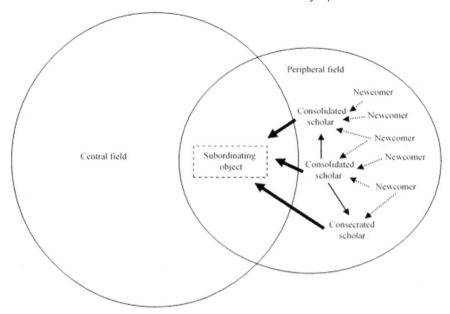

Figure 5.3 Consolidated and consecrated scholars as mediators within peripheral and central fields.

The circulation of scholars also exemplifies the disarticulated structure of networked fields. Without material resources to support travel abroad, local scholars are forced to obtain funds from international organisations (e.g. the Fulbright Commission) or from foreign universities or research centres. In both cases, the mediator role of local academics is missing, which not only hampers the possibility of exchange between local students and foreign scholars but also illustrates the basic, necessary labour conditions that foreign scholars require (and do not find in peripheral contexts) in order to be able to undertake serious professional academic work. Participation in international conferences seems to be almost impossible in a university system in which 90 per cent of the budget is devoted to the salary of local academics (Saviola 2008). Attendance at conferences and obtaining visiting professorships abroad depends more on the international links of scholars, reinforcing personal international connections (Becher and Trowler 2001), than on the support provided by local institutions, whose research and teaching agendas end up being set by external actors or individual scholars with enough academic or scientific capital.

The local network field of Argentine political science is structured through personal, local, and international contacts, and lacks an institutional structure of mediators. The absence of this illustrates the disarticulation between political scientists as well as the impossibility of regulating the conditions of entry that guarantee the inclusion of some members and

168 Centers and Peripheries in Knowledge Production

the exclusion of others without enough academic or scientific capital. As a consolidated scholar put it,

> [Argentine political science is] a corporation that does not know how to regulate the supply. [. . .] There is no entry ticket. In fact, there is no entry ticket to that club. So, the club does exist, and the entry ticket also exists, but is informal; it is located in another place. So, in reality the club which is worth participating in is not the one to which everybody has access. That's why they abandon it (15: 151–52).

The existence of only a few mediators is based on the assumption by scholars that it is perfectly possible to do research without funds (as political science seems to be a pure intellectual task) and that ideas end up being published sooner or later (it seems to be a matter of choosing the right place). In their words:

> Every year there is a call for research projects at this university, to support research, but *it's ridiculous because they give you the topic*, or big topics, and I'm not going to write about electric resources for 30,000 or 50,000 Argentine pesos [10,000 to 16,000 US dollars]. This is for an economist to do! I'm not going to do it! [. . .] I will not attach too much importance to them; I'm not interested. Q: Who are 'they'? A: The people who decide the research guidelines (41: 63–64; in translation).

Seen from abroad, the expectation is that only a few Argentine political scientists will attend international conferences, publish in mainstream journals, hold visiting professorships in prestigious metropolitan universities, and obtain resources from the philanthropic organisations of the central field (e.g. the Ford Foundation and the Rockefeller Foundation). Viewed from Argentina, and especially from the point of view of non-dominant actors, those scholars are famous, big names, leading and consecrated academics, but rarely are they mediators. The difference lies in the necessary material structure and elements that a social relationship, such as the role of mediator, actually requires. As Rammer has pointed out, 'one cannot imagine a mere political solution or social decision that is not mediated by data-processing, telephone calls, written documents, and bargaining techniques. Inversely, technology can be seen as "society made durable"' (Rammer 1999: 26; see also Latour 1991). Similarly, one cannot imagine the presence of a structure of mediators without electronic and printed journals appearing on a regular basis, full-time appointments that guarantee the availability of academics to serve as peer reviewers, travel grants to participate in international conferences, public and private research grants, a relatively strong local publishing industry, up-to-date libraries, scholarships, PhD programmes, research assistants, and office space where political science can be properly practiced.

Towards a Plurality of Translations   169

The paucity of mediators must not hide the fact that, when some conditions are met, some political scientists become dominant actors of the field. At least for peripheral scholars, the capital earned by obtaining a degree abroad, and by keeping in touch with foreign scholars, has been decisive in terms of its translation into bibliography, programmes, books, research, and conferences in the local field. Secondly, given the fragility of local institutions and the relatively short history of Argentine political science, consecrated scholars are network builders, not actors whose work adjusts to highly structured cultural and institutional systems.

Scholars in the periphery attempt to capitalise on their international contacts by translating them into different (local) cultural products: undergraduate curricula, conferences, visiting professorships, research, and publications. Further, scholars in the periphery face the problem of an international division of academic labour (Baber 2003; Alatas 2003), so only they can negotiate the meanings of the travelling objects (e.g. texts, grants, and lectures) within the local, peripheral field. In turn, this negotiation strengthens their position in the field but illustrates the subordinated position of the field in the international arena.

A scholar's consecration does not depend on his/her adaptability to the institutional structure of the field but, rather, on the capacity to build his/her own network and to transform it into an institution. The life of such institutions tends to be short and their strength rarely transcends the life and prestige of their creators (Vessuri 1997a; Kreimer 2000, 2006). The current attempt of another consecrated Argentine political scientist, Marcelo Cavarozzi, to institutionalise a School of Government at Universidad Nacional de San Martín (UNSM) is a clear example of this strategy. Nevertheless, the regular social, political, and economic crises in peripheral societies force scientists to keep on trying to develop institutional environments that favour innovation in social science.[34] In peripheral countries, such as Argentina, scientific activity is, to paraphrase Eliade, like the myth of the eternal return.

Conclusion

Argentine political scientists use foreign ideas in strategic ways to structure their own academic careers. They are taught that foreign knowledge has pre-eminence over local ideas, even though local knowledge is publically debated in Argentina. This predominance is based on, and at the same time reproduces, the international division of the academic world that has produced centres and peripheries of knowledge production and consumption. Throughout their careers, Argentine political scientists translate foreign knowledge into syllabi, research articles, conference presentations, and other scholarly works in order to reach dominant positions in the field. At the same time, the local institutional constraints, as well as the lack of material and symbolic resources, affect the process of introducing, using, and circulating foreign knowledge. Thus, both foreign knowledge and local academic labour conditions seem to be mutually influential.

1 MAIN POINTS FROM THE RESEARCH

This investigation has introduced three new ideas in the field of science and technology studies (STS) and the sociology of scientific knowledge. Firstly, it focused on peripheral social scientists, departing from traditional studies that revolve around natural sciences as practised in the developed world. Moreover, this research has used data from social scientists in the broad sense, i.e. it included life-histories of political scientists more inclined to humanities and a more normative and theoretical approach. This alternative focal point has permitted observation of the active role which scholars in the periphery play when internalising knowledge produced abroad. Further, it has permitted depiction of the periphery as a trading, or contact, zone and not merely as an area where metropolitan knowledge is uncritically appropriated, or as the passive recipient of cultural and academic imperialism.

Secondly, this study proposes some theoretical concepts to deal with the phenomenon of studying political science in the periphery. Firstly, the concept of asymmetrical translation refers to the process of transformation of the content and the form of foreign knowledge when introduced into a

Conclusion   171

peripheral context. Secondly, the notion of teaching technology refers to the socio-technical ensemble that humans and non-humans articulate with the aim of minimising dispersion of time and energy in multiple academic posts. These concepts are framed in a theoretical landscape in which science is rooted in power relations between nations and scientific fields.

Thirdly, this research employs a combination of methods and techniques of data gathering that had not previously been utilised to describe Argentine political science. Unlike prior analyses, based on personal interviews with prominent scholars and on the history of Argentine social sciences, this investigation has relied on life-histories of dominant and non-dominant actors in the field, as well as histories of political science, and studies of the Argentine university and science and technology systems. The result is a broader picture of the discipline in which micro-processes, mechanisms, and formal and informal rules permit observation of how foreign ideas are re-manufactured when introduced into Argentine political science. At the same time, life-histories, although focused on individuals and the narratives of their lives, have allowed us to observe some historical and more structural constraints such as the effects of the dictatorship on freedom of speech at universities or the consequences of the paucity of full-time researchers.

Although the working conditions in the university system influence all aspects of academic life, from recruitment of young scholars to the peer-reviewing system, this research has concentrated on the impact of foreign ideas that, once introduced in the local field, give rise to specific processes and patterns. Three assumptions underpin this international dimension of the local scholarly activity. Firstly, even though science has been considered to be an international activity since its origins, the increase in collaboration beyond national borders in the last twenty years has given rise to the idea of knowledge that travels around the world, contributing to the development of those countries that employ it. Thus, as Wagner has pointed out, the 'world of science [. . .] has changed from the national to the global level [and] self-organizing networks that span the globe are the most notable feature of science today' (2008: 2).

Secondly, the peripheral position of some countries has influenced the way in which their scholars interpret science and scientific development. While some academics defend an independent, autochthonous strategy that must focus on local problems and resources, others prefer an integrationist approach that positions local production as subordinated to, and co-ordinated with, foreign agendas, institutions, and knowledge. Furthermore, a constant tension exists in the periphery. While some scholars consider that the only source of legitimacy of their work is the recognition awarded by metropolitan academia through their institutions (i.e. journals and universities), others think they have to influence local government and social agendas in order to improve their environment. The first group tends to believe that the problems, methodologies, and theoretical frameworks proposed by academics in the centres of knowledge production ought to be

172 *Centers and Peripheries in Knowledge Production*

taken as the model for research and teaching. By contrast, the second group focuses on local needs and problems that, more often than not, do not inform the agenda of the metropolitan scholars. The result is contradiction that becomes a tension for academics in the periphery and this contradictory situation seems to be one important feature of carrying out scientific work in the periphery.

Thirdly, a glance at the citation patterns and teaching process in peripheral contexts permits an appreciation of the weight of foreign knowledge. Sustained by their infrastructure (e.g. large publishing houses and financially robust universities) foreign ideas travel more easily from their place of production to the rest of world. Outside the centre, this knowledge is translated into syllabi of university courses and research articles published in local journals. Thus, the production of peripheral scholars may be ignored by their metropolitan colleagues but the ideas coming from the centres of knowledge production have to be incorporated in the scholarly works of the periphery, producing an asymmetry that Chakrabarty has already described for historians: 'Third-world historians feel a need to refer to works in European history; historians of Europe do not feel any need to reciprocate' (1992: 2). This uneven relationship between scholars in the First and the Third World is the basis of what we have called asymmetrical translations.

2 SYNTHESIS

The focus of this research on the international dimension of the scholarly activity of Argentine political scientists has suggested that there are three stages in academic career development. Firstly, the training process of political scientists at the Argentine university system involves the development of an ability to distinguish between local and foreign production, a distinction that gives rise to a hierarchy of knowledge according to the place in which it has been produced. Secondly, young graduates enter into the academic labour market, a process that includes *ad honorem* (poorly paid) work and forces scholars to make a decision as to whether to stay in the country or leave for full-time postgraduate education abroad. Thirdly, the consolidation of the academic career takes place when scholars are able to make a living from university activities, which in most cases involves teaching at several institutions. Once academics are consolidated in their profession, the lack of institutional and economic support means that the connection with foreign scientific fields is disarticulated, and their careers depend more on the agendas and interests of foreign actors (e.g. metropolitan universities) than on the needs and preferences of local actors (e.g. the government and Argentine universities).

During the training years, Argentine political scientists are taught not only the theoretical framework from which reality has to be observed but also the practical concerns that affect the daily activity of political

Conclusion   173

scientists. From this, students learn how to distinguish between local ideas and foreign knowledge and the differentiation implies values and moral judgements as to the relevance, quality, complexity, and adequacy of both types of ideas. Empirical data suggest that there are at least five mechanisms to produce such a distinction. The first mechanism is to position local and foreign ideas differently in the curriculum, with the latter populating the syllabi of the main courses (e.g. political theory and comparative politics) and the former being part of secondary courses (e.g. Latin American history or Latin American political thought). Empirical evidence from the present study implies that foreign knowledge is perceived and presented as theoretically superior, general, and universal, and so professors structure their theoretical courses according to this knowledge and relegate local production to a lower level. For students, foreignness is equated with theory, which confirms that higher levels of theoreticity seem to be associated more with the place of certain ideas within a programme than with the inherent properties of texts or arguments.[1]

A second mechanism that produces a distinction between local and foreign knowledge is the repeated use of some foreign texts throughout the programme. Interviewees have recognised the place of some classic (e.g. Weber and Marx) and contemporary authors (e.g. Dahl and Sartori) in their training, since their texts are analysed again and again from the first year to the last year of undergraduate studies. This repetition has two main consequences. Firstly, it supports the assumption that these authors are the seminal figures of the discipline at an international level and that political science is approached in a more or less similar fashion in Argentina, France, Australia, and South Africa. Secondly, repetition produces a canonical effect, according to which the production of local knowledge is evaluated. This not only highlights some topics (e.g. transition to democracy in the 1980s) and methodologies (e.g. rational choice/formal analysis since the 1990s) but also proposes an order or organisation (Brown and Capdevilla 1999) for syllabi, courses, and even entire undergraduate or graduate programmes.

The third mechanism is the link between foreign knowledge and novelty. Ideas coming from centres of knowledge production provide trendy concepts and methodologies which local scholars are enticed to follow. Even though science is, by definition, an institutional framework that favours the production of original knowledge (Whitley 2006), such a framework has been fully consolidated only in developed countries, which implies that novelty—as defined according to metropolitan standards—is usually manufactured there. Furthermore, it is not surprising that those academics who are interested in theoretical innovation usually attempt to go to the centres of knowledge production for postgraduate education. The attraction of metropolitan institutions is thus based partly on the way in which such institutions and the knowledge produced there are depicted in the periphery by professors and researchers, particularly those who have spent time in the centres of knowledge production.

174 *Centers and Peripheries in Knowledge Production*

There is also a fourth mechanism, according to which foreign ideas are seen, in the periphery, as superior in terms of quality: they are just better. The difference in quality rests on some epistemological evaluation that permits some professors to judge local knowledge as more primitive, rustic, and simple. This apparent lack of rigour is rarely examined in detail and interviewees have only occasionally recognised the paucity of material and symbolic resources as reasons to produce underrated knowledge. However, when those who have undertaken postgraduate studies abroad were asked about their PhD experiences, they replied that they were more impressed by the material conditions of academic labour than by their professors. This suggests that, at least for those who hold PhDs from metropolitan institutions, better ideas have to be understood as better working conditions, which, at the same time, explains some of their anxiety concerning the prospect of Argentine political science ever reaching international standards.

The last mechanism through which a differentiation between local and foreign knowledge is produced is more personal and involves the connection between prestigious professors and the foreign ideas they introduce. When distinguished scholars use foreign knowledge, their students assume that such knowledge is superior to its local counterpart because they tend to value these professors over their fellow colleagues. The prestige of scholars is able to flow from the person to the texts used as a bibliography and, in the opposite direction the use of foreign texts tends to enhance the prestige of local scholars.

In chapter 3 it was shown that this subordinated position of local ideas does not imply cultural imperialism or absolute academic dependence. On the contrary, foreign knowledge is critically appropriated, through debates and negotiations that take place beyond the classroom or the boardroom, in places such as political meetings (e.g. in student centres), reading groups, local conferences, and non-institutional settings (e.g. cafés). Further, data show that such negotiations are only rarely translated into texts, and even when they are it is not easy for these ideas to find their way into local or foreign periodical publications. This pre-eminence of oral exchange confirms the findings of Canagarajah (2002) in relation to the difficulties of scholars in the periphery in developing a written culture. Such difficulties are not based on the intrinsic deficiencies of the scholars but on the lack of resources to produce work with the necessary quality to be published in journals based in the centres of knowledge production. For example, the lack of up-to-date libraries in developing countries hinders the chances of academics from these areas in making an adequate literature review, without which an article cannot be published in the metropolitan centres.

When students graduate, they have internalised a distinction between foreign and local knowledge that will condition many of their later decisions concerning scholarly life. In chapter 4 it was seen that the start of the academic career in Argentine political science is a process that implies establishing bonds with senior scholars who can offer posts at several

Conclusion 175

programmes or institutions. As time goes by, such bonds are transformed into positions within a Chair in which the senior scholar occupies the leading roles (e.g. Associate Professor or Professor) and the newcomers participate in teaching and research. However, since the first jobs are usually poorly paid, or ad honorem, newcomers have to face the problem of how to make a living from scholarly activities.

Many new professors have to obtain a job outside academia, trying to use their free time to teach and, if possible, undertake research. Others depend on family financial support (e.g. partners' income) or savings, which makes their position even more vulnerable to extra-academic factors. Yet others concentrate on obtaining as many academic posts as possible in order to avoid extra-mural jobs, but this strategy brings as a consequence the material impossibility of undertaking rigorous research, given the lack of time and the precariousness of their working conditions.

> At Universidad de Buenos Aires [. . .] full-time faculty do not even reach the 10 percent mark, while 90 percent of professors have second and third jobs. [In general] Argentine professors rarely have a decent room, they have no computers, poor libraries, and the classrooms are always too small for all the students, creating a poor learning environment. Even for full long-time faculty with assured institutional positions, salaries are still below the official poverty line. This means that the professors look for and find alternative ways of survival, in many cases in activities not related to their academic job, thus preventing them from reinforcing their scholarly education and upgrading their skills in the classroom or in the labs (Várnagy 2010: 165–68).

The three patterns observed allow us to conclude that the process of becoming a full-time academic in Argentine political science goes through a period during which centrifugal forces expel scholars from academia without consideration of their merits, potential, or intelligence.

In any case, the international connection of newcomers is subordinated to teaching duties and the decisions made by the senior professors. Newcomers have to teach the texts chosen by the professors of their Chair, which conditions the theories, methodologies, and philosophical assumptions with which they have contact. Originality in the work of the young scholars is thus discouraged, because they are oriented towards teaching instead of research and because their professors play the role of filters whose interests have predominance over those of the other members of the Chair. By definition, being part of a Chair is to accept the research and teaching agenda of the professors and to be in contact with foreign scholars and ideas solely through their lens.

Given the lack of material resources available with which to invite foreign colleagues or attend international conferences, international connections are always materialised in texts for young local scholars. This has at

176 Centers and Peripheries in Knowledge Production

least three important consequences. Firstly, there is a process of mystification of the institutions of the metropolitan centres. Scholars refer to them in terms of almost sacred places in which knowledge is produced, stored, and disseminated. Oxford, Sorbonne, and Harvard appear as sites of veneration, and labour conditions, both local and foreign, are ignored, giving rise to the idea that the academics in those places are more apt than others to generate novel ideas. Secondly, since texts are cultural goods manufactured by large publishing houses, the access of newcomers in peripheral fields to foreign ideas depends not only on the inner logic of metropolitan fields but also on the strategies and decisions of corporations that make the circulation of publications possible (e.g. Random House Mondadori). Academics in the periphery have access to the knowledge produced by their colleagues in the developed world but only in those cases in which large publishing houses decide to circulate such knowledge beyond the context of production. In this sense, there is a double condition that knowledge has to meet in order to travel abroad: (i) it has to be produced in the centres—predominantly in English or translated into other languages from English (Ortiz 2009)—and (ii) it has to be considered as commercially valuable by large publishing corporations. Thirdly, unlike face-to-face contact at conferences or academic visits, contact with foreign ideas through texts is passive because it does not allow peripheral scholars to engage in dialogue with the author but, rather, just disseminate his/her work. This academic debate, in which the scholar from the periphery negotiates the meaning of a text only at a local level (e.g. with her/his students or colleagues), is referred to as asymmetrical translation in this book; it implies a recognition of the power relations that are behind—and within—scientific fields.

In addition to the three strategies just mentioned, a fourth one requires that the scholar leaves the country for postgraduate education. This strategy permits scholars to remain as full-time academics, but in a different country where labour academic conditions for undertaking research are better. The empirical evidence found in this research suggests that newcomers pay particular attention to the material possibilities of postgraduate programmes and the institutions that offer them. They carefully analyse scholarship schemes and frequently compare options, between the small, selected group of countries and institutions of the centre. Intellectual features of the institutions, faculty, and programmes are clearly secondary, although they are not ignored. These become crucial when the scholars intend to remain in the foreign field after obtaining a PhD, because only in such a field, where specialisation is valued and demanded by universities, do departments of political science commonly search for scholars with specific research interests to occupy academic positions.

Due to their material solidity and world-wide known names, the most prestigious institutions tend to be the main target of scholars from the periphery when applying for postgraduate education. However, if it is not possible to obtain a place at these institutions, scholars opt for institutions

Conclusion 177

that offer more advantageous material conditions (e.g. research and teaching assistantships) or institutions with which the scholars have some contact, usually through the connections of the senior academics with whom they have worked.

There are at least four main consequences of choosing an international career-building strategy. Firstly, it requires that newcomers are part of one of the few local networks with international links. Interviewees with PhDs obtained abroad recognised that they had to move from one network to another one in order to acquire the necessary capital for becoming a successful applicant to an elite foreign institution. Capital, as Latour and Woolgar (1986) have shown, has to be seen not as an abstract concept, whose properties are socially assigned, but, rather, as a set of meaningful material elements that enact a particular network of people, processes, and objects. In this research capital was observed through letters of recommendation, research proposals, colleagues' reading of such proposals, phone calls between senior scholars, degrees at prestigious local institutions, proof readers, books and articles used to write the proposal, and local conferences. Furthermore, scholars move between networks in search of these elements; something that is itself conditioned by the capital previously accumulated, i.e. by the network enacted earlier.

Secondly, when newcomers decide to leave the country for postgraduate studies they have to be able to materialised foreign ideas into people, books, forms, phone calls, and e-mails. While texts tend to obscure the conditions of the production of knowledge through impersonal rhetoric, scholars ought to look in the opposite direction; that is, to recreate the person(s), institutions, and procedures behind the ideas. Put differently, they have to unpack knowledge. Where is quality of democracy studied? Who has published on republicanism recently? What methodologies are now being used to analyse public opinion? Which institutions offer scholarships? These are the 'who', 'where', and 'how' that scholars have to be able to answer. Responding to these questions correctly is, in terms of ANT, to enrol the correct actors into the network and, by achieving this, an application to a foreign academic institution is likely to be successful.

Thirdly, scholars who want to undertake postgraduate studies abroad must be able to learn and use appropriately the technicalities of the discipline as practiced in the field in which they want to study. This situation poses a tension between the local and foreign rules of the game, especially where both are substantially different. These technicalities include the correct use of the foreign language (generally, English), the specific procedures of academic writing (e.g. Chicago, APA, Harvard, MLA), the particularities of academic oral presentations and debates (e.g. avoiding gendered expressions), the dynamics of publication (e.g. journal submission and peer reviewing), expectations concerning PhD students (e.g. attendance at international conferences), and the ability to meet formal and informal deadlines (e.g. thesis submission). The knowledge and use of

178 Centers and Peripheries in Knowledge Production

technicalities is reinforced by the degree of standardisation of some academic procedures in the developed world (e.g. the GRE [Graduate Record Examination]), which oppose the lack of institutionalisation of such procedures in the periphery.

Fourthly, the lack of financial aid from Argentine universities and research centres for scholars who want to undertake postgraduate studies abroad means that they must depend entirely on the resources of foreign organisations (e.g. the Fulbright Commission and the British Council). This dependence is, however, not only material. More importantly, it means that scholars from the periphery may attend metropolitan institutions only when their research proposals are in accordance with the agendas and interests of the developed world organisations. Through financial aid, universities of the centre guarantee that their students, irrespective of their countries of origin, contribute to solving local problems and overcome the local needs of the centre, transforming these institutions into what Latour (1987) has called centres of calculation, in which knowledge from the entire world is concentrated. Seen from the periphery, this provides a discouraging outlook. Without a solid structure to support postgraduate studies abroad, developing countries cannot encourage scholars to investigate the topics that are relevant to their social, political, and economic agendas. Even though peripheral scholars go to the centres of knowledge production to carry out research concerning the political, social, or economic situation of developing countries, their research is often disregarded by local decision-makers and usually published abroad. More interesting is the fact that in countries of the developing world the systems of scientific and technological research, such as CONICET, tend to value foreign publications above their local counterparts.

The ultimate aim of the decision to either stay or go abroad seems to be to remain in the academic realm as a full-time scholar. This is just as much the case for those who stay in their own country, trying to be appointed to as many posts as possible, as for those who go abroad for postgraduate education. These similarities cannot hide the fact that, being in the periphery, Argentine political science seems to value highly the acquisition of a PhD abroad, especially in the centres of knowledge production. However, empirical evidence obtained from the present research has shown that holding a PhD from a prestigious university is not necessarily a ticket to an academic post in the university system. Many interviewees narrated the complex situation of returning to Argentina after obtaining a doctorate. In general, they pointed out that the process involves personal contacts with colleagues who can open up possibilities at local institutions, most of the time teaching at both undergraduate and graduate levels. It also implies negotiation, as well as difficulties in acquiring both office space and time for research. These scholars rarely achieve a full-time position soon after arrival, and this fact usually discourages Argentine political scientists who have gone abroad from returning to their homeland.

The data presented in chapter 4 suggest that a useful notion for understanding the dynamics of Argentine political science, in relation not only to its international connections but also to its internal organisation, is teaching technology. Following Bijker (1995), teaching technology is defined as the complex ensemble of humans (e.g. scholars and students), non-humans (e.g. syllabi and office space), and relationships (e.g. mentorship and taxicab professorship) that permit political scientists to remain in the academic field by minimising the dispersion that multiple positions produce. There are at least three advantages to the concept of teaching technology over others used to describe the dynamics of Argentine political science. Firstly, it takes into account the material elements that are necessary to undertake scholarly work. Secondly, it allows us to connect the strategies developed by academics to stay in the scholarly world by focusing on the management of time, resources, and relationships. Going abroad or remaining in Argentina point to the very same objective: becoming a full-time academic in a peripheral context. Finally, the concept of teaching technology, along with recognising the teaching-oriented nature of the Argentine university system, identifies the consolidation of an individual's academic career as the moment at which scholars are able to make a living from academia. When they master this technology, e.g. are able to use the same syllabi for courses in different universities, consolidation has been achieved.

Chapter 5 explores the characteristics of the international connections of Argentine political scientists once their careers have been consolidated. Empirical evidence shows that such connections rarely follow the intentions of local actors in the field but, rather, the interests and opportunities opened up by foreign organisations and scholars. This chapter deals with the links between Argentine political scientists and their colleagues abroad by illustrating the extent to which these links depend on foreign resources and agendas. Consequently, the behaviour of local actors, from the interpretation of a text to the decision to co-author a paper with a foreign scientist, seems to be random, opportunistic, haphazard, and beyond their own control. For Argentine political scientists, becoming a dominant actor in the field rarely involves having a gatekeeping role in terms of controlling the flow of people and objects (e.g. local journals) at an international level.

Chapter 5 also illustrates the weighted importance of Buenos Aires and Spain for Argentine political scientists, raising the issue of multiple, overlapping centres and peripheries. Within the local field, Buenos Aires is almost an obligatory passage point, since, even for important scholars in Rosario, Cordoba, and Mendoza, political science produced in Buenos Aires tends to be seen as superior, more rigorous, and more connected with international tendencies. This situation is reinforced at the local level by the concentration of universities, bookstores, publishing houses, and students in the metropolitan area which has become the main market—in academic and economic terms—for publications. On the other hand, Spain, which is a peripheral scientific field in the international landscape of political

180   *Centers and Peripheries in Knowledge Production*

science, plays a leading role for Latin American scholars. That role is based not only on its publishing houses and the size of its Spanish-speaking market, but also on its old metropolitan position during the colonial period. The special place occupied by Spain for Latin American countries rests on its control over the circulation of publications in Spanish, an issue influenced by linguistic similarities, as well as its material ability to translate foreign authors into Spanish. Furthermore, almost all translated titles in bookstores in Buenos Aires come from Spanish publishing houses while, at the same time, it is difficult to find a Colombian or Chilean book in those stores. This centralised system obstructs a South-South dialogue, such as that proposed by Santos (2009), and forces Argentine political scientists to be in touch with their Spanish colleagues, even though Spanish political science is not considered a centre for knowledge production at an international level.

Like the flow of texts, the circulation of scholars is mediated, stimulated, and produced by foreign organisations, such as the Fulbright Commission or the Agencia de Cooperación Internacional [Agency for International Cooperation]. Foreign scholars go to Argentina as visiting professors or researchers only infrequently, although sporadic encounters do take place at a few local universities. The lack of academic visitors makes the knowledge produced by local actors almost invisible to the members of the metropolitan scientific fields, something that is worsened by the difficulties in publishing in mainstream journals and in attending international conferences.

If incorporating foreign knowledge is difficult, making local knowledge known abroad is at least as hard. The paucity of schemes to support academic stays of Argentine political scientists abroad forces them to rely on financial support from the foreign institutions. Thus, the experiences abroad are usually the result of opportunistic contacts with foreign colleagues and almost never give rise to benefits for the local scientific field in general. Individually, visiting professorships allow Argentine scholars to keep their connections, to gather up to date data, to access databases, and to pursue collaborative work. Collaboration, however, has to be undertaken cautiously, because interviewees recognised the disparities that being in a peripheral scientific field implies.[2] The empirical evidence from the present research suggests that, following Shrum et al., collaboration does not always have positive effects:

> That collaborative work might somehow be preferable to other, presumably more individualistic ways of producing knowledge is based on the notion that synergies occur when participants work together, resulting in greater productivity or efficiencies. But that is to consider benefits without costs, as if there were no resources required to manage collaborations, no meetings and communication involved, and no time and energy devoted to teamwork and conflict management (Shrum et al. 2008: 202)

Conclusion   181

Publishing alone abroad, in the centres of knowledge production, is a rare achievement for Argentine political scientists. It demands time and additional commitment beyond the demands of their job(s) and many local scholars have neither. There are no institutional incentives and only a few universities (e.g. UTDT, UADE, UdeSA) have a system to reward academics for publishing in metropolitan journals, acknowledging the quality of such publications and the difficulties in trusting local journals in the same way. Those who have successfully published abroad recognise the rigour of the peer-reviewing process and the management of copyright, the material quality of the publication, as well as the scope of distribution that only metropolitan publishing houses can guarantee. The gap between the energy devoted to publishing abroad and the (lack of) recognition awarded by local institutions supports Caroline Wagner (2006)'s finding that personal reasons, more than structural or institutional incentives, form the basis behind scientists' productivity. Peripheral institutions just take advantage of these individual interests by relying on personal commitment to publish in international journals instead of developing a more stable and solid network of institutional connections with foreign fields that would help local academics to reach the most prestigious foreign publications. Nevertheless, the scarce interest in publishing abroad does not mean that international connections are not necessary or that they do not contribute to form a hierarchy of scholars within Argentine political science. On the contrary, they are crucial elements in the strategies of some academics to become leading actors of the field.

The international connections possessed by the majority Argentine political scientists may give the impression that Argentine political science is a more or less homogeneous field in which dominant actors do not exist. This is far from what was observed. There are powerful actors in the field, such as those who populate Chairs at the large, national universities or who hold full-time professorships at small, private universities within the metropolitan area of Buenos Aires. These academics control the internal flow of resources, mainly by being on committees at which scholarships and research grants are decided. They are also on the editorial board of the few local periodical publications, as well as being the more frequent contributors to those journals, which usually complicates the peer-reviewing process. Interestingly, the majority of the professors who hold important positions in the field, especially in Buenos Aires, have studied abroad, although there were many different reasons behind their decision to leave the country; from the dictatorship in the 1970s to the economic crisis of 2001. This tendency for those who have studied abroad to occupy the most significant posts cannot obscure the fact that the acquisition of a PhD abroad is not enough in itself to achieve a dominant position—and sometimes it can be a problem, as many interviewees mentioned when evoking their return to Argentina. The capital accumulated in metropolitan institutions has to be translated into connections, publications, research grants, invitations

182   Centers and Peripheries in Knowledge Production

to conferences, and a co-ordinated research agenda that is usually more focused on the problems and needs of the developed world than those of Argentina. Dominant positions are not based on scientists' records of publications in prestigious foreign journals or publishing houses, as if Argentine political science were part of a larger, international political science field where quality research is uniformly recognised. Rather, such positions are the result of translations that transform such a record into locally valued products, such as conferences, articles, and syllabi used and circulated in the local field. This is why some articles published in recognised journals of the developed world are then submitted by their authors, with minor or no changes, to local journals.

Chapter 5 concludes, from an analysis of successful Argentine political scientists, the three conditions that have to be met in order to become a dominant actor in the field. Firstly, empirical evidence identifies an intellectual condition, which represents the capacity of scholars to open new debates and propose timely responses to local political and disciplinary problems. The ability of scholars to recognise the most promising topics of research is combined with their capacity to see how these topics may respond to the problems of local political, social, and economic actors. However, their use of foreign theories and methodologies shows, once again, the tension between the local orientation towards problems and the scholarly requirement, characteristic of peripheral fields, of connections with foreign frameworks in order for peripheral ideas to be accepted as valid knowledge. This articulation between problems, research topics, and theories has to be complemented by the second condition, that is, the networking ability to organise people (e.g. colleagues, students, disciples) and objects (e.g. libraries, research grants, programmes) in a productive, innovative way. These networks are only occasionally situated in institutions, because the failure of institutionalisation in Latin America includes universities and the system of scientific and technological research. Some scholars have had the skill to group people around some programmes (e.g. FLACSO-Buenos Aires' MA in Social Science), even in disadvantageous conditions that include ad honorem work or job instability. Those who, alongside networks and intellectual niches, have been able to establish, extend, and maintain international connections are the dominant actors of the field. These scholars respond to international research agendas that allow them to obtain funds regularly, to attend international conferences, to participate in collaborative publications, and to become legitimate translators of some foreign authors, theories, or schools. Paradoxically, not all of these gatekeepers are mediators between scientific fields, because Argentina lacks a system of scientific and technological research that may provide an infrastructure to support constant, fluid exchange between countries. In this sense, although they may control the introduction of foreign ideas or scholars (by being in charge of the few institutions and publications with international links) into Argentina, they are rarely able to determine who leaves the country, and so, the extent of local political ideas being taken abroad. This process depends, rather, on the demand, needs and resources of foreign institutions and scholars.

3 LIMITATIONS OF THE RESEARCH

There are some limitations to this research that should be acknowledged. Firstly, the specific content of foreign ideas and their local translations has been overlooked. Obviously, differences in content imply different networks enacted; some of them more powerful or more extended. When peripheral scholars translate mainstream metropolitan political science to the local level, they enact a network made up of the most prestigious journals, some of the most powerful institutions and professional associations, as well as research grants from the most influential, and other, philanthropic agencies. On the contrary, networks whose actors belong to residual theoretical programmes are weaker and more unstable, which means that it is more difficult for the people, knowledge, and ideas to travel. Nevertheless, in both cases scholars employ the same strategies to deal with foreign knowledge and to structure their local career according to it.

Secondly, a quantitative analysis would shed light on the citation patterns and collaboration between local and foreign political scientists. Many recent studies have used social network analysis to present a picture of scientific disciplines in an era of increased intercommunication. However, this type of study was not preferred for the present research for three interconnected reasons. At a national level, there are few periodical publications devoted exclusively to political science, which hampers the possibility of obtaining proper generalisations. Further, these publications do not appear on a regular basis, making comparisons between them hard. Using international databases does not resolve the issue, since 416 articles were published by academics working in Argentine institutions between 1975 and February 2013 in the indexed academic journals, according to the Social Science Citation Index.[3] There does not seem to be a reliable source for general claims about Argentine political science production. A final reason to disregard quantitative analysis of publications has been pointed out by Shrum (1997), and refers to the lack of representativity of those scientists who publish frequently, especially in mainstream journals:

Visible scientists have a stronger orientation [than their less visible counterparts] towards international science, reporting more influence on problem selection and greater frequency in discussions with colleagues abroad as well as stronger agreement with views that are conventionally associated with international organizations and developed countries (1997: 232)

184 *Centers and Peripheries in Knowledge Production*

Despite this situation, a quantitative study could provide specificities for the existing networks. Are the members of a network who publish in English more concerned with metropolitan topics and methodologies than their colleagues who mainly publish in Spanish? Is there any difference in productivity between the networks whose members studied abroad and those composed of locally trained scholars? Do both networks understand productivity in the same way? To which countries are the local networks connected and what consequences does this have? Are local networks linked to the networks of other peripheral countries? These questions should be addressed in subsequent studies if a more complete landscape of Argentine political science is to be depicted (see Chernya et al. 2012).

Thirdly, linguistic problems were also undervalued in this research. This does not mean that language differences are not important or play no role in the international division of academic labour. As Ortiz (2004, 2009) has shown, the use of English as the lingua franca of the social sciences has vital consequences for the development of the social scientists in peripheral contexts. Further, the focus on language permits us to compare the situation of Argentine political science with other non-English speaking scientific fields, especially in Latin America. However, this treatment would also obscure the particularities of the Argentine university and science and technology systems, which have profound differences compared with those of other large Latin American countries, such as Brazil and Mexico. The cultural homogenisation that the predominance of one language presupposes is an acknowledged issue, but one that needs to be contextualised in terms of the institutions (or lack thereof) that enable and constrain the production of knowledge. This does not imply that studies concerning the distortion produced by the use—and abuse—of English are not necessary. On the contrary, this research could be substantially improved by taking into account those linguistic differences and also how they contribute to the structuring of academic careers.

4 OUTSTANDING QUESTIONS AND FUTURE RESEARCH

The mutual influence of academic labour conditions and foreign ideas is a broad topic that requires further thought. This research has opened up at least three new lines of inquiry:

(i) is it possible to generalise the findings of this type of research?
(ii) what are the policy implications from this research?
(iii) how do foreign organisations and scholars respond to the strategies of Argentine political scientists?

The first question calls for a comparative study that can provide information as to how other institutional frameworks condition research and teaching.

The analysis of the National System of Researchers (SNI) in Mexico or the National Council of Scientific and Technological Development (CNPq) in Brazil can be illuminative as to the impact of institutional design on the production and circulation of knowledge.

The second question demands a more complex answer, or perhaps an entire book. The main policy implications are:

(i) As long as Argentine political science relies heavily on part-time academics, it cannot establish a solid and stable system of publications that guarantees the quality of the scholarly products.[4]
(ii) Only if there is a material and symbolic infrastructure that gives rise to a national agenda and sustains the exchange with foreign countries will Argentina be able to influence the circulation of ideas, taking advantage of the presence of Argentineans in the most developed scientific fields (what has been referred to as the 'brain gain').
(iii) Undergraduate and postgraduate programmes in political science have to balance the weight of foreign and local knowledge, even favouring the (still scarce) local production, since this can be an important factor to encourage the development of strong scientific networks and institutions.
(iv) the entire university and scientific and technological research system requires higher degrees of institutionalisation, which means that the State must commit to transform personal and group initiatives into solid, reliable, and enduring institutions.

The question concerning the responses of foreign political scientists to the strategies of local ones forces us to think of the circulation of knowledge as a lasting process. Many scholars in the periphery have no opportunity for making their ideas visible to scholars working in the developed world, but, for those who do have this opportunity, the subsequent correspondence of their foreign colleagues may be highly productive. Actually, if the periphery is a contact zone, as Anderson and Adams (2008) have pointed out, some consequences of the contact may be found in the centre, producing cycles of cause and effect that may continue to endure. The study as to how peripheral scholars influence their metropolitan counterparts requires a trans-national analysis in which the researcher goes back and forth between differently-endowed scientific fields. Some recent literature has sought to describe the influence of the South on the North, and how Northern theory can be complemented by the development of Southern theorists (see Connell 2007; Connell and Wood 2002, 2005; Delpar 2007; Comaroff and Comaroff 2012). However, as Anderson and Adams (2008) have shown, this postcolonial, political sensibility is something missing in STS analyses.

The questions just raised make it clear that further research regarding the production of scientific knowledge in non-metropolitan countries is

186 *Centers and Peripheries in Knowledge Production*

necessary, because globalisation and the international economy have transformed knowledge into what is sometimes referred to as cognitive capitalism (Boutang 2008) or knowing capitalism (Thift 2005). Connell and Wood argued that 'as the political and economic agenda of neo-liberalism intensifies, the public funding of science declines and the problems of reproducing a scientific workforce in the periphery become more and more unmanageable' (2002: 189). Therefore, studying how science is practiced in the periphery, and how knowledge disseminates from the centre, sheds some light on the difficulties and opportunities that peripheral scientists face on a daily basis. The light, however, will illuminate not only the inequality of international power relations, the communication and reputation systems centred on the metropolis, and the hierarchies of scientific fields, but also the frequent and specific mistakes that actors in the periphery commonly make. The activity of disclosing veiled mechanisms of science is ultimately a cathartic exercise that puts scientists at the centre of the stage once more.

Notes

NOTES TO CHAPTER 1

1. ANT can be defined as a 'family of approaches to social analysis that rests on six core assumptions. First, it treats institutions, practices, and actors as materially heterogeneous, composed not only of people but also of technologies and other material. Second, it assumes that the elements making up practices are *relational*, achieving their shape and attributes only in interaction with other elements. [. . .] Third, it assumes that the network of heterogeneous relations and practices is a process. If structures, institutions, or realities are not continuously enacted then they disappear. Fourth, it therefore assumes that realities and structures are precarious in principle, if not in practice. Fifth, this implies that the world might be different, a suggestion that opens up interesting political possibilities. And sixth, it explores *how* rather than *why* realities are generated and maintained. This is because even the most obvious social causes are relational effects and therefore themselves subject to change' (Law 2006b: 4)
2. In the context of this research, *social world* is equivalent to what social world/arena theorists call *arena* (Strauss et al. 1964; Clarke 1991; Star and Griesemer 1989; Clarke and Star 2008). The same similarity can be pointed out in relation to the notion of *field* and *social world*.
3. Social world theorists argue that this is an ecological approach—instead of an individualistic one, such as ANT—because it does not underrate the relevance of the context (social world) in which the actors enrol, and are enrolled by, other actors.
4. The idea of the social world as an analytical device is close to Latour's network (Latour 2005). For him, 'the network does not designate a thing out there that would have roughly the shape of interconnected points . . . It is nothing more than *an indicator of the quality of a text* about the topics at hand' (2005: 129; emphasis in the original). The ability of the sociologist is what is at stake when a specific social world is suggested, proposed and traced.
5. This is important because the lack of local philanthropic organisations, as many have shown, has obliged Argentine social science to develop in accordance with the goals of metropolitan institutions, such as the Ford and Rockefeller foundations (Bulcourf and D'Alessandro 2002; González, 2000; Pereyra 2004). In his analysis of Argentine 'informal universities', as he calls the many small, private research centres, Lehmann has argued that '[a]lmost without realizing it, [social scientists] have built up an alternative [career path]—albeit one which is heavily dependent on the charity and to some extent the priorities of the international community who subsidize or

188 *Notes*

contract their work [. . .] The dependence on foreign financial support has meant that they are under pressure to do applied work, to do "action-research", to plan, to evaluate the myriad self-help projects which their sponsors are also financing' (1990: 184).

6. For an analysis of counter-hegemonic tendencies in sociology, see Keim (2011).

7. Actors such as WB, UNESCO, and IMF often contribute to this disarticulation by adding their interests and agendas to those of the local actors involved in the public policy (Borón 2006).

8. In the same way that Bourdieu's starting point is the social structure and the mechanisms through which it impacts on individual decisions (Seidman 2000: 148), our starting point is the international scenario of science (centres and peripheries) and how it affects the production of knowledge at the local level. As Swartz has pointed out, for Bourdieu 'the connections between fields, like the oppositions within fields, stem from structural factors, not the intentions of actors' (Swartz 1997: 134). This recognition of the relevance of structural factors, in Bourdieu's and in our claims, is what justifies the use of Bourdieu's main concepts to organise the arguments of this section.

9. If science had no structuring effects, its practices, at national and international levels, would not have any consequence on its historical and epistemological development, a thesis that has been rejected by historians and sociologists of science and technology (see, for example, Delbourgo and Dew [2008], Salvatore [2006], Schott [1998], Shapin and Schaffer [1985], Wagner, C. [2006], among others).

10. For example, Bourdieu's notion of structure is not equivalent to Latour's one. This situation is fixed in this research by stating a different idea of structure, one that is flexible enough to be studied as a network (and subject to the ongoing interplay of actors and objects) but at the same time is solid enough to influence and condition actors' decisions and behaviour.

11. The field of political science is embedded in the social sciences, for the purposes of this research. In turn, the social sciences are contained in the scientific field (which also includes exact and natural sciences).

12. The idea of struggle as an organising principle that structures scientific activity must not prevent us from mentioning that some actors, especially collective ones, such as universities, seem to play a fundamental role in the restructuring of current cognitive capitalism. 'The university is the institution in society most capable of linking the requirements of industry, technology, and market forces with the demands of citizenship. Given the enormous dependence of these forces on university-based experts, the university is, in fact, in a position of strength, not of weakness' (Delanty 2002: 113; cf. Readings 1996), or, even more explicitly, 'the university must be capable of giving society a cultural direction' (Delanty 2002: 155).

13. This rather inductive approach to science seems to be fruitful for studying the ways in which scientists organise themselves. For example, when interviewed about her study concerning the idea of excellence in the social sciences, Lamont states that she 'take(s) as a point of departure the individuals' understanding of the classification system in which he or she functions. Bourdieu starts with the structure of the field, which is predefined. This is my big disagreement with him' (Lalaki 2007: 93). The consequences of these differences will also be explored in chapter 2.

14. This idea of science is based on a weak realism or constructivist realism. Reality is something that, under certain conditions of stability, can be considered to be 'out there' (Latour 2005). However, in practice, reality is always in the making, that is, it is an ongoing process through which some entities

appear as long as the associations that support them can keep on working. When such associations weaken, the entities fade away, changing what we call 'reality' (Law 2006a). This can be readily identified in social science. As fields negotiate and reshape themselves, social worlds change and the 'real' social relationships are transformed. Consequently, science and other fields mould themselves and the social world at the same time, reinforcing the idea of a reality in the making (Golinski 2005; Latour 2005; Hacking 1999).

15. For theoretical insights as well as empirical analysis of disciplinary boundary work in peripheral contexts, see Chew (2005).

16. Scientific capital is 'a set of properties which are the product of acts of knowledge and recognition performed by agents engaged in the scientific field and therefore endowed with the specific categories of perception that enable them to make the pertinent distinctions' (Bourdieu 2004: 55). Each agent has a certain amount of capital that, along with other resources, gives him or her a particular position within the field. However, scientific capital is not a mere economic metaphor applied to science and it includes three sub-types. Two different types of scientific capital are produced and exchanged: what Bourdieu calls academic capital, and strict scientific capital. The former is based on the institutional positions occupied by scientists in the field; the latter refers to capital accumulated through 'distinctive contributions' to knowledge embodied in publications. For Bourdieu, strict scientific capital involves two sub-types according to the market or audience from which the scientists obtain recognition. Bourdieu maintains the strict scientific capital label for that achieved through the exchange with peers and other scientists of the field, while introducing the term intellectual capital for the one attained through the acclaim of the mass audience: what we call the public. Consequently, the position of actors in the field depends not only on their place in the social structure but also on the capital accumulated, both academic and scientific. See Delanty (2002: 93ff) on the place of the university as a site of struggle between different forms of capital.

17. Hodder claims that ANT, by referring to networks and symmetries, dissolves the object and by so doing it underrates the physical processes of things as well as their temporalities. 'So rather than talk of things and humans in meshworks or networks of inter-connections, it seems more accurate to talk of the dialectical tension of dependence and dependency, historically contingent' (2012: 94). With this tension, Hodder argues that agency and power are outcomes of entanglements rather than properties of things and humans.

18. For a detailed analysis of how theory informs distinctions that support a theoretical habitus see Brubaker (1993).

19. For some, networked science refers to the new organisation of scientific activities as a consequence of the impact of Internet and other information and communication technologies (Nielsen 2011).

20. Diversification of actors, however, increases competition between them, as Kauppi and Erkkilä (2011) has shown in their study of international university rankings.

21. Detailed descriptions of institutionalised fields can be found in Bourdieu (1988, 2003a, 2004), Lamont (1987), Knorr-Cetina (1981), Latour and Woolgar (1986), Galison (1987, 1997), Collins (1985), Lynch (1985), Pickering (1984), Ravetz (1971), Star and Griesemer (1989), Ziman (2000) and Haraway (1989). An up to date account of many of the research traditions opened by these studies can be found in Hackett et al. (2008). Whatever the theoretical perspective, from the classical post-Mertonian sociology of science to ANT, most scholars of STS are mainly concerned with institutionalised fields, generally located in developed countries.

190 Notes

22. See Ben-David (1984) and Barber (1967, 1978).
23. The other consequence of the distinction between community and the outside world is a set of rules that governs scientific life: universalism, communism, disinterestedness, and organised scepticism (Merton 1973).
24. Although some features of networked fields are shared by the exact, natural and social sciences, the focus of analysis here is the latter, which urges us to recognise that the others have some divergent characteristics, such as more stable and institutionalised working conditions, a more clearly defined career path, which includes obtaining a PhD, and undertaking postgraduate studies, a closer connection with centres of knowledge production, although playing a peripheral role within international research teams, and a higher dependence on material resources (García de Fanelli 2007; Kreimer 2006; Thomas and Dagnino 2005). In addition, the exact and natural sciences show higher degrees of functional and strategic dependence and a low degree of task uncertainty (Whitley 2006), even in peripheral contexts. Further, they rely on standardised procedures, encourage specialisation, and communicate through highly prestigious international journals, such as Science or Nature, which also promotes the use of English as the lingua franca.
25. Whitley (2006) seems to believe that low degrees of mutual dependence are the result of profound disagreements about the nature and features of sciences' subject matter. Thus, social sciences tend to be less structured than natural sciences because they study a more complex, varied, and changing object: society. A weaker realist assumption would be to believe that such a disagreement could be the outcome of many situations, amongst them the controversy about things that are (taken for) real at any given moment. Empirical data in this research will show that the different perspectives of political scientists are grounded not only in their theoretical or methodological positions but also in the way that their jobs and the field as a whole are structured.
26. Discrepancies between research groups usually end in sectarian conflicts, due to different interpretations and personal contacts. Research problems are taken as personal problems and, more frequently than not, every group tries to differentiate itself by adopting novel methodologies or strategic preferences.
27. See Delanty (2002: 110ff) on the role of teaching in modern university and its separation from research.
28. 'Theory' appears as a unifying element in the field, because almost all members were trained under similar theoretical perspectives. For a deeper discussion of this issue see chapter 3.
29. Political science in the Anglo-Saxon world seems to be a case of what Whitley has called 'partitioned bureaucracy', in which 'standardization of training programmes and skills in the central core enables the reputational elite to control research strategies and problem selection, but the lack of technical control over empirical phenomena—which is the basis for legitimacy claims in the wider social structure—threatens this theoretical coherence and closure' (2006: 160). As in neo-classical economics, Anglo-Saxon political science seems to be organised around the standardization and formalisation produced by following the theoretical principles of rational choice theory (Lamont 2009). The marginal place of rational choice theory in Argentine political science, along with the multiplicity of theoretical perspectives (Bulcourf and D'Alessandro 2002) obliges us to classify it as a polycentric oligarchy, a type of scientific field in which the 'technical control is still limited, and so results are relatively idiosyncratic to the local conditions of their production and interpretation [and] are exercised locally and through personal knowledge' (Whitley 2006: 160).

Notes 191

30. The absence of institutions and the proliferation of networks has a few benefits. While communities are self-contained entities able to produce a fixed identity, networks favour multiple standpoints, original solutions, and comparative analysis. Therefore, communities tend to be conservative and increasingly specialised and networks tend to evolve and be increasingly differentiated (Dal Fiore 2007). This could explain the ability of many people from developing social worlds to take advantage of all the opportunities that contact with developed social worlds may offer.

31. 'The majority of people said that foundations and foreign institutions are the main financing sources [of science and technology in Argentina] even though, in terms of objective indicators . . . the public sector is responsible for most of the expenditure in the area' (Polino et al. 2003: 9; in translation). In Argentina, only 17.6 per cent of respondents in a national survey as to the public perception of science and technology responded that the State was the main source for funding the sector and 50 per cent replied that foundations and foreign institutions were the main sources of funds. According to official statistics, 2.9 per cent of the expenditure in science and technology is made by non-profit organizations—such as foundations and foreign institutions—31 per cent by the private sector and more than 65 per cent by the State (SECyT 2007: 34). Although misinformation is not the same as disinterest, it is clear that, at least in Argentina, the public has a distorted perception concerning the dynamics of science and technology.

32. Because of this, any structure of centres and peripheries is, from the point of view of the architecture of complex systems, a scale-free network. For more details, see Barabási and Bonabeau (2003).

33. As data on productivity of Chilean scientists show, this structure seems to be reproduced in relation to publication. 'Research productivity is often concentrated among a few scholars: some 70% of the Chilean research articles were produced by less than 5% of professors' (Schiefelbein and Schiefelbein 2007: 169).

34. According to Hanchard (2003), Bourdieu's framework is not useful in application to the actual situation in Brazil, because it is based on what Charles Taylor called the 'incorrigibility thesis', a tendency to overestimate the nation-state and its cultural impact on society.

    Bourdieu and Wacquant's argument contains traces of the incorrigibility thesis, insofar as nationality or nation-ness serves as a form of cultural distinction (national history, politics and culture) which radically differentiates one national formation from another, in this case Brazil and Brazilians from the United States and US citizens. Their version of the United States thus contains vastly differentiated epochs and peoples who are united by their nation-ness but little else; the US state, its citizens, slaves, indigenous and other subject peoples, white ethnics, capitalists and laborers are not merely indistinguishable, but interchangeable (Hanchard 2003: 7).

35. Negotiation in this context refers to the academic debate of knowledge through the institutionalised means of communication of science (such as conferences, journals, workshops, and visiting professorships). This exchange is a negotiation because, when knowledge circulates, it is never appropriated without assessing its meaning, relevance, or usefulness. This implies that it is not necessary a counter-hegemonic, global social science, because Northern knowledge is actually negotiated but these negotiations have to be observed elsewhere (cfr. Keim 2011).

36. Translation without negotiation is not necessarily cultural imperialism, cultural colonialism, or intellectual dependency, even though it may degenerate to some of these forms of international exchange. Notwithstanding,

192 *Notes*

international contacts between academics are not always possible, negotiations of meanings and identities can be also the outcome of an internal process of communication. This process is not as rich as an international dialogue, but it opens up the possibility of avoiding acritical reception and repetition of (usually foreign) ideas.

37. Some examples may clarify the notion of translation in ANT. Latour (1988) has argued that the success of Pasteur's laboratory was based on his ability to translate the hygienists's interests (how to control infectious diseases) into his own interest (how to manipulate microbes), becoming a spokesperson for both parts. Law (1986b) has shown how the Portuguese vessels were able to translate the winds and the currents of the ocean into a propulsion force that helped the ships travel well beyond the coasts and circulate around the world. For him, the network formed by the vessels, the sailors, the wind, the ocean, the astrolabe, the stars, and the charts was responsible for the Portuguese expansion in the same sense that the king's interest and power. Moser and Law (1999) have used the idea of translation to describe the connection between Liv, a Norwegian disabled woman, and her wheelchair with which she has been able to organise her life as an autonomous adult. In a way, her wheelchair allows her to translate her interests (open the door or switch off the TV set) into a set of actions, technologically programmed, that guarantee her independence.

38. In the context of Callon's theory of translation, 'enrolment' is the result of a successful translation. In other words, it is the process through which an actor (spokesperson) makes other actors act in such a way that a particular objective can be pursued. When the spokesperson achieves this goal, then the other actors have been 'enrolled'.

39. Latour's description of the process of translation seems to require an intentional actor to play the role of enroller. His account looks like a military description of what generals would do in the battlefield, or what negotiators or politicians would do to convince people to accept their positions. Given that Latour accepts that humans and non-humans are, equally, mediators in any network, this ambiguity has motivated the criticism that he ultimately gives humans a more important role and surreptitiously perpetuates the difference between humans and non-humans. For further explanation of these criticisms see Ihde (2003a: 88–102) and Shapin (1998).

40. An in-depth analysis is presented in section 1.5 of this chapter.

41. What is a video camera? For the company that produces it, a commodity. For a mother, the object with which to record her son's best moments. For a political activist, a weapon. The difference does not lie in its technical components, but rather in its use in the social worlds where different actors interpret it flexibly and according to their realities.

42. This assumption about symmetry between fields or social worlds seems to underpin Bourdieu's (1999a) examples as to the circulation of ideas. He deals, essentially, with the French appropriation of Heidegger and the German importation of Deleuze and Foucault. Although he sees power relations implied in the circulation of ideas, his attention is drawn equally to institutionalised academic fields; German and French philosophy. Were he attentive to the exchange between the unevenly institutionalised fields, he could have seen 'structural' differences, such as those on which this research attempts to shed light.

43. 'As indicated by citation patterns, scientific research in the United States is the most central and most prestigious part of the scientific world-system. But scientific production in the United States is also characterized by the lowest percentage of foreign references, foreign co-authors, and publications

Notes 193

abroad. The percentages of foreign references in scientific articles and foreign publication in US citations are both about 25 percent. In Japan and the European countries the figure lies somewhere between 40 percent and 71 percent; for the developing countries it varies between 70 percent and 92 percent' (Heilbron 1999: 439; Schott 1991).

These figures show that scientific fields vary in relation to the relevance they assign to knowledge produced in foreign fields, giving rise to first-rate science (what is cited in central fields) and second-rate science (what is not cited there).

44. Canagarajah (2002: 102–4) tells the story of Raj, a friend at Jaffna University, in Sri Lanka. Raj took four months to prepare a research article concerning the way that languages are alternated by local people to redefine their roles and relationships. In the meantime three books appeared in North America on the same topic, which forced Raj to try to obtain them or, at least, look for reviews. The reasons behind the time it took Raj to write his work were many, but all of them non-academic. Amongst them, Canagarajah mentions the army marching in the city, the search for food for his wife and daughter, the absence of a salary (since the university had not paid salaries for several months), the need to give private tuition to students in his neighbourhood, continuing power cuts in the region, lack of access to up to libraries and databases (that conditioned the possibility of writing a decent introduction to his article in which he could discuss the recent development in the area), and even scarcity of paper. Even though the periphery is a heterogeneous region, the example illustrates how the conditions of academic labour affect the final outcome of scholars: their written pieces.

45. This sentence reviews Latour's framework but it is partially based on Bourdieu's claims. Bourdieu states, in relation to the circulation of texts, from where they were produced to where they are imported, that 'to publish what one loves is to strengthen one's position in a certain field, whether one likes it or not, whether one is aware of it or not, even if that effect was not part of the original intention . . . These exchanges can be understood as alliances, and function in the same way as relations involving force, hence they might be used to reinforce a dominated or threatened position' (Bourdieu 1999a: 223).

46. Following Thomas and Dagnino (2005), it is necessary to highlight that this movement of knowledge between different social worlds maintains three implicit meanings: (i) it involves the preservation of identity across different environments; (ii) it includes humans (actors as translators) and non-humans; and (iii) it deals with the 'syntactic effect' of displacing a signifier to a different context. Thomas and Dagnino call this last process 'transducción'. However, our notion of asymmetrical translations does not attempt to describe a transference from one social world to another but the difference in power relations between them, which condition the identity of the transferred knowledge. For this reason, asymmetrical translation seems to be closer to what Santos calls diatopic hermeneutics, a 'translation [that] impacts on knowledges and practices (and their agents); [an] interpretation between two or more cultures with the goal of identifying isomorphic concerns and the different answers they produce. A second kind of translation takes place between social practices and their agents. By impacting on practices, translation tries to create intelligibility between the forms of organisation and the objectives of action' (Santos 2009: 135–51; in translation). These translations should take place at the university as a obligatory passage point because the university 'no longer reflects the social transformations of modernity, but is itself now a major site in which different social projects are articulated' (Delanty 2002: 158).

194 *Notes*

47. An example will illustrate the point. The analysis of Portantiero (2000) about the legacy of Machiavelli in Gramsci's political theory is a thoughtful argument about the reasons of the failure of the State and the responsibilities of the most powerful political actors. The study shows how a scholar in the periphery may provide a lucid interpretation of the work of a metropolitan scholar and give us one insightful analysis of Machiavelli as a politician, as a voice committed to its time but also to the *raison d'état*, that is, the successful consolidation of the State. Portantiero's academic success, however, is only local, since his network, unlike, for example, Skinner (1993)'s or Viroli (1998)'s, has been weaker and smaller than that of his colleagues at the centres of knowledge production. Although Portantiero's study has been well read and debated and has also been taught in many political science programmes in Argentina, his ideas have rarely transcended the local field (with the exception of some countries in Latin America), which exemplifies the fact that negotiations (interpretations) are commonly internal processes in the peripheral fields and not an international debate of equally endowed participants.

48. If negotiations could be measured exclusively through co-authorship, it would be easy to prove this point. Wagner et al. point out that 'patterns of cooperation do not change quickly . . . Scientifically advanced countries share similar research profiles that stimulate collaboration among them, and these countries collaborate in all major scientific fields. Developing and lagging countries, in contrast, are more likely to specialize in a few areas of science, often in fields that relate directly to some national need' (Wagner et al. 2001: xiii). A general tendency emerges: 'scientists in advanced countries are most likely to collaborate with those in other advanced nations' (Wagner et al. 2001: xii). In addition, the wider the gap between countries, the lower the level of collaboration in terms of co-authorship. Scientifically advanced countries have little interaction with scientifically lagging countries. Moreover, we observed a drop in the number of papers resulting from collaborations between scientifically advanced and lagging countries compared with those of proficient and developing countries. However, our research shows that, at least in the United States, as much as $50 million per year is being spent by the US government on research about conditions or resources in scientifically lagging countries. The fact that collaborations have not emerged around these studies may indicate that local scientists are not able or available to work on these subjects (Wagner et al. 2001: xiii).

49. See Bourdieu (1999a) and Lamont (1987) to see examples of this type of analysis. Interestingly, exchange between uneven metropolitan fields do not give rise to asymmetrical translation, since both parts consider themselves as central. Weidemann, for example, argues that 'European research communities may deplore the scientific hegemony of the United States, yet they do not consider themselves peripheral, and Europeanization would hardly be considered "indigenization". European researchers may lament the general disinterest of US researchers in their contributions; this does not, however, prevent them from exhibiting the same pattern of ignorance of research done outside the Western world' (2010: 363–64).

50. In their analysis of natural history, Star and Griesemer (1989) recognise four types of boundary objects. There are *repositories*, objects that may contain heterogeneous entities; *ideal types*, which are useful for a diagram or scheme but need to be adapted to particular cases; *coincident boundaries*, objects with similar boundaries but different contents; and finally *standardised forms*, objects with a set of predetermined features that may carry unchanging information for long distances. This is not the only possible classification

of boundary objects, but it points clearly to the distinctive characteristics of flexibility and robustness.

51. This is why Star and Griesemer, in ANT's terms, claim that 'allies enrolled by the scientist must be disciplined, but cannot be *overly*-disciplined' (1989: 407). Spokespeople must know to what extent the interests and desires of their enlisted or networked actors have to be maintained and to what extent they can be negotiated.

52. Studies on international academic conferences could help fill the gap because in these events 'the international' is situated and can be traced (see Gross and Fleming 2011).

53. This figure appeared first in Spanish in Rodriguez Medina (2013).

54. Behind an article written in a metropolitan scientific field it is possible to find the work of the scholar, his/her research assistant(s) (sometimes a postgraduate student doing a PhD), an up to date library (with specialized personnel and strong connections for interlibrary loans), cutting-edge technology (such as the latest versions of software for qualitative or quantitative analysis), stable and proper working conditions, a structure of full-time faculty, peer-reviewed panels (for grants, appointments, and publications), and financially strong journals and publishing houses that enable a world-wide distribution. This entire network—not only the abstract 'idea'—travels to weaker fields and sets the local research and teaching agendas. The peripheral conditions of academic work impede scholars from enacting alternative, solid, strong networks where the reply—or the novel idea—can be inserted. Reality, at the end of the day, is what resists, what is sustained by the most powerful network (Latour 1988).

NOTES TO CHAPTER 2

1. Cf. Adelstein and Kugel 2004; Ziman 2000; Meadows 1997. Puiatti de Gomez states that a 'research article is the report of research in which the complex activities that took place [during the investigation] are reconstructed. The description of the process and that of the results and *successes* is relevant for the advancement and diffusion of science and knowledge' (Puiatti de Gomez 2007: 83; emphasis added in translation).

2. Constructivism, as used in this book, is not in conflict with the idea of structural features of the networks because there are characteristics of the assemblages that emerge and cannot be reduced to those of their constitutive parts (i.e. stability). In fact, by reconstructing the network, the researcher actively participates in the enactment of certain features and obscures others. Life-history is the method chosen in this research to produce the enactment of Argentine political science.

3. Unlike ANT theorists, we believe that consolidated networks acquire some specific features that may be called 'structural'. However, we agree with them in thinking that the structure/network enacted is more fluid, dynamic, and unstable than is usually thought by structuralist theorists.

4. This conception of society allows researchers in the social sciences to use biographies and life-histories. In this sense, Rustin argues that 'if [a biographical turn] occurs in social science on a significant scale, this requires that methodologies be developed (. . .) which enable societies and cultures to be studied from the individual "upwards", rather than from the social structure "downwards"' (2000: 45). These changes also imply an ontological turn, that is, the acceptance that 'the ontological assumption must be that individuals have agency, that biographies make society and are not merely

196 Notes

made by it' (Rustin 2000: 46). Thus biographies can be thought of as quasi-actants because they 'act as if they were "transcendental"' (Krarup and Blok 2011: 53).

5. Fischer-Rosenthal calls this 'biographical structuring'. For him, 'biographical structuring is *multi-relational*, it refers to and produces a network of events and options to be combined and continuously reinterpreted over a lifetime' (2000: 117; emphasis in the original).

6. According to Latour '[t]here is no difference between the "real" and the "unreal", the "real" and the "possible", the "real" and the "imaginary". Rather, there are differences experienced between those who resist for long and those who do not, those who resist courageously and those who do not, those who know how to ally or isolate themselves and those who do not' (1988: 159). Despite his vocabulary, Latour recognises the existence of 'real' things: those who last longer, who travel further, who group more allies. Strength is synonymous with the number of allies. Due to this, Latour can still be called a realist (as Kreimer 2005, has argued), but one who defends a relational notion of real (Law 2006a). The same perspective is used in this research.

7. All methodologies are useful for this purpose. Thompson has argued of historians that they 'are not methodological purists, but jackdaws; given a problem, they will seize on any evidence they can discover, and make the best of it. It is commonplace that the evidence will be patchy and biased, and the further back the period studied the more inadequate it is likely to be' (1981: 290). Law (2006a) generalized Thompson's description by saying that 'if much of reality is ephemeral and elusive, then we cannot expect single answers. If the world is complex and messy, then at least some of the time we're going to have to give up on simplicities. But one thing is sure: if we want to think about the messes of reality at all then we're going to have to teach ourselves to think, to practice, to relate, and to know in new ways' (2006a: 2).

8. In the classical literature on life history the relationships between humans and non-humans have already been addressed. Plummer (1983), for example, argues that the validity of life histories can be achieved through official records of biographical details. While Plummer presents an epistemological device to validate life-histories, we prefer to say that the person *and* the registered information constitute a network that enacts a determined reality. Thus, for Plummer, a criminal may tell a story and the researcher has to check that story against official documents. For us, a criminal *is* a criminal only if he or she is associated with an official document that states that the person has committed a crime. The difference lies ultimately between epistemology and ontology.

9. This is particularly important in the present research because many interviewees are consolidated scholars who may have a wider view of the discipline, the field, and the members of it.

10. Three of them were from Argentina and one was from Mexico.

11. For the purpose of sampling, the institutional affiliation of scholars holding multiple positions has been determined according to the time spent in each one. However, it is the experience of working at many sites which is most relevant for the goals of this research.

12. According to UBA's regulations, the regular positions within a *Cátedra* (Chair) are: Professorships: *Profesor Titular Plenario* (Full Professor, tenure-track position), *Profesor Titular* (Professor), *Profesor Asociado* (Associate Professor), and *Profesor Adjunto* (Assistant Professor); and Auxiliaries: *Jefe de Trabajos Prácticos* (Chief of Teaching Auxiliaries), *Ayudante de Primera* (First Auxiliary), and *Ayudante de Segunda* (Second Auxiliary). In turn,

Notes 197

there are three types of positions according to the time spent on academic activities: *dedicación exclusiva* (full-time, exclusive appointment), *dedicación semiexclusiva* (part-time appointment), and *dedicación parcial* (employment for specific courses). According to Hobert (2007: 1) there is another category: *de facto* professors, who are not recognised formally by the university at all. Other non-regular positions within the university system include *Profesor consulto* (Consulting Professor), *Profesor Contratado* (Term-contract Professor) or *Invitado* (Visiting Professor), *Docente Libre* (Free Teacher, in charge of new or ad hoc courses), *Docente Autorizado* (Authorised Teacher, assistant of professors who have finished the teaching training of any faculty), and two special appointments *Profesor Emérito* (Emeritus Professor) and *Honorario* (Honorary Professor). At UBA, there are 2,071 regular professors and auxiliaries (98.9 per cent) in the faculty of social sciences and only 23 non-regular positions (1.2 per cent).

13. Leiras et al. (2005) only make a general statement concerning political science produced in the provinces. They state that 'in the 1920s and 1930s, the height of the reformist tradition encouraged the opening of institutes, academies, journals, and faculties of Social and Political Sciences' (Leiras et al. 2005: 77; in translation). In a similar manner, Bulcourf and D'Alessandro (2003) refer to Mendoza's Faculty of Social and Political Sciences and Rosario's *Licenciatura* in Consular and Diplomatic Services simply as antecedents of academic political science in Argentina (Bulcourf and D'Alessandro 2003:141).

14. The lack of information, a consequence of the lack of consolidated institutions, is not only a problem for the SAAP. Many studies concur that there are important shortcomings in relation to information on gender in the science and technology system. 'Although many have clearly said that it is urgent to incorporate the variable "gender" into officially-produced statistics in Latin America, it seems that this situation (of paucity of information) has not changed and difficulties in collecting disaggregated data, even official data, still are an indicator of the lack of commitment to a topic that calls for attention' (Zubieta 2007: 85, in translation).

15. The website is available at http://www.educ.ar (Accessed 28 February 2013).

16. This second list was compared with the *Guia del Estudiante Edicion 2007* which appeared at the beginning of 2007. This guide is probably the most complete and up-to-date about universities and degrees in Argentina, and is published annually. Since 2009, on the other hand, nine new public universities have been created, although neither their organization nor their functioning seem to challenge the empirical findings of this research (Duffard 2012).

17. Information about the regulations for researchers at CONICET can be found on http://web.conicet.gov.ar/web/11716/3 (Accessed 27 February 2013).

18. This four-step process was a complex one, which involved in-depth reading and re-reading of data; organisation of field notes, memos, and other written accounts produced during fieldwork; constructing typologies; testing concepts against other empirical studies of Argentine academia; developing charts, diagrams, and other forms of illustration to make patterns more explicit; and re-reading the theoretical literature.

19. Scholarship on post-colonialism has already demonstrated that Argentine social science, as well as Latin American social science, is peripheral in relation to metropolitan centres (Lander 2003a, Coronil 2003; Castro-Gómez 2003; Quijano 2003; Mignolo 2007; Florez-Florez 2007). Scholars from metropolitan centres have also demonstrated the centre/periphery structure of international social science (Schott et al. 1998; Wallerstein 1996c; Tenbruck 1988). This book explores some of the institutional and non-institutional mechanisms through which the peripheral situation of Argentina is

198 *Notes*

produced and reproduced locally, paying particular attention to the ways in which knowledge in transit (Secord 2004) affects it.

20. A thorough depiction of the field requires the testimonies of both, dominant and non-dominant actors, and is the reason to discard bibliometric analysis, where dominant actors are overrepresented.

NOTES TO CHAPTER 3

1. 'Foreign ideas' is an expression referring, generally, to ideas generated in metropolitan or Western centres of knowledge production (Alatas 2003; Wallerstein 1996c). In chapter 1 it was shown that 'foreign' generally means Western, developed, or metropolitan.
2. Due to the scarcity of PhD programmes and the possibility of developing an academic career without holding a PhD, the focus of this chapter is on undergraduate education. Unless it is explicitly pointed out to be otherwise, the word 'student' in this chapter will refer to undergraduates.
3. The predominance of theoretical courses over others was clearly stated by a mature scholar at a public university in the metropolitan area of Buenos Aires who argued, 'during most of my undergraduate studies, the idea that only political theory and comparative politics were serious [specialties] was transmitted, but I don't know if this was done explicitly [by professors] at UBA. Public opinion [for example] was for superficial and shallow people who did not like to think . . . That is why I did not take a single course on Public Opinion [. . .]; it was like a prejudice' (39: 10; in translation).
4. It has been observed that many scholars tend to use the same texts they read as undergraduate students when selecting the bibliography for their syllabi. The influence of undergraduate readings on professors and their careers will be further explored in subsequent chapters.
5. For the purpose of this research, the work of Guillermo O'Donnell is part of the production of central scientific fields. As he recognised, when contacted as a potential interviewee, his written work was produced mainly during his time in the United States, so it can hardly be considered as a Latin American or Argentine product. This perspective is based on the idea, discussed in chapter 1, that knowledge is situated in its context of production; the scientific field and the social world from which it emerges. A different approach to political science, focused on Latin America and Argentina as research problems, and not as places of production of knowledge, can be found in Lesgart (2003).
6. The scientific status of political ideas was so important for local political scientists that on many occasions the predominance of foreign ideas seems to be located in their methodological prescriptions more than in their theoretical insights or conceptualisation. 'When I found social science, neither philosophy nor historical data [. . .] when I found hard data, then a love for [political science] appeared . . . [Mine] was an education based on *political science*, the Eastonian school, if you like, in Argentina. Something that cost too much argument amongst colleagues . . . But it was a very strong education (34:127; in translation; the emphasized expression was narrated in English by the interviewee)
7. This explains, for example, the canonical place of Sartori's *La Política* within Argentine political science.
8. The introduction of the rational choice paradigm and formalised political theory can also be seen as an attempt to bring in novel scientific ideas from abroad in order to modernise Argentine political science in the 1980s and

Notes 199

1990s. For that reason, labelling an idea or method as new is always a strategy to locate such an idea or method in the heart of the field (Baert 2012).
9. The influence of new ideas on students can be so strong that some scholars split the history of Argentine political science into 'modern' and 'pre-modern' stages, corresponding to the bibliography used in theoretical courses. A mature scholar at private universities in Buenos Aires mentions that, before the 1970s, the university at which he studied political science lacked a solid and differentiated core. However, he said 'I didn't read Mario Justo López's texts or the pre-modern theoreticians of political science (. . .) who played an important role in introducing some readings' (48: 30; in translation).
10. Latin American databases such as Scielo and Redalyc are trying to change this situation, but their future is still uncertain (Vessuri 2010).
11. See sections 1.4 and 1.5 in chapter 1.
12. There are no student-oriented journals in Argentine political science, although *POSTData* was born as an attempt to develop a journal where young researchers and even students could publish their work. However, economic reasons forced their editors to change the perspective, inviting consolidated scholars to submit their work instead of being a forum for undergraduates.
13. More information available at [http://www.saap.org.ar, accessed 15 February 2013]. There is no information of attendance to the tenth conference, held at Universidad Católica de Córdoba in 2011.
14. At this last conference in 2011, 50.4 per cent of participants were students (see http://www.saap.org.ar, accessed 24 February 2013). Probably because of the presence of Guillermo O'Donnell, some senior local scholars (e.g. Carlos Escudé and Carlos Acuña) and foreign academics (e.g. Scott Mainwaring and Manuel A. Garretón) were present at the 10th SAAP National Conference and contributed to its success. However, the death of O'Donnell in November 2011 will be a challenge for organisers of the 11th National Conference to be held at Universidad Nacional de Paraná (Entre Ríos) in July 2013.
15. The autonomy of Argentine universities means that each institution is free to decide what form of evaluation best suits its objectives and material possibilities. This makes it difficult to compare mechanisms of evaluation, but it is usually the case that neither written nor oral exams tend to motivate the creative, critical, academic writing that is necessary for an academic career, though usually developed at postgraduate level.
16. Only four out of thirty-three institutions in the sample have given professors individual or shared offices to meet students. Most of the scholars interviewed who have an office are also administrative staff, such as deans, heads of departments, head of programmes, and directors of institutes.
17. For some scholars, the debate could be channelled through student magazines and journals, sometimes funded by student centres.
18. By 'junior researchers' we mean both the undergraduate students and those recent graduates who have become part of a Chair and, by so doing, have entered the academic market and accepted the rules of the game, among which the pressure for publication stands out.
19. In Europe and North America undergraduates usually do not have publishing outlets, but this is due to the existence of an institutionalised structure of postgraduate programmes and a stabilised academic career that encourages publication only from postgraduate level onward. In contexts where there are but a few Masters and PhD programmes and the academic career starts in the last years of undergraduate studies, the pressure for publication begins earlier, but there is neither a market nor interest of the governmental agencies to sustain a structure of publications where students can publish their work.

200 Notes

20. Interestingly, the invisibility of internal debate was also a problem for a head of department at a private university in Buenos Aires. She says that 'for me, this programme had to be known by my peers . . . I'm talking about all professors that, regardless of whether they have a full time position at other universities, had to know of the existence of this programme. And for me the way to know something is by showing one's face in it. So the idea was, let's organise conferences and seminars and attend workshops and so on. Some professors of this university criticised this attitude because they said that we opened a space for others. The truth is, I accept that criticism because my idea was "Just know this programme"' (38:77; in translation). The passage makes clear that (in)visibility involves at the same time the (lack of) recognition of others—other scientists, other groups, other institutions—and the (lack of) acceptance that those others are a point of reference or, as Actor-Network theorists would say, an obligatory passage point.
21. Individual attempts have been made to encourage undergraduate students to write, and most interviewees have acknowledged that some professors really motivated them to write, academic articles. However, as is discussed in following chapters, the promotion of writing requires some specific labour conditions, such as full-time professors, who can conscientiously read and correct written pieces, well-equipped libraries, regular meetings between professors and students, physical spaces to meet (such as offices), and a manageable number of students per lecture course. Only a few institutions in the Argentine higher education system meet these requirements and this forces us to claim that, in general, political science students, at undergraduate level, are hardly ever stimulated to produce new knowledge.
22. In Baert (2012)'s words, they are intellectual interventions.
23. As one interviewee has put it, 'I work from 7pm to 7am. That's my life. So, a dark life, far away from the academic centres. I do imagine them. Yes, I do. I don't know Heidelberg (. . .) but I can even smell the wood that I'll never see, the wood of those desks from gothic times' (2: 68; in translation).
24. Probably because of this situation many post-colonialists believe that a Latin American thinking can be found in literature or literary studies, but not in the social sciences (Mignolo 2000; Lander 2003; Castro-Gomez 2007).

NOTES TO CHAPTER 4

1. This does not imply that personal connections are not important in developed countries where universities are highly institutionalized. However, the existence of widely spread media in which vacancies are listed help newcomers to know what institutions are recruiting scholars and, by so doing, they can better shape their networks of contacts to be eligible for the position.
2. Negotiations, however, may take place, especially when professors are interested in absorbing new ideas or perspectives advanced by newcomers (Ziman 1994), but this is far from being the rule.
3. The Ciclo Básico Común (Common Basic Cycle, CBC) is a set of core courses at the Universidad de Buenos Aires that is composed of six introductory courses for all new students. There are two general courses, two courses according to the Faculty (e.g. natural sciences), and two more according to the degree (e.g., within the Faculty of social sciences, communication, political science, sociology).
4. A senior scholar at a public university in Buenos Aires mentions that when he retired his Chair was composed of twenty-two members, seventeen auxiliaries and five Chiefs of auxiliaries (63: 21).

Notes 201

5. Appointments are divided into three types: full-time (forty hours a week of academic activities), half-time (twenty hours), and by courses (ten hours).

6. There are a few private institutions in Buenos Aires at which full-time appointments really mean a secure and stable job with proper labour conditions for teaching and research. Most Argentine political scientists, especially while passing through the first phase of their academic careers, only obtain part-time appointments that, in consequence, force them to be attentive to new job opportunities. Although statistical data concerning the different types of position (full-time or part-time employment for specific courses) are hard to find, UBA's figures show that 2,289 people hold a full-time position, 2,478 a part-time one, and 24,176 a by-course position (Universidad de Buenos Aires 2004: 74). Further, 20,000 people work as ad honorem teachers in the Argentine university system and, according to the Secretary of Academic Affairs at UBA, 17,006 (45.6 per cent) out of 37,300 positions at UBA are ad honorem. That is why Lorca (2004) argues that UBA functions miraculously thanks to the work of ad honorem professors and why Grüner (2012) has vehemently criticised how UBA is currently organised. To complicate the situation, the Chair system usually brings about a bottleneck that impedes newcomers and mature scholars from reaching the higher positions in the field. 'In countries with the tradition of the "Chair system", a relatively small number of academics are promoted to this high rank, and it is by no means certain that most academics will end their careers as full professors' (Altbach 2007a: 156).

7. A 'concurso' is the open, competitive examination through which universities make professorial appointments. It involves the analysis of the scholarly accomplishment of candidates, their experience in teaching and research, and sometimes a public lecture delivered by the prospective scholars.

8. The reasons for undertaking postgraduate studies may change in different historical periods but always refer to the necessity of enlarging the CV and not to the production of original ideas. During the last dictatorship, for example, some scholars found the State control over the public universities uncomfortable and frequently decided to take postgraduate studies in the few private universities that offered a master's or PhD (e.g. Universidad del Salvador and Universidad de Belgrano). Questioned about his experience in the PhD programme at a private university in Buenos Aires, a senior scholar remembers that 'I did my PhD during the years of the Proceso [dictatorship] when the greatest shelter for those of us who condemned both forms of violence, let's say, the shelter from escaping an ugly situation like that, was epistemology [and that is why] all of us ended up writing about that topic and doing the PhD, a three-year doctoral programme. We attended the seminars because we had nothing else to do; the public university did not provide any opportunities and [the experience] was interesting' (63: 46; in translation). The passage suggests that political reasons in the 1980s, as well as in the 1970s, played a similar role to that of restrictions of the academic market in the 1990s and 2000s.

9. In turn, according to testimonies of senior scholars interviewed for this research, 'institutional decisions' as to the organisation of a postgraduate programme in the hinterland are frequently based on 'personal contacts', which corroborate the networked nature of the field.

10. Those newcomers who are, in practice, in charge of a class often use the bibliography they discussed in undergraduate courses, so they also translate foreign ideas according to the selection made by the professors holding Chairs on undergraduate programmes.

11. The distance between the fields is not exclusively the responsibility of senior and mature scholars. The lack of symbolic and material resources

202 Notes

at universities, and the system of science and technology in the developing world, conspires to prevent scholars from attending international conferences and having high quality, widespread local journals in which to publicise their ideas. In fact, one role of gatekeepers in peripheral fields could be to concentrate resources as much as possible in order to include the standpoint of the periphery in the international agenda of science. This last interpretation, however, assumes that gatekeepers establish mechanisms regarding the production of local colleagues in order to articulate their research agendas and this does not seem to be the case, at least in relation to Argentine political science. Furthermore, while it is true that senior and mature scholars are also affected by the paucity of resources, they are probably the only actors in the fields with the capacity to advance a local, inclusive, and proactive national research agenda and to institutionalise local academic projects, such as postgraduate programmes and journals, that are still absent in the local political science field.

12. Currently there are eight PhD programmes in political science in Argentina: Universidad Nacional de Cuyo, Universidad Nacional de General San Martín, Universidad Nacional de Rosario, Universidad Nacional de Tucumán, Universidad Católica Argentina, Universidad Católica de Córdoba, Universidad de Belgrano, and Universidad Torcuato Di Tella (information available at http://web.siu.edu.ar/, accessed 14 February 2013). However, the quality of these programmes, as well as of their faculty, is far from even.

13. Source: CONICET [Available at http://web.conicet.gov.ar/documents/11722/42670414–26af-49cb-b357-acffb6a4ad6c, accessed 20 February 2013]

14. CONICET indicates that the numbers of scholarships for nationals to undertake PhD studies in areas where there are not consolidated programmes in Argentina in recent years have been sixty-eight (2000), seventy-five (2001), seventy-seven (2002), seventy-three (2003), sixty-four (2004), fifty-seven (2005), forty-one (2006), and zero (2007 and subsequent years to present). [Available at http://www.conicet.gov.ar/CIFRAS/indicadores/2006/indicadores_de_insumo2006/recursos_humanos/bec_tipo_beca.php, accessed 17 June 2009; and http://web.conicet.gov.ar/web/conicet.acercade.cifras/graficos, accessed 19 February 2013. The former website is no longer available, but according to CONICET's website (accessed 3 February 2013) only postdoctoral studies abroad are currently funded. Support for short-term stay programmes instead of doctoral studies seems to be the mechanism used by the government to contribute to the internationalization of Argentine science].

15. Even those who go abroad for their master's and PhDs end up studying the social, economic, and political problems of Argentina, or sometimes Latin America, frequently using a comparative perspective. Rarely do they focus on theory or other countries or regions.

16. Only one title of a PhD thesis awarded by University of California Berkeley in 1971 could not be obtained.

17. According to Latour '[t]here is no external referent. Referents are always internal to the forces that use them as touchstones [. . .] The interpretation of the real cannot be distinguished from the real itself because the real are gradients of resistance' (1988: 166). This weak realism, according to which objects and people are embedded in networks to enact a specific reality, obliges us to think that every act of interpretation (the connection between a text and its referent) is nothing but a newly proposed network of actors (exegetes) who are able to enrol other actors (texts, objects, graphs, tables, or maps). A detailed study of how referents are constructed through networks and why interpretation needs to be considered as a translation can be found in Latour (1999: 24–79).

Notes 203

18. Information concerning the reasons behind the decision of some scholars to remain in metropolitan fields could complement this research and provide another form of testing our findings. Where possible, such information was gathered through secondary resources (published interviews, autobiographies, and informal exchanges). However, collecting and analysing raw material concerning the trajectory of scholars who stayed abroad would also have required altogether different research.

19. The name of the programme is Internal Postdoctoral Scholarships for the Reinsertion of Researchers (see web.conicet.gov.ar/web/conicet.convocatorias.becas/repatriacion, accessed 17 February 2013).

20. Although it has been argued that peripheries are providers of data to the centres (Latour 1987; 1988; Richard 1998; Burawoy 2008), this research suggests that the opposite holds true: institutions from the centres serve as sites at which an academic career can be pursued and knowledge produced, as an alternative to the few posts available in the local field. Furthermore, almost all the interviewees who went abroad for postgraduate studies focused their research on Argentina or Latin America, which corroborates, at the same time, the idea that centres accumulate information from the peripheral nodes of the network, but also that the information already stored is attractive to scholars who use the metropolitan institutions to advance their own (locally oriented) scientific careers.

21. In central scientific fields time has also been problematized, since 'academic practice is rapidly disaggregating, or "unbundling", as a result of a variety of forces [which have allowed] the emergence of the "para-academic": staff who specialise in one element of academic practice' (Macfarlane 2010: 59).

22. Recent analyses of academic relationships have used theoretical frameworks from sociology and philosophy of technology in order to understand academic relationships that traditionally have been thought of as social relationships. On peer-reviewing as technology see Lamont (2009); in relation to teaching statistics and statistical reasoning as technology see Uprichard et al. (2008), and on collaboration between researchers as technology see Schroeder (2008).

23. According to Shapin and Schaffer (1985), it could be argued that teaching technologies have three dimensions. A material one that includes the use of apparatus required to teach and to do research (e.g. computers, software, classrooms), a literary one by means of which the result of use of the apparatus is reported in a more or less standard form (e.g. scientific paper, book chapter, textbooks), and a social one that takes into consideration the social rules and conventions around teaching and research in a particular context (e.g. teaching by undergraduates).

24. Time can be managed because it is 'a flattened and immanent scenario of connections, fluxes, and objective intensities', as Serres, according to Lash et al. (1998: 4), has sustained.

25. Some local consecrated scholars have been able to tangentially participate in the debates that have given rise to new knowledge, being an example of what Bijker (2001) calls 'high-included actors'. As far as this research concerns, newcomers are always 'low-included actors' for whom the technological device (e.g. a book published in the UK) is something given, packaged knowledge.

26. This situation explains the current debate within Argentine political science concerning the role of the SAAP, the professional organisation for political scientists. For some scholars, the activities of the association do not correspond to the segmentation of the field based on merits and recognition that are basic in science (Merton 1973; Bourdieu 2004) and that is why some academics have begun to talk of a 'Doctors' rebellion'. Although holding a PhD

204 *Notes*

is not an attribution exclusive to those who went abroad for postgraduate studies, the scarcity of PhD programmes in Argentina, as well as the difficulty of undertaking postgraduate studies while working under adverse conditions, makes it clear that the distinction between 'PhDs' and 'non-PhDs' is, to some extent, a struggle between those with foreign postgraduate education versus locally-trained political scientists.

NOTES TO CHAPTER 5

1. Peer-reviewing does not impede publications from having biases related to institutional affiliation, gender, age, and other socio-demographic factors (Meadows 1997).
2. This tendency is not homogeneous throughout the social sciences, since disciplines such as economics tend to value research articles more than books (Clemens et al. 1995).
3. Unlike newcomers, whose access to texts is mediated by mature and senior scholars, these academics have the endowed capital (Bourdieu 2004) to produce the necessary distinctions to acquire new texts according to their personal and professional interests. Since they are full members of the field, they are responsible for the selection of bibliography for undergraduate and graduate courses and for their own research projects and publications. However, this chapter shows that their work is to some extent conditioned by other actors in the local and foreign fields, who filter foreign ideas and contribute to the multiplicity of translations and translators. For more on how current decisions depend on previous articulations of objects and people, see Hodder (2012).
4. Perelman believes that 'on-line shopping in Argentina is new. [. . .] It is limited by the same factors that in general affect the development of e-commerce in the country: the lack of confidence on the circulation of personal data on the net and the fear of using credit cards for transactions. [. . .] Another problem is the inefficient postal service' (2003: 26). In addition, a recent decision to restrict the entry of foreign books into the country has affected individual and institutional actors (*The Economist* 2011; Bammel 2012). Empirical data mentioned in this research confirm the predisposition towards local shopping and question the real impact of the big online bookstores (e.g. Amazon.com) on the local political science field in Argentina.
5. This is obvious in a country where 79 per cent of the publishing houses are concentrated in the city and province of Buenos Aires (Centro de Estudios para la Producción 2005).
6. Between 1993 and 2004, 48 per cent to 52 per cent of Argentine importations of books came from Spain (Centro de Estudios para la Producción 2005: 28).
7. The difficulty of publishing on a regular basis is one of the common problems experienced in Argentine and Latin American journals (Cetto and Hillerud 1995). The publication of every new issue depends on procurement of funds, such as the small research grants provided by UBA (UBACyT). Ultimately, research grants are partially devoted to funding not only the academic journal but also the university press (e.g. Buenos Aires University Press [EUDEBA]). In this sense, the sustainability of the journal involves a complex system of reallocation of funds from the university that pervades the funding process and makes it susceptible to ups and downs that put the academic project at risk.
8. *POSTData* is another Argentine journal of political science, published since 1996, but not on a regular basis.

Notes 205

9. This helps explain why Argentine journals in political science have a wide range of topics, methodologies, and theoretical assumptions. The academic market is small enough to impede specialized journals from emerging and the difficulties in obtaining local and foreign contributions force editors to accept a very diverse range of articles.
10. Editors usually keep strong links with foreign colleagues for two reasons. First, the more international publications the journal has, the more widely sold it will be, since highly reputed actors of the field are the attractive stars who make the journal of interest to others. Second, editors in peripheral contexts usually feel the need for being acquainted with new trends and fashions in metropolitan fields in order to depict a wide landscape of the discipline.
11. One of the more successful journals in Argentine political science was *Agora*, now out of circulation. This journal was mainly devoted to translating articles from consecrated foreign authors whose works could thus be read in Spanish and known in Argentina (Bulcourf and D'Alessandro 2003). A consolidated scholar remembers that 'for me [the journal Agora] was something that gave identity to the discipline in the sense that [it allowed] a systematised thought process to be open for public debate. [. . .] Agora brought foreign intellectuals close, because Argentina has always been very parochial' (38: 65; in translation).
12. According to the Centro de Administración de Derechos Reprográficos de la República Argentina, the impact of photocopying on the Argentina higher education has been enormous. 98 per cent of students read photocopies and, from a survey conducted in Rosario, 38 per cent have never read an entire book. It has been argued that every year 2,552 million pages are photocopied in the country, which represents approximately 7 million books and costs US$100 million plus (see http://www.cadra.org.ar, accessed 20 February 2013).
13. Instead of reducing the knowledge gap between countries, the internet seems to be contributing to widening such a gap because it empowers major publishing houses, providing them with a technological platform that permits their journals to reach every corner of the planet. At the same time, even when access to metropolitan publications is possible, there still are the problems of costs and copyright, which widen the gap even more. Those who believe that Internet is a revolutionary tool for diffusion and circulation of knowledge tend to underrate the networked nature of technology (i.e. its permanent connection with institutions, regulations, people, and other objects such as databases or online bookstores) that forces us to pay attention, for example, to personal/institutional subscriptions, postal systems, or credit card use for online consumption.
14. Given their multifaceted subject matter, social scientists can usually publish their work in many different disciplines. The number of Argentine contributions is based on the analysis of the following neighbouring areas: political science, public administration, international relations, social sciences (interdisciplinary journals), and history of the social sciences. Nevertheless, it has to be noted that Argentine political scientists may have made contributions to other fields, such as anthropology or psychology, but these are rarely contributions to political science.
15. 'Between 1996 and 1999 the number of Argentine international co-authored articles—a good estimator of substantive research cooperation—grew almost 400 percent. With 1,200 international co-authored articles Argentina compares well with neighboring Chile but falls behind Brazil and Mexico' (Thorn 2005: 19). Co-authored articles can be an indicator that 'Argentine scholars are relatively well connected and respected internationally' (Thorn 2005: 20), but also that the publication of the article in metropolitan journals

206 *Notes*

demands a set of skills regarding textual and para-textual conventions that only those who have worked in, or those who have studied in, the First World possess (Canagarajah 2002).

16. The most cited article ever written by an Argentine scholar (with a foreign co-author) is Alchourrón and Makinson (1982), but it refers to an epistemological problem, i.e. the logic of theory change, a topic broad enough to be interesting for scholars in many disciplines, not only political science.

17. This article was cited only once in an Argentine journal, *Desarrollo Económico*, which may be an indicator that the impact factor refers more to colleagues in the discipline than to the relevance of the articles for the society under study.

18. Interestingly, there is an article that cites the original one, whose title does not contain any geographical delimitation: 'Unmet expectations: The cycle of convertibility'. However, this article was published in Spanish, in the Argentine journal *Desarrollo Económico*, by one of the original authors with two different co-authors. This simple analysis may suggest that only in the local field can scholars make universalistic claims for the titles of their articles because they have enough (local) capital to sustain such a risky decision.

19. For a detailed analysis of the organisation of Italian academia, see Clark (1977) and Gambetta (1998).

20. Exclusion does exist, but it is rarely related to the gate keeping functions of mediators and other dominant actors. Instead, exclusion is based on previous opportunities (or the lack thereof) for academics to obtain a PhD.

21. Information about postdoc scholarships can be found on CONICET's website (Available at web.conicet.gov.ar/web/conicet.convocatorias.becas/externas, accessed 20 February 2013)

22. The special nature of international conferences for peripheral scholars seems to suggest that negotiation of foreign knowledge usually happens locally within the local rules of the game.

23. The result is that mediator positions are filled by non-dominant members of the field, whose authority is not necessarily perceived as legitimate by their peers (cfr. Cole 1983).

24. In order to observe consecration in a peripheral scientific field such as Argentine political science, it has been necessary to focus on (i) the history of the discipline (Bulcourf and D'Alessandro 2002, 2003; Fernández 2002b); (ii) public speeches by the authorities of SAAP, such as his inaugural lecture at the 2007 Annual Meeting on Political Science (Fernández 2007), (iii) opinions by colleagues at many public events (Botana 2008; CEDES 2007; Saguir 1999), (iv) comments made by journalists, who help them to be more widely known (Uranga 2002), and (v) appointments by the government as members of a commission to evaluate the state of political science in Argentina (SECyT 1998).

25. Oszlak's work was located at the juncture of several publics, such as economists, sociologists, political scientists, lawyers, and politicians. The interest of the first four groups was in their own disciplinary problems, theories, and methodologies. The interest of politicians, however, was driven by Oszlak's analysis of problems, which were considered urgent in the political agenda of the government, especially that of Alfonsín.

26. 'The relationship between the structural, the political-institutional, and the ideological is the qualitative leap that appeared in the work of José Nun, Marcelo Cavarozzi, Oscar Oszlak and especially [. . .] of Guillermo O'Donnell' (Bulcourf and D'Alessandro 2003: 156, in translation).

27. Oszlak (1982) became obligatory reading in almost all undergraduate programmes and even in high schools, such as the (locally) prestigious Colegio

Notes 207

Nacional de Buenos Aires and Colegio Carlos Pellegrini, as part of a new historiography influenced by theoretical frameworks imported from political science and sociology.

28. Even today, FLACSO Buenos Aires does not have a full-time faculty, although many academics who work there have been linked to the institution for a long time. FLACSO pays scholars for teaching its postgraduate programmes, but they must obtain funds for their research and personal expenses through different channels, such as CONICET, the ANPCyT, and international philanthropic foundations (e.g. Rockefeller and Ford). Students' fees are used to sustain the costs of infrastructure, administrative staff, and the library. The prestige of the institution seems to be related to its long tradition of high-quality postgraduate programmes and the few research teams whose work has appeared in local and international publications.

29. This view of the local field supports Strasser's claims concerning international connections. Questioned as to the importance of keeping in touch with colleagues abroad, he replied that 'Yes, it's important. But I think that some of us have better personal abilities and dispositions [. . .]. It's necessary to have publications, degrees and that stuff, but it depends more on how much one really looks for' (16: 115; in translation). Once again, institutions are subordinated to personal networks and interests.

30. Floria recognises this when he says that 'the last thing I had read [from Dahl] was a paper on opposition in contemporary Europe. I had the idea of applying that framework to explain a long-standing debate concerning the May Revolution of 1810. Then Dahl told me "Please explain this to me because I haven't a clue about it"' (13: 66; in translation).

31. Marginality is clearly reflected, both in the importance that the debate may have had for foreign scholars' research agendas and in the transcendence that local historiography gives to the conference. Dahl (1989), for example, recognises in a footnote that some arguments and data for his book on poliarchy have been obtained from the work of colleagues in the periphery, whom he cites. For Bulcourf and D'Alessandro, this footnote 'constitutes a recognition [. . .] of the scientific studies undertaken in Argentina' (2003: 150). The fact that this one footnote can be interpreted as an acknowledgement of the entire field of Argentine political science is one of the reasons the importance of qualitative analysis in this research.

32. For a detailed analysis of the importance of seeking research funding in shaping research see Smith (2010).

33. In highly institutionalized scientific fields, gatekeepers play the role of mediators but also regulate the internal rules of the game. In a context in which the field has enough resources to sustain international connections, the people who control the flow of people and publications are those who become dominant actors locally and mediators of the foreign exchange. That is why, in metropolitan fields, any mediator is a gatekeeper even though not all gatekeepers are mediators (since some powerful positions are locally oriented).

34. While the impact of some political crises, such as the intervention of Argentine public universities in 1966 or the persecution of academics during the last military government (1976–1983), has been documented (Suasnábar 2004; Germani 2004; Invernizzi and Gociol 2003; Invernizzi 2005; Prego and Estebanez 2002; Terán 2004), the consequences of the economic crises of 1989–1990 and 2001–2002 have been less studied. It can be assumed that the crises have reduced the salaries of scientists in general, and political scientists in particular, and their access to cutting-edge bibliography or attendance at international conferences, as acknowledged by many scholars

208 *Notes*

who were interviewed. The institutional consequences of these crises have yet to be analysed.

NOTES TO THE CONCLUSION

1. This mechanism seems to parallel the strategy of peripheral scholars to situate their studies geographically through explicit clauses in their titles while their metropolitan counterparts usually make general claims in the titles, producing what Baber (2003) calls provincial universalism. Compare, for example, the study of Delamont and Atkinson (2001) of PhD students at US universities with the analysis of Vessuri (2007) of the training of scientists in Latin America. The former has no geographical delimitation and is entitled 'Doctoring Uncertainty: Mastering Craft Knowledge' while the latter is contextualised and entitled 'La formación de investigadores en América Latina' [The Training of Researchers in Latin America]. This difference in the use of geographical specifications is one of the rhetorical devices through which metropolitan knowledge becomes universal and peripheral knowledge remains local.
2. When collaboration takes place it is usually shaped by the norms of the most developed scientific field, in which, presumably, the work will ultimately be published.
3. Social Science Citation Index, accessed on 22 February 2013. Interestingly, the university where I work in Mexico has access to ISI Web of Knowledge but it is limited to a specific period: 1998–2013, which is not useful for my analysis. Given this, I had to access the index through the website of the German university where I was a visiting scholar in Spring 2013 in order to get these data. This is another reason to believe that the Internet, helpful as it is, will not solve most of the problems concerning the international circulation of knowledge.
4. CONICET and the universities are competitive actors in the Argentine scientific and technological research system because researchers have to be appointed to both institutions but receive only one salary, the greater one. That is why the installation of a structure of full-time academics would demand a profound transformation of this system, making it possible for scholars to consolidate the salaries provided by both organizations. The change would represent a significant increase in the income of political scientists working in academia in Argentina and would resolve the customary incompatibilities between the researcher position at CONICET and teaching position at a university.

Bibliography

Abel, R. and Newlin, L. (eds) 2002 *Scholarly Publishing. Books, Journals, Publishers, and Libraries in the Twentieth Century*, New York: Wiley.

Abend, G. 2006 'Styles of Sociological Thought: Sociologies, Epistemologies, and the Mexican and U.S. Quests for Truth', *Social Theory* 24(1): 1–41.

Abraham, I. 2000 'Postcolonial Science, Big Science, and Landscape' in R. Reid and S. Traweek (eds) *Doing Science + Culture*, New York: Routledge.

Acuña, C. 2000 'Entrevista', *PostData* 6: 233–45.

Adelstein, A. and Kugel, I. 2004 *Los Textos Académicos en el Nivel Universitario*, Buenos Aires: Universidad Nacional de General Sarmiento.

Alatas, S. F. 2003 'Academic Dependency and the Global Division of Labour in the Social Science', *Current Sociology* 51(6): 599–613.

Alatas, S. F. 2001 'The Study of the Social Sciences in Developing Societies: Towards an Adequate Conceptualization of Relevance', *Current Sociology* 49(2): 1–19.

Albornoz, M. 2007 'Argentina: Modernidad y Ruptura' in J. Sebastian (ed) *Claves del Desarrollo Científico y Tecnológico de América Latina*, Madrid: Fundación Carolina and Siglo XXI.

Alchourrón, C.E. and Makinson, D. 1982 'On the logic of theory change. Contraction functions and their associated revision function', *Theoria* 48(1): 14–37.

Altamirano, C. and Sarlo B. 1997 *Ensayos Argentinos. De Sarmiento a la Vanguardia*, Buenos Aires: Ariel.

Altamirano, C. and Sarlo B. 1983 *Literatura y Sociedad*, Buenos Aires: Hachette.

Altbach, P. 2007a 'Academic Challenges: The American Professoriate in Comparative Perspective' in A. Welch (ed.) *The Professoriate. Profile of a Profession*, Dordrecht: Springer.

Altbach, P. 2007b 'Empires of Knowledge and Development' in P. Altbach and J. Balán (eds) *World Class Worlwide. Transforming Research Universities in Asia and Latin America*, Baltimore: The Johns Hopkins University Press.

Altbach, P. and Balán, J. (eds) 2007 *World Class Worldwide. Transforming Research Universities in Asia and Latin America*, Baltimore: The Johns Hopkins University Press.

Anderson, W. and Adams, V. 2008 'Pramoedya's chicken: Postcolonial Studies of Technoscience' in E. Hackett, O. Amsterdamska, M. Lynch, and J. Wajcman (eds) *The New Handbook of Science and Technology Studies*, Third Edition, Cambridge, MA: MIT Press.

Araujo, S. 2003 *Universidad, Investigacion e Incentivos. La Cara Oscura*, La Plata, Arg.: Ediciones al Margen.

Baber, Z. 2003 'Provincial Universalism: The Landscape of Knowledge Production in an Era of Globalization', *Current Sociology* 51(6): 614–23.

Baert, P. 2012 'Positioning Theory and Intellectual Interventions', *Journal for the Theory of Social Behavior*, 42(3): 304–24.

210 Bibliography

Baert, P. 2005 *Philosophy of the Social Sciences. Towards Pragmatism*, Cambridge: Polity Press.

Baert, P. and Shipman, A. 2005 'University under siege? Trust and Accountability in the Contemporary Academy', *European Societies* 7(1): 157–85.

Balán, J. and García de Fanelli, A. M. 2002 'El Sector Privado de la Educación Superior' in R. Kent (comp.) *Los Temas Críticos de la Educación Superior en América Latina en los Años Noventa. Estudios Comparativos*, México: FLAC-SO–Chile, Universidad Autónoma de Aguascalientes, and Fondo de Cultura Económica.

Bammel, J. 2012 'Open Letter: Import restrictions on books threaten education, cultural diversity and human rights in Argentina', [Available at http://www.federacioneditores.org/0_Resources/Documentos/ARGENTINA_FINAL.pdf, accessed 20 February 2013].

Barabási, A.-L. and Bonabeau, E. 2003 'Scale–free Networks', *Scientific American* 288: 50–59.

Baranger, D. 2004 *Epistemología y Metodología en la Obra de Pierre Bourdieu*, Buenos Aires: Prometeo Libros.

Barber, B. 1978 *Science and the Social Order*, Westport: Greenwood Press.

Barber, B. (ed.) 1967 *Sociology of Science*, Glencoe: Free Press.

Barnes, B. 1982 *T. S. Kuhn and Social Science*, New York: Columbia University Press.

Barsky, O., Sigal, V., and Dávila, M. (coords) 2004 *Los Desafíos de la Universidad Argentina*, Buenos Aires: Siglo XXI.

Basalla, G. 1967 'The Spread of Western Science', *Science* 156(3775): 611–22.

Bazerman, C. 2000 *Shaping Written Knowledge: The Genre and Activity of the Experimental Article in Science*, http://wac.colostate.edu/books/bazerman_shaping/, accessed 25 June 2013.

Becher, T. and Trowler, P. 2001 *Academic Tribes and Territories. Intellectual Enquiry and the Culture of Disciplines*, Buckingham: The Society for Research into Higher Education and Open University Press.

Beigel, F. (ed) 2010 *Autonomía y dependencia académica. Universidad e investigación científica en un circuito periférico: Chile y Argentina (1950–1980)*, Buenos Aires: Biblos.

Beigel, F., Falero, A., Gandarilla Salgado, J. G., Kohan, N., Landa Vazquez, L., Martins, C. E., Nahon, C., Rodriguez Enriquez, C. and Schorr, M. 2006 *Crítica y Teoría en el Pensamiento Social Latinoamericano*, Buenos Aires: CLACSO.

Beltrán, G. 2005 *Los Intelectuales Liberales. Poder Tradicional y Poder Pragmático en la Argentina Reciente*, Buenos Aires: Eudeba.

Ben-David, J. 1984 *The Scientist's Role in Society: A Comparative Study*, Chicago: Chicago University Press.

Berger, P. and Luckmann, T. 1966 *The Social Construction of Reality*, Middlesex: Penguin.

Bertaux, D. 1981a *Biography and Society. The Life History Approach in the Social Sciences*, Beverly Hills, CA: Sage.

Bertaux, D. 1981b 'From the Life–History Approach to the Transformation of Sociological Practice' in D. Bertaux. *Biography and Society. The Life History Approach in the Social Sciences*, Beverly Hills, CA: Sage.

Bertaux, D. and Bertaux-Wiame, I. 1981 'Life Stories in the Baker's Trade' in D. Bertaux. *Biography and Society. The Life History Approach in the Social Sciences*, Bevery Hills, CA: Sage.

Bertaux, D. and Delcroix, C. 2000 'Case Histories of Families and Social Process: Enriching Sociology' in P. Chamberlayne, J. Bornat, and T. Wengraf (eds) *The Turn to Biographical Methods in Social Science. Comparative Issues and Examples*, London: Routledge.

Bibliography 211

Bertaux, D. and Thompson, P. 1997 *Pathways to Social Class. A Qualitative Approach to Social Mobility*, Oxford: Clarendon Press.

Beverly, J. 1999 *Subalternity and Representation. Arguments in Cultural Theory*, Durham, NC: Duke University Press.

Bielak, A. T., Campbell, A., Pope, S., Schaefer, K., and Shaxson, L. 2008 'From science communication to knowledge brokering: the shift from "science push" to "policy pull"' in D. Cheng, M. Claessens, T. Gascoigne, J. Metcalfe, B. Schiele, and S. Shi (eds) *Communicating science in social contexts: New models, new practices*, Amsterdam: Springer.

Bijker, W. E. 2001 'Understanding Technological Culture through a Constructivist View of Science, Technology, and Society' in S. Cutcliffe and C. Mitcham (eds) *Visions of STS. Counterpoints in science, technology and society studies*, Albany: State University of New York Press.

Bijker, W. E. 1995 *Of Bicycles, Bakelites and Bulbs. Toward a Theory of Sociotechnical Change*, Cambridge, MA: MIT Press.

Blanco, A. 2007 'La Temprana Recepción de Max Weber en la Sociología Argentina (1930–1950)', *Perfiles Latinoamericanos* 30: 9–38.

Blanco, A. 2004 'La Sociología. Una Profesión en Disputa', in F. Nieburg and M. Plotkin (comps) *Intelectuales y Expertos. La Construcción del Conocimiento Social en la Argentina*, Buenos Aires: Paidós.

Blumenfeld-Jones, D. 1995 'Fidelity as a criterion for practicing and evaluating narrative inquiry', *International Journal of Qualitative Research in Education* 8(1): 25–35.

Borón, A. 2006 'Prólogo' in F. López Segrera *Escenarios Mundiales de la Educación Superior. Análisis Global y Estudios de Casos*, Buenos Aires: CLACSO.

Borón, A. 2000 *Tras el Búho de Minerva. Mercado contra Democracia en el Capitalismo de Fin de Siglo*, Buenos Aires: Fondo de Cultura Económica.

Botana, N. 2008 'Presentación de Carlos Strasser, Profesor Emérito de FLACSO', http://www.flacso.org.ar/uploaded_files/Noticias/texto%20presentacion%20 Botana.pdf, accessed 24 June 2013.

Botto, M. 2006 'La concentración y la polarización de la industria editorial' in J. L. de Diego (dir) *Editores y políticas editoriales en Argentina, 1880–2000*, Buenos Aires: Fondo de Cultura Económica.

Bourdieu, P. 2004 *Science of Science and Reflexivity*, Cambridge: Polity.

Bourdieu, P. 2003a *Intelectuales, Política y Poder*, Buenos Aires: Eudeba.

Bourdieu, P. 2003b *Los Usos Sociales de la Ciencia. Por una Sociología Clínica del Campo Científico*, Buenos Aires: Nueva Visión.

Bourdieu, P. 1999a 'The Social Conditions of the International Circulation of Ideas' in R. Shusterman. *Bourdieu: A Critical Reader*, London: Blackwell.

Bourdieu, P. 1999b *The Logic of Practice*, Cambridge: Polity.

Bourdieu, P. 1988 *Homo Academicus*, Cambridge: Polity.

Boutang, Y. M. 2008 *Le Capitalisme Cognitif. La Nouvelle Grande Transformation*, Paris: Editions Amsterdam.

Boyer, E., Altbach, P., and Whitelaw, M. J. 1994 *The Academic Profession. An International Perspective*, Princeton: The Carnegie Foundation for the Advancement of Teaching.

Bowker, G. 2005 *Memory Practices in the Science*, Cambridge, MA: MIT Press.

Brink, P. and Wood, M. (eds) 1998 *Advanced Design in Nursuring Research*, Thousand Oaks, CA: Sage.

Brown, S. D. and Capdevila, R. 1999 'Perpetuum mobile: *substance, force and the sociology of translation*' in J. Law and J. Hassard (eds) *Actor-Network Theory and After*, London: Wiley-Blackwell.

Bryson, C. and Barnes, N. 2000 'The Casualisation of Employment in Higher Education in the United Kingdom' in M. Tight (ed.) *Academic Work and Life:*

212 Bibliography

What It Is to Be an Academic, and How This Is Changing, Amsterdam: Elsevier Science.

Brubaker, R. 1993 'Social Theory as Habitus' in C. Calhoum, E. LiPuma, and M. Postone (eds) *Bourdieu: Critical Perspectives*, Chicago: The Univesity of Chicago Press.

Bucchi, M. and Neresini, F. 2008 'Science and Public Participation' in E. Hackett, O. Amsterdamska, M. Lynch, and J. Wajcman (eds) *The New Handbook of Science and Technology Studies*, Third Edition, Cambridge, MA: MIT Press.

Buchbinder, P. 2004 *Historia de las Universidades Argentinas*, Buenos Aires: Sudamericana.

Bulcourf, P. and D' Alessandro, M. 2003 'La Ciencia Política en la Argentina' in J. Pinto (comp.) *Introducción a la Ciencia Política*, Buenos Aires: Eudeba.

Bulcourf, P. and D' Alessandro, M. 2002 'La Ciencia Política en la Argentina. Desde sus Comienzos hasta los Años 80', *Revista de Ciencias Sociales* 13: 139–230.

Bunge, M. 2000 *La Investigación Científica*, México: Siglo XXI.

Bunge, M. 1979 'Philosophical Inputs and Outputs of Technology' in G. Bugliarello and D. B. Doner (eds) *The History of Philosophy and Technology*, Urbana: University of Illinois Press.

Burawoy, M. 2008 'Reojoinder: For a Subaltern Global Sociology', *Current Sociology* 56(3): 435–44.

Burke, P. 2012 *A Social History of Knowledge. Volume II: From the Encyclopaedia to Wikipedia*, Cambridge: Polity Press.

Burke, P. 2002 *A Social History of Knowledge. From Gutenberg to Diderot*, Cambridge: Polity Press.

Busch, L. 2011 *Standards. Recipes for Reality*, Cambridge MA: MIT Press.

Bustamante, E. (coord.) 2003 *Hacia un Nuevo Sistema Mundial de Comunicación. Las Industrias Culturales en la Era Digital*, Barcelona: Gedisa.

Cabral, R. 2006 'International Politics and the Development of the Exact Sciences in Latin America' in J. J. Saldaña (ed.) *Science in Latin America*, Austin: University of Texas Press.

Caffarella, R.S. and Barnett, B.G. 2000 'Teaching Doctoral Students to Become Scholarly Writers: The Importance of Giving and Receiving Critiques', *Studies in Higher Education* 25(1): 39–52.

Calhoun, C., LiPuma, E., and Postone, M. (eds) 1993 *Bourdieu: Critical Perspectives*, Chicago, IL: The University of Chicago Press.

Callon, M. 1992. 'The Dynamics of Techno-economic Networks' in R. Coombs, P. Saviotti, and V. Walsh (eds) *Technical Change and Company Strategies*, London: Academic Press.

Callon, M. 1986 'Some elements of a Sociology of Translation: Domestication of the Scallops and the Fishermen of St. Brieuc Bay' in J. Law (ed.) *Power, Action, and Belief: A New Sociology of Knowledge?*, Keele: Sociological Review Monograph.

Callon, M. and Latour, B. 1992 'Don't Throw the Baby Out with the Bath School! A Reply to Collins and Yearly' in A. Pickering (ed.) *Science as Practice and Culture*, Chicago, IL: University of Chicago Press.

Camargo, A. A. 1981 'The Actor and the System: Trajectory of the Brazilian Political Elites' in D. Bertaux *Biography and Society. The Life History Approach in the Social Sciences*, Beverly Hills, CA: Sage.

Camic, C. 1995 'Three Departments in Search of a Discipline: Localism and Interdisciplinary Interaction in American Sociology, 1890–1940', *Social Research* 62: 1003–33.

Camic, C. and Gross, N. 2001 'The New Sociology of Ideas' in J. R. Blau (ed.) *Blackwell Companion to Sociology*, London: Blackwell.

Bibliography 213

Camic, C., Gross, N., and Lamont, M. (eds) 2011 *Social Knowledge in the Making*, Chicago, IL: The University of Chicago Press.

Camou, A. 1997 'Los Consejeros del Príncipe. 'Saber Técnico y Política en los Procesos de Reforma Económica en América Latina', *Revista Nueva Sociedad* 152: 54–68.

Campbell, R. A. 2003 'Preparing the Next Generation of Scientists: The Social Process of Managing Students', *Social Studies of Science* 33: 897–927.

Canagarajah, A. S. 2002 *A Geopolitics of Academic Writing*, Pittsburgh, PA: University of Pittsburgh Press.

Cardoso, F. H. and Falleto, E. 1973 *Dependency and Development in Latin America*, Berkeley, CA: UC Berkeley University Press.

Carelli Lynch, G. 2013 'La desigualdad entre Norte y Sur también divide el mapa editorial', *Clarín* 3 March [Available at http://www.clarin.com/sociedad/desigualdad-Norte-Sur-divide-editorial_0_875912524.html, accessed 3 March 2013].

Carnap, R., Hahn, H., and Neurath, O. 2003 'The Scientific Conception of the World: The Vienna Circle' in R. Scharff and V. Dusek (eds) *Philosophy of Technology: The Technological Condition. An Anthology*, New York: Blackwell.

Castro-Gómez, S. 2007 'Decolonizar la Universidad. La Hybris del Punto Cero y el Dialogo de Saberes' in S. Castro-Gómez and R. Grosfoguel (eds) *El Giro Decolonial: Reflexiones para una Diversidad Epistémica Más Allá del Capitalismo Global*, Bogotá: Siglo del Hombre Editores; Universidad Central, Instituto de Estudios Sociales Contemporáneos, Pontificia Universidad Javeriana, and Instituto Pensar.

Castro-Gómez, S. 2003 'Ciencias Sociales, Violencia epistémico y el Problema de la "Invención del Otro"' in E. Lander (comp.) *La Colonialidad del Saber: Eurocentrismo y Ciencias Sociales. Perspectivas Latinoamericanas*, Buenos Aires: CLACSO.

Castro-Gómez, S. and Grosfoguel, R. 2007 *El Giro Decolonial: Reflexiones para una Diversidad Epistémica Más Allá del Capitalismo Global*, Bogotá: Siglo del Hombre Editores; Universidad Central, Instituto de Estudios Sociales Contemporáneos, Pontificia Universidad Javeriana, and Instituto Pensar.

Castro-Gómez, S. and Mendieta, E. (coords) 1998 *Teorías sin Disciplina. Latinoamericanismo, Poscolonialidad y Globalización en Debate*, México: Porrúa.

Cavarozzi, M. 2006 *Autoritarismo y Democracia (1955–2006)*, Buenos Aires: Ariel.

CEDES (Centro de Estudios sobre el Estado y la Sociedad) 2007 'Round Table: CEDES' 30th Anniversary', http://www.cedes.org/ingles/institucional6.php, accessed 24 June 2013.

Centro de Estudios para la Producción 2005 *La Industria del Libro en Argentina*, Buenos Aires: Ministerio de Economía, http://www.buenosaires.gob.ar/areas/produccion/industrias/observatorio/documentos/libro_cep.doc, accessed 24 June 2013.

Ceriotto, L. 2012 'El 78 por ciento de los libros que se venden en el país son importados', *Clarín* 27 March 2012.

Cerutti Guldberg, H. 2000 'Perspectivas y Nuevos Horizontes para las Ciencias Sociales en América Latina' in J. Maerk and M. Cabrolie (coords) *¿Existe una Epistemologia Latinoamericana?*, México: Universidad de Quintana Roo and Plaza y Valdés.

Cetto A. M. and Hillerud K. I. (eds) 1995 *Publicaciones Científicas en América Latina*, México: Fondo de Cultura Económica.

Chakrabarty, D. 1992 'Postcoloniality and the Artifice of History: Who Speaks for "Indian" Pasts?', *Representations* 37: 1–26.

214   Bibliography

Chernya, L., Sierra, J., and Snyder, R. 2012 'Globalization, Money, and the Social Science Profession in Latin America', LASAForum 43(4): 3–6.

Chew, M. 2005 'Academic Boundary Work in Non-Western Academies. A Comparative Analysis of the Philosophy Discipline in Modern China and Japan', *International Sociology* 20(4): 530–59.

Chew, M. 2000 'Politics and Patterns of Developing Indigenous Knowledge under Western Disciplinary Compartmentalization: The Case of Philosophical Schools in Modern China and Japan' in M. Kusch (ed.) *The Sociology of Philosophical Knowledge*, London: Kluwer Academic Publishers.

Chiroleu, A. 2005 'La Educación Superior en la agenda de gobierno argentina en veinte años de democracia (1983–2003)' in E. Rinesi, G. Soprano and C. Suasnábar (comps) *Universidad: Reformas y Destinos. Dilemas de la Educación Superior en la Argentina y el Brasil*, Buenos Aires: Prometeo and Universidad Nacional de General Sarmiento.

Clark, B. R. 1987 *The Academic Life. Small Worlds, Different Worlds*, Princeton, NJ: The Carnegie Foundation for the Advancement of Teaching.

Clark, B. R. 1977 *Academic Power in Italy. Bureaucracy and Oligarchy in a National University System*, Chicago, IL: The University of Chicago Press.

Clark, W. 2006 *Academic Charisma and the Origins of the Research University*, Chicago, IL: The University of Chicago Press.

Clarke, A. 1997 'A Social World Research Adventure: The Case of Reproductive Science' in A.C. Strauss and J. Corbin (eds) *Grounded Theory in Practice*, London: Sage.

Clarke, A. 1991 'Social World/Arenas Theory as Organizational Theory' in D. Maines (ed.) *Social Organization and Social Process. Essays in Honor of Anselm Strauss*, New York: A. de Gruyter.

Clarke, A. and Star, S. L. 2008 'The Social Worlds Frameworks: A Theory/Methods Package' in E. Hackett, O. Amsterdamska, M. Lynch, and J. Wajcman (eds) *The New Handbook of Science and Technology Studies*, Third Edition, Cambridge, MA: MIT Press.

Clemens, E. S., Powell, W. W., McIlwaine, K., and Okamoto, D. 1995 'Careers in Print: Books, Journals, and Scholarly Reputations', *The American Journal of Sociology* 101(2): 433–94.

Coatsworth, J. H. 2006 'Estructuras, dotación de factores e instituciones en la historia económica de América Latina', *Desarrollo Económico* 46(182): 155–82.

Cole, S. 1983 'The Hierarchy of the Sciences?', *American Journal of Sociology* 89(1): 111–9.

Collins, H. M. 1985 *Changing Order: Replication and Induction in Scientific Practice*, Beverly Hills and London: Sage.

Collins, H. M. and Yearly, S. 1992a 'Epistemological Chicken' in A. Pickering (ed.) *Science as Practice and Culture*, Chicago, IL: The University of Chicago Press.

Collins, H. M. and Yearly, S. 1992b 'Journey into Space' in A. Pickering (ed.) *Science as Practice and Culture*, Chicago, IL: The University of Chicago Press.

Comaroff, J. and Comaroff, J. 2012 'Theory from the South: Or, how Euro-America is Evolving Toward Africa', *Anthropological Forum* 22(2): 113–31.

Connell, R. W. 2007 *Southern Theory. Social Science and the Global Dynamics of Knowledge*, Cambridge: Polity Press.

Connell, R. W. and Wood, J. 2005 'The Global Connections of Intellectual Workers. An Australian Study', *International Sociology* 20(1): 5–26.

Connell, R. W. and Wood, J. 2002 'Globalization and scientific labour: patterns in a life-history study of intellectual workers in the periphery', *Journal of Sociology* 38(2): 167–90.

Consejo de Decanos de las Facultades de Ciencias Sociales y Humanas de Universidades Nacionales 2005 *Crisis de las Ciencias Sociales de la Argentina en Crisis*, Buenos Aires: Prometeo.

Bibliography   215

Coraggio, J. L. and Vispo, A. (coords) 2001 *Contribución al Estudio del Sistema Universitario Argentino*, Buenos Aires: Miño y Dávila and Consejo Universitario Nacional.

Coronil, F. 2003 'Naturaleza del Poscolonialismo: Del Eurocentrismo al Globocentrismo' in E. Lander (comp.) *La Colonialidad del Saber: Eurocentrismo y Ciencias Sociales. Perspectivas Latinoamericanas*, Buenos Aires: CLACSO.

Coronil, F. 1998 'Más allá del Occidentalismo: Hacia Categorías Neohistóricas No-Imperialistas' in S. Castro-Gómez and E. Mendieta (coords) *Teorías sin Disciplina. Latinoamericanismo, Poscolonialidad y Globalización en Debate*, México: Porrúa.

Coser, L. A. 1975 'Publishers as Gatekeepers of Ideas', *Annals of the American Academy of Political Science* 421(5): 14–22.

Crane, D. 1972 *Invisible Colleges*, Chicago, IL: University of Chicago Press.

Cubo de Severino, L. (coord.) 2007 *Los Textos de la Ciencia. Principales Clases del Discurso Académico-Científico*, Córdoba, Arg.: Comunicarte.

Cutcliffe, S. and Mitcham, C. (eds) 2001 *Visions of STS. Counterpoints in science, technology and society studies*, Albany: State University of New York Press.

Cueto, M. 2006 'Excellence in Twentieth-century Biomedical Science' in J. J. Saldaña (ed.) *Science in Latin America*, Austin: University of Texas Press.

Dahl, R. 1989 La *Poliarquía. Participación y oposición*, Buenos Aires: Rei.

Dal Fiore, F. 2007 'Communities Versus Networks: The Implications on Innovations and Social Change', *American Behavioral Scientist* 50(7): 857–66.

De Diego, J. L. (dir.) 2006 *Editores y Políticas Editoriales en Argentina, 1880–2000*, Buenos Aires: Fondo de Cultura Económica.

De Sagastizábal, L. 2005 'Estudio comparativo de las editoriales universitarias de América latina y el Caribe', Instituto Internacional de la UNESCO para la Educación Superior en América Latina y el Caribe, http://unesdoc.unesco.org/images/0014/001494/149476so.pdf , accessed 24 June 2013.

De Sagastizábal L. and Esteves Fros, F. (comps) *El Mundo de la Edición de Libros*, Buenos Aires: Paidós.

Del Bello, J. C., Barsky, O., and Gimenez, G. 2007 *La Universidad Privada Argentina*, Buenos Aires: Libros del Zorzal.

Delamont, S. and Atkinson, P. 2001 'Doctoring Uncertainty: Mastering Craft Knowledge', *Social Studies of Science* 31(1): 87–107.

Delanty, G. 2002 *Challenging Knowledge. The University in the Knowledge Society*, Buckingham: Open University Press.

Delbourgo, J. 2011 'Sir Hans Sloane's Milk Chocolate and the Whole History of the Cacao', *Social Text* 29(1): 71–101.

Delbourgo, J. and Dew, N. (eds) 2008 *Science and Empire in the Atlantic World*, New York: Routledge.

Delpar, H. 2007 *Looking South: The Evolution of Latin Americanist Scholarship in the United States, 1850–1975*, Tuscaloosa: University Alabama Press.

Demir, I. 2011 'Lost in Translation? Try Second Language Learning: Understanding Movements of Ideas and Practices across Time and Space', *Journal of Historical Sociology* 24(1): 9–26.

Deneef, A. L. and Goodwin, C. 2007 *The Academic's Handbook*, Third Edition, Durham, NC: Duke University Press.

Denzin, N. K. (1970) *Sociological Methods: a Source Book*, Chicago, IL: Aldine Publishing Company.

Devés Valdés, E. 2003 *El Pensamiento Latinoamericano en el Siglo XX. Tomo 2: Desde la CEPAL al Neoliberalismo (1950–1990)*, Buenos Aires: Biblos.

Devés Valdés, E. 2000 *El Pensamiento Latinoamericano en el Siglo XX. Tomo 1: Del Ariel de Rodó a la CEPAL (1900–1950)*, Buenos Aires: Biblos.

De Gregori, T. 1978 'Technology and Economic Dependency: An Institutional Assessment', *Journal of Economic Issues* 12(2): 467–76.

216 Bibliography

Diani, M. 1995 *Green Networks: A Structural Analysis of the Italian Environmental Movement*, Edinburgh: Edinburgh University Press.

Diegues, M. and Wood, B. (eds) 1967 *Social Sciences in Latin America*, New York and London: Columbia University Press.

Dieterech, H. 2000 *La Crisis de los Intelectuales. Crisis en las Ciencias Sociales. La Tercera Vía en América Latina. Identidad Nacional y Globalización*, Buenos Aires: Editorial 21.

Doing, P. 2008 'Give Me a Laboratory and I will Rise a Discipline: The Past, Present, and Future Politics of Laboratoy Studies in STS', in E. Hackett, O. Amsterdamska, M. Lynch, and J. Wajcman (eds) *The New Handbook of Science and Technology Studies*, Third Edition, Cambridge, MA: MIT Press.

Dollard, J. 1935 *Criteria for the Life History*, New Haven, CT: Yale University Press.

Dos Santos, T. 1971 *La Estructura de la Dependencia*, Boston, MA: Extending Horizons.

Duffard, M.E. 2012 'Las universidades K: poca oferta académica y muchos contratos', *Clarin* 29 July, [Available at http://www.clarin.com/politica/universidades-poca-oferta-academica-contratos_0_745725538.html, accessed 15 July 2013].

Duque, R. B., Ynalvez, M., Sooryamoorthy, R., Mbatia, P. Dzorgbo, D-B S., and Shrum, W. 2005 'Collaboration Paradox: Scientific Productivity, the Internet, and Problems of Research in Developing Areas', *Social Studies of Science* 35: 755–85.

Dussel, E. 1995 *The Invention of the Americas: Eclipse of "The Other" and the Myth of Modernity*, New York: Continuum.

Economist, The 2011 'Keep Out', *The Economist* 24 September [Available at http://www.economist.com/node/21530136, accessed 20 February 2013]

Epstein, S. 1996 *Impure Science: AIDS, Activism and the Politics of Knowledge*, Berkeley: University of California Press.

Erickson, M. 2005 *Science, Culture and Society. Understanding Science in the 21st Century*, Cambridge, MA: Polity Press.

Evans, R. and Collins, H. 2008 'Expertise: From Attribute to Attribution and Back Again?', in E. Hackett, O. Amsterdamska, M. Lynch, and J. Wajcman (eds) *The New Handbook of Science and Technology Studies*, Third Edition, Cambridge, MA: MIT Press.

Featherstone, M. and Venn, C. 2006 'Problematizing Global Knowledge and the New Enciclopaedia Project', *Theory, Culture & Society* 23(2–3): 1–20.

Fernández, A. 2007 'Discurso de Apertura, 8vo Congreso Argentino de Ciencia Política', http://www.saap.org.ar/esp/page.php?subsec=congresos&page=congr esos-saap/octavo&data=VIII/discurso, accessed 25 June 2013.

Fernández, A. (ed.) 2002a *La Ciencia Política en Argentina. Dos Siglos de Historia*, Buenos Aires: Biebel.

Fernández, A. 2002b 'El Desarrollo de la Ciencia Política en la Argentina' in A. Fernández (ed.) *La Ciencia Política en Argentina. Dos Siglos de Historia*, Buenos Aires: Biebel.

Fernández, M. and Barbosa, S. 1996 *Tendencias Sociales y Políticas Contemporáneas. Perspectivas y Debates*, Santa Fé: Fundación Universidad a Distancia 'Hernandarias'.

Fernández Lamarra, N. 2007 *Educación Superior y Calidad en América Latina y Argentina. Los Procesos de Evaluación y Acreditación*, Buenos Aires: Universidad Nacional de Tres de Febrero and UNESCO.

Ferraroti, F. 2003 *On the Science of Uncertainty: The Biographical Method in Social Research*, Lanham, MD: Lexington Books.

Ferreira Furtado, J. 2008 'Tropical Empiricism: Making Medical Knowledge in Colonial Brazil' in J. Delbourgo and N. Dew (eds) *Science and Empire in the Atlantic World*, New York: Routledge.

Bibliography 217

Finkin, M. 2007 'The Tenure System' in A. L. Deneef, and C. D. Goodwin (eds) *The Academic's Handbook*, Third Edition, Durham, NC: Duke University Press.

Fischer-Rosenthal, W. 2000 'Biographical Work and Biographical Structuring in Present-day Societies' in P. Chamberlayne, J. Bornat, and T. Wengraf (eds) *The Turn to Biographical Methods in Social Science. Comparative Issues and Examples*, London: Routledge.

Florez-Florez, J. 2007 'Lectura No Eurocentrica de los Movimientos Sociales Latinoamericanos. Las Claves Analiticas del Proyecto Modernidad/Colonialidad' in S. Castro-Gomez, S. and R. Grosfoguel (eds) *El Giro Decolonial: Reflexiones para una Diversidad Epistémica Más Allá del Capitalismo Global*. Bogotá: Siglo del Hombre Editores; Universidad Central, Instituto de Estudios Sociales Contemporáneos, Pontificia Universidad Javeriana, and Instituto Pensar.

Forero Pineda, C. 2002 'Partnership on the New World Science Stage', paper presented at the International Seminar on North-South and South-South Research Partnership, Cartagena de Indias, Colombia, http://www.kfpe.ch/download/columbia/Clemente_Forero_e.pdf, accessed 25 June 2013.

Foray, D. 2006 *The Economics of Knowledge*, Cambridge, MA: MIT Press.

Forster, R., García, G., González, H., Lewkowickz, I., and Tatian, D. 2004 *Qué Piensan los que Piensan. La Transmision de Conocimiento,* Buenos Aires: Altamira.

Fortes, J. and Lomnitz, L. 2005 *La Formación del Científico en México. Adquiriendo una Nueva Identidad*, México: Siglo XXI and Universidad Nacional Autónoma de México.

Foucault, M. 1979 *Discipline and Punish*, New York: Vintage Books.

Fox, N. 2011 'Boundary Objects, Social Meanings and the Success of New Technologies', *Sociology* 45(1): 70–85.

Frondizi, R. 2005 *La Universidad en un Mundo de Tensiones. Misión de las Universidades en América Latina*, Buenos Aires: Eudeba.

Fujimura, J. H. 2000 'Transnational Genomics: Transgressing the Boundary Between the "Modern/West" and the "Premodern/East"' in R. Reid and S. Traweek (eds) *Doing Science + Culture*, New York: Routledge.

Fujimura, J. H. 1992 'Crafting Science: Standardized Packages, Boundary Objects, and "Translation"' in A. Pickering (ed) *Science as Practice and Culture*, Chicago, IL: The University of Chicago Press.

Gadamer, H. G. 1998 *Verdad y Método*. Salamanca: Sígueme.

Gagnon, N. 1981 'On the Analysis of Life Accounts' in D. Bertaux *Biography and Society. The Life History Approach in the Social Sciences*, Beverly Hills, CA: Sage.

Gaillard, J. 1994 'The Behaviour of Scientists and Scientific Communities' in J. J. Salomón, F. Sagasti, and C. Sachs-Jeantet (eds) *The Uncertain Question. Science, Technology, and Development*, Tokyo: United Nations University Press.

Gaillard, J., Krishna, V. V., and Waast, R. (eds) 1997a. *Scientific Communities in the Developing World*, New Delhi: Sage.

Gaillard, J., Krishna, V. V., and Waast, R. 1997b 'Introduction: Scientific Communities in the Developing World' in J. J. Gaillard, V. Krishna, and R. Waast. (eds) *Scientific Communities in the Developing World*, New Delhi: Sage.

Galceran Huguet, M. 2007 'Reflexiones sobre la Reforma de la Universidad en el Capistalismo Cognitivo', *Nómadas* 27: 86–97.

Galison, P. 2001 'Material Culture, Theoretical Culture, and Delocalization' in J. W. Scott and D. Keates (eds) *Schools of Thought. Twenty-Five Years of Interpretive Social Science*, Princeton, NJ: Princeton University Press.

Galison, P. 1997 *Image and Logic. A Material Culture of Microphysics*, Chicago, IL: University of Chicago Press.

Galison, P. 1987 *How Experiments End*, Chicago, IL: University of Chicago Press.

218 Bibliography

Gambetta, D. 1998 'Concatenation of Mechanisms' in P. Hedström and R. Swedberg (eds) *Social Mechanisms. An Analytical Approach to Social Theory*, Cambridge: Cambridge University Press.

Gandarilla Salgado, J. G. (comp) 2007 *Reestructuración de la Universidad y del Conocimiento*, México: Universidad Nacional Autónoma de México.

Garcés, F. 2007 'Las Políticas del Conocimiento y la Colonialidad Lingüística y Epistémica' in S. Castro-Gómez and R. Grosfoguel (eds) *El Giro Decolonial: Reflexiones para una Diversidad Epistémica Más Allá del Capitalismo Global*, Bogotá: Siglo del Hombre Editores; Universidad Central, Instituto de Estudios Sociales Contemporáneos, Pontificia Universidad Javeriana, and Instituto Pensar.

García de Fanelli, A. 2009 'La movilidad académica y estudiantil: reflexiones sobre el caso argentino', in S. Didou Aupetit and E. Gérard (eds.) *Fuga de cerebros, movilidad académica, redes científicas. Perspectivas latinoamericanas*, México: IESALC-CINVESTAV-IRD.

García de Fanelli, A. 2007 'The Challenge of Building Research Universities in Middle-Income Countries: The Case of the University of Buenos Aires' in P. Altbach and J. Balán (eds) *World Class Worldwide. Transforming Research Universities in Asia and Latin America*, Baltimore, MD: The Johns Hopkins University Press.

García de Fanelli, A. 2005 *Universidad, Organización e Incentivos. Desafíos de la Política de Financiamiento frente a la Complejidad Institucional*, Buenos Aires: Miño y Dávila y Fundación OSDE.

Garciadiego Dantan, A. 1998 'El Editor de Publicaciones Académicas ¿Una Especie en Peligro de Extinción?' in A. M. Cetto and O. Alonso (comps) *Revistas Científicas en América Latina / Scientific Journals in Latin America*, México: Fondo de Cultura Económica.

Gentili, P. and Levy, B. 2005 *Espacio Público y Privatización del Conocimiento. Estudios sobre Políticas Universitarias en América Latina*, Buenos Aires: CLACSO.

George, A. L. and Bennett, A. 2005 *Case Studies and Theory Development in the Social Science*, Cambridge, MA: MIT Press.

Gerson, E. 1983 'Scientific Work and Social World', *Knowledge: Creation, Diffusion, Utilization* 4(3): 357–77.

Germani, A. A. 2004 *Gino Germani. Del Antifascismo a la Sociología*, Buenos Aires: Taurus.

Giardinelli, M. 2004 *El País y sus Intelectuales. Historia de un Desencanto*, Buenos Aires: Capital Intelectual.

Giddens, A. 1990 *Central Problems in Social Theory. Action, Structure and Contradiction in Social Análisis*, Hong Kong: MacMillan.

Gieryn T. F. 1999 *Cultural Boundaries of Science: Credibility on the Line*, Chicago, IL: University of Chicago Press.

Gieryn, T. F. 1995 'Boundaries of science' in S. Jasanoff, G. Markle, J. Petersen, and T. Pinch (eds) *Handbook of Science and Technology Studies*, Thousand Oaks, CA: Sage.

Gläser, J. 2003 'What Internet Use Does and Does Not Change in Scientific Communities', *Science Studies* 16(1): 38–51.

Glaser, B. G. and Strauss, A. 1967 *The Discovery of Grounded Theory: Strategies for Qualitative Research*, Chicago, IL: Aldine.

Golinski, J. 2005 *Making Natural Knowledge. Constructivism and the History of Science*, Chicago, IL: University of Chicago Press.

Gómez-Escalonilla, G. 2003 'Libro y Entorno Digital: un Encuentro de Futuro' in E. Bustamente (ed) *Hacia un Nuevo Sistema Mundial de Comunicación. Las Industrias Culturales en la Era Digital*, Barcelona: Gedisa.

Bibliography 219

González, H. 2000 *Historia Crítica de la Sociología Argentina. Los Raros, los Clásicos, los Científicos, los Discrepantes*, Buenos Aires: Colihue.

Goodsell, C. T. 1988 *The Social Meaning of Civic Space. Studying Political Authority through Architecture*, Lawrence: University Press of Kansas.

Gray, C. H. 2002 *Cyborg Citizen: Politics in a Posthuman Age*, New York: Routledge.

Gross, A., Harmon, J., and Reidy, M. 2002 *Communicating Science. The Scientific Article from the 17th Century to the Present*, Oxford: Oxford University Press.

Gross, N. and Fleming, C. 2011 'Academic Conferences and the Making of Philosophical Knowledge', in C. Camic, N. Gross, and M. Lamont. (eds) *Social Knowledge in the Making*, Chicago, IL: The University of Chicago Press.

Grüner, E. 2012 'La insensatez de la UBA ante sus maestros', *Clarín* 28 August [Available at http://www.clarin.com/opinion/insensatez-UBA-maestros_0_763723690.html, accessed 20 February 2013].

Guilhot, N. 2007 'Reforming the World: George Soros, Global Capitalism and the Philanthropic Management of the Social Sciences', *Critical Sociology* (33): 447–77.

Gunter, F. 1967 *Capitalismo y Subdesarrollo en América Latina*, New York: Monthly Review Press.

Hackett, E., Amsterdamska, O., Lynch, M., and Wajcman, J. (eds) 2008 *The New Handbook of Science and Technology Studies*, Third Edition, Cambridge, MA: MIT Press.

Hacking, I. 1999 *The Social Construction of What?*, Cambridge, MA: Harvard University Press.

Hammersley, M. and Atkinson, P. 1989 *Ethnography: Principles in Practice*, London: Routledge.

Hanchard, M. 2003 'Acts of Misrecognition: Transnational Black Politics, Anti-Imperialism, and the Ethnocentrisms of Pierre Bourdieu and Loïc Wacquant', *Theory, Culture & Society* 20(4): 5–29.

Haraway, D. 2004 *The Haraway Reader*, New York: Routledge.

Haraway, D. 1989 *Primate Visions: Gender, Race, and Nature in the World of Modern Science*, New York: Routledge.

Harding, S. 1998 *Is Science Multicultural? Postcolonialisms, Feminisms, and Epistemologies*, Bloomington: Indiana University Press.

Harper, R., Mahar, C., and Wilkes, C. 1990 *An Introduction to the Work of Pierre Bourdieu. The Practice of Theory*, London: MacMillan.

Hedström, P. and Swedberg, R. (eds) 1998 *Social Mechanisms. An Analytical Approach to Social Theory*, Cambridge: Cambridge University Press.

Heilbron, J. 1999 'Towards a Sociology of Translation. Book Translation as a Cultural World-System', *European Journal of Social Theory* 2(4): 429–44.

Helmke, G. and Sanders, M. 2006 'Modeling Motivations: A Method for Inferring Judicial Goals from Behavior', *The Journal of Politics* 68:867–78.

Henderson, A. 2002 'The Growth of Printed Literature in the Twentieth Century' in R. Abel and L. Newlin (eds) *Scholarly Publishing. Books, Journals, Publishers, and Libraries in the Twentieth Century*, New York: Wiley.

Henderson, K. 1999 *On Line and On Paper: Visual Representations, Visual Culture, and Computer Graphics in Design Engineering*, Cambridge, MA: MIT Press.

Henry, L, Mohan, G., and Yanacopulos, H. 2004 'Networks as Transnational Agents of Development', *Third World Quarterly* 25(5): 839–55.

Hermanowicz, J. C. 2009 *Lives in Science. How Institutions Affect Academic Careers*, Chicago, IL: The University of Chicago Press.

Hermanowicz, J. C. 2007 'Argument and Outline for the Sociology of Scientific (and Other) Careers', *Social Studies of Science* 37: 625–46.

220 Bibliography

Hermanowicz, J. C. 1998 *The Stars are not Enough. Scientists: Their Passions and Professions*, Chicago, IL: The University of Chicago Press.

Hess, D., Breyman, S., Campbell, N., and Martin, B. 2008 'Science, Technology, and Social Movements' in E. Hackett, O. Amsterdamska, M. Lynch, and J. Wajcman (Eds) *The New Handbook of Science and Technology Studies*, Third Edition, Cambridge, MA: MIT Press.

Hill, K. Q. and Leighley J. E. 2005 'Science, Political Science, and the American Journal of Political Science' in K. Renwick Monroe (ed.) *Perestroika! The Raucous Rebellion in Political Science*, New Haven, CT: Yale University Press.

Hitchin, L. and Maksymiw, W. 2012 'Story spaces: a methodological contribution', *New Technology, Work and Employment* 27(1): 65–77.

Hobert, R. 2012 'Apuntes para la comprensión del clientelismo académico', *La Revista del CCC*, 14/15 [Available at http://www.centrocultural.coop/revista/exportarpdf.php?id=301, accessed 1 March 2013].

Hobert, R. 2007 'Entre el Portazo y la Zanahoria. La Docencia por el Honor en la UBA', *Revista Apuntes de Investigacion del Centro de Estudios en Cultura y Politica*, 12, http://webiigg.sociales.uba.ar/globalizacioncultural/publicaciones/pdf/hobert/ad-honorem-hobert.pdf, accessed 24 June 2013.

Hodder, I. 2012 *Entangled. An Archaeology of the Relationships between Humans and Things*, Singapore: Wiley-Blackwell.

Hofmeister, W. and Mansilla, H. C. F. (eds) 2003 *Intelectuales y Política en América Latina. El Desencantamiento del Espíritu Crítico*, Rosario: Homo Sapiens.

Holstein, J. A., and Gubrium, J. F. 2002 'Active Interviewing' in D. Weinberg (ed) *Qualitative Research Methods*, Oxford: Blackwell.

Honigmann, J. 1970 'Sampling in Ethnographic Field Work', in R. Naroll and R. Cohen (eds) *A Handbook of Method in Cultural Anthropology*, New York: Natural History Press.

Horowitz, I. L. 1970 *Sociological Self-Images: A Collective Portrait*, Oxford: Pergamon.

Iaryczower, M., Spiller, P. T., and Tommasi, M. 2002 'Judicial Independence in Unstable Environments, Argentina 1935–1998', *American Journal of Political Science* 46(4): 699–716.

Ihde, D. 2003a *Bodies in Technology*, Minneapolis: University of Minnesota Press.

Ihde, D. 2003b 'A Phenomenology of Technics' in R. Scharff and V. Dusek (eds) *Philosophy of Technology: The Technological Condition. An Anthology*, New York: Blackwell.

Ihde, D. 1998 *Expanding Hermeneutics. Visualism in Science*, Evanston, IL: Northwestern University Press.

Ihde, D. 1991 *Instrumental Realism. The Interface between Philosophy of Science and Philosophy of Technology*, Bloomington: Indiana University Press.

Invernizzi, H. 2005 *"Los Libros son Tuyos". Políticos, Académicos y Militares: La Dictadura en Eudeba*, Buenos Aires: Eudeba.

Invernizzi, H. and Gociol, J. 2003 *Un Golpe a los Libros. Represión a la Cultura durante la Última Dictadura Militar*, Buenos Aires: Eudeba.

Izaguirre, I. 2005 'Acerca de un Maestro. Gino Germani, Fundador de la Sociología Argentina', *Sociologias* 7(14): 492–503.

Jacob, M. 2008 'Science, Global Capitalism, and the State', in J. Delbourgo and N. Dew (eds) *Science and Empire in the Atlantic World*, New York: Routledge.

Jamison, A. 1994 'Western Science in perspective and the Search for Alternatives' in J. J. Salomón, F. Sagasti, and C. Sachs-Jeantet (eds) *The Uncertain Question. Science, Techonology, and Development,* Tokyo: United Nations University Press.

Bibliography 221

Jasanoff, S. 2008 'Making Order: Law and Science in Action', in E. Hackett, O. Amsterdamska, M. Lynch, and J. Wajcman (eds) *The New Handbook of Science and Technology Studies*, Third Edition, Cambridge, MA: MIT Press.

Jasanoff, S. 1995 *Science at the Bar: Law, Science, and Technology in America*, Cambridge, MA: Harvard University Press.

Jenkings, R. 1992 *Pierre Bourdieu*, London: Routledge.

Kandel, V. 2002 'El Estudio Académico de la Ciencia Política. El caso de la Universidad de Buenos Aires' in A. Fernández (ed.) *La Ciencia Política en Argentina. Dos Siglos de Historia*, Buenos Aires: Biebel.

Kasza, G. 2005 'Quantitative Methods. Reflections on the Files of Recent Job Applicants' in K. Renwick Monroe (ed.) *Perestroika. The Raucous Rebellion in Political Science*, New Haven, CT: Yale University Press.

Kauppi, N. and Erkkilä, T. 2011 'The Struggle Over Global Higher Education: Actors, Institutions, and Practices', *International Political Sociology* 5: 314–26.

Keating, P., Cambrosio, A., and MacKenzie, M. 1991 'The Tools of the Discipline: Standards, Models and Measures in the Affinity-Avidity Controversy in Immunology' in A. Clarke and J. Fujimura (eds) *The Right Tools for the Job. At Work in Twentieth-Century Life Sciences*, Princeton, NJ: Princeton University Press.

Keim, W. 2011 'Counterhegemonic currents and internationalization of sociology. Theoretical reflections and an empirical example', *International Sociology* 26(1): 123–45.

Keim, W. 2008 'Social sciences internationally: The problem of marginalisation and its consequences for the discipline of sociology', *African Sociological Review* 12(2): 22–248.

Kemple, T. M. and Mawani, R. 2010 'The Sociological Imagination and its Emperial Shadows', *Theory Culture & Society* 26(7–8): 228–49.

Kent, R. (comp) 2002 *Los Temas Críticos de la Educación Superior en América Latina en los Años Noventa. Estudios Comparativos*, México: FLACSO-Chile, Universidad Autónoma de Aguascalientes, and Fondo de Cultura Económica.

Kerz, M. 1996 'Sobre las Claves Políticas de la Transición: Carlos A. Floria' in J. C. Agulla (ed) *Ideologías políticas y ciencias sociales. La experiencia del pensamiento social argentino*, Buenos Aires: Instituto de Derecho Público, Ciencia Política y Sociología, Academia Nacional de Ciencias de Buenos Aires and Sigma.

Knorr-Cetina, K. 1981 *The Manufacture of Knowledge. An Essay on the Constructivist and Contextual Nature of Science*, New York: Pergamon Press.

Kohli, M. 1981 'Biography: Account, Text, Method' in D. Bertaux (ed) *Biography and Society. The Life History Approach in the Social Sciences*, Beverly Hills, CA: Sage.

Krarup, T. M. and Blok, A. 2011 'Unfolding the social: quasi-actants, virtual theory, and the new empiricism of Bruno Latour', *The Sociological Review* 59(1): 42–63.

Kreimer, P. 2006 '¿Dependientes o Integrados? La Ciencia Latinoamericana y la Nueva Division Internacional del Trabajo', *Nómadas* 24: 199–212.

Kreimer, P. 2005 *De Probetas, Computadoras y Ratones: La Construcción de una Mirada Sociológica sobre la Ciencia*, Bernal, Arg.: Universidad Nacional de Quilmes.

Kreimer, P. 2000 'Ciencia y Periferia. Una Lectura Sociológica' in M. Montserrat (ed) *La Ciencia en la Argentina entre Siglos. Textos, Contextos e Instituciones*, Buenos Aires: Manantial.

Krotsch, P. (org) 2002 *La Universidad Cautiva. Legados, Marcas y Horizontes*, La Plata, Arg.: Ediciones al Margen.

Krotsch, P. 2001 *Educación Superior y Reformas Comparadas*. Bernal, Arg.: Universidad Nacional de Quilmes.

222 Bibliography

Kuhn, M. 2010 'Facing a Scientific Multiversalism—Dynamics of International Social Science Knowledge Accumulations in the Era of Globalization', in M. Kuhn and D. Weidemann (eds) *Internationalization of the Social Sciences. Asia—Latin America—Middle East—Africa—Eurasia*, Bielefeld: Transcript Verlag.

Kuhn, T. S. 1962 *The Structure of Scientific Revolutions*, Chicago, IL: The University of Chicago Press.

Kumar, D. 1980 'Patterns of Colonial Science in India', *Indian Journal of History of Science* 15(1): 105–13.

Lago Carballo, A. and Gómez Villegas, N. 2006 *Un viaje de ida y vuelta. La edición española e iberoamericana (1936–1975)*, Madrid: Siruela.

Lalaki, D. 2007 'Rehabiliting the Importance of the Non-cognitive: An Interview with Michèle Lamont', *International Journal of Politics, Culture and Society* 19: 91–103.

Lamont, M. 2009 *How Professors Think. Inside the Curious World of Academic Judgment*, Cambridge, MA: Harvard University Press.

Lamont, M. 1987 'How to Become a Dominant French Philosopher: The Case of Jacques Derrida', *The American Journal of Sociology* 93(3): 584–622.

Lamont, M. and Molnár, V. 2002 'The Study of Boundaries in the Social Science', *Annual Review of Sociology* 28: 167–95.

Lander, E. (comp) 2003a *La Colonialidad del Saber. Eurocentrismo y Ciencias Sociales. Perspectivas Latinoamericanas*, Buenos Aires: CLACSO.

Lander, E. 2003b 'Ciencias Sociales: Saberes Coloniales y Eurocéntricos' in E. Lander (comp) *La Colonialidad del Saber. Eurocentrismo y Ciencias Sociales. Perspectivas Latinoamericanas*, Buenos Aires: CLACSO.

Landerman, M. 2001 'Trayectorias Académicas Generacionales: Constitucion y Diversificación del Oficio Académico. El Caso de los Bioquímicos de la Facultad de Medicina', *Revista Mexicana de Investigacion Educativa* 6(11): 33–61.

Larrain, J. 2000 *Identity and Modernity in Latin America*, Cambridge: Polity.

Lash, S., Quick, A., and Roberts, R. (eds) 1998 *Time and Value*, Oxford: Blackwell.

Latour, B. 2005 *Reassembling the Social. An Introduction to Actor-Network Theory*, Oxford: Oxford University Press.

Latour, B. 1999 *Pandora's Hope: Essays on the Reality of Science Studies*, Cambridge, MA: Harvard University Press.

Latour, B. 1991 'Technology is Society Made Durable' in J. Law (ed.) *A Sociology of Monsters: Essays on Power, Technology and Domination*, Keele: Sociological Review Monograph No. 38.

Latour, B. 1988 *The Pasteurization of France*, Cambridge, MA: Harvard University Press.

Latour, B. 1987 *Science in Action. How to Follow Scientists and Engineers through Society*, Cambridge, MA: Harvard University Press.

Latour, B. and S. Woolgar 1986 *Laboratory Life. The Construction of Scientific Facts*, Princeton, NJ: Princeton University Press.

Law, J. 2006a *After Method. Mess in Social Science Research*, London: Routledge.

Law, J. 2006b 'Actor Network Theory' in B. S. Turner (ed.) *The Cambridge Dictionary of Sociology*, Cambridge: Cambridge University Press.

Law, J. 1999 'After ANT: complexity, naming and topology', in J. Law and J. Hassard (eds) *Actor-Network Theory and After*, London: Wiley-Blackwell.

Law, J. (ed) 1986a *Power, Action, and Belief: A New Sociology of Knowledge?*, Keele: Sociological Review Monograph.

Law, J. 1986b 'On the Methods of Long-Distance Control: Vessels, Navigation and the Portuguese Route to India' in J. Law (ed.) *Power, Action, and Belief: A New Sociology of Knowledge?*, Keele: Sociological Review Monograph.

Bibliography 223

Law, J. and Hassard, J. (eds) 1999 *Actor-Network Theory and After*, London: Wiley-Blackwell.

Law, J. and Hetherington, K. 2002 'Materialities, Spatialities, Globalities', in M. Dear and S. Flusty (eds) *Spaces of Postmodernity: Readings in Human Geography*, London: Wiley-Blackwell.

Law, J. and Urry, J. 2004 'Enacting the Social', *Economy and Society* 33(3): 390–410.

Lehmann, D. 1990 *Democracy and Development in Latin America. Economics, Politics and Religion in the Post-war Period*, Philadelphia, PA: Temple University Press.

Leiras, M., Abal Medina, J. M., and D' Alessandro, M. 2005. 'La Ciencia Política en Argentina: el Camino de la Institucionalización dentro y fuera de las Aulas Universitarias', *Revista de Ciencia Política* 25(1): 76–91.

Lesgart, C. 2003 *Usos de la Transición a la Democracia. Ensayo, Ciencia y Política en la Década del 80*, Rosario: Homo Sapiens.

Lesgart, C. 2002 'Ciencia Política y Producción de la Idea de Transición a la Democracia' in A. Fernández (ed.) *La Ciencia Política en Argentina. Dos Siglos de Historia*, Buenos Aires: Biebel.

Lesgart, C. and Ramos, M. J. 2002 'La Temprana Creación del Estudio Universitario de la Política en Rosario. Itinerarios Institucionales', in A. Fernández (comp.) *La Ciencia Política en la Argentina. Dos Siglos de Historia*, Buenos Aires: Babel.

Licha, I. 2007 'Investigación Científica y Desarrollo Social en America Latina', in J. Sebastián (ed) *Claves del Desarrollo Científico y Tecnológico de América Latina*, Madrid: Fundación Carolina and Siglo XXI.

Lightfield, E. T. 1971 'Output and Recognition of Sociologists', *American Sociologist* 6:128–33.

Livingstone, D. N. 2007 'Science, Site, and Speech: Scientific Knowledge and the Spaces of Rhetoric', *History of the Human Sciences* 20(2): 71–98.

Livingstone, D. N. 2005 'Text, Talk, and Testimony: Geographical Reflections on Scientific Habits', *British Journal for the History of Science* 38: 93–100.

Livingstone, D. N. 2003 *Putting Science in its Place. Geographies of Scientific Knowledge*, Chicago, IL: The University of Chicago Press.

López Segrera, F. 2006 *Escenarios Mundiales de la Educación Superior. Análisis Global y Estudios de Casos*, Buenos Aires: CLACSO.

López Segrera, F. 2003 'Abrir, Impensar, y Redimensionar las Ciencias Sociales en América Latina y el Caribe. ¿Es Posible una Ciencia Social no Eurocéntrica en Nuestra Región?' in E. Lander (comp) *La Colonialidad del Saber. Eurocentrismo y Ciencias Sociales. Perspectivas Latinoamericanas*, Buenos Aires: CLACSO.

Lorca, J. 2004 'El Milagro del Funcionamiento de la UBA se basa en los ad honorem', *Pagina12*, 6 July, http://www.pagina12.com.ar/diario/universidad/10–37660–2004–07–08.html, accessed 25 June 2013.

Luchilo, L. 2010 'Internacionalización de investigadores argentinos: el papel de la movilidad hacia España', *Revista Iberoamericana de Ciencia, Tecnología y Sociedad* 6(16): n/p.

Luchilo, L. 2007 'Migraciones de Científicos e Ingenieros Latinoamericanos: Fuga de Cerebros, Exilio y Globalización', in J. Sebastián (ed) *Claves del Desarrollo Científico y Tecnológico de América Latina*, Madrid: Fundación Carolina and Siglo XXI.

Luhmann, N. 1992 *Die Wissenschaft der Gesellschaft*, Frankfurt: Suhrkamp.

Lynch, M. 1985 *Art and Artifact in Laboratory Science: A Study of Shop Work and Shop Talk in a Research Laboratory*, New York: Routledge Kegan & Paul.

Lynch, M. and Jasanoff, S. 1998 'Contested Identities: Science, Law and Forensic Practice' (Special Issue), *Social Studies of Science* 35(2): 269–311.

224 Bibliography

Macfarlane, B. 2010 'The Morphing of Academic Practice: Unbundling and the Rise of the Para-academic', *Higher Education Quarterly* 65(1): 59–73.

Maerk, J. 2000 'La "Ciencia *Cover*" en las Ciencias Humanísticas y Sociales en América Latina' in J. Maerk and M. Cabrolie (coords) *¿Existe una Epistemología Latinoamericana?* México: Universidad de Quintana Roo and Plaza y Valdés.

Maines, D. (ed) 1991 *Social Organization and Social Process. Essays in Honor of Anselm Strauss*, New York: A. de Gruyter.

Malamud, A. and Freidenberg, F. 2012 'La diáspora politológica: Patrones imprevistos de emigración y retorno al Cono Sur', *LASA Forum* 43(4): 7–9.

Marradi, A., Archenti, N., and Piovani, J. 2007 *Metodología de las Ciencias Sociales*, Buenos Aires: Emecé.

Marshall, C. and Rossman, G. 1995 *Designing Qualitative Research*, Thousand Oaks, CA: Sage.

McFarlane, C. 2006 'Crossing Borders: development, learning and the North-South divide', *Third World Quarterly* 27(8): 1413–437.

McGinty, S. 1999 *Gatekeepers of Knowledge: Journal Editors in the Sciences and the Social Sciences*, New York: Bergin & Garvey.

McLeod, R. 1996 'Passages in Imperial Science. From Empire to Commonwealth' in W. Storey (ed) *Scientific Aspects of European Expansion*, Aldershot: Variorum.

McLeod, R. 1975 'Scientific Advice for British India: Imperial Perceptions and Administrative Goals, 1898–1923', *Modern Asian Studies* 9(3): 343–84.

Meadows, A. J. 1997 *Communication Research*, London: Academic Press.

Melkers, J. and Kiopa, A. 2010 'The Social Capital of Global Ties in Science: The Added Value of International Collaboration', *Review of Policy Research* 27(4): 389–414.

Merton, R. K. 1973 *The Sociology of Science: Theoretical and Empirical Investigations*, Chicago, IL: Chicago University Press.

Meyer, M. 2010 'The Rise of the Knowledge Broker', *Science Communication* 32(1): 118–27.

Michael, M. 2006 *Technoscience and Everyday Life*, Buckingham: Open University Press.

Mignolo, W. 2007 'El Pensamiento Decolonial: Desprendimiento y Apertura', in S. Castro-Gomez and R. Grosfoguel (eds) *El Giro Decolonial: Reflexiones para una Diversidad Epistémica Más Allá del Capitalismo Global*, Bogotá: Siglo del Hombre Editores; Universidad Central, Instituto de Estudios Sociales Contemporáneos, Pontificia Universidad Javeriana, and Instituto Pensar.

Mignolo, W. 2006 'Espacios Geográficos y Localizaciones Epistemológicas: La Ratio entre la Localización Geográfica y la Subalternización de Conocimientos', http://www.javeriana.edu.co/pensar/Rev34.html, accessed 25 June 2013.

Mignolo, W. 2003 'La Colonialidad a lo Largo y a lo Ancho: el Hemisferio Occidental en el Horizonte Colonial de la Modernidad' in E. Lander (comp.) *La Colonialidad del Saber: Eurocentrismo y Ciencias Sociales. Perspectivas Latinoamericanas*, Buenos Aires: CLACSO.

Mignolo, W. 2002 'The Geopolitics of Knowledge and the Colonial Difference', *South Atlantic Quarterly* 101(1): 57–96.

Mignolo, W. 2000 *Local Histories/Global Designs. Coloniality, Subaltern Knowledges, and Border Thinking*, Princeton, NJ: Princeton University Press.

Mignolo, W. 1993 'Colonial and Postcolonial Discourse: Cultural Critique or Academia Colonialism?', *Latin American Research Review* 28(3): 120–34.

Mihic, S., Engelmann, S., and Wingrove, E. 2005 'Making Sense in and of Political Science. Facts, Values, and "Real" Numbers' in G. Steinmetz (ed) *The Politics*

Bibliography   225

of *Method in the Human Sciences. Positivism and its Epistemological Others*, Durham, NC: Duke University Press.

Miles, M. B. and Huberman, A. M. 1994 *Qualitative Data Analysis: An Expanded Sourcebook*, 2nd edition, Thousands Oaks: Sage.

Miller, N. 1999 *In the Shadow of the State. Intellectuals and the Quest for National Identity in Twentieth-century Spanish America*, London: Verso.

Mody, C. and Kaiser, D. 2008 'Scientific Training and the Creation of Scientific Knowledge', in E. Hackett, O. Amsterdamska, M. Lynch, and J. Wajcman (eds) *The New Handbook of Science and Technology Studies*, Third Edition, Cambridge, MA: MIT Press.

Mollis, M. (comp) 2003 *Las Universidades en América Latina: ¿Reformadas o Alteradas? La Cosmética del Poder Financiero*, Buenos Aires: CLACSO.

Montgomery, S. L. 2000 *Science in Translation: Movements of Knowledge Through Cultures and Time*, Chicago, IL: The University of Chicago Press.

Morgan, C., Campbell, B., and Teleen, T. 2012 'The Role of the Academic Journal Publisher and Open Access Publishing model', *International Studies Perspectives* 13: 228–34.

Moser, I and Law, J. 1999 'Good passages, bad passages', in J. Law and J. Hassard (eds) *Actor-Network Theory and After*, London: Wiley-Blackwell.

Mouzelis, N. 1988 'Marxism or Post-Marxism?', *The New Left Review* 167(1): 107–23.

Munck, R. 1992 'The Democratic Decade: Argentina since Malvinas', *Bulletin of Latin American Research* 11(2): 205–16.

Murmis, M. 2005 'Sociology, Political Science, and Anthropology: Institutionalization, Professionalization and Internationalization in Argentina', *Social Science Information* 44(2–3): 227–82.

Nadal, J. and García, F. 2005 *Libros o velocidad. Reflexiones sobre el oficio editorial*, Madrid: Fondo de Cultura Económica.

Naishtat, F., García Raggio, A. M., and Villavicencio, S. 2001 *Filosofía de la Universidad y Conflicto de Racionalidades*, Buenos Aires: Colihue.

NSF (National Science Foundation) 2008 'Science and Engineering Indicators', http://www.nsf.gov/statistics/seind08/figures.htm#ch4, accessed 20 June 2013.

Nieburg, F. and Plotkin, M. (comps) 2004a *Intelectuales y Expertos. La Construcción del Conocimiento Social en la Argentina*, Buenos Aires: Paidós.

Nieburg, F. and Plotkin, M. 2004b 'Intelectuales y Expertos. Hacia una Sociología Histórica de la Producción del Conocimiento sobre la Sociedad en la Argentina' in F. Nieburg and M. Plotkin (comps) *Intelectuales y Expertos. La Construcción del Conocimiento Social en la Argentina*, Buenos Aires: Paidós.

Nieburg, F. and Plotkin, M. 2004c 'Los Economistas. El Instituto Torcuato Di Tella y las Nuevas Elites Estatales en los años Sesenta' in F. Nieburg and M. Plotkin (comps) *Intelectuales y Expertos. La Construcción del Conocimiento Social en la Argentina*, Buenos Aires: Paidós.

Nielsen, M. 2011 *Reinventing Discovery: The New Era of Networked Science*, Princeton, NJ: Princeton University Press.

Nowotny, H. 1994 *Time: The Modern and Postmodern Experience*, Cambridge: Polity Press.

Nye, M. J. 2006 'Scientific Biography: History of Science by Another Means?', *Isis* 97: 322–29.

O'Donnell, G. 1998 'Polyarchies and the (un)rule of law in Latin America', Working paper, Notre Dame, IN: The Hellen Kellogg Institute for International Studies, University of Notre Dame.

O'Donnell, G. 1996 'Otra institucionalización', *La Política: Revista de Estudios sobre el Estado y la Sociedad* 2: 5–28.

226 Bibliography

O'Donnell, G. 1992 'Delegative Democracy?', Working paper, Notre Dame, IN: The Hellen Kellogg Institute for International Studies, University of Notre Dame.

O'Donnell, G., Schmitter, P., and Whitehead, L. (eds) 1986 *Transitions from Authoritarian Rule*, 4 vols, Baltimore, MD: The Johns Hopkins University Press.

Oromaner, M. 1983 'Professional Standing and the Reception of Contributions to Economics', *Research in Higher Education* 19(3): 351–62.

Ortiz, R. 2009 *La Supremacía del Inglés en las Ciencias Sociales*, Buenos Aires: Siglo XXI.

Ortiz, R. 2004 'As Ciências Sociais e o Inglês', *Revista Brasileira de Ciências Sociais* 19(54): 5–23.

Oszlak, O. 2005 'State Bureaucracy: Politics and Policy', in T. Janoski, R. Alford, A. Hicks, and A. Schwartz (eds) *Handbook of Political Sociology*, Cambridge: Cambridge University Press.

Oszlak, O. 1984 *Teoría de la Burocracia Estatal. Enfoques Críticos*, Buenos Aires: Paidós.

Oszlak, O. 1982 *La formación del Estado argentino. Orden, progreso y organización nacional*, Buenos Aires: Editorial de Belgrano.

Oszlak, O. 1979 'Notas Críticas para una Teoría de la Burocracia Estatal', *Desarrollo Económico* 19(74): 211–50.

Parmar, I. 2012 *Foundations of the American Century: The Ford, Carnegie, and Rockefeller Foundations in the Rise of American Power*, New York: Columbia University Press.

Patton, M. Q. 2001 *Qualitative Research and Evaluation Methods*, Thousand Oaks, CA: Sage.

Payne Katt, T. 1997 'A Learning Journey (In Progress): A Personal Biographical Ethnography', in E. T. Stringer, M. F. Agnello, S. C. Baldwin, L. McFayden Christensen, D. L. Philb Henry, K. I. Henry, T. Payne Katt, P. Gathma Nason, V. Newman, and R. Petty, *Community-Based Ethnography: Breaking the Traditional Boundaries of Research, Teaching, and Learning*, Philadelphia, PA: Lawrence Erlbaum.

Perelman, P. 2003 *Componente: Industria de Generación de Contenidos y Bienes Culturales*, Buenos Aires: Ministerio de Economía and CEPAL, http://www.eclac.org/argentina/noticias/paginas/8/12238/Resumen336BienesCult.pdf, accessed 25 June 2013.

Pereyra, D. 2004 *American Organizations and the Development of Sociology and Social Research in Argentina. The Case of the SSRC and the Rockefeller Foundation (1927–1966)*, New York: Rockefeller Archive Center.

Pérez Lindo, A. 2003 *Universidad, Conocimiento y Reconstrucción Nacional*, Buenos Aires: Biblos.

Pickering, A. 1995 *The Mangle of Practice. Time, Agency and Science*, Chicago, IL: University of Chicago Press.

Pickering, A. (ed.) 1992 *Science as Practice and Culture*, Chicago, IL: University of Chicago Press.

Pickering, A. 1984 *Constructing Quarks: A Sociological History of Particle Physics*, Edinburgh: Edinburgh University Press.

Pinch, T. 1986 *Confronting Nature: The Sociology of Solar Neutrino Detection*. Dordrecht: Reidel.

Pinto, J. (comp) 2003 *Introducción a la Ciencia Política*, Buenos Aires: Eudeba.

Plotkin, M. 2006 *La Privatizacion de la Educacion Superior y las Ciencias Sociales en Argentina*, Buenos Aires: CLACSO.

Plummer, K. 1983 *Documents of Life*, London: George Allen and Unwin.

Bibliography   227

Polanyi, M. 1958 *Personal Knowledge. Towards a Post-Critical Philosophy*, New York: Routledge & Kegan Paul.

Polino, C., Vaccarezza, L., and Fazio, M. E. 2003 'Indicadores de Percepcion Publica de la Ciencia. Aplicación de la Experiencia RICYT/OEI en la Encuesta Nacional de Argentina y Comparacion Internacional', http://www.science.oas.org/ricyt/interior/normalizacion/VItaller/M1_Percp/polinodoc.pdf, accessed 25 June 2013.

Polkinghorne, J. 2007 *Exploring Reality: The Intertwining of Science and Religion*, New Haven, CT: Yale University Press.

Portantiero, J. C. 2000 'Gramsci, lector de Maquiavelo', in T. Várnagy (ed) *Fortuna y Virtud en la República Democrática. Ensayos sobre Maquiavelo*, Buenos Aires: CLACSO.

Porter, T. M. 2006 'Is the Life of the Scientist a Scientific Unit?', *Isis* 97: 314–21.

Pratt, M. L. 1991 'Arts of the Contact Zone', *Profession* 91: 33–40.

Prebisch, R. 1950 *The Economic Development of Latin America and its Principal Problems*, New York: United Nations Press.

Prego, C. and Estebanez, E. 2002 'Modernización Académica, Desarrollo Científico, y Radicalización Política' in P. Krotsch (org) *La Universidad Cautiva. Legados, Marcas y Horizontes*, La Plata, Arg.: Ediciones Al Margen.

Puiatti de Gómez, H. E. 2007 'El Articulo de Investigacion Cientifica' in L. Cubo de Severino (coord) *Los Textos de la Ciencia. Principales Clases del Discurso Académico-Científico*. Córdoba, Arg.: Comunicarte.

Quijano, A. 2007 'Colonialidad del Poder y Clasificacion Social' in S. Castro-Gómez and R. Grosfoguel (eds) *El Giro Decolonial: Reflexiones para una Diversidad Epistémica Más Allá del Capitalismo Global*, Bogotá: Siglo del Hombre Editores; Universidad Central, Instituto de Estudios Sociales Contemporáneos, Pontificia Universidad Javeriana, and Instituto Pensar.

Quijano, A. 2003 'Colonialidad del Poder, Eurocentrismo y America Latina' in E. Lander (comp) *La Colonialidad del Saber: Eurocentrismo y Ciencias Sociales. Perspectivas Latinoamericanas*, Buenos Aires: CLACSO.

Quiroga, H. 2003 'Intelectuales y Política en Argentina. Notas sobre una Relación Problemática' in W. Hofmeister and H. C. F. Mansilla (eds) *Intelectuales y Política en América Latina. El Desencantamiento del Espíritu Crítico*, Rosario: Homo Sapiens.

Raj, K. 2010 *Relocating Modern Science: Circulation and the Construction of Knowledge in South Asia and Europe, 1650–1900*, New York: Palgrave Macmillan.

Ramírez, G. 2007 'Estado del Desarrollo Científico y Tecnológico de Chile' in J. Sebastián (ed) *Claves del Desarrollo Científico y Tecnológico de América Latina*. Madrid: Fundación Carolina and Siglo XXI.

Rammer, W. 1999 'Relations that Constitute Technology and Media that Make a Difference: Toward a Social Pragmatic Theory of Technicization', *Techne: Research in Philosophy and Technology* 4(3): 23–43.

Rappert, B. 2006 *Controlling the Weapons of War: Politics, Persuasion and the Prohibition of Inhumanity*, London: Routledge.

Rappert, B., Balmer, B., and Stone, J. 2008 'Science, Technology, and the Military: Priorities, Preoccupations, and Possibilities', in E. Hackett, O. Amsterdamska, M. Lynch, and J. Wajcman (eds) *The New Handbook of Science and Technology Studies*, Third Edition, Cambridge, MA: MIT Press.

Ravetz, J. R. 1971 *Scientific Knowledge and Its Social Problems*, Oxford: Clarendon Press.

Readings, B. 1996 *The University in Ruins*, Cambridge, MA: Harvard University Press.

228   Bibliography

RICYT (Red de Indicadores de Ciencia y Tecnología), Indicadores de Ciencia y Tecnología en Iberoamérica, http://www.ricyt.org, accessed 25 June 2013.

Reed-Danahay, D. 1997 *Auto/ethnography: Rewriting the Self and the Social*, Oxford: Berg.

Renwick Monroe, K. (ed) 2005 *Perestroika. The Raucous Rebellion in Political Science*, New Haven, CT: Yale University Press.

Ribeiro Durham, E. 2002 'Introducción. Los Estudios Comparativos de la Educación Superior en América Latina', in R. Kent (comp) *Los Temas Críticos de la Educación Superior en América Latina en los Años Noventa. Estudios Comparativos*, México: FLACSO-Chile, Universidad Autónoma de Aguascalientes, and Fondo de Cultura Económica.

Richard, N. 1998 'Intersectando Latinoamérica con el Latinoamericanismo: Discurso Académico y Crítica Cultural' in S. Castro-Gómez and E. Mendieta (coords) *Teorías sin Disciplina. Latinoamericanismo, Poscolonialidad y Globalización en Debate*, México: Porrúa.

Rinesi, E., Soprano, G., and Suasnabar, C. (comps) 2005 *Universidad: Reformas y Destinos. Dilemas de la Educación Superior en la Argentina y el Brasil*, Buenos Aires: Prometeo and Universidad Nacional de General Sarmiento.

Riquelme, G. C. 2006 *Educación Superior, Demandas Sociales, Productivas, y Mercado de Trabajo*, Buenos Aires: Miño y Dávila and Universidad de Buenos Aires.

Roberts, L. 2011 *Centres and Cycles of Accumulation in and Around the Netherlands during the Early Modern Period*, Bielefeld: Verlag.

Robertson, B. 2002 *Biographical Research*, Buckingham: Open University Press.

Rodriguez Medina, L. 2013 'Objetos subordinantes: la tecnología epistémica para construir centros y periferias', *Revista Mexicana de Sociología*, 75(1): 7–28

Rodriguez Medina, L. 2009 'Algunos apuntes para una geopolítica del conocimiento', in A. López Cuenca (ed) *¿Desea Guardar los Cambios? Propiedad Intelectual y Tecnologías Digitales: Hacia un Nuevo Pacto Social*, Córdoba: Centro Cultural España-Córdoba.

Rodriguez Medina, L. 2008a 'Relaciones precapitalistas en las prácticas científicas en Argentina', *Nómadas* 29: 64–78.

Rodriguez Medina, L. 2008b 'Las ideas no se matan (pero hay que saber guardarlas). Bibliotecas personales, académicos y notas sobre la materialidad de las ideas', *Studia Politicae* 14: 87–108.

Rodriguez-Pose, A. 2006 'Commentary', *Environment & Planning* 38: 603–10.

Rossi, U. 2008 'Being here and there: in-betweeness, double absence, and the making of a multi-layered academic citizenship', *Area* 40(3): 401–6.

Rudolph, S. H. 2005 'The Imperialism of Categories: Situating Knowledge in a Globalizing World', *Perspectives on Politics* 3(1): 5–14.

Rustin, M. 2000 'Reflections on the Biographical Turn in Social Science' in P. Chamberlayne, J. Bornat, and T. Wengraf (eds) *The Turn to Biographical Methods in Social Science. Comparative Issues and Examples*, London: Routledge.

Saguir, E. 1999 'Entrevista', *POSTData* 5: 307–18.

Saítta, S. 2004 'Modos de Pensar lo Social. Ensayo y Sociedad en la Argentina (1930–1965)' in F. Nieburg and M. Plotkin (comps) *Intelectuales y Expertos. La Construcción del Conocimiento Social en la Argentina*, Buenos Aires: Paidós.

Saldaña, J. J. (ed) 2006 *Science in Latin America. A History*, Austin: University of Texas Press.

Salomón, J. J., Sagasti, F., and Sachs-Jeantet, C. (eds) 1994 *The Uncertain Question. Science, Techonology, and Development*, Tokyo: United Nations University Press.

Salvatore, R. (comp) 2006 *Los Lugares del Saber. Contextos Locales y Redes Transnacionales en la Formación del Conocimiento Moderno*, Rosario: Beatriz Viterbo Editora.

Bibliography 229

Sanchez A. and William E. 2007 'La Universidad Sin Organos. Capitalismo Cognitivo y Transformacion Empresarial de la Universidad Colombiana', *Nómadas* 27: 34–46.

Sanchez Ramos, I., and Sosa Elizaga, R. (coords) 2004 *América Latina: Los Desafíos del Pensamiento Crítico*, México: Universidad Nacional Autónoma de México and Fondo de Cultura Económica.

Santos, B. S. 2009 *Una Epistemología del Sur. La Reinvención del Conocimiento y la Emancipación Social*, México: CLACSO and Siglo XXI.

Sapsed, J. and Salter, A. 2004 'Postcards from the Edge: Local Communities, Global Programs and Boundary Objects', *Organization Studies* 25(9): 1515–534.

Sarlo, B. 2001 *La Batalla de las Ideas (1943–1973)*, Buenos Aires: Ariel.

Saviola, C. 2008 'La UBA dice que salió del rojo y espera menos conflictos', *Clarín* 17 February, [Available at http://edant.clarin.com/suplementos/zona/2008/02/17/z-03215.htm, accessed 25 June 2013]

Schaffer, S., Roberts, L., Raj, K., and Delbourgo, J. 2009 *The Brokered World: Go-Betweens and Global Intelligence, 1770–1820*, Sagamore Beach, MA: Watson Publishing.

Schiefelbein, E. and Schiefelbein, P. 2007 'Improve Teaching Methods or Perish. Issues Confronting the Academic Profession in Latin America' in A. Welch (ed) *The Professoriate. Profile of a Profession*, Dordrecth: Springer.

Schott, T. 1998 'Ties Between Center and Periphery in the Scientific World-System: Accumulation of Rewards, Dominance and Self-Reliance in the Center', *Journal of World-Systems Research* 4: 112–44.

Schott, T. 1993a 'World Science: Globalization of Institutions and Participation', *Science, Technology, & Human Values* 18(2): 196–208.

Schott, T. 1993b 'Performance, Specialization and International Integration of Science in Brazil: Changes and Comparisons with Other Latin America and Israel', Sao Paulo: Escola de Administração de Empresas, Fundação Getúlio Vargas, and World Bank

Schott, T. 1991 'The World Scientific Community: Globality and Globalization', *Minerva* 29: 440–62.

Schott, T. 1988 'International Influence in Science. Beyond Center and Periphery', *Social Science Research* 17: 219–38.

Schott, T., Kugel, S., Berrios, R., and Rodriguez, K. 1998 'Peripheries in World Science: Latin America and Eastern Europe' in M. Epitropoulos and V. Roudometof (eds) *American Culture in Europe. Interdisciplinary Perspectives*, Westport, CT: Praeger.

Schroeder, R. 2008 'e-Sciences as research technologies: reconfiguring disciplines, globalizing knowledge', *Social Science Information* 47(2): 131–57.

Schwartz-Shea, P. 2005 'The Graduate Student Experience. "Hegemony" or Balance in Methodological Training?' in K. Renwick Monroe (ed) *Perestroika. The Raucous Rebellion in Political Science*, New Haven, CT: Yale University Press.

Scott, A. 2008 'Governing Disciplines: Reform and Placation in the Austrian University System', paper presented at Centre for the Research in the Arts, Social Sciences and Humanities, Cambridge University, 12 May.

Scott, P. 2007 'From Professor to "Knowledge Worker": Profiles of the Academic Profession', *Minerva* 45: 205–15.

Sebastián, J. (ed) 2007a *Claves del Desarrollo Científico y Tecnológico de América Latina*, Madrid: Fundación Carolina and Siglo XXI.

Sebastián, J. 2007b 'Introducción. Análisis de la Evolución del Desarrollo Científico y Tecnológico de América Latina' in J. Sebastián (ed) *Claves del Desarrollo Científico y Tecnológico de América Latina*, Madrid: Fundación Carolina and Siglo XXI.

Secord, J. A. 2004 'Knowledge in transit', *Isis*, 95: 654–72.

230 Bibliography

SECyT. 2007 'Indicadores de Ciencia y Tecnología en Argentina', http://www.mincyt.gov.ar/indicadores_2006/publicacion/indicadores_2006.pdf, accessed 28 March 2009.

SECyT. 1998 *Informe sobre el estado de la ciencia política en la Argentina*, Buenos Aires: SECyT.

Seidman, S. 2000 *Contested Knowledge. Social Theory Today*, Malden, MA: Blackwell Publishing.

Serrafero, M. 2002 'Las Ciencias Sociales', in Academia Nacional de la Historia, *Nueva Historia de la Nación Argentina*, Volume X, Part 4: La Argentina del Siglo XX c. 1914–1983, Buenos Aires: Planeta.

Shapin, S. 2008. *A Scientific Life. A Moral History of a Late Modern Vocation*, Chicago, IL: The University of Chicago Press.

Shapin, S. 1998 'Placing the View from Nowhere: Historical and Sociological Problems in the Location of Science', *Transactions of the Institute of British Geographers* 23(1): 5–12.

Shapin, S. 1992 'Discipline and Bounding: The History and Sociology of Science as Seen Through the Externalism-Internalism Debate', *History of Science* 30: 333–69.

Shapin, S. and Schaffer, S. 1985 *Leviathan and the Air-pump*, Princeton, NJ: Princeton University Press.

Shetty, S. 2007 'The Job Market: An Overview' in A. L. Deneef and C. D. Goodwin (eds) *The Academic's Handbook*, Third Edition, Durham, NC: Duke University Press.

Shils, E. 1988 'Center and Periphery: An Idea and Its Career, 1935–1987' in L. Greenfeld and M. Martin (eds) *Center. Ideas and Institutions*, Chicago, IL: The University of Chicago Press.

Shinn, T., Spaapen, J., and Krishna, V. (eds) 1995 *Science and Technology in a Developing World*, Dordrecht: Kluwer Academic Publisher.

Shrum, W. 1997 'View From Afar: "Visible" Productivity of Scientists in the Developing World', *Scientometrics* 40(2): 215–35.

Shrum, W., Genuth, J. and Chompalov, I. 2008 *Structures of Scientific Collaboration*, Cambridge MA: MIT Press.

Shusterman, R. (ed) 2005 *Bourdieu: A Critical Reader*, London: Blackwell.

Sigal, S. 2002 *Intelectuales y Poder en Argentina. La Década del Sesenta*, Buenos Aires: Siglo XXI.

Sisto, Campos, V. 2007 'Managerialismo y Trivializacion de la Universidad', *Nómadas* 29: 8–21.

Sisto Campos, V. 2005 'Flexibilización Laboral de la Docencia Universitaria y la Gest(ac)ion de la Universidad sin Órganos. Un Análisis desde la Subjetividad Laboral del Docente en Condiciones de Precariedad' in P. Gentili and B. Levy (comps) *Espacio Público y Privatización del Conocimiento. Estudios sobre Políticas Universitarias en América Latina*, Buenos Aires: CLACSO.

Skinner, Q. 1993 *Machiavelli and Republicanism*, Cambridge: Cambridge University Press.

Smith, K. 2010 'Research, policy, and funding—academic treadmills and the squeeze on intellectual spaces', *British Journal of Sociology* 61(1): 176–95.

Solleiro, J. L., Castanon, R., Montiel, M., and Luna, K. 2007 'Evolución del Desarrollo Científico y Tecnológico de América Latina: México' in J. Sebastián (ed) *Claves del Desarrollo Científico y Tecnológico de América Latina*, Madrid: Fundación Carolina and Siglo XXI.

Sorá, G. 2004 'Editores y Editoriales de Ciencias Sociales: un Capital Específico' in F. Nieburg and M. Plotkin (comps) *Intelectuales y Expertos. La Construcción del Conocimiento Social en la Argentina*, Buenos Aires: Paidós.

Bibliography 231

Spivak, G. C. 1988 'Can the Subaltern Speak?' in C. Nelson and L. Grossberg (eds) *Marxism and the Interpretation of Culture*, Urbana: University of Illinois Press.

Star, S. L. and Griesemer, J. R. 1989 'Institutional Ecology, "Translations" and Boundary Objects: Amateurs and Professionals in Berkeley's Museum of Vertebrate Zoology, 1907–1939', *Social Studies of Science* 19: 387–420.

Stichweh, R. 1996 'Science in the System of World Society', *Social Science Information* 35: 327–40.

Strasser, C. 2012 'Entrevista', *PostData* 12(Agosto): 229–41.

Strauss, A. C. 1982 'Social Worlds and Legitimation Processes', in N. Danzin (ed) *Studies in Symbolic Interaction 4*, Greenwich: JAI Press.

Strauss, A. C. 1978 'A Social Worlds Perspective' in N. Danzin (ed) *Studies in Symbolic Interaction 1*, Greenwich: JAI Press.

Strauss, A. C. and Corbin, J. (eds) 1997 *Grounded Theory in Practice*, London: Sage.

Strauss, A. C., Schatzman, L., Bucher, R., Erlich, D., and Sabshin, M. 1964 *Psychiatric Ideology and Institutions*, Glencoe: Free Press.

Suasnábar, C. 2004 *Universidad e Intelectuales. Educación y Política en la Argentina (1955–1976)*, Buenos Aires: FLACSO-Manantial.

Suchman, L. 2008 'Feminist STS and the Sciences of the Artificial', in E. Hackett, O. Amsterdamska, M. Lynch, and J. Wajcman (eds) *The New Handbook of Science and Technology Studies*, Third Edition, Cambridge, MA: MIT Press.

Sverisson, A. 2001 'Translation network, knowledge brokers, and novelty construction: Pragmatic environmentalism in Sweden', Acta Sociologica 44: 313–27.

Swales, J. 1990 *Genre Analysis. English in Academic and Research Settings*, Cambridge: Cambridge University Press.

Swartz, D. 1997 *Culture & Power. The Sociology of Pierre Bourdieu*, Chicago, IL: The University of Chicago Press.

Taschwer, K. 1996 'Science as system vs. science as practice: Luhmann's sociology of science and recent approaches in science and technology studies (STS)—a fragmentary confrontation', *Social Science Information* 35(2): 215–32.

Taylor, S. J. and Bogdan, R. 1998 *Introduction to Qualitative Research Methods. A Guidebook and Resource*, New York: John Wiley & Sons.

Tenbruck, F. 1988 'Shifting Centers and Peripheries: The Role and Responsibility of American Social Science' in L. Greenfeld and M. Martin (eds) *Center. Ideas and Institutions*, Chicago, IL: The University of Chicago Press.

Terán, O. (coord) 2004 *Ideas en el Siglo. Intelectuales y Cultura en el Siglo XX Latinoamericano*, Buenos Aires: Siglo XXI.

Thagaard, T. 1986 *Scientific Communities*, Oslo: University of Oslo.

Thomas, H. and Dagnino, R. 2005 'Efectos de transducción: una nueva crítica a la transferencia acrítica de conceptos y modelos institucionales', *Ciencia, Docencia y Tecnología* 31: 9–46.

Thomas, W. I., and Znaniecki, F. 1958 *The Polish Peasant in Europe and America*, 2 vols, New York: Dover Press.

Thompson, E. C. 2006 'Internet-Mediated Networking and Academic Dependency in Indonesia, Malaysia, Singapore and the United States', *Current Sociology* 54(1): 41–61.

Thompson, J. B. 1991 *Ideology and Modern Culture: Critical Social Theory in the Era of Mass Communication*, Stanford: Stanford University Press.

Thompson, P. 1981 'Life Histories and the Analysis of Social Change', in D. Bertaux (ed) *Biography and Society. The Life History Approach in the Social Sciences*, Beverly Hills, CA: Sage.

Thorn, K. 2005 *Science, Technology and Innovation in Argentina. A Profile of Issues and Practices*, Working paper, Washington, DC: World Bank.

Thrift, N. 2005 *Knowing Capitalism*, London: Sage.

232 Bibliography

Tight, M. (ed) 2000 *Academic Work and Life: What It Is to Be an Academic, and How This Is Changing*, Amsterdam: Elsevier Science.

Torres Salcido, G. 2000 'Disciplina e Interdisciplina en las Ciencias Sociales Hoy', in J. Maerk and M. Cabrolie (coords) ¿*Existe una Epistemología Latinoamericana?* México: Universidad de Quintana Roo and Plaza y Valdés.

Turner, S. P. and Turner, J. A. 1990 *The Impossible Science. An Institutional Analysis of American Sociology*, London: Sage.

Universidad de Buenos Aires 2004. *Censo Docente.04*, Buenos Aires: Secretaría de Asuntos Académicos, Universidad de Buenos Aires, www.uba.ar/institucional/censos/Docente2004/censo_docente.pdf, accessed 25 June 2013.

Universidad Nacional de Entre Ríos 2007 *Nuestra historia,* http://www.uner.edu.ar/institucional/2/nuestra-historia, accessed 25 June 2013.

Uprichard, E., Burrows, R., and Byrne, D. 2008 'SPSS as an "inscription device": from causality to description', *The Sociological Review* 56(4): 606–22.

Uranga, W. 2002 '¿Por qué Oscar Oszlak?', *Pagina 12*, 4 February, http://www.pagina12.com.ar/diario/elpais/subnotas/1497–851-2002–02–04.html, accessed 25 June 2013.

Uribe, R., Guerrero, S., and Steenkist, R. 2005 *La Edición de Libros en las Universidades de América Latina y el Caribe, 2004–2005*, Bogotá: Centro Regional para el Fomento del Libro en América Latina y el Caribe.

Vaccarezza, L., Polino, C., and Fazio, M. E. 2004 'Hacia una medición de la percepción pública de la ciencia en los países iberoamericanos' http://www.ricyt.org/interior/difusion/pubs/elc/15.pdf, accessed 29 March 2009.

Várnagy, T. 2010 'The Americanization of Argentine and Latin American Social Sciences', in M. Kuhn and D. Weidemann (eds) *Internationalization of the Social Sciences. Asia—Latin America—Middle East—Africa—Eurasia*, Bielefeld: Transcript Verlag.

Verran, H. 1999 'Staying true to the laughter in Nigerian classrooms' in J. Law. and J. Hassard (eds) *Actor-Network Theory and After*, London: Wiley-Blackwell.

Vessuri, H. 2010 'The Current Internationalization of the Social Sciences in Latin America: Old Wine in New Barrels?', in M. Kuhn and D. Weidemann (eds) *Internationalization of the Social Sciences. Asia—Latin America—Middle East—Africa—Eurasia*, Bielefeld: Transcript Verlag.

Vessuri, H. 2007 'La Formación de Investigadores en America Latina' in J. Sebastián (ed) *Claves del Desarrollo Científico y Tecnológico de América Latina*, Madrid: Fundación Carolina and Siglo XXI.

Vessuri, H. (comp) 2006a *Universidad e Investigación Científica. Convergencias y Tensiones*, Buenos Aires: CLACSO.

Vessuri, H. 2006b 'Academic Science in Twentieth-century Latin America' in J. J. Saldaña, (ed) *Science in Latin America*, Austin: University of Texas Press.

Vessuri, H. 1997a 'Science for the South in the South. Exploring the Role of Local Leadership as a Catalyst of Scientific Development', in T. Shinn, J. Spaapen, and V. Krishna (eds) *Science and Technology in a Developing World*, Dordrecht: Kluwer Academic Publisher.

Vessuri, H. 1997b 'Bitter Harvest. The Growth of a Scientific Community in Argentina' in J. Gaillard, V. Krishna, and R. Waast (eds) *Scientific Communities in the Developing World*, New Delhi: Sage.

Vessuri, H. 1994 'The Institutionalization Process' in J. J. Salomón, F. Sagasti, and C. Sachs-Jeantet (eds) *The Uncertain Question. Science, Techonology, and Development*, Tokyo: United Nations University Press.

Vessuri, H., Martínez Larrechea, E., and Estévez, B. 2001 'Los Científicos Sociales en Venezuela. Perfil Bibliográfico e Implicaciones de Política', *Cuadernos del Cendes* 48: 89–121.

Bibliography 233

Villanueva, E. F. 2002 'La Articulación entre Sistema Científico y Sistema Universitario, ¿es un Dilema?', *Revista de Estudios sobre la Ciencia y la Tecnología* 9(19): 25–40.

Viroli, M. 1998 *Founders of Modern Political and Social Thought*, Oxford: Oxford University Press.

Wacquant, L. 2013 'Bourdieu 1993: A Case Study in Scientific Consecration', *Sociology* 47(1): 15–29.

Wagner, C. 2008 *The New Invisible College. Science for Development*, Washington, DC: Brooking Institution Press.

Wagner, C. 2006 'International Collaboration in Science and Technology: Promises and Pitfalls' in L. Box and R. Engelhard (eds) *Science and Technology Policy for Development. Dialogues at the Interface*, London: Anthem Press.

Wagner, C., Brahmakulam, I., Jackson, B., Wong, A., and Yoda, T. 2001 *Science and Technology Collaboration: Building Capacity in Developing Countries?*, Santa Mónica, CA, Arlington, VA, and Pittsburgh, PA: RAND Corporation, http://www.rand.org/pubs/monograph_reports/2005/MR1357.0.pdf, accessed 20 June 2013.

Wagner, C. and Leydesdorff, L. 2005 'Network Structure, Self-Organization and the Growth of International Collaboration in Science', *Research Policy* 34(10): 1608–618.

Wagner, I. 2006 'Career Coupling: Career Making in the Elite World of Musicians and Scientists', *Qualitative Sociology Review* 2(3): 78–98.

Wallace, B. A. 2007 *Hidden Dimensions. The Unification of Physics and Consciousness*, New York: Columbia University Press.

Wallerstein, I. 1996a 'El Eurocentrismo y sus Avatares' in I. Wallerstein, *Conocer el Mundo. Saber el Mundo. El Fin de lo Aprendido. Una Ciencia Social para el Siglo XXI*, México: Siglo XXI.

Wallerstein, I. 1996b 'Las Estructuras del Saber, o De Cuantas Maneras Podemos Saber' in I. Wallerstein, *Conocer el Mundo. Saber el Mundo. El Fin de lo Aprendido. Una Ciencia Social para el Siglo XXI*, México: Siglo XXI.

Wallerstein, I. 1996c 'Eurocentrism and its Avatars: The Dilemmas of Social Science', Keynote address at ISA East Asian Regional Colloquium, 'The Future of Sociology in East Asia', 22–23 November, Seoul, Korea.

Wallerstein, I. 1987 *World-system Analysis*, Stanford: Stanford University Press.

Wallis, K. C. and Poulton, J. L. 2001 *Internalization*, Buckingham: Open University Press.

Weidemann, D. 2010 'Challenges of International Collaboration in the Social Sciences', in M. Kuhn and D. Weidemann (eds) *Internationalization of the Social Sciences. Asia—Latin America—Middle East—Africa—Eurasia*, Bielefeld: Transcript Verlag.

Welch, A. (ed) 2007a *The Professoriate: Profile of a Profession*, Dordrecht: Springer.

Welch, A. 2007b 'Challenge and Change: The Academic Profession in Uncertain Times' in A. Welch (ed) *The Professoriate: Profile of a Profession*, Dordrecht: Springer.

Welch, A. 2007c 'From Peregrinatio Academica to Global Academic: The Internationalisation of the Profession' in A. Welch (ed) *The Professoriate: Profile of a Profession*, Dordrecht: Springer.

Welch, A. 2007d 'Conclusion: New Millennium, New Milieu?' in A. Welch (ed) *The Professoriate: Profile of a Profession*, Dordrecht: Springer.

Welch, A. 1997 'The Peripatetic Professor: The Internationalisation of the Academic Profession', *Higher Education* 34: 323–45.

Whitley, R. 2006 *The Intellectual and Social Organization of the Sciences*, Oxford: Oxford University Press.

234 Bibliography

Whitley, R. 1982 'The Establishment and Structure of the Sciences as Reputational Organizations' in N. Elias, H. Martins, and R. Whitley (eds) *Scientific Establishments and Hierarchies*, Dordrecht: Reidel Publishing.

Whitley, R. 1985 'Knowledge Producers and Knowledge Acquirers: Popularisation as a Relation Between Scientific Fields and Their Publics' in T. Shinn and R. Whitley (eds) *Expository Science: Forms and Functions of Popularisation*, Dordrecht: Reidel Publishing.

Wilbur, H. M. 2007 'On Getting a Job', in A. L. Deneef and C. D. Goodwin (eds) *The Academic's Handbook*, Third Edition, Durham, NC: Duke University Press.

Winner, L. 2004 'Trust and Terror: The Vulnerability of Complex Socio-Technical Systems', *Science as Culture* 13(2): 155–72.

Wolin, S. 1969 'Political Theory as a Vocation', *American Political Science Review* 63: 1062–82.

Wolin, S. 1968 'Paradigms and Political Theory' in P. King and B. C. Parakh (eds) *Politics and Experience*, Cambridge: Cambridge University Press.

Yarrow, T. 2008 'Life/History: Personal Narratives of Development Amongst NGO Workers and Activists in Ghana', *Africa: The Journal of the International African Institute* 78(3): 334–58.

Zanca, J. A. 2006 *Los Intelectuales Católicos y el Fin de la Cristiandad. 1955–1966*, Buenos Aires: Fondo de Cultura Económica and Universidad de San Andrés.

Ziman, J. 2000 *Real Science. What is and What it means*, Cambridge: Cambridge University Press.

Ziman, J. 1994 *Prometheus Bound. Science in a Dynamic Steady State*, Cambridge: Cambridge University Press.

Zubieta, J. 2007 'Las científicas latinoamericanas y sus avatares para posicionarse en la esfera de la ciencia y la tecnología' in J. Sebastián (ed) *Claves del Desarrollo Científico y Tecnológico de América Latina*, Madrid: Fundación Carolina and Siglo XXI.

Index

A

Academic career 5, 8, 10, 22, 41, 47, 76, 77, 92, 95–97, 99, 101, 105, 110, 120, 126–128, 130, 131, 150, 170, 172, 174, 179, 184, 198 (n2), 199 (n15, n19), 201 (n6), 203 (n20)

Academic clientelism 100

Academic imperialism 170

Academic labour 5, 95, 102, 119, 131, 170

and 'argentinisation' 120

and full-time scholarship 59, 98, 101–103, 111, 130, 145, 147, 149, 151, 168, 171, 175–179, 181, 195 (n54), 197 (n12), 200 (n21), 201 (n5, n6), 207 (n28), 208 (n4)

international circulation of 149–157

international division of 5, 42, 71, 87, 92, 93, 96, 98, 107, 110, 169, 170, 184

and job instability 25, 182

local division of 98

and office space 6, 18, 46, 55, 80, 95, 126, 147, 148, 151, 155, 156, 161, 168, 178, 179, 200 (n21)

and taxi-cab professorship (also multiple appointments) 8, 102–105, 108, 117, 120, 125, 126, 130, 139, 147, 171, 189, 196 (n11)

and working conditions 26, 116, 118–120, 125, 147, 151, 160, 162, 171, 174, 175, 190 (n24), 195 (n54)

Actor-Network Theory (also ANT) 2, 4, 7, 10, 11, 16, 18, 19, 30, 32, 33, 42, 46, 61, 63, 70, 85, 87, 123, 124, 140, 177, 187 (n1),

189 (n17, n21), 192 (n37), 195 (n51, n3)

Ad honorem work 26, 59, 96, 99, 102, 110, 115, 160, 161, 172, 175, 182, 201 (n6)

Argentine political science 7–9, 27, 47–49, 57, 58, 62–65, 67, 68, 73, 75, 81, 83–85, 89, 91, 93, 94, 96, 99–103, 105, 111, 124, 125, 128–131, 138, 146–148, 157, 158, 161–164, 166–169, 171, 174, 175, 178, 179, 181–185, 190 (n29), 195 (n2), 198 (n7), 199 (n9, n12), 202 (n11), 203 (n25), 205 (n11), 206 (n24), 207 (n31)

B

Biographical ethnography 45

Biographical structuring 196 (n5)

Biographical turn 195 (n4)

Bookstore 132, 137, 148, 179, 180, 204 (n4), 205 (n13)

Border thinking 90, 91, 123

Boundary object 2, 7, 11, 32–37, 40, 63, 194–195 (n50)

C

Canon 72, 83, 86, 107, 173, 198 (n7)

Capital 11, 15–18, 21–24, 33, 109, 130, 169, 177, 181, 204 (n3), 206 (n18)

Academic capital 8, 21, 63, 76, 99, 136, 158, 167–169, 189 (n16)

Intellectual capital 18, 21, 22, 189 (n16)

Scientific capital 3, 17, 18, 22, 23, 63, 167–169, 189 (n16)

Social capital 105, 128

Symbolic capital 114

236 *Index*

Career bonding 8, 97, 101–104

Centre (also central field) 1, 2, 4–6, 10, 11, 13, 16, 21, 28, 31, 39–43, 60, 64–66, 70–74, 78, 88, 90, 107, 109–124, 127, 130, 132, 133, 143–149, 154, 163, 164, 167–174, 176, 178–181, 185, 186, 188 (n8), 190 (n24), 191 (n32), 192–193 (n43), 194 (n47, n49), 197 (n19), 198 (n1, n5), 200 (n23), 203 (n20, n21)

Chair 5, 8, 9, 60, 84, 91, 97–104, 107–109, 114, 128, 130, 149, 175, 181, 196 (n12), 199 (n18), 200 (n4), 201 (n6, n10)

Classroom 46, 51, 55, 69, 78, 79, 81–83, 85, 87, 89, 91, 92, 94, 97, 98, 108, 119, 126, 174, 175, 203 (n23)

Co-authorship 1, 38, 44, 124, 143–146, 150, 153, 179, 192 (n43), 194 (n48), 205 (n15), 206 (n16, n18)

Coffee houses (also cafés) 46, 51, 55, 78, 80, 85, 87, 94, 174

Consecration (also consecrated scholars) 60, 63, 68, 81, 135, 153, 158, 160–164, 166–169, 203 (n25), 205 (n11), 206 (n24)

   And intellectual condition 9, 158–160, 182

   And international condition 9, 158, 162–165

   And networking condition 9, 158, 160–162

Constructivism 195 (n2)

Critical appropriation (also negotiation) 7, 8, 11, 29, 30, 34–37, 70, 78–86, 89, 169, 174, 191 (n35), 191–192 (n36), 194 (n47), 200 (n2), 206 (n22)

Curriculum 70, 92, 164, 173

D

Desarrollo Económico 83, 206 (n17, n18)

Diatopic hermeneutics 193 (n46)

Dominant agents (also dominant actors and dominant positions) 9, 17, 18, 30, 60, 68, 96, 114, 129, 131, 135, 150, 157, 159, 161, 163, 168–171, 179, 181, 182, 198 (n20), 206 (n20, n23), 207 (n33)

E

Ethnographic analysis 44–46

F

Foreign knowledge 5–8, 29, 40, 85, 88, 109, 127, 130, 131, 139, 141, 157, 170, 172–174, 180, 183, 206 (n22)

Functional dependency 25, 130, 190 (n24)

G

Gatekeeper (also gatekeeping) 9, 48, 165–169, 179, 182, 202 (n11), 207 (n33)

Grant 18, 23, 26, 42, 66, 90, 95, 96, 123, 129, 147, 153, 158, 159, 164, 165, 168, 169, 181–183, 195 (n54), 204 (n7)

H

Habitus 16, 19–21, 42, 88, 94, 111, 189 (n18)

I

Identity (also identity-building) 11, 18, 31, 33, 35–37, 44, 51, 52, 89, 90, 92, 128, 143, 191 (n30), 193 (n46), 205 (n11)

In-depth interview 7, 46, 47, 49, 55

Informal university 26, 187 (n5)

Interactionism 16–18, 21, 35, 39, 50, 51, 63

International collaboration 38, 104

International conferences 37, 81, 107, 125, 136, 149, 152, 153, 163, 164, 167, 168, 175, 177, 180, 182, 202 (n11), 206 (n22), 207 (n34)

J

Journal editor 126, 133–138, 166, 199 (n12), 205 (n9, n10)

   As mediator 139–141

L

Library 5, 6, 31, 51, 64, 83, 95, 118, 119, 126, 132, 134, 137, 139, 140, 147, 148, 151, 163, 164, 168, 174, 175, 182, 193 (n44), 195 (n54), 200 (n21), 207 (n28)

Life-history 6–9, 45–49, 51–56, 62, 100, 124, 170, 171, 195 (n4), 196 (n8)

   and credibility 53–65

   and informants 55

   and principle of saturation 52, 56, 61

   and reliability 53–65

Index 237

and representativity (also sampling) 56–61
and settings 55

M

Mediator 9, 109, 129–132, 135, 138, 139, 146, 148, 150–153, 155, 165–169, 182, 192 (n39), 206 (n20, n23), 207 (n33)

N

Networks 2, 4, 8, 10, 16, 28, 32, 37–39, 42, 57, 58, 63, 67, 68, 86, 87, 96, 97, 101, 104–122, 124, 126–130, 135, 138, 139, 154, 156, 157, 160, 161, 165, 166, 171, 177, 182–185, 189 (n17), 191 (n30), 195 (n54, n2, n3), 200 (n1), 202 (n17), 207 (n29)
  International networks 97, 110–122, 127, 128
  International networks as perceived by foreign scholars 116–119
  Local networks 104–110, 127, 129, 130, 177, 184
Newcomer 59–61, 96–99, 101, 102, 104, 106–117, 122, 126–128, 130, 132, 138, 175–177, 200 (n1, n2), 201 (n6, n10), 203 (n25), 204 (n3)

O

Obligatory passage point 30, 32, 87, 95, 124, 129, 179, 193 (n46), 200 (n20), 201 (n8)

P

Para-academic 125, 203 (n21)
Participant observation 6, 7, 46, 49, 54–56, 89
Periphery (also peripheral field) 1, 2, 4–6, 10, 11, 13, 15, 21, 23, 25–30, 32, 37, 40, 42, 58, 60, 65–68, 70–72, 74, 75, 87, 90, 91–93, 97, 98, 107, 109, 115–117, 120–126, 132, 133, 140, 141, 144, 146, 147, 149–155, 163, 165, 167, 169–174, 176, 178–186, 189 (n15), 190 (n24), 193 (n44), 194 (n47, n49), 195 (n54), 197 (n19), 202 (n11), 203 (n20), 205 (n10), 206 (n24), 207 (n31), 208 (n1)
Post-colonialism 2, 4, 14, 191 (n36), 197 (n19), 200 (n24)

PostDATA 83, 84, 199 (n12), 204 (n8)
Preferential attachment 28, 130, 143, 158
Prestige 3, 23, 34, 76–78, 90, 93, 100, 127, 143, 145, 165, 166, 169, 174, 207 (n28)
Public (of science) 14, 15, 27, 28, 80, 123, 127, 189 (n16), 191 (n31), 206 (n25)
Publishing industry (also publishing houses) 22, 23, 75, 89, 103, 131–137, 140, 141, 147, 148, 158, 166, 168, 172, 176, 179–182, 195 (n54), 199 (n19), 204 (n5, n7), 205 (n13)

R

Rational choice 75, 76, 190 (n29), 198 (n8)
Repetition 72, 78, 86, 88, 173, 192 (n36)
Revista Argentina de Ciencia Política 83

S

SAAP (Sociedad Argentina de Análisis Político) 55, 61, 81, 83, 103, 152, 162, 197 (n14), 199 (n12, n14), 203 (n26), 206 (n24)
Scale-free networks 28, 191 (n32)
Scholarly work 11, 12, 36, 37, 40, 42, 74, 80, 88, 100, 101, 104, 148, 160, 170, 172, 179
Scientific field 1, 3, 4, 9–30, 37, 38, 40, 42, 44, 45, 56, 58, 66, 67, 69, 70, 81, 90, 92–94, 96, 98, 101, 103, 106, 109–111, 120, 122–124, 127, 129, 135, 141, 148, 157, 158, 162, 171, 172, 176, 179, 180, 182, 184–186, 188 (n11), 189 (n16), 190 (n29), 193 (n43), 194 (n48), 195 (n54), 198 (n5), 203 (n21), 206 (n24), 207 (n33), 208 (n3)
  Institutionalised scientific field 16, 21–24, 27, 35, 42, 110, 111, 126, 135, 148, 151, 158, 189 (n21), 192 (n42)
  Networked scientific field 16, 21–30, 35, 42, 69, 91, 100, 103, 111, 129, 136, 146, 148, 161, 165, 167, 189 (n19), 190 (n24), 201 (n9)
Scientific practice (also scientific activity) 1, 4–6, 10, 13, 14, 16, 17, 19–21, 23–25, 38, 46, 50, 53, 67–69, 71, 88, 115, 120,

238 *Index*

125, 126, 169, 171, 172, 177, 186, 187 (n1), 188 (n9, n12), 193 (n46), 203 (n21)
Social world 2, 7, 11–15, 18, 21, 24, 29, 32–38, 40, 42, 44, 48, 52, 87, 88, 91, 187 (n2, n3, n4), 189 (n14), 191 (n30), 192 (n41, n42), 193 (n46), 198 (n5)
Social network analysis 75, 183
Socio-technical ensemble 19, 125, 126, 151, 156, 158, 171, 179
Strategic dependency 25, 190 (n24)
Student centre 78, 79, 85, 88, 94, 174, 199 (n17)
Studia Politicae 83
Subordinating object 7, 36, 40, 42, 69, 90, 93, 96, 98, 109, 132
Syllabi 8, 70–72, 76, 87, 126, 127, 135, 140, 153, 170, 172, 173, 179, 128, 198 (n4)

T

Teaching by undergraduates 8, 97–101, 203 (n23)
Teaching technology 8, 122–128, 130, 131, 139, 140, 147, 156, 171, 179
and time 126–128

Temas y Debates 83
Ticket of entry (also conditions of entry) 11, 17, 21–23, 96, 100, 106, 167, 168, 178, 204 (n4)
Training process 8, 25, 63, 69, 70, 73, 78, 85, 88–93, 98, 99, 115, 172, 173, 190 (n29), 208 (n1)
Transducción 193 (n46)
Translation 7, 10, 11, 19, 29, 30, 31, 39, 40, 42, 44, 63, 70, 71, 78, 79, 81, 84–87, 92, 109, 114, 116, 119, 120, 129, 130, 132, 134, 135, 141, 143, 158, 163–166, 169, 170, 172, 176, 182, 183, 191 (n36), 192 (n37, n38, n39), 193 (n46), 194 (n49), 202 (n17), 204 (n3)
Asymmetrical translation 7, 30, 35–37, 42, 71, 85, 87, 143, 163–165, 170, 172, 176, 193 (n46), 194 (n49)
Symmetrical translation 33–36
Triangulation 49, 53, 55, 67

U

Uncertainty 25, 26, 121, 166, 190 (n24), 208 (n1)

CPSIA information can be obtained
at www.ICGtesting.com
Printed in the USA
JSHW011454201219
3107JS00006B/141